The Aristocratic Ideal
and
Selected Papers

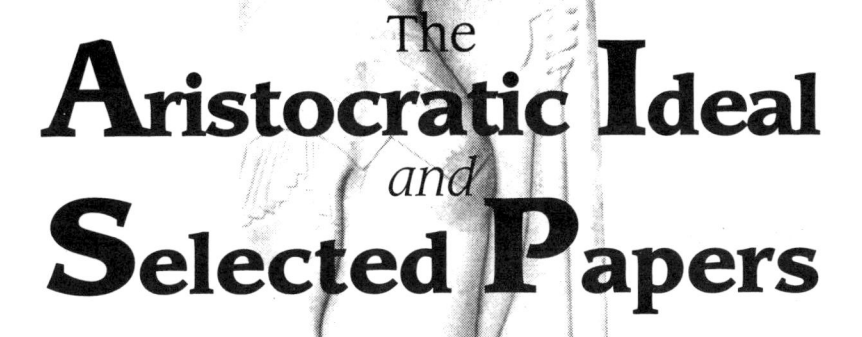

by
Walter Donlon

Bolchazy-Carducci Publishers, Inc.
Wauconda, Illinois

General Editor
Laurie K. Haight

Cover Design
Charlene M. Hernandez

Cover Illustration
Stele of Aristion, 510–500 B.C.
Photograph by Raymond V. Schoder, S.J.
from *Masterpieces of Greek Art*
By permission of Ares Publishers, Inc., Chicago, Illinois

© 1999 Bolchazy-Carducci Publishers, Inc.

Bolchazy-Carducci Publishers, Inc.
1000 Brown St., Unit 101
Wauconda, IL 60084 USA

http://www.bolchazy.com

Printed in the United States of America
1999
by Trade Service Publications

ISBN 0-86516-411-8

Library of Congress Cataloging-in-Publication Data

Donlan, Walter.
    The aristocratic ideal and selected papers / Walter Donlan.
        p.   cm.
    Originally published: Lawrence, Kan. : Coronado Press, 1980.
    Includes bibliographical references and index.
    ISBN 0-86516-411-8 (alk. paper)
    1. Aristocracy (Social class)—Greece—Attitudes—History. 2.
  Class consciousness—Greece—Attitudes. 3. Greece—Civilization—To
146 B.C. I. Title.
    HT653.G8 D65 1998
    305.5'2—dc21   98-14706
                                                          CIP

To my father and mother

PREFACE TO THE 1999 EDITION

Since 1980, when *The Aristocratic Ideal in Ancient Greece* was first published, the number of studies in Greek social history and thought has grown considerably. Also, the scope of research has broadened to include dimensions of Greek society that were previously not much studied or were taken for granted. As a result, some traditional assumptions about class and class relationships in early Greece have come under question. This scholarship and many fruitful discussions with colleagues have led me to change my mind on several points. I take this opportunity to mention briefly my afterthoughts and their significance to my study of class attitudes in the literature of the eighth through fifth centuries BC.

It is gratifying that many now agree with my premise that the social system represented in the *Iliad* and *Odyssey* has close affinities to the level or stage of political integration that anthropologists call the "chiefdom." Others, however, emphatically disagree with this historical reading of the Homeric poems. The old controversy concerning the "use of Homer as history," which was heated in 1980, continues unabated today, and is, if anything, even more complicated. One important aspect of the debate, does, however, appear to have been largely resolved. A majority of social historians today inclines towards M. I. Finley's essential argument (*The World of Odysseus* [1954, 1978]) that the epics present a coherent and internally consistent social system which must have some relationship to an actual society. Although the vexed question of how we may use the epics to tell us about the Dark Age and early Archaic period will be with us for a long time to come, few would deny that the *Iliad* and *Odyssey* are major sources for sociological study of Greek culture and thought at the juncture of pre-history and history.

On the important issue of the placement in time of Homeric society, I no longer follow Finley's dates of the tenth and ninth centuries BC. I would now place the social background of the poems close to the time of their composition, though not exactly contemporaneous. My present view is that during the later eighth century, when the poems were being composed, much of Greece was undergoing rapid social change, as chiefdom societies evolved into aristocratically governed city-states. The oral bards, however, did not (possibly because of the constraints of their traditional material), incorporate the structural changes of their "own day" into their songs. I see, in other words, a time-lag between the social structures that were emerging in the late eighth-century and those of the narratives. With others, then, I place Homeric society around 800 BC, a generation or two before the "final" composition of the *Iliad* and *Odyssey*, yet still within the contemporary audiences' collective memory. Along this line, I am now convinced that the concepts of civic community and of the leaders' responsibility for the good of the entire community were highly developed by the end of the ninth century BC rather than "muted" as I said (again following Finley) in the book (see pp. 8–9). In 800 BC the *polis*-community was effectively in place, poised for its transformation into the *polis*-state. (I expand on these points later in this Preface.)

Viewing the city-state form of polity as a rapid evolution from the chiefdom form makes for an easier transition to the class attitudes observed in the seventh century. It explains, for example, how the city-state elites could so easily appropriate the ideal of the warrior elites of the epics as the model of their self-presentation. So too, the expressions of outrage in Hesiod's *Works and Days* (ca. 700 BC) against the "gift-devouring" *basileis*—the local aristocrats of that day—are more readily understood if we consider that the quasi-egalitarian chiefdom had only recently given way to a more stratified, non-reciprocal regime. The idealized "just" *basileus*, whom Hesiod clearly connects with the "more righteous and better" race of heroes that preceded the present, dismal "race of iron," still existed in living memory. The recent emphasis on the effect of "poetic selection" on the structure of epic narrative corroborates this view. Hesiod appropriated the figure of the traditional *basileus* for his class ideology by foregrounding the leader's role as righteous judge and caretaker of the people while excluding from his narrative the image of the *basileus* as the honor-obsessed warrior-chief (see pp. 26–31).

The realization that poems emphasize or omit certain elements and aspects of the societies they describe has also led to a reevaluation of the theory of the "hoplite revolution." It was because Homer selected the chiefs and put them in the foreground of battle that critics assumed that aristocratic "champions" did the real fighting, while the ordinary Dark-Age soldiers stood back as a "mob" of ineffective nonentities. The appearance of the hoplite and the phalanx formation, it was thought, brought about a radical readjustment of the power relations between the ruling aristocracy and the people, and was primarily responsible for both the conception and implementation of egalitarian citizenship. When I wrote *The Aristocratic Ideal*, the theory of a "hoplite revolution" in the seventh century was widely accepted. Studies of battles in Homer have shown, however, that they were fought by massed foot-troops, drawn up in a loose sort of "proto-phalanx." In this knowledge, I would now soften the distinctions I made between the pre-hoplite and hoplite phases of military conduct (see pp. 39–40, 70, 74). In fact, that the mass of non-elite fighting men played a much more important military role in the pre-*polis* society than was previously thought provides further support for my contention that a deeply rooted "spirit of egalitarianism" informed *polis* life from the very beginning, and that this ideology was a prime factor in the curbing of aristocratic power (p. 19).

Critics have also become increasingly less inclined to read the highly personal, autobiographical statements of the Archaic Age poets literally. According to this revision, poets adopted a particular *persona* which stood for and expressed a certain outlook. We need not suppose, for example, that a "Hesiod" and his brother "Perses" actually quarreled over the inheritance of their paternal *klêros* (the family's farmland). We may rather read the *Works and Days* as a programmatic poem that proclaims a message of justice and fair-dealing in a time when the reciprocal ties between leaders and led, still available in memory, have deteriorated. The narrator assumes the role of the teacher of *dikê* to his "brother," cast as the exponent of the *hybris* of the *basileis* whose pawn he has become. In a similar vein, the *Theognidea* may be seen not simply as a miscellany (frequently contradictory) of aristocratic sentiments from the seventh to the early fifth century, compiled around a core of verses by an historical Theognis of Megara, but as an organic work-in-progress, reflecting the ongoing discourse within the panhellenic aristocracy over their place and role in a changing society. Thus for us the shifting values and internal conflicts of the traditional ruling elite come together in the multivalent *persona* of the aptly named "Theognis," whose poetic program includes both the chastisement and the regeneration of his class. The same may be said of the anti-elitist maxims that accrued around the name of Phocylides ("This, too, from Phocylides . . ."). Needless to say, this generic perspective is attractive to the social historian, for by depersonalizing it gives a broader voice to the aristocratic and anti-aristocratic attitudes expressed by individual writers.

Finally, if I were writing this book today, I would "read" at greater length and more carefully the material evidence: vase painting, sculpture, grave monuments, burial gifts, cult deposits, domestic architecture, and other relics of social class behavior. While analyses of the social content of Greek art largely confirm my reading of the literary texts, they also provide nuances that I missed. To take one obvious example, the genre scenes of aristocratic life on late Archaic and Classical vases were certainly an expression of elite exclusiveness, yet the vases were not bought exclusively by aristocrats. Clearly their ownership by non-elites indicates at the least a fascination with aristocratic high-life among the general public, but also perhaps suggests a certain acquiescence to aristocratic pretensions that their birth, wealth, and breeding did make them superior. Such quasi-acceptance of elite self-representation helps to explain why even in the radical democracy of the Athenians, the *dêmos* continued to choose men from the ancient nobility to lead them.

While the outstanding progress that has been made towards a fuller understanding of how *polis* society evolved during the Archaic and early Classical periods has altered my views in several specifics, it has nevertheless confirmed my central thesis about the attitudes of superiority during that time. The ideological construct we call the aristocratic ideal was far from static, but rather was an evolving standard, which appears in the literature as a series of flexible "defensive" stances taken in reaction to the challenges to aristocratic hegemony and values posed from below.

The articles reprinted in this volume represent the development of my views on class relations and class attitudes in early Greek society. I have concentrated on the Dark Age (Homeric) chiefdom, because I came to believe early on that this long phase of Greek political history was the formative period of the city-state, and that understanding it is the key to understanding how the *polis* came into being and how the structures, institutions and ideologies of the early *polis* evolved and developed.

As I presently see things, the loosely articulated chiefdom system that is depicted in the epics prevailed throughout most of Greece in one form or another from the eleventh to the early eighth century. The image of a simple economy and government slowly advancing towards more complex economic and political relations is borne out by the archaeological record of the Protogeometric through Middle Geometric periods (ca. 1050–760 BC). The archaeology of the Late Geometric period (ca. 760–700) shows societies in many parts of the Greek world experiencing remarkable growth and development. Population was increasing; the economic gap between the leaders and mass of people was widening; the office of paramount *basileus* was on the way to being replaced by colleges of magistrates, and separate communities were coalescing into single political units. The time-lag phenomenon, as I mentioned above, would account for the exclusion of these major developments from the *Iliad* and *Odyssey*. Let us be clear about this. Our epics probably do incorporate some contemporary material (urban features, for example, and perhaps colonization), but I am doubtful that we can infer from the internal evidence that the *Iliad* and the *Odyssey* were commenting on structural changes as they were occurring.

Some scholars, however, do just that, interpreting, for example, the apparently contradictory expressions of elite dominance and egalitarian outlook found in the texts as literary representation of social class tensions within the emerging *poleis* during the late eighth century, or even the seventh (to which some assign the poems). Herein lies the crux of today's Homeric Question: to what extent did, or could, "Homer" and his contemporaries inject into their narrative tales events and ideas that ran counter to their inherited traditional poetics? I prefer, for example, to explain the tensions among the leaders (*basileis*) and between the *basileis* and the people (*dêmos*) as endemic to pre-state chieftain societies. The chiefdom model offers a satisfactory explanation for the coexistence in the epics of a formal, legitimated hierarchy, subject to internal shifts, and a stipulated relationship of reciprocity between the *basileis* and the *dêmos*, which contains elements of egalitarianism. Such an arrangement is most characteristic of immature chiefdoms, where chiefs have limited coercive powers.

I conclude, as do others, that in 800 BC the chieftain societies contained most of the civic and communal functions of the early city-state. In my articles I have attempted to describe social life in the late Dark Age and to explore why and how a system of local *basileis* headed by a paramount *basileus* evolved, within a few generations, into a system of impersonal magistracies and boards, which distributed leadership roles among a wealthy nobility. The articles I have selected for this volume cover major aspects of social life, some of which loom large in the epic narratives, while others are pushed into the background. The topics include community and its constituent elements (*dêmos*, *oikos*); economic, social, and political relationships among the elite and between the elite and the people (power and authority, the "embedded" economy, gift-giving and exchange, guest-friendship, *hetairoi*-bands, land use and land-tenure); and the values and attitudes that inform, validate, or contradict the social structure (honor and shame, the ideal of personal achievement and the agonistic spirit, obligation, and insistence on reciprocity).

Reciprocity, I have found, is the basic standard for all kinds of social relationships in Homeric society. The ancient principle of reciprocity inherited from the simple chiefdoms of the Dark Age became severely undermined in the city-state societies, as the economic and social divisions between the aristocratic leaders and the ordinary citizens widened. Consciousness of this rupture, as I tried to show in *The Aristocratic Ideal*, initiated the ideological conflicts recorded in the literature of the Archaic and Classical city-states.

It was not so long ago that historians could pronounce impossible the quest for the origins of the city-state form of government. "As a matter of fact the process of the emergence of the *polis* eludes us entirely and it could hardly be otherwise" (M. M. Austin and P. Vidal-Naquet, *Economic and Social History of Ancient Greece* [1977] 51). The outlook is no longer so gloomy. I have come to believe, as others have, that the step from the pre-state society to the city-state society, though momentous in terms of later Greek history, was not a mysterious process, but rather a rapid sequence of political change within an existing social structure whose outlines are fairly clear to us. I would assert, therefore, that for historians concerned with the origins and early development of the *polis*-state the most fruitful line of inquiry bears on the nature of and the changes in the relations of power among the levels of the society and the attitudes generated by those changes. I hope that this volume will be of some use to teachers and students interested in the dynamics of social and ideological evolution within a single culture over a long period of time.

Irvine, California
October 1998

ACKNOWLEDGMENTS

I should like to thank Bonnie Kounas of Coronado Press for kindly releasing the rights to *The Aristocratic Ideal in Ancient Greece* and Ladislaus J. Bolchazy and Bolchazy-Carducci Publishers for undertaking the reissue of the book and inclusion of my articles. Special gratitude goes to the Editor, Laurie K. Haight.

Permissions from the following publishers to reprint material from their publications is gratefully acknowledged.

The University of Chicago Press: From *The Iliad of Homer*, translated by Richmond Lattimore. Copyright 1951.

Harper Collins Publishers: From *The Odyssey of Homer*, translated by Richmond Lattimore. Copyright 1965.

Harvard University Press and The Loeb Classical Library: From *Hesiod, the Homeric Hymns and Homerica*, translated by H. G. Evelyn-White. Copyright 1914.

Penguin Books Ltd. (Penguin Classics): From *Thucydides. History of the Peloponnesian War*, translated by Rex Warner. Copyright 1954.

I also acknowledge with thanks the following journals and publishers for permission to reprint my articles.

Gaetano Macchiaroli Editore for "Changes and Shifts in the Meaning of *Demos* in the Literature of the Archaic Period," *La Parola del Passato* 135 (1970) 381–395.

Franz Steiner Verlag Stuttgart GmbH for "The Tradition of Anti-Aristocratic Thought in Early Greek Poetry," *Historia* 22 (1973) 145–154.

The Johns Hopkins University Press for "The Structure of Authority in the *Iliad*," *Arethusa* 12 (1979) 51–70.

Scandinavian University Press for "The Pre-State Community in Greece, *Symbolae Osloenses* 67 (1989) 5–29.

Phoenix, Journal of the Classical Association of Canada, for "The Unequal Exchange Between Glaucus and Diomedes in Light of the Homeric Gift Economy," *Phoenix* 43 (1989) 1–15.

Museum Helveticum for "Homeric *Temenos* and Land Tenure in Dark Age Greece," *Museum Helveticum* 46 (1989) 129–145.

Colby Quarterly for "Duelling with Gifts in the *Iliad*: As the Audience Saw It," *Colby Quarterly* 29 (1993) 155–172.

Black Rose Books, Montréal, Québec for "Chief and Followers in Pre-State Greece," in *From Political Economy to Anthropology,* ed. D. Tandy and C. Duncan (1994) 34–51.

TABLE OF CONTENTS

Preface to 1999 Edition v

Acknowledgements xi

Introduction to The Aristocratic Ideal in Ancient Greece xv

THE ARISTOCRATIC IDEAL IN ANCIENT GREECE
    Chapter One, The Ideal of the Warrior-Aristocrat 1
    Chapter Two, The Old Ideal under Challenge 35
    Chapter Three, The Crisis of Identity: Theognis and Pindar 77
    Chapter Four, The Aristocratic Ideal in the Classical Period 113
    Chapter Five, Aristocratic Life-Style in the Fifth Century 155
    Notes to the Text 181
    Index 213

SELECTED PAPERS
    Changes and Shifts in the Meaning of Demos in the Literature
        of the Archaic Period 225
    The Tradition of Anti-Aristocratic Thought in Early Greek
        Poetry 237
    The Structure of Authority in the *Iliad* 249
    The Unequal Exchange Between Glaucus and Diomedes
        in Light of the Homeric Gift-Economy 267
    The Pre-State Community in Greece 283
    Homeric τέμενος and the Land Economy of the Dark Age 303
    Duelling with Gifts in the *Iliad*: As the Audience Saw It 321
    Chief and Followers in Pre-State Greece 345

Bibliography of Works by the Author 359

INTRODUCTION TO THE ARISTOCRATIC IDEAL IN ANCIENT GREECE

MODERN INTERPRETERS of the intellectual and cultural history of ancient Greece turn instinctually and inevitably to the artists and thinkers whose achievements have ranked them high above the mass of ordinary men. More often than not these great figures represented the convictions and prejudices of a narrow group within the society as a whole. In the surviving treasures of Greek art one is tempted to see the plastic or graphic extension of the same point of view. The gleaming stone temples house statues of gods cast in the image of highborn men and women; sculpture and painting depicted gods and heroes in attitudes of serene aloofness or noble youths and maidens in graceful action or elegant repose. The bitter drudgery of a hard life eked out from stony soil was seldom celebrated in literature and art. The unspectacular lives of the countless thousands of "ordinary" people, and their attitudes and values, sparsely recorded and difficult to recover, resonate hardly at all in the researches of modern scholars.

The tendency to define the essence of a culture in terms of its highest refinement can lead to a distorted view of the dynamics of that culture. In one of the most influential books written in this century about the cultural ideals of Greece, the late Werner Jaeger could say,

> All later culture, however high an intellectual level it may reach, and however greatly its content may change, still bears the imprint of its aristocratic origin. Culture is simply the aristocratic ideal of a nation, increasingly intellectualized. (*Paideia* I, p. 4).

But is this true?

We must remind ourselves that the Parthenon, which still crowns the ancient citadel of Athens, was the product of Athenian democracy's proudest hour, and that the enormous gold and ivory statue of Athena, which once dominated its interior, carried the helmet, spear and shield of the citizen-soldier. The very gold that sheathed her body was part of the treasury of the people, the *dēmos,* to be used in an emergency as the sovereign people voted it. Athena herself was no remote queen nor a symbol of the lofty intellect, but the patron of the potters and other artisans who labored daily in the city below. According to the ancient myth her gift to Athens was the olive tree, whose oil filled the potters' jars and provided a cash crop for the farmer-soldiers who manned the ranks; her animals were the owl and the snake, homely creatures which represented the life forces of a simple agrarian community.

It is necessary, too, to recall that the god at whose festivals the Athenians watched the tragedies and comedies of the great playwrights was not the aloof, aristocratic Apollo, but Dionysos, a cthonian, a rural vegetative god, who, despite the antiquity of his worship, was often regarded as a late interloper to the Olympian pantheon. Athena and Dionysos were part of the Greek ideal; in origin and essence they are not representative of a specifically aristocratic ideal.

We must be very careful, therefore, not to confuse the aristocratic ideal with the ideals of the whole of the Greek culture; they are not one and the same, although at many points they coincide. When it is realized that the aristocratic ideal is essentially the product of a particular class and not a national ideal, its development and the forces and stresses which shaped it are more easily apprehended.

The Greek aristocratic ideal did not, as Jaeger and others have assumed, give Greek culture its definitive form. Rather, it was itself shaped by opposing forces in Greek society, and it developed and changed in response to pressures on the social class which was its focus. We can go further and say that the resultant pattern of social and intellectual attitudes, usually identified as the Greek aristocratic ideal, was not a static or constant phenomenon, but that it evolved, at times by almost imperceptible shifts, into a final phase which was, in very many respects, quite different from its early stages.

This book is neither a constitutional history nor a formal study of political institutions of Greek states, but an exploration of the patterns of social attitudes and values of one subgroup — the aristocratic class. Nor have I attempted to substitute for the traditional view of Greek society a new theory of social development, but merely to shift the perspective somewhat, to show how totally the aristocratic pattern of thought was a class phenomenon and to indicate its dependence on the often fast-moving and important social and cultural changes experienced in the Greek world during the period from 800 to 400 B.C.

In short, I wish to present the Greek aristocratic ideal as a "defensive" standard, whose proponents were constantly and consistently aware of the challenges to their values posed by the larger society, and who reacted by altering their own scheme of values. The aim, which in time became increasingly self-conscious, was both to prove the superiority of the upper class and to impose a particular set of values on the society as a whole. That this attempt was successful, to some extent at least, is indicated by the fact that modern observers of ancient Greece have continued to confuse the "Greek ideal" with the "Greek aristocratic ideal."

Finally, it is hoped that those whose main interests lie outside the area of Greek studies will gain some insight into the process of Greek social evolution. Hellenic society provides a fruitful model of study for the social scientist, first because of the very high level of self-consciousness and historical awareness that possessed the ancient Greeks, and secondly, because we are far enough removed to be objective in our assessment of the social drama, and to trace its evolution over a lengthy period of time.

In some ways this is an "old-fashioned" book. As its subtitle affirms, it is a study of *attitudes* — primarily the "thought-world" of a remarkably homogeneous upper stratum, contrasted, where possible, with the outlook of those who were not of the privileged few. Attitudes are primarily a function of reflection; as such they are most apparent in the literary sources. Other evidence for human attitudes are the surviving monuments — from temples to safety pins — and demographic information gleaned from these and other sources. Where it was feasible, I have made reference to this valuable material, which supplements (and sometimes corrects) the written record. However, such information is often difficult to assess, and reliable statistical or demographic data hardly exist. In like manner, other areas of ancient studies, such as political history, religious cult, prosopography, which are closely entwined with the evolution of the aristocratic ideal, are used to supplement the literary expression of social attitudes, without losing sight of the restricted purpose of this study: the isolation of the sociopsychological currents that accompanied the main flow of events in the Greek world from 800 to 400 B.C.

◊

One last word: As every student of ancient Greece is painfully aware, a disproportionate amount of the available literary data comes from Athenian writers, and is related to social and political problems in

Athens. Such an emphasis is unavoidable, but we can be reasonably sure that the attitudes discernible in our Attic sources are representative of attitudes of Greeks in other communities.

Ω

The Aristocratic Ideal in Ancient Greece

CHAPTER ONE
The Ideal of the Warrior-Aristocrat

THE ULTIMATE ORIGINS of the Greek aristocratic ideal lie buried in the obscurity of Greece's prehistory; but in the poems of Homer, at the dawning of the historical era, we find the elements of the ideal already articulated. The great epics, the *Iliad* and *Odyssey*, composed about 750 B.C., reflect the culture of an "Heroic Age."

There continues a lively debate among scholars about the historical validity of the "world of Homer." For some, the epics, which were the products of centuries of oral development, reflect the institutions and material culture of the Mycenaean era, which ended with the widespread destruction of numerous centrally controlled, highly bureaucratic, "palace" complexes around 1200 B.C. (the time of the Trojan war). For others, they depict the society of a subsequent Dark Age, between 1100 and 900, while others see the epics as more or less contemporary records of the time of final composition, the eighth century B.C. A number of scholars reject these alternatives, maintaining that the poems are fictional amalgams of material background, institutions, and values, drawn from the whole period, from late Mycenaean to after 750 B.C., and therefore useless as historical or social evidence.

Whether the society portrayed in Homer was a "real" one, mirroring an actual society, in space and time (as I believe), or not, there can be no disagreement about one fact. The cultural standards and attitudes found in the *Iliad* and *Odyssey*, that make up what is called the "Heroic Ideal," had a profound effect on the conceptual universe of all subsequent generations of Greeks from the late eighth century on. Historically "real" or not, the epic system of values was very real to the Greeks of the Archaic and Classical periods (and beyond), who had no doubts about the literal existence of the events, characters and behavioral standard depicted in the epics. For them, Achilles, Odysseus, Hector,

---

N.B. NOTES TO THE TEXT appear last, with running heads to indicate to what page(s) they refer.

and the other heroic figures spoke and acted just as Homer (about whose existence there was no doubt either) said. And, for the post-Homeric Greeks, especially for those of higher status, the norms of individual behavior contained in the Homeric warrior-ideal constituted a paradigm which they assumptively accepted as right and proper. The evolution of the Greek aristocratic ideal, formed on the model of the ideals embodied in the Homeric epics, is the story of how the upper-class Greeks conformed to, deviated from, or altered this fundamental set of normative values in response to changing social realities.[1]

The historical culture itself, the source from which this warrior "code" arose, is only dimly perceived by us. I believe, with Finley and others, that the institutional background of the *Iliad* and *Odyssey* is essentially the experience of Greeks on the mainland, Aegean islands, and the coast of Asia Minor in the tenth and ninth centuries B.C. While many of the culture's features (architecture, weaponry and modes of fighting, use of metals, etc.) are Dark Age retrojections into a dimly remembered Mycenaean past, the political, economic, social and ideological systems belong to this period. The social system was one of chiefdoms, of a not advanced type, which exhibited many elements of an egalitarian, non-stratified tribal structure. The economic base of the culture was stockbreeding (cattle, sheep, goats, swine), along with agriculture (grain, vine, olives). These Greeks lived in small, unprepossessing, mud-brick villages, usually unwalled, with farm plots and pasturage outside. The central societal institution, however, was not the clan-village, but the household, *oikos*, a patrilineal corporation, consisting of the male *oikos*-head, his immediate family, dependents and slaves. The *oikos* was almost completely self-sufficient economically, and enjoyed much political autonomy also. Heads of wealthy (in flocks, land and treasure) and powerful lineages were called *basileis*, a word that is commonly rendered as "kings." Although the Homeric *basileus* was anachronistically vested with some of the trappings of the powerful Mycenaean overlord, the *wanax* (a title that is occasionally applied to some human leaders and to the gods, in Homer), the texts show the Homeric *basileus* to correspond to the model of the tribal chief in all respects. The chief of the most dominant lineage was the paramount, also called simply *basileus*, a "first among equals," to whom other *basileis* and their corporations were tied in a complex system of reciprocities, rather typical of primitive chiefdoms.

It is of fundamental importance to stress at the outset that the epic system of values was formulated within the kind of social organization

The Ideal of the Warrior-Aristocrat

that anthropologists term "simple" or "primitive." This does not imply that the Greeks of the Dark Age were intellectually or artistically "savage" (one need only refer to the high technical and aesthetic standards of Geometric pottery — or to the epics themselves). It is simply that the ethical superstructure of a pre-literate tribal culture, characterized by a pre-market economy and a pre-state polity, is the valuative statement of the underlying structure. Thus, the "heroic ideal," like the social structure itself, was essentially tribal, reflecting the values of a society in which physical skill, courage, and leadership were the prized attributes, high rank was attained or maintained by accomplishment in an atmosphere of individual competition for prestige, set within the context of a rigidly prescribed system of obligation and counter-obligation. As the result of a variety of structural and historical causes (which cannot be explored here), the dominant ethos of the high-ranking Homeric individual revolved around success in war; accordingly, the main concern of the epics is the great deeds of men in battle or contest.[2]

With the evolution of more complex social structures after 700 B.C., especially with the emergence of the state form, the *polis* (the rudiments of which can be traced in the epics), the focus of activity of the ruling stratum shifts in conformance. Nevertheless, the standard of success, the agonistic impulse, and, indeed, the tribal form itself, exhibit a remarkable tenacity throughout Greek history. Despite the enormous changes that took place within Greek culture during the four centuries covered by this survey, the upper-class Greeks of the late fifth century B.C., in their reflections concerning human behavior and the relations between men, continued to take as their assumptive starting point the complex of received beliefs embedded in the heroic ideal.

Because the purpose of this study is the relatively narrow one of tracing the evolution of the aristocratic ideal, it will be necessary to abstract, somewhat artificially, the ideal from its social matrix. I hope this will not present too many conceptual difficulties to the reader, who is asked to keep in mind that, although detailed discussion of the social forces behind attitudes and changes in attitudes must be severely limited, those forces were the operative causes of the world of thought that we are describing.

Before the various aspects of the heroic ideal are described in detail, a brief explanation of a tool useful in the study of social concepts is in order.[3] In the Greek language (as in English) there are certain "key" words, highly charged with social and ethical implications. Very important among these are the groups of adjectives and nouns that signify "good" and "bad" — fundamental notions in any social order. A study of these and similar terms, observed over a long period of time, affords valuable clues to the shiftings of cultural values. In Homer, for example, the chief epithets of approbation, *agathos* and *esthlos,* which are inadequately translated as "good," refer mostly to excellence in some physical sphere and are almost always related to warcraft. Thus one is said to be "*agathos* at the war-cry," or "*esthlos* in close fighting."[4] Hence, frequently the best translation in Homer for these two adjectives is simply "brave." Not surprisingly, the word that indicates "bad" *(kakos)* is often best rendered in the epics as "cowardly."[5] These words later operate within a more broadly social or ethical-moral sphere, but in Homer there is practically no trace of these broader significations. According to the value system of the Homeric fighter a man was judged "good" or "bad" by the standards of physical prowess, and their attendant psychological states.

The Homeric hero in war was inspired by a single purpose: to win personal glory and honor *(timē, kydos)* for himself by means of valorous deeds performed on the field of battle. Accordingly, the goal of every activity, practically without exception, was the recognition of self by peers as a good warrior. This ideal operated even in areas where, according to the modern sense of values, different motivations would seem to apply. The acquisition of wealth, for example, which was a major preoccupation of the epic warriors, and about which they talked endlessly, was not prompted by greed: such a motivation belongs to market economies. The possession of great wealth was a conspicuous sign of success — visible proof of prowess and leadership. It was also the means by which prestige and rank were enhanced, since it enabled the holder to give valuable gifts to guest-friends *(xeinoi)* and to reward followers, thereby insuring and increasing loyalty and dependency.

The wealth of the early Greek world was in flocks and land, the property of the *oikos,* controlled by the *oikos*-head. Aside from normal natural increase, wealth was acquired or added to in the form of booty from war raids (animals, captives, metal, luxury objects); the warrior-chief shared in the general distribution of spoils, and, as leader, was awarded an extra share as his special prize *(geras).*[6] As a general rule, therefore, one grew rich, stayed rich or became richer, by fighting; the successful warrior was a wealthy man, and, conversely, a rich man was a successful warrior. The clear and definite impression of the Homeric age's attitude towards wealth is that it was regarded both as the tangible proof of a man's excellence and a means of increasing reputation and standing, not as a primary goal in itself.

The Ideal of the Warrior-Aristocrat 5

One rather odd (to us) form of non-landed wealth in the epics, cumbersome bronze tripods or cauldrons, is explainable only in terms of display and exchange. These and other treasures were "laid up" *(keimē-lia)*, not as misers' hoards, but as proof of status and attainment. Equally significant are the elaborate rituals of gift giving, in which the exchange of such objects of value confirmed the standing of the warriors and served to cement social relations among them. In short, the "social" motives for the acquiring of goods had greater force than purely "economic" motives. When, according to legend, Ajax went mad with rage and frustration because Odysseus, not he, was awarded the arms of the dead Achilles, it was not on account of the value of the prize, but because these would have been the outward signal to all the world that he was, indeed, the heir to the fame and glory of Achilles.[7]

This emphasis on the visible proof of success demonstrates the importance of opinion in determining status as a warrior; how one "seemed" not what one "was" was the index of a man's worth. In fact, one "was" what one seemed to others. Homer allows his warriors many moments of self-doubt as they ponder whether to stay or to run; always it is how they will appear to others which determines their decision to risk their lives.[8] There is not one character in Homer who possesses perfect internal security. The Homeric warrior cannot say: "I know my own worth, and I do not care what others say about me," since he could, in fact, see himself only in terms of what others said about him. Past success counted for little; men who displayed great courage over long periods of time might suddenly be accused of outright cowardice because of a momentary hesitation.[9] Seldom, if ever, does a warrior defend himself by appealing to past performance, for worth is always measured by the present moment, and the individual Homeric hero appears never to be in disagreement with this imposed necessity for constant justification. A.W.H. Adkins has put the matter succinctly: "The Homeric hero cannot fall back upon his own opinion of himself for his self only has the value which other people put upon it."[10] And because of this total dependency on honor which can only be realized in terms of public opinion — "what people say" — all other appeals to action fade before the need to prove oneself. Thus Hector, the greatest of the Trojan heroes and the bulwark of his city, even when he was urged by those most closely connected to him, his family, not to expose himself to certain death in combat with Achilles, could reply only in terms of his heroic honor.[11] Fear of failure, that is, loss of public approbation, is the reverse of the need for appearing successful, and acts as an equally powerful motivating factor of personal behavior. For this reason Homeric society has been termed a "shame culture" as opposed to a "guilt culture."[12]

External valuation extends to other areas, too. For example, how one looked in the simple physical sense was not separable from the true self. Thus it can be said of a stranger that "He looks like a *basileus.*" Needless to say, this is said only of someone who was a *basileus.*[13] The importance of physical appearance is underscored in the *Odyssey*, where, to hide his identity, Odysseus is disguised by Athena as a beggar. Yet, even after he slew the suitors, having revealed himself as the absent chief, his wife, Penelope, appears unable to recognize him because of his "evil rags."[14] No less significant in this regard is the fact that the only "commoner" who plays a role in the *Iliad,* the obstreperous Thersites, is described as physically repulsive. This is sufficient, apparently, to stamp him as socially inferior.[15] We shall see that external appearance as an index of human worth, already firmly established in Homer, continues as a constant theme in the developing aristocratic self-conception.

The emphasis on physical prowess and the honor which it wins does not preclude, but presupposes, intelligence and resourcefulness. Cunning in stratagem and trickery, along with facility in public speaking, were desirable attributes. Nevertheless, it is clear in Homer that intelligence is not separate from physical ability but is integral to it. The ideal is a combination of physical excellence (which includes good looks as well as strength) and mental agility. Some, like Odysseus, who is most often called "resourceful" and "of many counsels," or the wise old Nestor, have the latter ability to a higher degree; others, like Ajax, are primarily men of action, not noted for skill in planning and persuading. The intimate connection between body and mind is readily seen in the characterizations of heroes. Hector praises Ajax for his "stature, strength and wisdom" (*Iliad* 7.288-89). Diomedes is called by Nestor "mighty in battle, and in counsel *(boulē)* best among your age group" (*Iliad* 9.53-54). Hector kills a warrior who is described as better by far than his father "in all sorts of *aretai,* both in swiftness of foot and in fighting, and in intelligence *(noos)* among the first of the Mycenaeans" (*Iliad* 15.641-43). Priam tells the god Hermes (disguised as a human) that he is "admirable in form and beauty *(eidos),* and wise in *noos*" (*Iliad* 24.376-77). Conversely, Elpenor is said by Odysseus to have been "not overly courageous in war nor sound in wit" (*Odyssey* 10.552-53).

Odysseus gives a capsule description of himself that sums up the nexus of attributes considered necessary for the complete hero. He tells his men that they had escaped the brute strength of the Cyclops "through my *aretē* (i.e. courage and skill), my *boulē* (counsel, advice) and my *noos* (intelligence)" (*Odyssey* 12.211). The most succinct statement of the composite ideal is Peleus' charge to Phoenix to teach the young Achilles "to be both a speaker of words and a doer of deeds" (*Iliad* 9.443).[16] There is, however, also an awareness that few, even among heroes, achieve the ideal of the perfect combining of body and mind. Once Odysseus rebukes Achilles:

> you are stronger than I am and greater by not a little with the spear, yet I in turn might overpass you in wisdom *(noēma)* by far . . .
> (*Iliad* 19.217-19, Latt.)[17]

Elsewhere Homer had Odysseus lecture a rude young Phaeacian—saying first that the gods do not give gifts to all men alike "neither in stature nor yet in brains or eloquence." The hero goes on to say that one man is inferior in appearance *(eidos)*, but a superb speaker, and wins honor thereby; another has *eidos* like the gods but no ability in speaking,

> as in your case the *eidos* is conspicuous, and not a god even would make it otherwise, and yet the *noos* there is worthless.
> (*Odyssey* 8.167-77, Latt.)

These examples, which evidence a certain tension between the realms of the physical and the mental, reinforce our impression that the Homeric world set little stock by mere brute strength or even that it commended simple physical ability, but sought its highest ideal in the combining of skill (with the attendant proper mental attitude, courage) and intelligence.[18] Even in the mental sphere, however, the emphasis is on action. The notion of introspective intellectuality is simply nonexistent in Homer. The thinking portion of the hero's make-up is directed toward the deed: tactical planning, trickery, persuasion in council. Naturally, excellence in these things, as in the other areas of activity, leads to the primary goal of personal fame, either at the moment, or, very importantly, after death.

The conception that excellence was a function of both body and mind, so vividly expressed in the Homeric poems, sank deep into the Greek consciousness, and remained integral to the self-perception of the aristocrats of the Archaic and Classical periods that followed. However, the tension, already observable in Homer, between "mere" appearance and the reality of accomplishment, and between physical and mental ability (which leads to the more abstract formulation of the dichotomy between action and thought) was to have a profound effect on the aristocratic ideal.

When we probe more deeply into the warrior-ideal we find aspects of human behavior that differ markedly from those of the later Greek aristocrats. A case in point is the muted sense of identity with, and responsibility to, the wider community. In general, private considerations tend to override public concerns in Homer. The hero feels his responsibility to self and expanded self (family, friends) much more heavily than to any larger group (tribe, community). When the Achaean chiefs appeal to the sulking Achilles' sense of loyalty to the whole of the Achaean army he can respond only in terms of his offended honor.[19]

Among the Trojans, fighting on home territory, identification with the community is naturally more pronounced. But even here the focus is relatively narrow. They fight "for their children and for their wives" (*Iliad* 8.57). Hector tells his allied forces that they were summoned "to save the wives of the Trojans and their little children from the war-loving Achaeans" (17.223-24); of course, their reward for this service will still be glory for themselves (line 232). Agenor, in his challenge to Achilles, says that the Trojans "will stand before our beloved parents, our wives and our children, to defend Ilion" (21.587-88, Latt.).[20]

Appeal may, in fact, be made to a larger circle of relationships and responsibilities. Hector seeks to inspire the Trojans to valor:

> He has no dishonor when he dies defending his country *(patrē)*, for then his wife shall be saved and his children afterwards, and his house and property shall not be damaged.
> (*Iliad* 15.496-98, Latt.)

He urges a Trojan warrior to fight: "we must kill them, or else sheer Ilion be stormed utterly by them, and her citizens *(politai)* be killed" (15.557-58, Latt.). Paris is told by Hector (3.50) that Helen is

> to your father a big sorrow, and your city *(polis)* and all your people *(dēmos)*.[21]

In a moving simile from the *Odyssey* the homesick Odysseus weeps,

> As a woman weeps, lying over the body of her dear husband, who fell fighting for her city *(polis)* and people *(laoi)* as he tried to beat off the pitiless day from city *(asty)* and children.
> (*Odyssey* 8.523-25, Latt.)

The Ideal of the Warrior-Aristocrat

Poulydamas, one of the Trojan counsellors, having observed a disturbing omen, urges Hector to proceed cautiously. Hector's reply (*Iliad* 12. 243),

One bird sign is best, to fight in defense of our country *(patrē)*,

is the closest the epic comes to expressing the notion of loyalty to the community as an abstract ideal. It is Hector, above all, who appears as a spokesman for responsibility to the community, but even his frame of reference is restricted. And it is instructive to note that the ruling family of Troy, including the patriarch, Priam himself, views the loss of Hector in personal terms.[22]

Naturally, the fact that loyalty to a larger group *can* be appealed to means that a concept of broader social obligation existed, but the main motivation remains personal and familial. In the final analysis, even Hector is concerned mostly with his own fame; his family comes next, Troy last (*Iliad* 6.447-65). The wider community, which to a later generation of Greeks will become the main focus of manly activity, does not yet exist. As M.I. Finley says, "the community could grow only by taming the hero and blunting the free exercise of his prowess, and a domesticated hero was a contradiction in terms."[23]

The reasons for this ambiguity are to be found in the nature of the political organization of Homeric society. The segmental tribal design, made up of numerous small, autonomous corporations (*okoi* and lineages) headed by chieftains jealous of their independence, tended to be centrifugal and atomistic. In such a polity loyalty was concentrated in a narrow sphere of kin and followers, hence the great importance of "friendship," *philotēs*, as a value and as a motive for behavior. The "immature" chiefdoms which integrated these groups were politically fragile and subject to dissolution (as in Odysseus' chiefdom at Ithaca). The *polis*-form, which begins to become visible in the eighth century, eventually provided a focus of communal solidarity as kinship and corporation loyalty yielded to a sense of the unified community of citizens. Even then, however, *oikos* and lineage retained much of their autonomous and divisive nature, with the result that even the Classical *polis* was rent by factional conflict among leading families for hegemony. The evolving aristocratic ideal had to face this ethical dilemma which surfaced after 700 B.C. in the form of tension between narrow class interest and the ideal of fealty to a collective whole. Such a straitened frame of reference, centered on self and the small circle of kin and close associates, as opposed to the larger sphere of cooperative responsibility, influenced the whole of the Homeric individual's pattern of activity.

A whole range of emotional responses, which we associate with "chivalric" behavior — truth-telling, honesty, mercy towards a fallen foe or for the defenceless — or the more "tender" aspects of human relations, like affection, pity, kindness, are certainly not lacking in the Homeric scheme of values. The epics do not reflect a world of unrestrained barbarity, despite the violence and bloodshed which are the constant background of the poems. But such traits have little priority, and go quickly by the board if they conflict with the aims of success. In the Judaeo-Christian system of ethics heaven is the guardian of these virtues, but in the Homeric world the gods evince little concern for "personal" morality; ethico-religious restraints on uninhibited human behavior are minimal, and the sphere of divine interest in human-to-human behavior is quite narrow. There are passages in the epics where it is taken as a self-evident fact that the gods punish men when they commit acts which transgress the rights of other men. But such passages are rather few in number, and there is little sense that fear of heavenly retribution provided much motivation.[24] In the *Iliad* there is a simile which describes a destructive storm sent by Zeus:

> in a deep rage against mortals after they stir him to anger because in violent assembly they pass decrees that are crooked, and drive righteousness *(dikē)* from among them and care nothing for what the gods think . . .
>
> (*Iliad* 16.386-88, Latt.)

Zeus and the other gods are also concerned with the keeping of oaths and the punishing of oath-breakers (*Iliad* 3.276-80, 298-301; 4.155-68; 19.258-65). Once the soldiery of both sides asks Zeus to impose the judgment of death on either Paris or Menelaus as the cause of the many evils brought by the war (*Iliad* 3.320-23).

In the *Odyssey,* which perhaps reflects a somewhat more "progressive" stage of ethical development, the restraining influence of the gods over the actions of men appears stronger. Nestor relates to Telemachus (3.132-34, Latt.) that Zeus "devised a sorry homecoming for the Argives, since not all were considerate *(noēmones)* nor righteous *(dikaioi)."* There are, in the *Odyssey,* several other references to the displeasure of the gods at men's injustice, but, on closer examination, they are all seen to occur within the context of the code of hospitality and the treatment of strangers and suppliants. "All strangers and beggars are from Zeus" is the formula used to express the religious injunction (*Odyssey* 6.207-208; 14.57-58). Odysseus tells a story that once a king of Egypt rescued him, as a suppliant, from the hands of the angry citizens of the land Odysseus' men had just plundered, for "he regarded the wrath of Zeus, the Protector of Strangers, who especially is angered at evil deeds" (14.283-84). It should be noted that the "evil deeds" *(kaka erga)* refer not to the rapine and slaughter committed by Odysseus' sailors but to the slaying of a suppliant. Odysseus' swineherd, Eumaeus, describes the suitors of Penelope, who are greedily devouring Odysseus' livestock, as men

> who do not have in their minds the vengeance of the gods, nor pity. The blessed gods do not love cruel deeds, rather they honor justice *(dikē)* and the righteous deeds of men.
> (14.82-84; cf. 20.214-16)

The "crime" of the suitors is precisely that they violated the societal norms of reciprocity and hospitality — dramatically symbolized by the mistreatment of the beggar Odysseus. Antinous, the most arrogant of the suitors, hurls a footstool at Odysseus as he is begging (a social sin that is repeated on two other occasions by other suitors). Odysseus puts a beggar's curse on Antinous (17.475-476); the other suitors are upset at the breach of socio-religious custom:

> What if he is somehow a god from heaven; and, indeed, gods, putting on all sorts of shapes, likening themselves to strangers from other lands, visit cities, watching over the violence *(hybris)* and lawfulness *(eunomia)* of men.
> (17.484-87)

The most vivid expression of this main province of divine interest in human wrongdoing is found in a dialogue between Odysseus and the Cyclops. Odysseus entreats him:

> Respect the gods, O best of men. We are your suppliants, and Zeus the guest god, who stands behind all strangers with honors due them, avenges any wrong towards strangers and suppliants.
> (*Odyssey* 9.269-71, Latt.)

The Cyclops, completely remote from any civilized human responsibility, answers:

> Stranger, you are a simple fool, or come from far off, when you tell me to avoid the wrath of the gods or fear them. The Cyclopes do not concern themselves over Zeus of the aegis, nor any of the rest of the blessed gods . . .
>
> (9.273-76, Latt.)[25]

His refusal to respond to the claims of religious custom shows the Cyclops as a creature outside the pale of correct human association, while the suitors, by negating the claims, show themselves as betrayers of the norms of proper social behavior. Thus their punishment may be seen as divine requital for their impiety.[26]

On a broader scale, however, religious sanctions on human-to-human behavior, which are powerful factors in later Greek ethical development, are not a major part of the heroic ethic. Once again the causes are to be sought in the structure of the social organization. Within the bounds of tribal corporations — family, household, lineage, clan — the relations between individuals and subgroups are maintained by social mechanisms that require no appeal to "higher" authority. Within such tightly knit segments anti-social acts like murder, adultery, robbery, theft, etc., are self-evidently bad, because they threaten group stability and must be put to right. Balance and redress operate within the confines of the social units concerned. Murder, for example, is a problem between the families of the killer and the slain; the instrumental goal is social harmony.

> And, indeed, a man accepts recompense *(poinē)* from the killer of his brother or of his dead son; and the slayer remains among his *dēmos,* having paid back much; and the man's heart and proud spirit are held in check because he has received recompense.
>
> (*Iliad* 9.632-36)

The alternative to peaceful settlement is blood feud or exile of the killer (See *Iliad* 15.430; 23.85; *Odyssey* 24.430-37). In the same way, an adulterer balances the wrong he has done by paying the adulterer's fine *(moichagria, Odyssey* 8.332). In such cases "justice" and a fair dealing," operating within the context of the reciprocal nature of primitive societies, need no divine superstructure for reinforcement.

It is in the dealings of stranger with stranger that divine concern with human behavior manifests itself most: the keeping of oaths, the rules for the treatment of strangers, suppliants and beggars, and the uses of hospitality (the violations of which are also a diminution of the gods'

The Ideal of the Warrior-Aristocrat

own *timē*). Because these situations are beyond the control of tribal mechanisms of redress and amelioration, a "transcendent" morality is required.

The beginnings of a sense of divinely ordained "justice" within the community itself or as a universal conception governing all men, however rarely expressed, is significant. It reflects both the reality of wider contact among Greeks from different geographical areas (around 900 B.C., according to archaeologists), and also the needs of a society in structural flux. The main characteristic of the chiefdom form of polity is that it gathers separate and essentially autonomous groups under a kind of "centralized" government, with the paramount as head, thus making all the subgroups of the community interdependent. More formal and more complex institutions to settle disputes are required, because social problems involve a number of segments and disparate points of view, not amenable to the direct "justice" of kinship groups. The formal proceedings for adjudicating a dispute over blood price depicted on the Shield of Achilles (*Iliad* 18.497-508), with a gathering of the people, a "jury" of elders, and an "umpire," illustrate the beginnings of an institutionalized process of justice. At the same time, the unstable Homeric chiefdom has difficulty keeping the autonomous corporations "in check," and in times of social upset the delicate centralized system breaks down. At Ithaca, because of the paramount's long absence, no assembly of the people had been held for twenty years. When Telemachus, Odysseus' son, finally convokes an assembly, he is frustrated because the combined political power of the suitors (members of independent *oikoi*) overcomes the centralized process of arbitration. The only "solution" is a recourse to force — the slaying of either Telemachus or the suitors, and a narrowly averted civil war. Finally, as social stratification increases, together with decline of local kinship groups, the individual of lower status finds himself adrift and at the mercy of powerful men. For all these reasons the abstract idea of universal justice, promoted by the gods, finds expression.

In the Homeric poems these forces are at work, but in muted fashion. Thus, apart from infrequent mentions of social justice in the broad sense, and in the concern over the breakdown of public order in the *Odyssey*, which prompts cries to heaven (couched, we note, in terms of transgression of the norms of sociability, especially of hospitality), the concept of "righteousness" and of divine sanction for its observance is limited to situations that occur outside the limits of the tribal order. The "necessity" for imposing the restraints of divinely ordained right, which originates in the regulation of intertribal behavior, on the community itself, betokens an important social change, the significance of which becomes evident with Hesiod and the seventh century.

A key feature of the Homeric social system was a highly developed pattern of social behavior between eminent men from different tribal groups: an elaborate etiquette of gift exchange, stylized eating and drinking ceremonial, and modes of polite address. These formed a complex system of guest-friendship *(xeniē)*, which afforded individual protection in a hostile tribal world, fostered the expansion of "foreign" contact and increased the prestige of individuals and their *oikoi*.[27] In addition, the ceremonial aspect gave a kind of psychological protection to the ideal; everyone took part in a solemn charade which insured the validity of the heroic conventions. All heroes treat one another as heroes, even when they are enemies; the bond which linked heroic warriors together was the unity of the code, which transcended tribal and even ethnic boundaries. This common feeling helps to explain why the *Iliad* displays practically no cultural differences between Greek and Asiatic, despite the obvious real disparities which must have existed. By the same token, the Trojan war is hardly portrayed as a "national" war, and seldom is the motivation for the conflict ever felt as "patriotic." Rather the war is perceived as a private quarrel between two feuding high-ranking households. Later Greeks would make much of the fact that this was the first clash of Europe and Asia, East and West, Greek and barbarian, but the Homeric epics reflect almost identical societies on both sides. Homer seems scarcely aware of the fact that Greeks and Trojans would speak different languages.[28] Thus, even when it is projected on an "international" scale, unity of aristocratic culture is the important factor: Hector is as much a Greek warrior-aristocrat as Achilles and the motivations for their actions are exactly the same.

An example of this common identification is seen in the encounter between the Lycian Glaukos and the Greek Diomedes in *Iliad* 6.119ff. They meet on the field of battle as enemies; Diomedes is impressed with Glaukos' bravery, and, suspecting that he may be a god, asks him his lineage. Glaukos gives the history of his family, after which Diomedes cries that his ancestor, Oeneus, and Glaukos' grandfather, the hero Bellerophontes, had been guest-friends: "Therefore," he continues:

> I am your friend and host in the heart of Argos; you are mine in Lykia when I come to your country. Let us avoid each other's spears, even in the close fighting.
>
> (*Iliad* 6.224-26, Latt.)

The Ideal of the Warrior-Aristocrat 15

Then they exchange gifts and go off to seek other foes—another clear indication that the heroic ethos, with its complicated norms of social behavior, supersedes all other considerations as an impetus to action. A scene such as this also points up the greater importance that ties of friendship and personal loyalty within the fraternity of the warrior élite had over tribal and communal bonds. In this case Glaukos and Diomedes find the host-guest system a more compelling determinant of behavior than the requirements of mortal combat. What prompted Achilles finally to reenter the battle was his need to avenge the death of his companion Patroclus and not any sense of loyalty to the Greek army.

It is in light of these considerations that the Homeric treatment of lineage must be viewed. The ability to trace descent from heroes of the past was important in two directions. It acted as a spur to the individual, who felt that he had to live up to his own illustrious warrior-ancestors, and it helped to establish the warrior's credentials as warrior, identifying him as a member of the closed fraternity, enabling him to "trade" on his status. However, claim to personal excellence on the grounds of lofty ancestry was seldom possible. In the first place, ancestry was usually traced back no further than three or four generations—and the majority of the Homeric genealogies mention grandfather or simply father.[29] But, more importantly, success had to be won by the individual on his own account. Rarely does a warrior give his lineage in order to impress others with his eminence—and at times the point of a recited genealogy seems to be the necessity for the hero to meet the standards of excellence set by his forebears. Thus, after the long narrative of his ancestor Bellerophon, Glaukos says:

> But Hippolochos begot me, and I claim that he is my father; he sent me to Troy, and urged upon me repeated injunctions, to be always among the bravest, and hold my head above others, not shaming the generation of my fathers, who were the greatest men in Ephyre and again in wide Lykia. Such is my generation and the blood I claim to be born from.
>
> *(Iliad 6.206-11, Latt.)*

When Diomedes says, "I also boast that I am by birth the son of an *agathos* father" (*Iliad* 14.113), he appears to be claiming that he is a good man because of his ancestry. Actually, Diomedes sets forth his lineage as a compensation for his youth (line 112), specifically his uncertainty about his ability to offer counsel to the other, older, leaders. Having given his genealogy, he says:

> Therefore, you could not call me a coward *(kakos)* and a weakling by birth, and dishonor my spoken counsel, when I speak out well.
>
> (4.126-27)

What Diomedes means, having listed three generations of ancestors who were brave warriors, is that his pedigree, full of fighting men, makes his battle counsel meritorious. Although he has proved his worth as an *agathos* on his own merits, the fact that he could point out others of like ability in his family enhances his claims to these qualities. In this respect, a very important one, the Homeric warrior ideal differed from the later aristocratic ideal in which noble ancestry was appealed to as automatic evidence of class superiority.[30] The epic attitude shows the genesis of this idea, but for the Homeric warrior high descent was not a guarantee of worth, as may be seen from a passage in the *Iliad* where Agamemnon, fearful that Menelaus would be chosen by Diomedes for the dangerous spying mission in the Trojan camp, advises Diomedes:

> Do not, out of the reverence in your heart, leave behind a better man, and, yielding to reverence, take the worse, looking to birth — not even if he is more chiefly *(basileuteros)*.
>
> (*Iliad* 10.237-39)

Menelaus' higher birth status makes him no less the worse man *(cheirōn)*. For another indication that high birth was regarded mainly as a spur to achievement we may turn to the prayer of Hector for his infant son:

> Zeus, and you other immortals, grant that this boy, who is my son, may be as I am, pre-eminent among the Trojans, great in strength, as I am, and rule strongly over Ilion; and some day let them say of him: "He is better by far than his father," as he comes in from the fighting; and let him kill his enemy and bring home the blooded spoils, and delight the heart of his mother.
>
> (*Iliad* 6.476-81, Latt.)[31]

Moreover, should success be lacking, for any reason, ancestry counted for nothing whatever. Paris, despite his lofty birth, was despised by Greeks and Trojans alike, because of his softness. In addition, the sudden mutability of fortune in a world governed by physical force made the accident of birth less dependable. For an illustration of this we can turn to the fears of Andromache regarding the prospects of Astyanax after Hector has been killed:

The day of bereavement leaves a child with no agemates to befriend him. He bows his head before every man, his cheeks are bewept, he goes, needy, a boy among his father's companions, and tugs at this man by the mantle, that man by the tunic, and they pity him, and one gives him a tiny drink from a goblet, enough to moisten his lips, not enough to moisten his palate. But one whose parents are living beats him out of the banquet hitting him with his fists and in words also abuses him: Get out, you! Your father is not dining among us."
(*Iliad* 22.490-98, Latt.)

Although Odysseus' son Telemachus was the acknowledged heir to the rule of Ithaca, all knew that if one of the suitors prevailed Telemachus would lose not only the chiefdom but his property besides.[32] And the community at large was apparently quite content to sit back and watch the warrior-chiefs quarrel among themselves, without thought of interference. One may be born the son or daughter of a chief, but a pirate raid or kidnapping could reduce one's status to that of a slave.[33] At the funeral of Hector, Andromache considers the fate of the Trojan women who will be taken as slaves when Troy is ultimately captured; she laments her own misfortune and that of her child Astyanax:

and among them I shall also go, and you my child, follow where I go, and there do much hard work that is unworthy of you, drudgery for a hard master...
(*Iliad* 24.732-34, Latt.)

The prime requisites for political rule, as for military success, were personal prowess and ability to lead.[34] Thus, in the confused situation at Ithaca, the young Telemachus was physically (and psychologically) inadequate to cope with the suitors; the old chief, Odysseus' father Laertes, was powerless; and even Odysseus himself could not simply return and claim his office, but had to regain it by slaying the suitors. By the same laws of personal excellence it was also possible to raise one's social status. In an interesting passage in the *Odyssey,* Odysseus, disguised as a beggar, tells the fictitious story of how he, born the bastard son of a Cretan noble, with only a tiny inheritance, gained great fame, wealth and power because he was a good warrior.[35] And when Odysseus was preparing to fight the suitors he made two of his slaves, the swineherd Eumaeus, and the cowherd Philoetius, henchmen in his struggle to regain the chiefdom, promising that:

> If by my hand the god overmasters the lordly suitors, then I shall get wives for you both, and grant you possessions and houses built next to mine, and think of you in the future always as companions of Telemachos, and his brothers.
>
> (*Odyssey* 21.213-16, Latt.)

These are, however, the only hints of "upward mobility" in the Homeric poems. Although fame and position are won by virtue of a strong right arm, the epics reflect a society which had already begun to turn the corner from individual achievement, dependent solely on skill and prowess, toward the idea of a social class in which membership alone allowed one to claim excellence *(aretē)*. Although the self-image of the Homeric aristocrat centers on personal ability and the glory that can be won only by individual merit, it has already become clear that one must be a member of the "club" in order to compete. There are no sharply defined class distinctions yet; rather Homer tends to obscure the faceless mass of "ordinary" people. While they are not unimportant, they serve mainly as background to the exploits of the heroes. Homer never suggests that they are inferior;[36] nevertheless their role, both in war and peace, is played down. They are the *dēmos*, the people, or *laos*, the host, rather passively reflecting the greatness of the individual warrior-chiefs, who have already begun to appear aware of themselves as a distinctive group.

Again we can look to comparative anthropology for a clearer perspective. In anthropological terms, the "ranked" society of the tribal chiefdom had just begun to move in the direction of the "class" or "stratified" society of the archaic aristocratic state. In the "egalitarian" social structure which exists at the level of band or tribe there is equal access to status positions (and, of course, to economic resources as well). In such societies a great hunter or warrior will achieve status distinction, but this status is neither transferable nor inheritable. Each generation can (and must) achieve status on its own. We have seen clear evidence of this egalitarianism surviving in Homer. In "ranked" societies, usually signalled by the appearance of chiefs, rank is "built-in" as it were. The office of chief is often hereditary (as in Homer); chiefs, and their families, consequently have structured greater access to prestige. Usually those who work closely with the chief (his companions and followers), and their families, share in this ranking, constituting a kind of nobility (or, "proto-nobility"). In such an organization may be discerned the beginnings of an hereditary class sytem, in which an upward change in status becomes difficult to achieve. Although ranked societies exhibit differential access to prestige, access to goods remains equalitarian; that is, all free members of the community have equal access to the group's production. In Homer, for example, the spoils of war and raid are distributed evenly, sometimes by lot, to all the warriors. However, those of high rank, the leaders, are awarded an extra, or choice portion *(geras)*, as their due. This inequality amidst equality ("chiefly due") confers greater prestige and an edge of wealth (which can be used to reward, and thereby to increase, one's following), and has a redundant effect on the ranking system. A "class" society, on the other hand, restricts access to economic resources as well as to high status; not every type of person has an equal chance to acquire land, animals and other goods. Only in such a system is it possible to speak of "nobles" and "commoners," "the rich" and "the poor" as formally conceived social categories. Within the context of these schematic societal models, the social structure of the Homeric world conforms, as we have already observed, to the ranked chiefdom, which also exhibits a number of features of the egalitarian tribal scheme.

The purpose of this brief examination of evolutionary models, besides "fixing" Homeric society more firmly along the spectrum of these types, is to emphasize that the Homeric Greeks did not attain the level of the stratified or class society. Nor did the Greeks ever really evolve such a social system. As we shall see, the Greek aristocracy later developed a "class consciousness," and some of the mannerisms of a true ruling class. Economically and politically, in some parts of the Greek world, the élite managed to acquire for a time something like a monopoly of economic resources and status positions. Nevertheless, the state forms which eventually emerged from the declining chiefdoms of the late Dark Age retained to a remarkable degree elements of the early tribal system — especially a profoundly rooted spirit of egalitarianism.

Certainly, contrary to an often expressed view, the political system which forms the background of the epics is not a highly stratified feudal order of "barons" and "peasant masses." The common people are not regarded as social inferiors — there is, in fact, no birth or class nomenclature in Homer. The role of the people, though passive for the most part, does not imply submissiveness to their leaders. It must be remembered that the rank and file are also given the epithet *aristoi* (best), and that they, too, are called "heroes."[37] The crew that sailed with Odysseus on his voyage home from Troy were not all noble warriors; most of them were ordinary soldiers, but they had the love and respect of their captain, who called them his companions and friends.[38] The war-leader was still, in the old tribal sense, the "shepherd of the people," "leader of the host," and mutual dependency and respect are evident. High rank, with its attendant honors, was, in a real sense, still a gift of the community at large; conversely, if a leader abused his privileges, he was accountable to the people. This reciprocity is summed up in a famous conversation between Sarpedon, chief of the Lycians, and Glaukos, his second in command. Why, Sarpedon inquires of Glaukos, do the Lycians give us such great honor—first place at the feasts, choice meats, respect like the gods, and

> a great piece of land by the banks of Xanthos, good land, orchard and vineyard, and ploughland ...

The question is a rhetorical one and Sarpedon answers it himself:

> Therefore it is our duty in the forefront of the Lykians to take our stand, and bear our part of the blazing of battle, so that a man of the close-armoured Lykians may say of us: "Indeed, these are no ignoble men who are lords of Lykia, these *basilēes* of ours, who feed upon the fat sheep appointed and drink the exquisite sweet wine, since indeed there is strength of valour in them, since they fight in the forefront of the Lykians."
>
> (*Iliad* 12.310-21, Latt.)

There is more than an implication in these words that should they fail in their duties they would no longer merit the honors they received. The chiefs were not simply single champions fighting alone; their primary military function was to lead and inspire the warriors, who were not an insignificant rabble, but fellow tribesmen, able and willing to judge their leaders. The "man of the Lykians" does not say that his leaders fight for him, but that they "fight in the forefront." And when the commons do act they act decisively and as free men.[39]

Only once in Homer is there any sign of strain in the easy alliance between noble warriors and ordinary soldiers. In *Iliad* 2, Thersites, a commoner,[40] verbally abuses the supreme commander of the Greeks, and is beaten by Odysseus for his presumption. Generations of scholars have tried to extract from this incident far-reaching conclusions regarding the social organization of Dark Age Greece. Much of the controversy centers on whether or not a "commoner" had the right to speak in the assembly. Those who deny this possibility assert that otherwise

The Ideal of the Warrior-Aristocrat

Odysseus would not have humiliated him. But, as Homer himself says, Thersites had done this before—he was always abusing Odysseus and Achilles (whom he now defends); and the fact that he was allowed to finish his speech would seem to show that speaking out was not unthinkable. It seems easiest to say that Thersites had a "right" (probably not used much) to speak out, but that he overstepped the bounds of tribal custom not only by speaking his mind, but by urging a specific course of action—in this case to abandon the war and return home. In any event, this is the only sign of open societal tension in either epic, and it would be unwarranted to read into it anything beyond the simple fact that the Homeric soldier was a free man who usually obeyed his leaders and took their advice, but demurred when conditions seemed to warrant it.[41]

To what extent the ordinary people subscribed to the warrior-code is not easy to say, since their voice is so seldom heard. We may suspect that their outlook was different. The outburst of Thersites, for example, reveals a point of view that is clearly contrary to the ethic of the aristocratic warrior, and is worth quoting in full:

> Son of Atreus, what thing further do you want, or find fault with now? Your shelters are filled with bronze, there are plenty of the choicest women for you within your shelter, whom we Achaians give to you first of all whenever we capture some stronghold. Or is it still more gold you will be wanting, that some son of the Trojans, breakers of horses, brings as ransom out of Ilion, one that I, or some other Achaian, capture and bring in? Is it some young woman to lie with in love and keep her all to yourself apart from the others? It is not right for you, their leader, to lead in sorrow the sons of the Achaians. My good fools, poor abuses, you women, not men, of Achaia, let us go back home in our ships, and leave this man here by himself in Troy to mull his prizes of honour that he may find out whether or not we others are helping him. And now he has dishonoured Achilleus, a man much better than he is. He has taken his prize by force and keeps her. But there is no gall in Achilleus' heart, and he is forgiving. Otherwise, son of Atreus, this were your last outrage.
>
> (*Iliad* 2.225-42, Latt.)

The whole tenor of Thersites' speech is non-heroic—the only reference to the code is his statement that Agamemnon has dishonored *(atimēsen)* Achilles.

Aside from this, a number of further points can be made about the speech. First of all, for Thersites, the object of fighting was simply to amass booty. Second, he makes no bones of the fact that the spoils are won by people like him, the ordinary soldier. Third, he takes for granted that Agamemnon's motive for the war is greed and nothing more. Fourth, he confidently assumes that it is the mass of the army who are the mainstay of the expedition. Finally, and perhaps most importantly, he takes Agamemnon to task in the strongest terms for failing in his duty as a leader. When he says that it is not seemly "for you, being the leader *(archos)*, to bring the sons of the Achaeans into evil," he is stating the principle that the commander has a responsibility to lead properly; should he fail in this his troops have the right to repudiate him. This attitude, stated explicitly here, is very similar to the implicit recognition of it by Sarpedon in the passage quoted earlier (above, page 20). The poet seems anxious to point out to his audience that Thersites' views were not shared by the rest of the Achaean troops, for he had them say after Odysseus has beaten Thersites:

> Come now: Odysseus has done excellent things by thousands, bringing forward good counsels and ordering armed encounters: but now this is far the best thing he ever has accomplished among the Argives, to keep this thrower of words, this braggart out of assembly. Never again will his proud heart stir him up, to wrangle with the princes *(basileis)* in words of revilement.
> (*Iliad* 2.272-77, Latt.)

But Homer appears to be protesting too much here, and we may safely believe that in his total lack of sympathy with the heroic code of honor, and in making Agamemnon accountable for his failures of leadership, Thersites reflected the sentiments of the non-aristocratic host. There is, in fact, no good reason to suppose that the code of personal glory should operate at the lower level of society, although many historians tend to regard as self-evident that the cultural ideals of the warrior-heroes were accepted universally throughout the society.[42]

Otherwise, the few glimpses of ordinary life in the epics show a preoccupation with the daily crises of earning a living or the simple pleasures of life in an agricultural society. An important fact, often not sufficiently stressed, is that in societies based primarily on subsistence, or near subsistence, agricultural economy (as ancient Greece always was for the most part), the mere filling of the belly was the constant preoccupation of the vast majority of the population. In outlook, the great

The Ideal of the Warrior-Aristocrat

figures of the *Iliad* and *Odyssey* had moved far beyond that stage; glory, not food, was their chief concern, and it is this simple fact perhaps more than anything else that separates them from the mass of men. There is a passage in the *Iliad* which casts this difference into vivid relief. After the death of Patroclus, Achilles resolved to fight and was eager to begin. Odysseus, the man of practical reason (the most "ordinary-minded" of the heroes), insisted that the army have breakfast first. In anger Achilles retorts:

> Food and drink mean nothing to my heart but blood does, and slaughter, and the groaning of men in the hard work.
> (*Iliad* 19.213-14, Latt.)

Odysseus answers him from a wisdom that is far older than the ideal of glory in war:

> There is no way the Achaians can mourn a dead man by denying the belly. Too many fall day by day, one upon another ... and all those who are left about from the hateful work of war must remember food and drink ...
> (*Iliad* 19.225-31, Latt.)

While the host eats, Achilles abstains from mere food—Athena distils nectar and ambrosia, the sustenance of the immortals, into his breast to sustain his strength. But the theme of the empty belly is a constant motif of "lower class" thought throughout Greek literature, and one can observe its occurrence frequently, often in conscious opposition to the more exalted aristocratic ideal.

We may sum up the Homeric aristocratic ideal by saying that worth or excellence, *aretē*, was conceived of in the physical sphere almost exclusively, most specifically in terms of prowess as a warrior. The aim of the high-status warrior was public recognition of his ability. The Homeric proto-aristocrat endlessly competed with his fellows for prestige *(kydos, timē)*, with the goal of being recognized as "best" *(aristos)*; his greatest fear was failure and its accompanying communal humiliation. Responsibility and loyalty were directed towards his immediate family and the corporate household *(oikos)*, extending outward to a small circle of friends and companions *(philoi, hetairoi)*. Other attributes and qualities might be prized or considered desirable, but they were either adjunct to or proof of fighting skills and the *timē* these won. Wealth was a by-product of prowess, a sign of success, and a means of increasing one's influence. Mental excellence was important, but mainly as an aid to action. A handsome or prepossessing exterior was the obvious accompaniment of size and strength and of the status that they commanded. Descent from gods or from other great warriors was both proof of ability and incentive to excel further. All sociopsycological responses, such as loyalty, kindness, pity, mercy, affection, fair dealing, responsibility to others, were manifested to a greater or lesser degree, depending on the demands of the primary goal of aggrandizement of self, family, and followers. The sense of membership in an exclusive group of like-minded men, regardless of tribal affiliation, was prominent.

As the aristocratic self-conception was altered by time and circumstances these earliest components of the Greek aristocratic ideal appear in a state of considerable flux, with now one, now another set of values dominating. In assessing the heroic ideal it is difficult to exaggerate the "singlemindedness," as Finley calls it, in which

> everything pivoted on a single element of honor and virtue: strength, bravery, physical courage, prowess. Conversely, there was no weakness, no unheroic trait, but one, and that was cowardice and the consequent failure to pursue heroic goals.[43]

But this, it must be stressed, is a warrior's ideal, refined to an extraordinary degree. Just as Achilles' overly intense dedication to the requirements of heroic honor proved too extreme even for his fellow heroes, so also there is good reason to question the extent to which ordinary men shared the code. Certainly the degree of their dedication to the values of the military élite must have been considerably less. From the little evidence given us in the Homeric poems about the "man of the *dēmos*" we know that his conception of society emphasized the responsibility of the leader towards his followers. That this attitude prevailed in peace as well as war is shown by a speech of the "beggar" Odysseus to Penelope:

> your fame goes up into the wide heaven, as of some *basileus* who, as a blameless man and god-fearing, and ruling as lord over many powerful people, upholds the way of good government, and the black earth yields him barley and wheat, his trees are heavy with fruit, his sheepflocks continue to bear young, the sea gives him fish, because of his good leadership, and his people prosper under him.
>
> (*Odyssey* 19.108-14, Latt.)

The Ideal of the Warrior-Aristocrat

These remarkable lines, like the speech of Thersites and the dialogue between Sarpedon and Glaukos, give a glimpse of the leader as perceived by the ordinary person. If the *basileus* is "god-fearing," "upholds justice *(eudikia),*" and exercises "good leadership," his people *(laoi)* prosper. This triad of virtues plays a negligible role in the ethos of the aristocratic champions.[44]

At the same time we see little evidence that those outside the dominant group felt disposed to challenge its pre-eminence or to offer a "counter-ideal." In a world where physical might was the decisive factor the great warrior enjoyed a natural superiority, universally recognized and unchallenged. From this natural superiority flowed all the perquisites of wealth, status and respect, ungrudgingly given so long as there was no violent interference with the rights of those who ranked below. In the epics there are very few signs of disagreement between rulers and ruled; at most we can see fairly plainly that the heroic ideal of personal honor was not shared by all elements of the society.

Finally, all that has been said of the Homeric warrior-élite must be put firmly in a proper sociological perspective. I have called these chiefs and "outstanding men" *(exochoi)* "aristocrats," and their value system an "aristocratic ideal," mostly for want of better terms. Just as Homeric society was not "feudal" in the post-Roman European sense (despite certain analogies, which misled earlier scholars), so Homer's "rulers and counsellors" were but fledgling aristocrats, and their attitudes had not hardened into the code of a stratified "class." As Starr and others have pointed out, the epics themselves and the findings of archaeology reveal that the Dark Age aristocrat was no powerful "prince" or "baron." His economic superiority was only relative, his material life-style not vastly different from that of his fellow tribesmen. Because of the fragile nature of the chiefdom form itself the political authority of the *basileus* was severely limited. Despite the obvious self-awareness of these men as a group apart, in the absence of a true class society the Homeric "aristocratic ideal" could not have been a conceptualized ideological superstructure intended to differentiate a "nobility" from the "masses." We may thus conclude with Starr, that

> ... the Homeric world had not yet traveled all the way toward the elaboration of an aristocratic ethos, i.e., an obligatory pattern of life and values *consciously* conceived and shared by a limited group which considered itself "best" and the claims of which were generally accepted, even cherished, by other elements of society.[45]

That time had not yet come, but it was not far off.

◊

When we turn from Homer to the next important figure of Greek literature, Hesiod, we can note signs of social tension. Hesiod was a farmer, who lived and composed his poetry around 700 B.C., shortly after, or perhaps at the same time as, the final composition of the *Odyssey*. The "world" of Hesiod is an exactly contemporary one; Hesiod is a direct witness of his own time, which is later, perhaps by four, five or six generations, than the historical period reflected in the Homeric epics. His father, he tells us, pressed by poverty, had emigrated from Asia Minor to the mainland of Greece, settling near the town of Ascra in Boeotia, which Hesiod calls "bad in summer, horrid in winter, good at no time," and there took up farming. The living was not much better in Boeotia, and the picture of daily life that we get from Hesiod is one of unremitting toil for small reward. Still, Hesiod was not poor; he would rank as a fairly prosperous independent freeholder by the standards of the early seventh century B.C. in Greece. The life of harsh manual labor, the lot of the marginal farmer, has changed little since then. Countless millions have lived (and live) just as Hesiod described in his long poem, *The Works and Days*—few have looked at the world from the perspective of a warrior-chief. For this reason it is not surprising that there is no trace at all in Hesiod of the Homeric warrior ideal. Prowess and glory are foreign concepts to the farmer whose main concern is a full stomach and whose idea of wealth is a full barn. The *Iliad* opens with an invocation to the Muse to sing the wrath of Achilles. Hesiod heard the Muses, too; on Mount Helicon, as he was tending his flocks, they summoned him to compose, addressing him thus:

> Shepherds of the wilderness, wretched things of shame, mere bellies . . .
>
> (*Theogony* 26)[46]

The reproach of the Muses underlines the difference between the aristocratic outlook, obsessed with prestige, and the peasant's constant preoccupation with survival. Pride, honor, glory, immortality, self-doubt had small place in Hesiod's world; his message was simple: work hard and you will be "wealthy."

> If your heart within you desires wealth, do these things and work with work upon work.
>
> (*Works and Days* 381-82)

For the Homeric hero abundant wealth was a sign of eminence, for Hesiod wealth was a decent living and not having to borrow. The

The Ideal of the Warrior-Aristocrat

warriors of the epic moved in a world of elaborate courtesy, gift exchange and complicated personal obligations; Hesiod distrusted his neighbors, preached a stingy parsimony, and quarreled with his own brother over their inheritance. Homeric women were valued possessions, respected and fought over; for Hesiod woman is an evil. The Trojan elders, when they sight Helen, who was the cause of untold woe, say:

> Surely there is no blame on Trojans and strong-greaved Achaians if for long time they suffer hardship for a woman like this one.
> (*Iliad* 3.156-57, Latt.)

To Hesiod, Pandora, the primal woman, was a curse from the gods.[47] Examples could be multiplied, but these suffice to show how far removed was Hesiod's outlook from the "refined" view of Homer.

There is one important point of contact between the two worlds that helps also to underline the differences in outlook. On several occasions Hesiod talks about the *basileis;* these are not the high-souled, glory-obsessed warriors of Homer; rather they are local big-men, whom Hesiod calls "gift-devouring." They accept bribes and are interested only in their own might, not the welfare of the people. To his brother, Perses, who had cheated Hesiod of his inheritance, he says:

> For we had already divided our inheritance, but you seized the greater share and carried it off, greatly swelling the glory of our bribe-swallowing *basileis* who love to judge such a cause as this.
> (*Works and Days* 37-39)

Later in the same poem he comes to the theme again:

> There is a noise when Justice *(Dikē)* is being dragged in the way where those who devour bribes and give sentence with crooked judgements take her. And she, wrapped in mist, follows to the city and haunts of the people, weeping, and bringing evil *(kakon)* to men ...
> (*Works and Days* 220-23)

Concern over the greed of the leader and his responsibility to the people not to lead them into evil had formed the substance of Thersites' charge against Agamemnon. So, here the two poets meet in the authentic voice of the independent peasant and the common soldier.

Twice Hesiod speaks of the truly good rulers; but his descriptions do not match the Homeric ideal of personal glory and fame:

> All the people *(laoi)* look towards him while he settles causes with true judgements: and he, speaking surely, would soon make wise end even of a great quarrel; for therefore are there *basileis* wise in heart, because when the *laoi* are being misguided in their assembly, they set right the matter again with ease, persuading them with gentle words.
>
> *(Theogony* 84-90)

The chiefly qualities commended here are wisdom and fairness, dispensed with a gentle concern. Another description, highly reminiscent of the simile from the *Odyssey* quoted above (19.108-14), depicts the just leader as bringing his people into prosperity and peace:

> But they who give straight judgements to strangers and to the men of the land, and go not aside from what is just *(dikaion)*, their polis flourishes, and the *laoi* prosper in it: Peace, the nurse of children, is abroad in their land, and all-seeing Zeus never decrees cruel war against them. Neither famine nor disaster ever haunt men who do true justice; but light-heartedly they tend the fields . . . the earth bears them victual in plenty . . . their wooly sheep are laden with fleeces; their women bear children like their parents. They flourish continually with good things . . .
>
> *(Works and Days* 225-36)

As we have seen, Justice, the fair dealing between men and men, is much on Hesiod's mind, an ethical concept which is missing almost entirely from the *Iliad* and the *Odyssey*. Also, Justice is given very strong divine sanction by Hesiod; his Zeus, unlike the Zeus of Homer, is vitally concerned with justice in general and with the punishment of mortal wrongdoing. Justice, Law and Peace are the children of Zeus *(Theogony* 901-903). At the beginning of the *Works and Days* we are told that Zeus

> easily makes strong and easily crushes the strong man; easily he humbles the conspicuous and raises the obscure; easily he straightens the crooked and withers the arrogant . . .
>
> (Lines 5-7, translation mine)

In a passage that goes much farther than anything in Homer he says that Zeus gives punishment *(dikē)* to those who commit violence *(hybris)* and cruel deeds. Often a whole community *(sympasa polis)* suffers for the evil deeds of a *kakos* man, with famine, plague, destruction of their army, their walls, and their ships *(Works and Days* 238-47). He admonishes the leaders in the strongest terms:

> O *basileis*, mark well this *dikē*, you also; for the deathless gods are near among men and note all those who oppress one another with crooked judgements and do not heed the anger of the gods. For upon the bounteous earth Zeus has thrice ten thousand immortals, watchers of mortal men, and they keep watch on judgements *(dikai)* and cruel deeds *(schetlia erga)* as they roam, clothed in mist, all over the earth.
>
> (Translation mine)

Dikē sits beside her father, Zeus, and tells him of men's injustice

> until the *dēmos* pays for the mad folly of *basileis*, who, evilly minded, pervert judgement and give sentence crookedly. Keep watch against this, *basileis*, and make straight your judgements, you who devour bribes; put crooked judgements altogether from your thoughts.
>
> (*Works and Days* 248-64)

The social priorities of Homer and Hesiod are evident on a grander, theological, level. Homer's Olympus is a mirror of the heroic world on earth: the gods banquet, boast and quarrel like the mortals below — indeed, they mingle with the heroes and sometimes even battle with them. Hesiod's Olympus is an island of calm in a harsh universe. His great cosmological tale, the *Theogony*, recounts the slow, often grim, evolution from primeval chaos and savage passion to order and stability, where, finally, a Zeus mindful of justice sits on the throne. So, it is by opposites and contrasts that we perceive Hesiod's assessment of the aristocratic ideal. It should be clear by now that the heroic value system was the ideal of a small group, not of the society as a whole. On the few occasions when Homer allows the lower class outlook to show through, we see a non-responsive, almost negative reaction to the ideal; for Hesiod that ideal hardly exists.

In the considerable span of time that separated the world of the *Iliad* and the *Odyssey* from the contemporary experience of Hesiod, the social fragmentation already apparent in the epics had increased. The chiefdom form of polity, unstable by its nature, had not evolved into the centralized monarchy or the feudal state, but into a system of local aristocracies. According to the late Karl Polanyi, the tribal order, with its integrative institutions and bonds of reciprocity, was yielding to a "crude individualism."

The traditional political structure of tribal settlements had been viciously distorted by the "gift-devouring princes," who now failed to return the law and justice that was their responsibility. The empty forms of chieftainship remained; but meaning and content were gone. The tribal obligations expressed by those forms had faded. Justice became an abstract ideal to be pursued, and was no longer the institutional setting for the life of the tribe.[48]

The pessimism that came with the consciousness of "tribal decay" is vividly captured in Hesiod's famous description of the retrogression of humankind. In successive stages, from a "golden race," in primordial times, when men "lived like gods," without sorrow or toil, through a constantly degenerative process a "silver race" was replaced by a race of bronze, culminating in the present "iron race."

> Thereafter, would that I were not among the men of the fifth generation, but either had died before or been born afterwards. For now truly is a race of iron, and men never rest from labour and sorrow by day, and from perishing by night; and the gods shall lay sore trouble upon them.
>
> (*Works and Days* 174-178)

Interestingly, Hesiod breaks this regressive ordering of metal races by placing a "god-like race of hero-men" between the bronze and the iron race of his own day. These "demi-gods" *(hēmitheoi)*, "more righteous and better" *(diakaioteron kai areion)* than those who had preceded them, were the Homeric race of warriors who fought at Thebes and Troy, now dwelling in ease in the "Isles of the Blessed." This revealing bit of social history shows that Hesiod was grimly aware of the breakdown of the stable order of the tribal community, in which mutual responsibility afforded even the lowliest beggar some measure of security. In times to come, he predicts,

> The father will not agree with his children, nor the children with their father, nor guest with his host, nor comrade with comrade; nor will brother be dear to brother as aforetime. Men will dishonour their parents as they grow quickly old, and will carp at them, chiding them with bitter words, hard-hearted they, not knowing the fear of the gods. They will not repay their aged parents the cost of their nurture, for might shall be their right: and one man will sack another's city. There will be no favour for the man who keeps his oath or for the just or for the good; but rather men will praise the evil-doer

The ideal of the Warrior-Aristocrat

and his violent dealing. Strength will be right and reverence will cease to be; and the wicked will hurt the worthy man, speaking false words against him . . .

(*Works and Days* 182-94)

The preceding race of heroes, when the chiefdom form was still sufficiently viable to integrate the community and to ameliorate the divisiveness of atomistic individualism, was, for Hesiod, a nostalgic exception to what he sees as the inexorable decay of human morality.[49]

In spite of his pessimism, Hesiod is aware of the possibility of a new type of social ordering, in which "community" might once again prevail. But community henceforth is to be the association of neighbor and citizen, not the community of kinship. The reciprocity of a changing order must be accomplished outside of the paternalistic beneficence of the corporation head or the mutual assistance of the clan.

Call your friend to a feast; but leave your enemy alone; and especially call him who lives near you: for if any mischief happen in the place, neighbours come ungirt, but kinsmen stay to girt themselves.

(*Works and Days* 342-45)

In a world in which strife and competition are constant, when "neighbor view with neighbor, hastening after wealth" (*W&D* 23), and the *basileus* is likened to a hawk who terrorizes the powerless nightingale (*W&D* 202-12), then neighborliness and fairness must be strictly observed.

Take fair measure from your neighbor and pay him back fairly with the same measure, or better, if you can; so that if you are in need afterwards, you may find him sure.

(*Works and days* 349-351)

Nevertheless, neighbors do not always cooperate. A person in want may go begging "to other men's houses" in vain (*W&D* 395); "grieving in heart, with your wife and children, you may seek a living among your neighbors, and they do not care" (*W&D* 399-400):

For it is easy to say: 'Give me a yoke of oxen and a waggon,' and it is easy to refuse: 'I have work for my oxen.'

(*Works and Days* 453-54; cf. 477, 706)

When we consider the social forces at work at the end of the eighth century—the waning of kinship-community, the uncertainty of mutuality from fellow villager, the spirit of selfish competition, the increase of status and wealth differentiation, land scarcity and rising population — it is easy to understand Hesiod's insistence on the need for justice sanctioned by the gods, and his emphasis on individual moral responsibility.

Hesiod's concern with ethical relations is especially reflected in word usage. It was noted that in the epics the words for good *(agathos, esthlos)* and bad *(kakos)* referred almost exclusively to the sphere of physical excellence and bravery. In fact, the epithet of highest commendation, *agathos,* is used only of high-status warriors, never of the rank and file. In Hesiod, on the contrary, these words never refer to physical excellence, and often have a decidedly ethical-moral connotation.

For example, Hesiod pairs *agathos* with the adjective for "just" *(dikaios),* a combination not found in Homer.[50] In another place he says:

> A *kakos* neighbor is as great a plague as an *agathos* one is a great blessing; he who enjoys an *esthlos* neighbor has a precious possession. Not even an ox would die but for a *kakos* neighbor.
> (*Works and Days* 346-48)

It is plain that good and bad here are defined in terms of a simpler ethos which stresses service, cooperation and fair dealing, with no reference at all to the qualities that make a Homeric man *agathos.* Equally in the ethical sphere is this usage:

> Do not get a name either as lavish or churlish; as a friend of *kakoi* or as a slanderer of *esthloi.*
> (*Works and Days* 715-16)[51]

Again, in Hesiod the adjective *aristos* (best) has a force lacking in Homer, in a passage where "quiet" intellectual competence is given great value:

> That man is altogether best *(panaristos)* who considers all things himself and marks what will be better afterwards and at the end; and he, again, is *esthlos* who listens to a good advisor; but whoever neither thinks for himself nor keeps in mind what another tells him, he is an unprofitable *(achreios)* man.
> (*Works and Days* 293-297)

The Ideal of the Warrior-Aristocrat

Hesiod's notions of ability and success *(aretē)* and of the good man have no reference at all to the heroic conception of these. *Aretē* consists in being a successful farmer; the good man *(agathos anēr)* is one who is capable, efficient, prudent and cooperative within the narrow sphere of agrarian life.[52]

It is clear that the semantic differences in the uses of terms of approval and disapproval betoken a rift in social perceptions. We cannot, of course, make too much of these differences; given the disparity of subject matter, time, and perspective, between Homer and Hesiod certain differences are inevitable. Accordingly, the terminology of merit is used differently by different groups in the community. Hesiod does not record a radical change in values nor is he consciously rebutting the traditional claims of the *agathos;* he simply reflects the ethical norms of his portion of the society of his own time. If, in all respects, Hesiod saw the world through a peasant's eyes, most certainly he advocates no change in the political structure. In this sphere his sole concern is that the leaders respond to communal needs, hence his preoccupation with justice and the divine machinery which would ensure that justice.[53]

◊

In summary: the differences of outlook in Hesiod and Homer are attributable to a number of interconnected factors. Most obvious is the simple fact that a warrior-leader and a small or middling farmer will view their environment differently. Structural changes in Greek society, however, are of greater account in the differences in attitudes expressed. The transition from the tribal chiefdom to the "aristocratic" polity witnessed the passing of the kinship order and the economic and social stability that such an order represented. Social differentiation, competition, craft specialization, private property, indebtedness, social alienation, are all evident in Hesiod's assessment of contemporary life. What the material and technological causes were that led to the replacement of the security of a kinship society by the insecurity of a territorial society are too complex and too uncertain to speculate on here. Certainly, the slow evolution from an economy based primarily on stockbreeding to one that was principally agricultural, attained by Hesiod's time, was a key factor. A dramatic rise in population around the middle of the eighth century, the result, surely, of the increase in food production, seems to have led to a land shortage, and, in turn, to the export of surplus population in the form of colonization. An increase in foreign trade and in the manufacture of goods for export (also connected with the colonizing movement), the import of luxury items from the East, richer finds in graves and sanctuaries, attest to a general rise in prosperity, but most especially among the upper stratum.[54]

The beginning of the stratified society, in which access to fundamental resources is restricted to certain groups, signals important changes in ethico-religious values. According to a recent theory, when a society is marked by unequal distribution of wealth — individual ownership of property, debt relations, and economic stratification — supernatural sanctions governing human behavior are likely to emerge and to become prominent; hence, the apparent paradox that "the ethical systems of advanced literate cultures are supernaturalistic to a greater degree than those of preliterate cultures."[55]

As yet there is no sign that the two concepts of *aretē*, despite the increasing differences, had become polarized. One supposes that when an eighth- or early seventh-century aristocrat called himself a "good" man the term embraced essentially the range of qualities of the Homeric *agathos,* and that the same would be true, *mutatis mutandis,* of the peasant concept of the *agathos.* Where we do see active evidence of discontent or protest is when the contrasting points of view come into abrasive contact—as in the case of a Thersites, whose expressions of quarrelsome independence earn him blows from the spokesman of the traditional order, or in a Hesiod, when he is affected personally by the power of the "bribe-devouring" *basileis.* So long as the society as a whole remains relatively stable—with an aristocratic warrior-group which protects the weaker members of the community from outside aggression, and a peasant-group that recognizes the inherent "superiority" of its leaders, accepting protection with gratitude, and offering in return its loyalty and respect—and, so long as neither group attempts to exceed its place in the order, the friction points will be few. But once the delicate balance is broken: when, for example, the leaders fail in their responsibilities by using their power and wealth to oppress or to aggrandize themselves at the expense of the people, or when the larger mass of the populace begins to intrude itself into spheres of activity formerly confined to the aristocrats, assuming, say, an important military role, or attempting to gain political control, then the social fabric shows signs of wear, and active strife results. That is what happens during the next two centuries in Greece. Naturally, the expressed values of the competing groups will be reshaped radically in the process of adjusting to the social changes.

Ω

CHAPTER TWO

The Old Ideal under Challenge

AS A RESULT of the pressure of considerable social, economic and political ferment in the Greek world during the next two centuries, important changes occurred in the pattern of values professed by the aristocratic class. The main evidence for social attitudes during this period, which extends from about the first quarter of the seventh century to around 500 B.C., is literary. Unfortunately, the so-called lyric poets of the seventh and sixth centuries B.C. have come down to us in very fragmentary form, and we possess only a tiny quantity of this major artistic outpouring. Because the seventh century was the beginning of the historically self-conscious stage of Greek culture, the testimony of the direct literary remains is supplemented by the prose writings of later Greeks, especially the historians of the fifth, fourth and later centuries, who have preserved for us something resembling a coherent account of the events of the period. In addition to the "researches" of these historiographers and antiquarians, inscriptions on stone and bronze, a much fuller archaeological record, and a scattering of other sources have given us the data to reconstruct the main outlines of the evolution of Greek thought during the Archaic Age, as it is called.

Few periods of history before the modern era have experienced so rapid a pace of social and intellectual change as the Archaic and early Classical Ages, a rate of evolution that appears all the more remarkable because of the few advances in the technological sphere. In many ways it was a truly revolutionary age, but change was not, as it often is in human history, the result of new techniques. Aside from the momentous transition from bronze to iron, there were no "revolutions" in agriculture, industry or practical science; most technical skills (many of which were borrowed in the first place) were already known, and were merely refined. Even the extraordinary discoveries in natural science and mathematics achieved by the sixth- and early fifth-century Greek "physicists," were founded on the practical wisdom of the ancient Near

East—and became highly abstract intellectual constructs which had little material application. The enormous energy of the Greeks of the Archaic Age exploded in all directions save that of technology; the "revolution" was one of ideas, aesthetics and politics, in which technological innovation played only a subsidiary role.[1]

Small-farm agriculture, based on traditional farming techniques, had become the principle mode of production by Hesiod's time, and remained so, essentially unchanged, for centuries thereafter. The manufacture of goods, trade, shipbuilding, and other "industrial" activities became important economic factors after 800 and expanded rapidly after 700, but never came close to rivaling agriculture as a source of livelihood. It has recently been estimated that the percentage of the population of Greece engaged in agriculture was over eighty and may have been as high as ninety percent.[2] This does not mean that trade, commerce and manufacture were insignificant; however small the portion of the population that was involved, the pursuit of wealth by these and other means (e.g. mercenary service, piracy) was an important social phenomenon, to which we shall have occasion to refer later.

As a general rule, the small or medium independent farm was the base of economic existence in Greece. There were exceptions to this norm (as in Sparta), and in the course of the Archaic Age in many Greek states there came to be a concentration of land in the hands of a few wealthy landowners, which provoked social unrest. Nevertheless, individual possession of land (which essentially defined citizen status) was the standard pattern as well as the ideal. The enduring quality of this ideal is seen in the frequently raised cry for the redistribution of land — whenever inequality in land ownership became severe. The sociopsychological effects of this economic fact were momentous, for it meant that change during these turbulent years took place against the background of a generally static and stable rural economy and within the context of a value system based on an agrarian way of life and the ideology of ownership of land as the criterion of citizenship. Its chief manifestation was a prevalent notion of equality (realized in many variations and degrees, of course). There were other consequences: the gap between rich and poor never became a yawning gulf; there never developed a large and powerful merchant class, nor a class of permanently oppressed peasants; Greece knew neither plantations nor teeming urban centers. The social stratification that emerged with the evolution from the tribal design to the "aristocratic" state did not result in a formal class system. No Greek, however elevated his status, ever had a title before his name; no citizen of the many small *poleis* ever thought of himself as an "inferior."

In spite of their dominant position in the archaic polis, aristocrats could not automatically assume the mantle of class superiority. The aristocratic ideology had to conform to the social realities, which meant that from the very beginning its evolution was adaptive. In formal terms: "A code of ethics is merely an aspect of a social system. It is merely a mechanism of social control. As social systems evolve, so will their ethical counterparts." Or, to put it another way, "the social systems are the independent [variables], the ethical systems the dependent, variables."[3] The evolution of the social system itself is still not well understood, and the brief sketch that follows must, of necessity, be highly selective and simplified.

Around 750 B.C. a number of major processes are evident: a steep rise in population, the beginning of a long wave of overseas colonization, a sharp increase in trading activity, and the emergence of the polis or "city-state." They are all related, of course, although their causal connections are elusive. I have already suggested that the rise in population was the effect of greater productivity due to the change from a stockbreeding to an agrarian base. Colonization (which itself implies the existence of some kind of systematic organization) appears to have been primarily a response to surplus population and land shortage, but is also connected to the increase in trade and commerce. Most historians agree that by 700 B.C. there was a general rise in the level of prosperity throughout the Greek world. We know from the evidence of grave goods that the upper stratum had developed the taste for and the means to acquire expensive trade luxuries after 800 B.C. In addition, there is good reason to posit the existence of a "middle" group of fairly well-off farmers (among whom was Hesiod) and a fair number of moderately prosperous artisans and traders, gathered in the slowly growing urban clusters.

The polis, or "city-state," form of social organization was the principal political development of the period. Unfortunately, its origins and early form are poorly known. A polis was both more and less than a "city," more and less than a "state," as we use these terms today. It can be defined as "an independent group of people occupying an area with definite borders," but considering that the rather small geographical area which was inhabited by Greek-speakers eventually held 1500 of these units, ranging from small villages with surrounding populations in the hundreds to true urban centers, with corresponding diversity of institutions, simple categorization is impossible. The single, overreaching characteristic of all *poleis*, large or small, was the self-identification of its members with the group; the life of a "citizen," *politēs*, in its every aspect, was bounded by this identification. It is perhaps not too sweeping a generalization to say that all elements of the preceding tribal life, psychological as well as material, were subsumed in the polis. Thus, not only did the polis provide the systematic framework of a man's military, legal, political and property relations, it also determined his religious worship, his marriage customs and his recreational and aesthetic pursuits.[4]

The evolution from a kinship-and-loyalty tribal system to a territorial unit which undercut the traditional bonds of social integration and united town and countryside into a single entity with institutionalized political authority, did not occur uniformly. The story of Greek constitutional development is the story of hundreds of separate communities whose growth was determined by local and regional variables. In some remote areas the older tribal structure *(ethnos)* survived almost unchanged; some states, like Sparta, were curious hybrids combining elements of both forms. Despite this unevenness, a general model of political evolution is discernible. The tribal chief, *basileus*, whose nascent centralized political authority (as we have seen) had eroded in the face of competing claims by lesser chiefs, lost his preeminent leadership which passed to corporate control by the powerful lineages in the community. By about 700 B.C. the very office of *basileus* had virtually disappeared, except as one of a number of (usually annual) magistracies into which the powers of the chief had dispersed. There was no "ruler"; political leadership of the early polis was in the hands of men from dominant descent groups, large landholders, who held exclusive control of the political and military offices, cult associations, and the legal machinery. These were the "aristocrats," whose power base, as before, lay in their households *(oikoi)* and in the wider associations of lineage *(genos)* and phratry, corporations which figure more prominently in the polis than in the chiefdom.

The jealous competition for hegemony in the polis among the aristocratic lineages gave rise to long-standing rivalries and temporary and shifting alliances, leading to feuds, which often broke out into that internal warfare *(stasis)* which all Greeks dreaded, but which appears to us as a normal characteristic of polis life through the centuries. In their jockeying for position and prestige aristocratic lines naturally sought to increase their bases of wealth and influence, inevitably at the expense

The Old Ideal under Challenge

of non-aristocrats. Signs of class conflict, the result of political and economic exploitation by the ascendant aristocracies, are evident from the time of Hesiod on. Sporadically there arose in various Greek states individual strong men, usually men of wealth and ancestry, called *tyrannoi*, "tyrants," who opportunistically grasped political power for themselves and attempted to establish family dynasties. Ranged against their fellow aristocrats and playing on the discontent of the medium and small farmers, tyrants often appeared as defenders and "champions of the people" (as Aristotle calls them), whose acquiescence to their rule was necessary.[5]

If, as many scholars maintain, the appearance of tyrants points to reaction against aristocratic oppression of the populace, the role of the people in the tyrants' rise to power demonstrates no less the lower classes' potential for political leverage. To understand the evolution of the aristocratic ideal it is important to emphasize that at the very time men of wealth and family were trying to widen the gap between themselves and others — to become a true aristocratic class — those below this stratum were affected by the same dynamic processes at work in the society. The sense of individualism and self-awareness, restless vitality, probing curiosity (both the cause and the effect of the dramatic social changes we have sketched) touched all free men of the new polis.

At some time between 700 and 650 B.C. a change in military tactics had far-reaching consequences. The older style of fighting, like that portrayed in the *Iliad,* consisted of opposing groups, loosely organized, with a majority of the combatants armed haphazardly and lightly. The decisive fighting was done by individual warriors who were heavily armed and well protected, in many cases operating as cavalry. The outcome of a battle was decided, not by the lightly-armed mass, but by these individual aristocrats, successors of the Homeric warriors. In the new tactical system a large body of infantry, each soldier heavily armed with helmet, breastplate, shield and greaves* and wielding a long spear, stood in close formation, shield to shield, in deep ranks. This formation, called the phalanx, moved in unison and was able to overpower any existing opposing force. An individual, or knots of individuals, as well as the cavalry forces then in use, would be powerless against the concerted thrust of the bristling lances. So the phalanx and the heavily armed infantryman (*hoplitēs,* from *hopla,* arms) became, like any successful military innovation, the prevailing mode of warfare.

----

*Armor for the leg below the knee.

Clearly, the new phalanx was intimately bound up with the emerging polis; the military innovations and the socioeconomic structure developed in tandem. The phalanx presupposes, first of all, a rather large number of men. The principle of the phalanx is relatively simple: the deeper the formation the more pressure it exerts, and the longer the front line the more easily the enemy could be outflanked. So, the more hoplites a city could muster the more successful it was in warfare. Second, the phalanx requires that the large number of men necessary to man it have sufficient wealth to provide their own heavy equipment and the leisure and inclination to train together as a cohesive body.

The very existence of this new style of fighting implies that changes were taking place in the values of the society.[6] When the single warrior becomes part of a "team," the old ideal of personal glory must yield to the ideal of collective glory; the community rather than the individual becomes the focus of brave deeds. Another important social implication is the introduction of equality into the ranks. A relatively poor man of undistinguished family, whose property qualification may have been barely sufficient for the furnishing of his panoply, might find himself fighting alongside a wealthy man from an eminent family. The poor man could be the hero of the day, the "nobleman" the coward. Under the impulse of comradeship in arms and the sense of belonging to a civic unit, the scope for distinction on the basis of wealth or birth alone was reduced. In times of peace the noble would find his fellow hoplites demanding a share in the affairs of the polis which they defended in war, or at least insisting that they be treated fairly and not be subject to exploitation, either economic or political.[7]

Under the impact of the military innovations and the accompanying social awareness on the part of the "ordinary" soldiers, the old Homeric warrior ideal shows signs of change. Bravery and skill in battle are still the principle values of the soldiers, but it is a new and "non-heroic" kind of bravery that is celebrated by the poets. The essential requirement of success with the phalanx is that the hoplite stand firm in the compact ranks and not give ground; and so, in the literature after 700 B.C. the heroic individual fighter yields pride of place to the cooperative infantryman. A Spartan poet, Tyrtaeus, writing about 650 B.C., exhorts his countrymen, who had just begun to fight in the new formation:

> Let each man hold, standing firm, both feet planted on the ground, biting his lip with his teeth, covering with the belly of his broad shield his thighs and legs, his breast and shoulders . . . let each man,

Closing with the enemy, fighting hand-to-hand with long spear or sword, wound and take him; and setting foot against foot, and resting shield against shield, crest against crest, helmet against helmet let him fight his man breast to breast, grasping the hilt of his sword or of his long spear.

(Fr. 8.21-34, Diehl)[8]

It is only natural that a different emphasis is now placed on the potent Greek notion of *aretē*. In the poems of Tyrtaeus *aretē* is no longer the daring individual success, the flash of personal brilliance; the impulse towards cooperative action altered the older values, and *aretē* for Tyrtaeus is simply the ability to stand firm in ranks:

For a man is not *agathos* in war, unless he endure seeing the bloody slaughter, and standing close reach out for the foe. This is *aretē*, this the best and loveliest prize for the young man to win. A common good this, for the whole polis and all the *dēmos*, when a man holds, firm-set among the fighters, unflinchingly ...

(Fr. 9.10-17D)

In Tyrtaeus' Sparta the soldier is exhorted to fight and die for his country, his polis, not for individual glory or for plunder, which enhance a man's status. Glory there was, but it could be stated only in terms of the community. Here again, the words of Tyrtaeus illustrate the shift in emphasis:

For it is a fine thing *(kalon)* for an *agathos* man to die, falling among the front-fighters, fighting for his fatherland ...

(Fr. 6.7.1-2D)

The man who falls among the front-fighters and loses his dear life, bringing glory to his town and the people *(laoi)* and his father, struck many times in front through the breast and bossy shield and breastplate—him both young and old alike bewail, and the whole polis is distressed with grievous longing; and his tomb and children are famed among men, and his children's children and his family to come. And never does his goodly fame perish, nor his name, but even though he is under the earth he is immortal because he stood firm, acted bravely, and was fighting for his land and children when violent Ares struck him down.

(Fr. 9.23-34D)

Another early poet, Callinus of Ephesus in Asia Minor, a near contemporary of Tyrtaeus, speaks in identical terms:

> For it is an honorable and glorious thing for a man to fight for his land and children and wife against the enemy . . .

Callinus also says (in the same poem) that the man who dies at home:

> is not dear to the *dēmos* nor regretted,

but the good warrior:

> him both great and small lament if he die, for a stouthearted man, when he is dead, is a grievous loss to all the *laos*, and alive he is like a demi-god.
>
> (Fr. 1D)[9]

A side consequence of this altered ideal is the new belief that death for a "higher cause," that is, the polis, is a good thing. This is in sharp contrast to the Homeric belief that one's own life was particularly valuable. Homer's heroes never considered dying for a "cause," and a sentiment like this one by Tyrtaeus would seem impossibly extreme to the most valiant of the epic figures:

> Make life your enemy, and the black spirits of death dear as the rays of the sun.
>
> (Fr. 8.5-6D)

The idea of dedication to the community was not completely new in the seventh century; we saw its genesis in Homer, especially among the Trojans and Hector, the most communally oriented of the epic heroes. Nevertheless, Hector thought still in terms of the segmental tribe – his concern was for the close circle of family, not for the territorial community. Tyrtaeus calls the new *aretē* a *xynon esthlon,* a "common good," a concept that does not appear in the epics.

We recall that the Homeric warrior's primary goal was fame among men for great exploits. Glory is also sought by the new polis warrior, but it can be earned only by service to the state, and the peer group that awards it is no longer a small circle of similarly minded heroes, but the *whole* community. In the seventh century, then, the notion of personal greatness recedes, and the idea of civic approbation takes its place. One of the natural effects of this process was that valor, fame and glory became localized. Homer's heroes sought a transcendental "fame among men"; the polis fighter can expect a more homely reward:

> All honor him *(timaō)* both young and old, and he goes down to Hades having had much joy; growing old he stands out among the townspeople, and no one wants to harm him, in his honor or his rights, and all yield place to him on the benches, both the young, his age-mates, and those who are older.
> (Tyrtaeus fr. 9.37-42D)

With the major elements of the heroic ideal thus transmuted, it is not surprising to find that other qualities which formed an important part of the traditional ideal are similarly downgraded. Again we turn to Tyrtaeus, who says things which would have been incomprehensible to the epic hero, but which reflect perfectly the polis ideal. At the beginning of one of his poems he lists skills and accomplishments which were, in epic terms, proof of a man's goodness — skill in running and wrestling, great strength, fleetness of foot, bodily beauty, vast wealth, political power, eloquence — and says he would not praise a man that had these:

> not even if he had all fame *(doxa)* except savage valor.
> (Fr. 9.1-9D)

As Werner Jaeger says, Tyrtaeus "recast the Homeric ideal of the single champion's *aretē* into the *aretē* of the patriot..."[10]

It is important to stress that this is not so much a rejection of the code of the aristocratic warrior as it is a transvaluation. Essentially the Tyrtaean scheme subsumes all the excellence of the fighting man into the single cause of service to the whole community. The effect on the aristocratic ideal of this restrictiveness was bound to be drastic. For when all the citizens of the polis, aristocrats and non-aristocrats alike, are exhorted to dedicate their manly abilities to the common cause, and when honor is conferred, not as the consequence of individual superiority but for ability to further the common good, then a recasting of the old priorities is demanded. Put another way, when the aristocratic *aretai* cease to command universal approbation, that is, cease to be functionally valuable, and if the aristocratic group wishes to retain its superior position in the community's regard, then it must seek other ways of demonstrating its superiority.

Hesiod's poetry showed us a section of society which simply did not concern itself, except at the points of abrasive contact, with the ideals of an aristocratic group. Tyrtaeus' Spartan ideal shows essentially the same element of society encroaching on the aristocratic *aretai,* and dramatically reducing their scope. This means, of course, that now the areas of possible tension between groups are liable to increase, as the cultural values of the noble class become subject to closer and more critical scrutiny in contrast to the new criterion of usefulness to the society as a whole.

While Tyrtaeus and Callinus were speaking for the new civic awareness of duty to a common cause, other voices began to be heard, which more directly challenged aristocratic assumptions. Archilochus of Paros is the first truly individual figure in Greek literature. We possess only bits and fragments of this master poet, compared by later Greeks to Homer himself, but even these remnants show us a man of intense personal feeling who expressed himself in a new and important way. The facts of his life are obscure, and even his dates are uncertain. As well as can be established, he lived and wrote around 650 B.C. His father was an important member of the Parian aristocracy, who led a colony to the northern island of Thasos; his mother was a slave. Archilochus led a wandering life; he himself took part in the colonizing of Thasos; he may have been a mercenary, but that is not certain. What is certain is that he spent most of his life as a soldier:

> In my spear is my kneaded bread, in my spear my Ismarian wine. I drink leaning on my spear.
>
> (Fr. 2D)

He was both soldier and poet (fr. 1D):

> I am a squire of the lord of war, Enyalius, and I understand the lovely gift of the Muses,

a fighter, drinker, lover, of a swashbuckling kind — a match in these qualities to any Homeric figure. But, in all respects he was a man of the new Greece, the world of the polis and of the hoplite infantryman, of restless energy and psychological uncertainty. Archilochus' poetry (like that of Tyrtaeus) is full of epic phrases and formulas, but the thought is quite otherwise. His view of a soldier's life was almost totally the reverse of Homer's idealized world of personal glory and brilliance, for Archilochus not only rejected the epic conventions, he mocked them.

The Old Ideal under Challenge

The astounding difference in outlook may be seen in some famous lines, which were considered shocking even by later generations:

> Well, some Thracian is enjoying my shield which I left — I didn't want to and it was a perfectly good one — beside a bush. But I saved myself. What do I care about that shield? The hell with it, I'll get another one just as good.
>
> (Fr. 6D)

Nowhere in Homer do we find this sort of cynicism or ironic self-mockery. To the Homeric warrior, who lived in a constant agony of self-doubt about his own bravery, to abandon arms and flee was a sign of cowardice and failure; to have broadcast it, as Archilochus did, would have been unthinkable.[11] But Archilochus' poetry is full of such "anti-heroic" reaction. One by one he slights the cherished tenets of the epic ideal. On comrades in arms, he writes:

> A mercenary, Glaukos, is a friend — as long as he's fighting.
>
> (Fr. 13D)

On the glory of combat:

> Seven fell dead whom we caught in pursuit, we the thousand slayers.
>
> (Fr. 61D)

On posthumous glory:

> There's no respect or fame from townsmen when you're dead. It's the praise of the living we want — while we're alive. A dead man gets the worst of it — every time.
>
> (Fr. 64D)

In the epic scheme of values physical appearance was not only important, but decisive in determining status. Archilochus explodes that notion in these lines:

> I don't like a general who is big or who walks with a swagger, or who glories in his curly hair, cut-off moustache. Give me a man who's little, bandy-legged, feet firm on the ground, full of heart.
>
> (Fr. 60D)

There is no question of Archilochus' bravery; he was a soldier, and a good one. He simply removed the aura of romanticism from warfare, seeing the world as it really was and his robust, earthy view of life illustrates the new mood of realism which characterized the age. For Homer all things and all places were ideally good;[12] Hesiod, though, had no illusions about miserable Ascra, and Archilochus says much the same about Thasos:

> She stands, like the backbone of an ass, crowned with a savage wood.
>
> (Fr. 18D)

And in a fragment about his native Paros he says:

> Never mind Paros, and those figs, and the life of the sea.
>
> (Fr. 53D)

Paradoxically, this attitude of negative realism did not contradict the new spirit of communal patriotism. For all their heroic idealism the Homeric warriors were motivated mainly by their own self-centered desire for personal glory; according to legend Archilochus died defending his homeland, Paros.[13]

The difference between the Archilochean and Homeric expression of values seems immense — all the more so because Archilochus' diction, as well as many of his themes, were those of the Homeric epos. So severe a divagation from traditional standards is a testimony to the structural changes that had taken place in Greek society. The mood of pessimism born of the insecurity produced by the transition from a kinship to a territorial system that we observed in Hesiod has its counterpart in Archilochus' salty iconoclasm a generation or so later. But what Hesiod lamented, Archilochus accepted as natural. To some modern critics Archilochus was a rebel who completely disdained the norms of behavior he had inherited. It is perhaps more correct to view him as a transitional figure, not rejecting but modifying a scheme of values which, although still vital, could not stand unaltered in the face of new realities, uncertainties and ambiguities.[14] The very act of "rejecting" old certitudes demonstrates their continuity. A recent work on Archilochus expresses this point of view. Archilochus may have parodied and mocked the tradition, but he was not "anti-heroic; nor one died and mocked the tradition, but he was not anti-heroic; nor one who entirely rejected the 'honour' code that in one form or another has permeated Greek society . . . down to the present day. Archilochus continued and modified the cultural traditions embodied in the epic."[15]

To this assessment we may add a further thought. By 700 B.C. the epic ideal against which Archilochus pointedly ranged his own view of reality already had the character of a stylized ethos, which aristocrats, fully conscious now of social division, had appropriated for themselves. By mocking the "code" of the warrior-élite, Archilochus challenged one basis of the aristocracy's claim to superiority, not in a "partisan" way, as if he were some anti-aristocratic ideologue, but as an ironic critic of a concept which had become artificial and outmoded by the realities of societal change. The new generation of critics, forceful and outspoken in their opposition to the potent (but static) norms of upper-class behavior — and Archilochus was the first, not the only one — brought about a radical reshaping of the aristocratic ethos. A testament to the lasting quality of the sting administered to the enduring mirage of the Homeric ideal is the harsh attack launched against Archilochus by Plato's cousin Critias, a thoroughgoing oligarch, some 250 years later. Critias censures the unrestrained nature of Archilochus' own self-revelations: his slavish birth, his poverty, his intemperateness and sexual excesses, and, "what is even more disgraceful than this, [is the admission] that he threw away his shield."[16] This enumeration of character defects (which reveals, by the way, the fifth-century aristocratic version of the traditional norms) focuses especially on Archilochus' lack of restraint in both deed and word, a characteristic that will become one of the main props of the evolving aristocratic ideal.

In his own way Tyrtaeus mirrored the restructuring of traditional norms of manly worth, but, like the Homeric warrior (and the later aristocrats), he was profoundly motivated by the epic notions of shame and respect for public opinion *(aidōs)*. A lack of concern about "what people say," which was the essence of Critias' attack, is prominent in Archilochus and highlights the uprooting of tradition and the sense of isolated individualism characteristic of the age:

> Aisimides, no one would enjoy very many delightful things if he cared about the reproaches of the *dēmos*.
>
> (Fr. 9D)

Tyrtaeus, for whom discipline and respect for authority were paramount, urged the Spartans to obey their leaders, a notion quite similar to the Homeric conception of the ruler's position.[17] A statement by Archilochus on a public leader defies the tradition:

> And now Leophilos is ruling, and Leophilos has the power; to Leophilos goes everything, and Leophilos is listened to.
>
> (Fr. 70D)

Who Leophilos, "dear to the people," was we do not know; but he was either a real individual or a type of the popular leader. In any case, we note a lessening of respect for what is termed today public authority.[18] The same attitude of irreverence for what is conventionally great is seen in a fragment of Archilochus in which, according to Aristotle, the speaker is a carpenter:

> The wealth of golden Gyges means nothing to me; I've never been envious, nor am I jealous of the works of the gods; I've no desire for a mighty tyranny — for these things are beyond my vision.
>
> (Fr. 22D)

Gyges, the king of Lydia, was proverbial for his wealth and power; Charon, the carpenter, is the "little man" who thumbs his nose at the exalted.

Another fragment of Archilochus seems at first glance to be out of keeping with his customary tone of cynical realism:

> O Zeus, father Zeus, yours is the rule of heaven, and you watch over the deeds of men both vile and lawful; and the violence *(hybris)* and justice *(dikē)* of the wild beasts is your concern, too.
>
> (Fr. 94D)

But when we recall Hesiod's obsession with the same subject, these impassioned lines which make Zeus the arbiter of justice are not at all surprising. Cries for justice, for fair dealing, have their origin from below the ruling stratum. Archilochus was not a peasant farmer, but he was definitely alienated from the traditional ideals of the aristocratic class. The only commoner whose feelings were expressed in the *Iliad,* namely Thersites, was concerned with the same thing, the unfairness of the high-handed Agamemnon in distributing the spoils. We must hear in these appeals to a higher power for equity the voice of an emerging social consciousness raised in opposition to a ruling class, just as later the terms connoting equality become catchwords of the fledgling Greek democracies.[19]

Other evidence of Archilochus' concern for social justice is seen in the remnants of his Fables, or animal tales, in which the speakers are animals. Attempts to reconstruct these poems from the few lines we possess have been largely unsuccessful, but they appear to be concerned with social problems. The genre of the Fable is certainly "popular" in origin. The best-known of the fable writers, Aesop, is said to have been a slave who lived during the sixth century B.C. The first extant example of this folk genre is found in Hesiod's *Works and Days* where he tells the fable of the Hawk and the Nightingale, which is specifically concerned with social injustice. Archilochus' fragment on justice, quoted (opposite), is from his animal tales.[20]

Both the concern for justice and the various questionings of the heroic ideal may be seen as indications of an increasing element of social tension in the seventh century. An important clue to the form which this tension was taking is seen in a one-line fragment from Archilochus' animal tales. A fox addresses a deer:

Pass on, for you are of noble birth *(gennaios)*.

(Fr. 97)

In this line occurs the first recorded instance in Greek of a word meaning "of noble birth." In all of Homer and Hesiod neither this word nor any other words for high birth are found — surely no coincidence. The aristocratic warriors of the Homeric poems constituted a noble class of merit which was just beginning to identify itself as a social class based on claims of birth and inherited wealth; but this process had not advanced far enough for a formulation of aristocratic terminology to develop. In fact, in the Homeric epics, surprisingly little is said about noble birth, despite the interest on the part of the heroes in genealogy; conversely, there was practically no attempt to prove individual or group superiority on the basis of blood lines.[21] The superiority of the Homeric warrior-aristocrat was self-presumptive, and there were no rival claimants to challenge their natural pre-eminence. As a consequence of the emergence of the aristocratic state the lines of division had obviously deepened, so that words like *gennaios* can appear, which, if they do not betoken a completely new set of aristocratic priorities, at least indicate an explicitness not seen before.

Thus, as the claims of worth made by the other than noble segment of society increase — claims which either supersede the older aristocratic values or subsume them into the new communal ideology — signs of an aristocratic "reaction" surface. The emergence of terms of social distinction based on hereditary factors is one aspect of this reaction.

Whereas in the *Iliad* and *Odyssey* self-conscious expression of social division was absent or almost totally muted, in Hesiod there appear some indications of "class" consciousness. In an address to Perses, for example, the adjective *esthlos* is contrasted with another word, *deilos,* both of which take on social colorations different from their usual Homeric and Hesiodic usage:

> But you, Perses, listen to right *(dikē)* and do not foster violence *(hybris);* for *hybris* is bad for a *deilos* man. Even the *esthlos* cannot easily bear its burden, but is weighed down under it when he has fallen into delusion *(atē)*.
>
> (*Works and Days* 213-16)

Deilos is found frequently in Homer, signifying "unlucky," "unfortunate," "miserable." In this passage it seems to have the meaning "unfortunate" in the more generalized sense of a man in unfortunate circumstances, i.e. a poor or weak man. *Esthlos* also appears to have an extended meaning here; these moralizing lines are preceded by the fable of the Hawk and the Nightingale, which was addressed to the *basileis* and which tells how the weak must submit to the strong. They, in turn, are followed by a reference to the violators of Justice, "those who devour bribes and give sentences with crooked judgments" (220–21). Logically, then, the word *esthlos* had something of a technical force, the "distinguished," "prosperous" man, an extension of the physical or ethical qualities normally contained in it. And if Hesiod is giving the "title" *esthlos* to the man who is materially successful or powerful, we must conclude that such words had, by the early seventh century, gained some popular currency as socio-economic terms.[22]

A more obvious illustration is provided by Callinus (fr. 1D), who says that the brave soldier who dies in battle is mourned by the whole people, both by the great man *(megas)* and the little man *(oligos)*. In Homer the words *megas* and *oligos* could only refer to physical size or strength, never, as here, to social or economic condition. These are isolated and scrappy indications, but their force is undeniable. During the first half of the seventh century B.C. the Greek world was developing a socio-political vocabulary.

The beginning of a vocabulary of social differentiation, the signs of popular discontent with the ruling structure, the questioning of the warrior ideal, and the substitution of a communal ideal in its place, all point to an awareness of a deepening cleavage in the social structure. The most ominous sign of social division in the seventh century, however, is the evidence of an increasing disparity in wealth. In broadest terms, the assumption of control of civic and religious institutions by the aristocratic families gave them the means to increase their holdings. These same families, it is safe to say, also participated in and were enriched by the growth of trade and commerce. Concomitantly, many of the small farmers began a slow slide to impoverishment or to dependency on their wealthy neighbors, the inevitable result of social stratification. I hasten to add that this scenario was not acted out in the same way or at the same pace everywhere in the Greek world. We know very little of the history of most Greek *poleis* in this period, and to pretend to be sure of the causes of social change would be a grave mistake. We must be careful neither to exaggerate the extent of economic incongruence (see above, pages 36-37) nor to rely on explanations of modern economic theory. For example, the amount of surplus that could be generated to support an unproductive group will have been small, while to speak of "capital" and "investment" is a modernist fallacy. Some farmers will have remained well-off; others beside the aristocracy (farmers as well as non-aristocratic entrepreneurs) enjoyed the fruits of a general increase in wealth. There were never economic "classes" in the strict Marxian sense among free citizens; and by 500 B.C. "the solid backbone of the citizenry of most Greek *poleis* consisted of small and medium farmers who cultivated their *kleroi* in ancestral fashion . . ."[23] Still, one fact of major importance is indisputable. By 700 B.C. the aristocratic landowners were *relatively* much wealthier than the rest of the farmers. Increasingly, social tension will be expressed in the form of economic inequality; "rich" and "poor" become semantic categories for the first time.

On the other hand, the increase in power and wealth of the aristocracy did not take place in a vacuum. As we have seen, counterforces were operating. After 650 B.C. the "knightly" warrior, the individual fighter of great prowess, no longer held center stage, because of the changes in military tactics. The emerging civic consciousness, closely connected to the new military formation, also had its effect; the free peasantry was not about to become an oppressed class at the same time it was fighting the polis' battles. The old tribal egalitarianism both reinforced and was reinforced in turn by these factors. Aristocrats, who were no less bound by the organic unity of the polis, could not, however much they may have wished, distance themselves too far above their fellow *politai;* a frequent counterdose to aristocratic exploitation was tyranny, itself a demonstration of the people's ultimate power.

Very few states, in fact, were able completely to restrict civic participation to a narrow group of hereditary aristocrats; some broadening of the base of government occurred in most *poleis* in the course of the seventh and sixth centuries. Nevertheless, even in the most advanced democratic *poleis,* where civic offices were eventually opened to the whole of the citizenry, political leadership continued to be dominated by aristocrats or by the wealthiest citizens. Indeed, in a good many states, a small group, relatively much wealthier, retained control of the political machinery throughout the classical period — and beyond. But no matter how oligarchical the government of his polis may have been, the free citizen was never less than that; no *politēs* was ever a member of a downtrodden mass.

Some of the shifts in attitudes caused by these social variables have already been mentioned. Certain key aspects of the old aristocratic ideal, which was founded in the natural superiority of the tribal warrior-leader, were being challenged or transvalued at the very time aristocrats were attempting to establish their superiority in a self-conscious way. One very important new element is already evident: a consciously expressed feeling among the nobles that their superiority was based on birth. Another change in the aristocratic ideal surfaces at this time; the emergence of an emphasis on a particular style of life. The Homeric poems, for all their concentration on wealth and display, show that the warrior-élite enjoyed a material standard distinguishable from that of their lesser neighbors only in degree, a fact that is confirmed by the archaeological record of the tenth and ninth centuries. Basically they were prosperous landowners who lived a better, but not essentially different life, than the smaller farmers. Homeric heroes were not above performing the simplest of manual labor, and their interests (aside from battlecraft and related activities, where the gulf was wide) were pretty much those of the society as a whole. Beginning in the eighth, and increasingly in the course of the seventh century, however, a greater emphasis on a specifically aristocratic style of life becomes evident. On the finest pottery (the kind meant for consumption by wealthy buyers) motifs depicting the gods and heroes of Greek legends are increasingly popular. By the last decade of the seventh century, when the black-figure technique of vase painting was beginning to prevail, heroic motifs dominate, and scenes depicting contemporary aristocratic life appear with greater frequency, especially the youthful warrior with his horses and (now obsolete) chariot. Through the sixth century these themes are continued; depicted are heroic legends, aristocrats in fine clothing,

The Old Ideal under Challenge

scenes of revelling, athletic contests, youths riding or leading horses, hunting or arming scenes.[24] Speaking of this early period, the fifth-century historian, Thucydides, tells us:

> The Athenians were the first to give up the habit of carrying weapons and to adopt a way of living that was more relaxed and more luxurious. In fact the elder men of the rich families who had these luxurious tastes only recently gave up wearing linen under-garments and tying their hair behind their heads in a knot fastened with a clasp of golden grasshoppers: the same fashions spread to their kinsmen in Ionia, and lasted there among the old men for some time.
> (Thuc. 1.6.3)[25]

These developments in the life-style of the upper class — in dress, ornamentation, hair styling, and customs — give the clear impression of overt manifestations of class consciousness. One of the "new" attitudes provides an excellent illustration. In the Homeric epics there are only the barest hints of male homosexuality;[26] Hesiod never alludes to boy-love, and Archilochus, who lived in a warrior-society, appears not to have had any male lovers. But increasingly in the aristocratic literature of the seventh and sixth centuries pederasty plays a prominent role, and the importance placed on homosexual attachments becomes a distinguishing characteristic of the aristocratic culture.[27]

Another indication of change from the older ideal is a trend towards a certain "softness" noted in the literature of the archaic period. In general this takes the form of a shift from primary emphasis on martial qualities to a mode of life that celebrated style and manners. The rejection by Archilochus of the dandified general (fr. 60D) had implied a type of aristocratic officer who consciously strove to *look* the part: tall, posturing, long-haired, carefully shaved. Xenophanes, an Ionian philosopher who wrote during the last half of the sixth century, criticizes the upper class of his native city of Colophon:

> Having learned useless luxuries from the Lydians, while they were still free from hateful tyranny, they would go into the place of assembly wearing robes of all-purple — a thousand of them, no less — boastful, glorying in their well-dressed long hair, drenched with the perfume of elaborate scents.
> (Fr. 3D)[28]

Another poet, earlier than Xenophanes, has this to say about the wealthy citizens of the island of Samos:

> And so they would go, their locks carefully combed, into Hera's precinct, covered in their splendid cloaks, sweeping the ground with their snow-white robes, with golden grasshoppers adorning their topknots. And their long-flowing hair, bound in golden ties, would swing in the breeze, and around their arms were fancy bracelets.
>
> (Asius fr. 13 Kinkel)

These are lines written in criticism, but they serve as reflection of a newer, more pronounced, emphasis by the upper class on a style of living which separated them much more sharply from their less privileged fellow citizens. In the poetry of Mimnermus, an Ionian from Colophon, who wrote in the last third of the seventh century, a preoccupation with love and youth and the horrors of old age is strikingly evident:

> But what life, what joy is there without golden Aphrodite? Let me die when these no longer matter — secret love and its honey-sweet gifts and bed — these are the flowers of youth, alluring to men and women alike. But when grievous old age comes, that makes a man both foul and ugly, then evil cares wear out his heart, and he no longer joys in looking at the sun's rays, but is hateful to boys, dishonored by women. God has made old age a wearisome thing.
>
> (Fr. 1D)

Archilochus had written about love, to be sure, and phrases like "secret love," and "honey-sweet gifts," were not original with Mimnermus.[29] What is different in these lines above is that Mimnermus makes love and youth the focal point of existence, and old age its greatest evil. We must caution against placing undue emphasis on one man's hedonistic philosophy; nevertheless these ideas, expressed by an aristocratic poet, are at the furthest remove possible from either the heroic values or the claims of community on a man's energies.

It is important to note Mimnermus' different usage of certain key words. He says that old age makes a man both foul *(aischros)* and ugly *(kakos)*. These words, which in Homer (or in Tyrtaeus, for that matter) would refer to cowardly behavior, are given an aesthetic reference.[30] Similar is the use of the word "dishonored" *(atimastos)*, another powerful term. Honor *(timē)* is always used to indicate peer evaluation within the context of success or failure; here dishonor is the consequence of growing old, and the context is a private relationship.[31] We can compare a two-line fragment of Mimnermus which conveys much the same message:

The Old Ideal under Challenge

> Though he was surprisingly fair, when youth has gone by, not even a father is loved or honored *(timios)* by his sons.
>
> (Fr. 3D)

In another poem (fr. 5D) the brief period of youthful bloom *(hēbē)* is called "honored" *(timēessa)*, while old age is "painful and misshapen *(amorphon)* ... hateful and without honor *(atimon)*" and makes a man "unknown" *(agnōstos)*. Not only is the traditional vocabulary of merit given new applications, even the standard observations on human life have been altered to reflect a more restricted vision. In fr. 2D the Homeric image of the transitory nature of life — the race of men is like the seasonal changes (*Iliad* 6. 146-49) — is narrowed to mean the brevity of youth. It is in this poem that we read the startlingly pessimistic sentiment:

> But when this time of spring has passed it is better to die straight off than live (lines 9-10).[32]

In these poems the worth of a man is expressed in terms of externals — youth and beauty; there is no feeling either for the old standard of success or the newer standard of service. Mimnermus was no mere voluptuary, of course; other fragments are of a martial and patriotic nature,[33] but it is true, nevertheless, that his later reputation in antiquity was as a love poet, and that this is a new direction in Greek values.

Another Ionian poet, Anacreon of Teos, writing about a century later, devoted himself almost entirely to erotic and convivial themes. Here the "softness" is in full flower, and Anacreon abandons the hardy virility of the traditional aristocratic ethos for the pleasures of wine, song, and love. In style, as well as in choice of subject, Anacreon's verses have a langorous, almost passive, quality. In a short poem, imitative in form of Archilochus' biting satire on Leophilos, but totally different in theme, he says:

> Kleoboulos is the one I love, Kleoboulos I go mad for,
> Kleoboulos I keep looking at.
>
> (Fr. 359 Page)[34]

A sense of how much the old values had yielded to new ones is evident in an anecdote told about Anacreon. When asked why he wrote hymns, not to the gods but to boys, Anacreon is said to have replied: "Because they are our gods." In a prayer that offended the religious sensibilities of a late philosopher he invokes Dionysus:

I beseech you, come kindly to me, heeding a prayer that will find favor, and be a good counsellor to Kleoboulos, that he, O Dionysus, may accept my love.

(Fr. 357.6-11 Page)

Many other examples of Anacreon's charmingly lighthearted view of life and love could be quoted, but this poem, to a reluctant girl, may be taken as typical:

Thracian filly, why do you look askance at me and run away from me, and think that I am not at all wise? Please know that I could put a bridle on you quite well, and holding the reins could ride you around the race-course. But now you graze in the meadows, frisking and playing, for you do not have a skilled horseman to mount you.

(Fr. 417 Page)

Anacreon's delicate approach to passion may be taken as typical of the aristocratic concentration on style and manner.[35] More basically, perhaps, there is an impulse toward restraint, a feeling that passions should be controlled:

I love, and then again, I do not love, I am mad, and not mad.

(Fr. 428 Page)

This is, in fact, "court" poetry. Anacreon spent considerable time as the guest of Polycrates, the tyrant of Samos (who reigned *ca.* 535-523 B.C.); on Polycrates' death, the tyrant of Athens sent for him. Surrounded by the elegant young aristocrats of the tyrants' circles he wrote endlessly of love and the pleasures of a leisured class, grace and charm *(charis)* the hallmark of his poetry:

For boys would love me for my songs, since I sing charming things, and charming things are what I know how to say.

(Fr. 402c Page)

In one poem real and undisguisedly deep feeling is apparent:

My temples are already gray, my head is white, graceful youth is no longer by me, and my teeth are old. There is no longer much time left of sweet life. For this I weep often, fearing Tartarus, for the pit of Hades is terrible, and the road down to it is hard; and further, once a man has descended there is no way back again.

(Fr. 395 Page)

We are reminded immediately of Mimnermus and his hatred of old age. Anacreon sees in the symptoms of his body's decay the portent of eternal death; for him, as for Mimnermus, the fleeting of "graceful youth" and its eternal beauty is the real evil of life. In his almost single-mindeded devotion to love and beauty, good company and good manners, in his concentration on luxury and his avoidance of the serious in favor of light and inconsequential topics, delivered in a tone of slightly mocking irony and detachment, Anacreon stands as a living symbol of the genteel elegance affected by aristocrats (young and old) in the waning years of the Archaic Age.[36]

A slightly younger contemporary of Anacreon, Ibycus, wrote on the same subjects. A native of Rhegium in Italy, and an aristocrat, Ibycus also was at the court of Polycrates. He was, we can gather from the few extant fragments, a remarkably gifted poet, full of sensuous imagery and a keen observer of nature. Naturally, love was his main concern; in fact, Cicero calls him more amorous even than Anacreon, whose (the latter's) poetry Cicero characterized as *tota amatoria*. In one poem of Ibycus, Love comes like the Northwind from Thrace, and with "parching madness, dark and fearless, shakes me to the bottom of my heart with his might" (fr. 286 Page). In another poem on the onslaught of love he compares himself to an old champion race horse who unwillingly draws his chariot to the contest (fr. 287 Page). The characteristic fear of death is expressed in this fragment: "It is not possible to find a medicine for life for those who are dead" (fr. 313 Page).

The veneration of youth and beauty, and the celebration of love and wine and pleasure, so strikingly characteristic of aristocratic archaic poetry, had become, by the middle of the sixth century, important components of the aristocratic "thought world." One cause of the emphasis on the softer aspects of life by aristocratic poets in the seventh and sixth centuries was the vacuum created by the displacement of individual success as the primary psychological requirement of the society. Many of the traditional aristocratic excellences had been taken over, altered, or made untenable by a growing "middle class," pragmatically oriented to what was of benefit to the whole community. The polis, in other words, with its much larger number of useful citizens, had co-opted many of the values of the warrior-aristocrat.

At the same time, the ancient motivation of the aristocracy — the desire for prestige and public esteem — remained unchanged. Their economic superiority gave aristocrats the means to outshine, and even to dazzle, their less fortunate contemporaries. The museums of the

Western world today are full of the products of this urge: tripods and cauldrons, sometimes massive, statues, armor, stelae — almost all of them public dedications, intended to impress. The keeping of horses and chariots, now long outmoded as tools of battle, is simply the most obvious of the various kinds of display; and when a Greek nobleman's chariot team won a victory at one of the pan-Hellenic games, what he gained in return for expensive outlay was prestige and honor, the same *kydos* and *timē* after which the warrior-aristocrats of the Dark Age had so single-mindedly strive. It is important to stress that the relatively lavish expenditure (we must keep in mind that even the wealthiest family was rich only by Greek standards) was concentrated in buildings and objects for public display, things that all citizens could look at and admire, not on private homes and furnishings, which do not become extravagant until well into the Classical period. And that, of course, was the point. Ostentation, whether material or personal or cultural, has as its primary objective social differentiation. In a society in which the group, now institutionalized into a single organic entity, is the inescapable focus of all human activity, the means of differentiation are severely canalized. Thus the adoption of a style of life that is unmistakably "superior" assumes great importance.[37]

Greek choral lyric provides an interesting example of the connections between public display and personal or familial honor. Choral lyric was pre-eminently a phenomenon of the Archaic Age (although its greatest master, Pindar, lived until 438 B.C.). The choral ode was sung and danced by a large chorus of boys and girls (fifty is a common number) of the polis. It was thus a communal art form and an expression of the collective whole. It was also expensive, requiring elaborate costumes, payment of the poet and choirmaster and musicians. Whatever the occasion, civic, religious, or personal, the expense was borne privately. In his capacity as provider *(chorēgos)* an aristocrat both performed a public office and gained distinction in the polis for himself and his family. Choral lyric

> could only flourish where it found a well-established circle of art-loving *dilettanti* which was capable of appreciating and producing these difficult choral dances. It presupposed a society which could afford money, leisure and cultivation of the mind, and which took pleasure in elaborate and splendid performances.[38]

The aristocratic concentration on refinement and culture did not mean that the older ideal had been abandoned. One of its most eloquent

The Old Ideal under Challenge

spokesmen was Alcaeus, a nobleman from the island of Lesbos, who lived and wrote around 600 B.C. But even in Alcaeus, who was an aristocrat to the core, the old values are touched by the new ideas. As conscious as he was of his own class he could only view the turmoil of his native Mytilene as a citizen vitally concerned with his polis, its people and its institutions. Once, when he was in exile from Mytilene, he wrote these plaintive lines:

> I, poor wretch, live a rustic's life, yearning to hear the Assembly summoned, O Agesilaidas, and the Council; what my father and my father's father have grown old possessing, among these citizens who wrong each other, from these things I am outcast, an exile on the boundaries.
>
> (Fr. 130.16-24 L-P)[39]

What Alcaeus longs for most are the Council and Assembly, the living heart of the polis. In another poem, that has come down in a paraphrase by a later author, he says that "it is not stones nor timbers nor the craft of the carpenters, but, wherever there are men who know how to defend themselves, there are walls and a polis" (fr. 426 L-P). These words recall in some sense the old heroic ideal of bravery, but their main focus is the polis; Alcaeus, like Tyrtaeus, understood that the duty of fighting men is to defend the community. Another line from a much-mutilated papyrus fragment expresses the same sentiment:

> For men are the warlike tower of a polis.
>
> (Fr. 112.10 L-P)

The political battles of which Alcaeus speaks with so much passion were most probably not in the nature of true civil (i.e. class) war; they were partisan squabbles among the aristocratic families of Lesbos jockeying for political control.[40] On the other hand, it would be incorrect to depict the non-aristocratic population as merely passive spectators of aristocratic infighting without concern or participation. It is important to note that Alcaeus was sufficiently a man of the new polis to couch his rhetoric in terms of the larger community. Thus, in a poem directed against a former political ally, turned enemy, he says:

> Let us abate our soul-consuming discord and intestine *(emphylos)* fighting, which some Olympian has roused, bringing the *dāmos* to ruin, but to Pittacus giving glory, his heart's desire.
>
> (Fr. 70.10-13 L-P)

And in another poem on the same Pittacus he speaks of "rescuing the *dāmos* from distress" (fr. 129.20 L-P). Now, in both poems *dāmos*, the Aeolic form of "people," refers not to the "commons" but to the whole of the citizen body of Mytilene.[41] Indeed, in both poems Pittacus is accused of "devouring the polis," which shows that for Alcaeus polis is equivalent to *dāmos*, the human element of the state. So, this most aristocratic of men spoke, perforce, the idiom of public service, even when he meant the internal quarrels of a ruling élite.

Nevertheless, despite this wider sense of public concern, the much narrower world of the older heroic ideal had the most appeal for Alcaeus. In a long fragment the poet describes some armor, stored in his house, which he hopes will be used in the battles with his political rivals:

> The great house is agleam with bronze, and the whole roof is full-dressed with shining helmets, and from them white horsehair plumes wave down — adornments for the heads of men. Shining greaves of bronze hang round and hide the pegs — defense against the arrow's might. Corslets of new linen and hollow shields lie thrown upon the floor. By them are blades from Chalcis, and beside them many belts and tunics. These we may not forget, since first we stood to this our task.
>
> (Fr. 357 L-P)

Both the language and the spirit are heroic, but an air of unreality has been noted in the description. According to Page, Alcaeus' armory is "eccentric and relatively old-fashioned,"[42] and in this romantically vivid depiction of the armor of the single champion (there is no mention of the hoplite spear) we may perhaps detect an evocative, reminiscent, feeling, as if the poet himself suspected that the day for such bravura had passed. Could it be that even for an Alcaeus the Homeric warrior ideal had become a relic, an echo?[43] Another of his poems curiously mixes the old epic attitudes with a sense of insouciance regarding heroic exploits. It is addressed to his brother Antimenides, who had just returned from mercenary service with King Nebuchadrezzar of Babylon in his campaign against Jerusalem.

> From the ends of the earth you are come, with your sword-hilt of ivory bound with gold . . . Fighting beside the Babylonians you accomplished a great feat, and delivered them from distress, killing a warrior who lacked only one palm's breadth of five royal cubits.
>
> (Fr. 350 L-P)

The old Ideal under Challenge 61

Alcaeus' obvious delight in describing his brother's weapon and the height of the giant (eight feet, four inches) reflect a Homeric interest in the manly achievements of the individual warrior, but there is also no denying here what Bowra calls a "touch of gaiety in the treatment of war."[44] We are not surprised, then, that Alcaeus himself communicates in a poem to a friend how in a battle with the Athenians he had thrown away his arms and escaped whole (fr. 428 L-P). This Archilochean gesture (above, page 45) shows that the rigid heroic code of honor, even for Alcaeus, had lost much of its force; the glory of combat no longer commanded the same single-minded devotion from the aristocrat that it had earlier. True passion is reserved for politics (or for love).

A much clearer index of the evolving aristocratic ideal is seen in his characterization of his political enemy, Pittacus. We know little about Pittacus; he was, perhaps, the son of a Thracian nobleman who had attained a position of importance in Mytilene. At one time, in Alcaeus' youth, Pittacus joined the faction to which Alcaeus' family belonged, to drive out the reigning tyrant, Melanchros. Later, the alliance broke up and Pittacus associated himself with another tyrant, Myrsilus, to rule in Mytilene. When Myrsilus died Alcaeus recorded his savage jubilation at the event:

> Now must a man get drunk, and drink with might and main, for Myrsilus is dead . . .
> (Fr. 332 L-P)

Sometime after this, apparently, Pittacus was elected by the people of Mytilene to be *aisymnētēs,* or governor, for ten years, while Alcaeus ate out his heart in bitter exile. Pittacus' "betrayal" of the faction and the oaths of alliance he had sworn, plus his obvious popular appeal enraged Alcaeus. It is significant that in his denunciation of Pittacus the poet could think of no worse epithet than "base-born."

> The base-born *(kakopatridēs)* Pittacus they have set up as tyrant of that polis, spiritless and ill-starred; all together they shout his praises.
> (Fr. 348 L-P)[45]

Some lines in another fragment also appear to be a gibe at Pittacus' low birth:

> Have you, the son of such a woman, the reputation that free men, born of *esthloi* parents have . . . ?
> (Fr. 72.11-13 L-P)

These fragments have occasioned much controversy over whether Pittacus actually was a "commoner" or not. All the facts at our disposal (there are not many), however, show that Pittacus belonged to the best Mytilenian society into which he was accepted at the highest level.[46]

Clearly, the reason Alcaeus called Pittacus (and his other opponents) *kakopatridēs* was that by this time noble birth had become one of the most important manifestations of membership in the aristocracy. By impugning Pittacus' ancestry Alcaeus, so to speak, drummed him out of the nobility. *Kakopatris* was not the only name that Alcaeus called Pittacus. We are told that he described him as "splay-foot," "cracked-foot," "braggart," "pot-belly," "midnight glutton," and "unkempt." Other references apparently allude to Pittacus' (and his father's) heavy and intemperate drinking.[47] If our assessment of Alcaeus as one who clung tenaciously to an older conception of the good man is correct, then it is easy to see why Pittacus would be for him the antithesis of the ideal. Pittacus' foreign birth may have been the nominal basis for his being termed *kakopatridēs*, but this allegation (like the derogatory references to his appearance and habits) was after the fact. One charge levelled against Pittacus by Alcaeus, repeated several times, was that he was an oath-breaker and betrayer of comrades, a cardinal offense in the scheme of Homeric values.[48] Pittacus' real sin, accordingly, was the abandonment of the code: rejecting the narrow group, courting popular favor, and, as *aisymnētēs* (which for Alcaeus meant *tyrannos*), instituting measures that had anti-aristocratic overtones.[49]

The fact that Alcaeus chose to castigate his enemies in this particular way is significant evidence for the evolution of the aristocratic self-image. High birth and identification with a particular style of life had become more and more the indispensable proofs of an upper-class gentleman; even the inference that these were lacking was sufficient to raise serious doubts about one's position (and worth) in the society. From later sources we know that during the archaic period descriptive epithets for social groups were employed which had similar implications. In various parts of Greece, aristocrats styled themselves *eupatridai* (sons of noble fathers), *hippobotai* (horse rearers), *hippeis* (knights), *gēomoroi* (landowners), reflecting their pride of family, wealth, the aristocratic passion for horseflesh, while the lower classes were called "the naked," "club bearers," "dusty feet."[50]

The "proper" things – dress, ornamentation, hair style, the cultivation of the skills of hunting and riding, and athletics, playing a "gentleman's" musical instrument, the ability to compose spontaneously at

The Old Ideal under Challenge 63

drinking parties, knowing when to be moderate in drink and speech and (equally important) when to carouse and speak intemperately, had all become, by the beginning of the sixth century B.C., integral to the aristocratic pattern of behavior. We have already seen these ideas reflected in the poems of Mimnermus and Anacreon, full of the praises of wine and song, flowers and youths. Alcaeus is no exception, for he did not confine his lively spirit merely to political invective. A significant portion of the fragments that remain are devoted to the pleasures of drinking and friendship, and in later antiquity he had a reputation as an author of ardent love poems to boys.[51] Alcaeus, in short, may be taken as representative of the Greek aristocrat of the mid-Archaic Age: a combination of the older heroic ideal of glory and honor and the newer notions of partisan politics, pride of blood, class consciousness — all blended with a sense of nostalgic loss, bewilderment at social changes, retreat into transient pleasures. Hubert Martin's assessment is apt:

> The extant fragments lead us to conclude that Alcaeus never extended his moral vision beyond a world of masculine camaraderie and partisan politics, a world of loyalty to faction and sympotic fellowship. Yet within the narrow confines of Alcaeus' poetic cosmos, wine is a lofty and beneficent sign, conferring whatever joy and comfort this world has to offer.[52]

Still, the aristocratic concentration on pleasure was not unalloyed. Correctness of style, even here, was the moderating "form" that gave restraint and decorum to what otherwise might have degenerated into unseemly licence. Just as Alcaeus lashed out at the immoderateness of Pittacus' personal habits, so Anacreon cautions:

> But come, let us no longer pursue this Scythian kind of drinking, with din and uproar over the wine, but drink in moderation between beautiful hymns.
> (Fr. 356(b) Page)[53]

On the other hand, the inability of the lower classes to carry these things off well is lampooned by Anacreon:

> Once he wore a shabby tunic and a wasp-like headdress, and wooden dice in his ears, and about his ribs a bare ox-hide (the unwashed covering of a miserable shield), and mixed with bread-sellers and easy

whores, and made a fraudulent living — the low Artemon. Often his neck was in the pillory or stretched on the wheel. Often his back was scourged with the leather whip, and his hair and beard pulled out. But now he goes around in a carriage, the son of Cyce, wearing golden earrings, and carries an ivory parasol, just like a woman.

(Fr. 388 Page)[54]

We do not know who this Artemon was; clearly he is an example of rags-to-riches success, but for the aristocratic Anacreon he was a vulgar nobody, who, when he became prosperous, still could not disguise his low origins. In another fragment Anacreon appears to be satirizing the pretensions of a common man:

I asked the perfume-maker Strattis if he would wear his hair long.

(Fr. 387 Page)[55]

As a contrast to these attitudes we have some remarkable fragments of a man who was surely one of the strangest products of the lyric age of individualism. Hipponax of Ephesus, was, so far as is known, a man of good birth who had fallen on hard times. Exiled from his native city in the middle of the sixth century B.C., and penniless, he wrote bitingly satiric verses, the effect of which appears quite opposite to the aristocratic gentility of the day. While others concentrated on propriety, manners and beauty, Hipponax wrote scurrilous and obscene lampoons of his enemies and parodied his poverty, seeming almost to glory in his own abjectness:

Hermes, dear Hermes, son of Maia, lord of Cyllene, I pray you, for I am quite chilly, give a cloak to Hipponax, and a shirt, and sandals, and winter shoes, and sixty staters of gold hidden inside the house.

(Fr. 24a D)

In another fragment he insults the god of wealth:

Ploutos never came to my house — for he's quite blind — and said to me, 'Hipponax, I'm giving you thirty minas of silver, and lots else besides.' For he's foolish in the head.

(Fr. 29D)

Other lines of Hipponax, with their savage realism and abundant use of lower class slang, gave a glimpse of the life or the ordinary man and are dramatic evidence that in archaic literature there existed a kind of

The Old Ideal under Challenge 65

counter-tradition to the courtly postures of aristocratic poets like Mimnermus, Anacreon and Ibycus.[56]

Attitudes like those of Hipponax not only underscore the differences in outlook between the upper and lower classes, they also point to an increasing sense of worth on the part of the "little man," the small farmer and the medium tradesman/artisan, who had begun to formulate a social philosophy and who had found articulate spokesmen for his values.[57] As aristocrats place greater emphasis on external polish and at the same time betray a tendency towards a certain soft escapism, those who wrote in a non-aristocratic context reflect a common-sense ideal that stresses the real and the useful, and increasingly mistrusts pomp, luxury and mere appearance. Even in the sparse fragments of the lyric poets enough of this practical philosophy has come down to us to be easily identifiable. The process began early and continued through the archaic period. In the seventh century Archilochus, Tyrtaeus and Callinus had criticized aristocratic values or had recast them by stressing what was of benefit to the whole community. The sixth-century poet Xenophanes (*fl. ca.* 530 B.C.) found fault with the useless display, luxury and arrogance of the noblemen in his city, even implying that these things led to the conquest of Colophon.[58] In another poem, similar to one by Tyrtaeus, Xenophanes lists the various skills of athletes — ability in the foot race, the pentathlon, boxing, the pancratium,* chariot racing — and the glory that these win. He complains that the honors would be undeserved, for his own "wisdom" (as a poet and thinker) is superior. He concludes:

> For neither if there were a good boxer among the people, or one good at the pentathlon or in wrestling, or even in swiftness of foot (and this is the most honored of all the deeds of strength in the contests), would the polis be in better order *(eunomia)*. Small joy would it be for the polis if an athlete won by Pisa's banks, for these things do not fatten the treasury of the polis.
>
> (Fr. 2.15-22D)

By criticizing the skill of the athlete (who, at this time, would usually be a nobleman) Xenophanes attacks one of the bases of the aristocratic ideal, in both its old and new forms: its emphasis on physical prowess and individual prestige. For him the real test of worth is usefulness to the polis. Alcaeus' poetry was full of the bitter quarrels for power in

---
*An athletic contest involving both boxing and wrestling.

his native city; such divisiveness is rejected by Xenophanes in a poem on the proper behavior at banquets:

> Praise the man who, when he drinks, displays good things *(esthla)*, how he has memory, and strives after *aretē*. Do not speak of the battles of Titans or Giants or Centaurs, phantasies of old, or of violent discord *(stasis)* for there is nothing useful in these things. What is good is always to give respect to the gods.
> (Fr. 1.19-24D)

Again, the touchstone of value is the notion of what is useful. The word Xenophanes uses, *chrēstos,* almost always means "useful to the community," and in rejecting not only modern political strife *(stasis)* but even the mythological tales of violent intestine discord (motifs that recur again and again on the fine vases of the period), Xenophanes puts the highest premium on civic order and harmony.[59]

Xenophanes was a philosopher, and most of his poems have universal, cosmic implications; accordingly, his criticisms of aristocratic values appear somewhat detached and intellectual. A contemporary, another Ionian, Phocylides of Miletus, has a more homely touch. In the few fragments of his that have survived the common-sense views of the "ordinary" Greek of the mid-sixth century B.C. are more readily seen. His maxims, delivered in a plain unadorned style, reflect a point of view markedly different from the values expressed by the aristocratic poets of his day. For example, wealth and luxurious living, matters of great importance to the nobles of the archaic period, are reduced to the simplest level by Phocylides:

> If you desire wealth then farm a fertile piece of land; for a farm, they say, is the horn of Amaltheia.
> (Fr. 7D)

By equating wealth with a decent plot of farmland, Phocylides echoes faithfully the uncomplicated economic concerns of peasants since time immemorial. Equally instructive is an exchange of views, also from the mid-sixth century, which serves to underline this basic difference in outlook. An aristocratic drinking song, attributed to a certain Pythermus, contained this line:

> Except for gold, all the rest is nothing.
> (Fr. 910 Page)

The Old Ideal under Challenge

This was answered by some lines ascribed either to Ananius or to Hipponax:

> If someone shut up a lot of gold in a house, and a few figs, and two or three men, he'd soon know how much better figs are than gold.
> (Ananius fr. 2D)

Aretē (skill and its attendant accomplishments) was a constant preoccupation of the nobility of the Archaic Age; it is given a wholly different priority in this peasant precept by Phocylides:

> Seek a livelihood; and when you have a living, *aretē*.
> (Fr. 9D)

Since the heroic age "What people say" had been a motivating factor both for aristocrats concerned with their personal glory, and for those whose chief concern was the whole community. Phocylides naturally expresses this idea in communal terms:

> And this from Phocylides. Friend must consider with friend what citizens *(politai)* whisper around.
> (Fr. 5D)

This contrasts with the somewhat waspish disclaimer of the aristocratic Anacreon:

> I am not now firm-set nor easy-going with the townsmen
> (fr. 371 Page),

to which we may compare a similar thought by Mimnermus:

> Pleasure your own heart; for of the critical *politai* one will speak you evil, another good.
> (Fr. 7D)

Aristocratic concern with external appearance is criticized in these lines by Phocylides:

> Many men give the appearance of soundness, by behaving with propriety; but they are really lightweights.
> (Fr. 11D)

Phocylides was the first poet we know of who directly attacked the notion of high birth as a sufficient index of real worth:

> And this from Phocylides. What good is noble birth *(genos eugenes)* for those who lack grace in words and counsel?
>
> (Fr. 3D)

The ordinary man sets his sights piously low, eschewing pretence and pride in favor of stability, whether it is his polis —

> And this from Phocylides. A small polis, dwelling orderly on a height is greater than foolish Ninevah
>
> (fr. 4D)

or his own place in the polis:

> Much advantage to those who are the middle; I want to be middle in the polis.
>
> (Fr. 12D)

One striking statement preserved in Phocylides is dramatic evidence that for some Greeks a revaluation of the traditional conception of *aretē* had taken place. Since Hesiod, non-aristocratic writers had placed great emphasis on justice; in a remarkable fragment Phocylides equates the abstract idea of justice *(dikaiosynē)* with *aretē*:

> In *dikaiosynē* is summed up all *aretē*.
>
> (Fr. 10D)[60]

The new spirit of independence and sense of worth of the non-noble citizen is reflected in an unexpected source. Solon, famed as the great lawgiver of Athens, and an aristocrat, was elected chief magistrate *(archōn)* in 594 B.C. with apparently extraordinary powers to effect political and economic reforms. It is not possible to discuss in detail Solon's far-reaching legislative measures, designed to head off political and economic disaster, but a brief outline of conditions there will help to illuminate the statesman's words. When Solon became archon the wealthy upper class not only controlled political and religious offices but was also exploiting its natural economic advantages. Many of the small farmers had mortgaged their lands to their prosperous neighbors; because of debt some were reduced to a condition of dependency, having to pay a portion of their annual produce to the mortgage holders;

The Old Ideal under Challenge

and some, having offered their own persons as surety for debt, and being unable to pay, had even been sold as slaves. Chief among Solon's economic measures was the cancelling of debts owed on land and persons and the forbidding of future debt-slavery by making it unlawful to contract debts on the security of one's person. He thus saved the free peasant population of Attica from possible economic ruin at the hands of the noble landowners. He also made important constitutional changes, creating four new "classes" of citizenship based on annual wealth instead of birth, strengthening the citizen assembly, and instituting a strong popular court.

Because we are better informed about Athens than about any other Greek polis, it is well to pause briefly here and compare the historical background of the situation at Athens with what has been said in general about institutional development in Greece — always keeping in mind, of course, that all *poleis* evolved in response to their own particular socioeconomical circumstances and at their own pace. The territory of Attica, which comprised the polis of Athens, was very large by Greek standards (1000 square miles), consisting of three plains divided by high hills and containing a number of separate settlements. In the Dark Age these communities were ruled by tribal chiefs *(basileis)*. According to later Athenian tradition, one ranking chief, Theseus, effected a "combining" *(synoikismos)* of the separate towns and villages into a single state, with the largest town, Athens, as its center. For the classical Athenians this unification took place at a very early date (Theseus, whose very existence is problematical, would have lived before the Trojan War), but modern opinion holds that, while *synoikismos* may have begun relatively early, it was a gradual process that occurred mostly during the eighth century and was not totally completed until after 700 B.C. Unification will have been the work of strong chiefs attempting to mold a centralized chiefdom. Following the pattern observed elsewhere, the ranking lineage (the Medontidai) supplied the dominant chief, until at some time (about 750) his power was eroded by competing chiefs who instituted other offices — *archōn* (leader), *polemarchos* (war-leader) — which incorporated the political and military functions of the *basileus*, who retained only minimal authority, mainly religious. The stages in the change from a "centralized" chiefdom (never firmly established, as we have seen) to a system of collegial authority distributed among heads of lineages are obscure to us. Scholars disagree over the details and the chronology, but the general outlines are plain enough. By about 700 B.C. the Attic communities had been formed into a single state, "the Athenians," controlled by powerful local descent groups by means of annually elected magistrates and other aristocratic bodies, such as the Council of the Areopagus. In Athens, as in other aristocratic Greek states, the ruling families competed among themselves, each family group, with its local dependents, trying to solidify and increase its circle of power and influence. In the process the *eupatridai* ("descendants of noble fathers") exploited their position to the economic and political disadvantage of the common citizens. One result of this infighting was the attempt by one or another of the aristocrats to usurp authority as a *tyrannos* with the support of the discontented farmers. In 632 Cylon, a wealthy eupatrid, whose prestige was high because of a recent Olympic victory and whose power base had been enlarged by marriage to the daughter of Theagenes, the new tyrant of nearby Megara, attempted such a coup, aided by his kinsmen, his followers, and men supplied by his father-in-law. It failed, presumably because of insufficient support from the people, whose grievances had not reached the point of active withdrawal of allegiance from their local leaders. The continuing economic and political distress caused by the incessant feuding and competition for prestige among the nobility, together with a growing consciousness of unity, the result of the polis form itself and the hoplite "reform," gave rise to calls for relief measures. One such step was the reduction to writing and public posting in 621 B.C. of at least some parts of unwritten custom/law, hitherto arbitrarily enforced and unevenly interpreted by heads of kinship groups. The "law code" of Draco had the effect of concentrating the process of justice in the state itself to some extent, thereby partly diminishing the exclusive and hereditary exercise of legal authority by local aristocrats. Lawgivers like Draco were a phenomenon of the seventh century in a number of Greek states; their reforms were regarded as a democratizing influence by the later Greeks, and most modern opinion agrees.

By 600 B.C. in Athens the economic woes of the small farmers reached the point where they would either have degenerated into a position of total dependency on the wealthy landowners or have resorted to civil war. The worsening social crisis, which brought forth the call for redistribution of the land in Attica, inspired the extraordinary spate of relieving legislation by Athens' second great lawgiver. It remains only to add that while Solon's reforms did avert the bloody *stasis* he warned about and did save the free peasantry (who also formed the bulk of the hoplite force), the root causes of the economic inequality were not extirpated. Athens later experienced her own tyranny when Pisistratus, a

The Old Ideal under Challenge

prominent eupatrid, after two abortive attempts succeeded in establishing himself as tyrant in 546, with broad-based popular support. Such were the prelude and aftermath to Solon's appearance in history, a scenario which, in this general form, was common to many Greek states of the Archaic Age.

Although he styled himself a mediator between the two opposing groups in the state, it is quite clear that Solon's sympathy was with the non-noble element in Athenian society.[61] In his poems many of the now familiar themes of a tradition hostile to aristocracy are evident. Especially prominent is his characterization of the nobles as greedy and unjust. In a long philosophical poem Solon states the principle that while wealth is good it must be gained righteously. Wealth that the gods give will last, but,

> that which men seek through violence *(hybris)* comes not orderly, but persuaded against its will by unjust *(adika)* deeds it comes, and ruin is quickly mixed in.
>
> (Fr. 1.11-13D)[62]

He returns to this topic later in the same poem:

> But of wealth no limit is set that men can see; for those of us now who have the greatest means are doubly eager; for who could satisfy all?
>
> (Fr. 1.71-73D)

In another fragment, composed before he completed his reforms, Solon severely lectures the powerful:

> The townsmen themselves, persuaded by wealth, wish to destroy a mighty polis through their foolishness. The mind of the leaders of the *dēmos* is *adikos,* and many woes are at hand for them to suffer because of their great *hybris.* For they do not know how to keep from excess, nor to conduct in decency and in peace the present pleasures of their feasts . . . and they grow rich, persuaded by *adika* deeds . . .
>
> (Fr. 3.5-11D)

He goes on in the poem to accuse the nobles of public and private plundering, and of disregard for *Dikē*. These things cause "an inescapable wound to the whole polis" which will soon fall into an evil servitude; civil discord and war will result. He makes references to the aristocratic political "clubs" which he calls "dear to the unjust." He finally makes an appeal to "good order" *(eunomia)* which checks excess and *hybris,* straightens crooked judgments, tames arrogant deeds, stops faction and strife (12-39). Solon cautions the wealthy in lines that remind us of Phocylides' wish to be midmost *(mesos)* in the polis:

> You who have pushed into an excess of many good things, calm the strong heart in your breasts, and put your high thoughts in bounds *(metrioi).* For we shall never yield, nor will all be good for you.
> (Fr. 4.5-8)

The catalogue of aristocratic faults is impressive: greed, injustice, violence, excess, love of luxury, factionalism, arrogance. The ills these produce are stated in terms of the harm to the whole community. Solon in his poems reflects faithfully the major elements of the common man's view of the aristocracy.

Solon himself was enough of an aristocrat to employ aristocratic terminology; nobles are *agathoi* or *esthloi,* non-nobles are *kakoi.*[63] In other respects, too, he was representative of his class. Two fragments survive which are typical of his milieu:

> Until in the lovely flowering of youth he love a boy *(paidophileō),* desiring thighs and sweet mouth.
> (Fr. 12D)

And,

> The works of the Cyprus-born are dear to me, and of Dionysis and of the Muses; these make good cheer for men.
> (Fr. 20D)

No less aristocratic is this thought:

> Happy the man who has dear children, single-hooved horses, hunting dogs and a guest-friend from a foreign land.
> (Fr. 13D)

Despite these aristocratic sentiments Solon's outlook differed greatly from that of his contemporaries. Mimnermus had written

> Without disease and grievous cares, I hope that the fate of death may find me at sixty years.
> (Fr. 6D)

The Old Ideal under Challenge

This typical piece of pessimism was corrected by Solon in a fragment containing the line,

> May the fate of death find me at eighty years

and which ends,

> I grow old ever learning many things.[64]
>
> (Fr. 22D)

Not only in his major legislative and economic reforms, which diminished the power and influence of the old nobility and increased that of the *dēmos*, but also in his minor measures Solon evidenced concern about unbridled aristocratic influence. Like those of Pittacus and other lawgivers and tyrants, they were aimed at curbing aristocratic excess. Later commentators mention his laws against overly lavish funeral expenses, regulation of the prizes and emoluments given to victors in the games and his distrust of the high honors accorded athletes.[65] Modern historians, echoing the ancient controversy, still argue whether Solon was really a "democrat" or an "oligarch." Aside from the fact that these terms (and hence the concepts) did not yet exist in Greece, what is known of Solon's life and career shows plainly that he was an aristocrat, brought up in the old traditions, who recognized that these values would have to yield to new currents of social changes. As a statesman he knew that the good of the *total* community was the truly important concern; thus equally abhorrent to him were civil discord *(stasis)*, rule by one man, the nobility's greed for wealth and power, and the *dēmos*' attempts to seize power themselves. He was, in this respect, a mediator:

> I stood, casting a strong shield over both sides, and I allowed neither to win unjustly.
>
> (Fr. 5.5-6D)

And,

> I took my stand between them, like a boundary stone in the midst of no man's land.
>
> (Fr. 25.8-9D)

But, instinctively perhaps, his greatest sympathy was with the common man. Once, in a complete reversal of the usual aristocratic terminology, he calls the poor *agathoi* and the rich *kakoi:*

For many *kakoi* are rich, and *agathoi* poor; but we will not exchange with them *aretē* for wealth . . .

(Fr. 4.9-11D)

This is a very strong statement. Not only does Solon identify himself with the *agathoi* poor, he places wealth in direct opposition to *aretē*. According to the old epic-aristocratic system of values wealth was an essential ingredient of *aretē*, but by now this latter concept had been modified to the extent that wealth could be depicted as an impediment to it.[66]

◊

The evidence discussed in this chapter shows a pattern of attitudes that was evolving steadily and in a particular direction. At the beginning of the seventh century aristocratic groups enjoyed political, social and economic advantages that gave them great power in the developing Greek states. But the urge for domination, inherent in the traditional agonal code of superiority, led to factionalism among aristocratic families; their struggles for prestige among themselves resulted in economic oppression of the people as the nobles competed for the small surpluses of production that would solidify and enlarge their power base. Although the economic expansion of the seventh and sixth centuries did increase the available resources and raise the general level of prosperity, the steadily growing wealth of aristocratic families merely accelerated their need for more; increasingly aristocrats were perceived as greedy and unjust, provoking discontent and giving rise to anti-aristocratic reaction. At the same time, the polis, which by its very nature emphasized the unity and solidarity of its citizen body, provided a counterforce against rampant individualism and the social disorder that resulted from the centrifugal effect of aristocratic factionalism. Also, the new prosperity was shared to some extent both by the small group of non-aristocratic artisans and traders and by the moderately prosperous middling farmers, who still had little share in the governance of the state. The hoplite "revolution" was intimately connected with these factors. On the one hand it made the small and middling farmer the bulwark of the polis' security and diminished the traditional role of the warrior-élite; on the other hand, it fueled the feeling of worth and importance of the ordinary spearman in the ranks. Economic distress among the free peasantry threatened their ability to participate in the phalanx, thus posing a danger to the polis at the very time that warfare between city-states began to increase. These interacting forces led to

The Old Ideal under Challenge

the phenomenon of tyrants, lawgivers and elected semi-tyrants (such as Pittacus and Solon) who promoted the welfare of the majority against the privilege of the dominant class. During the sixth century, as a result of the manifold social pressures unleashed by the transition from tribe to polis, "the upper classes tended to lose part of their political and economic preeminence."[67] Many of these same forces insured the persistence of the ancient egalitarianism, despite the aristocracy's attempt to establish itself as a true ruling class of birth and wealth. As Polanyi perceptively noted, "The *demos* was heir to the tribal tradition of equality. The dichotomy between the *demos* and the oligarchs was fundamentally a continuance of the archaic distinction between the tribe and the manorial households that grew up outside the tribal confines."[68]

By the middle of the sixth century B.C. the old aristocratic certitudes no longer had their previous force; many of the stoutly held tenets of the traditional value system had come under fire, had been taken over (appropriately transvalued) by the mass of citizens, or had been subsumed into a communal ideal which could be claimed by all free citizens. The aristocratic class, its prestige lessened, had reacted by altering its frame of values in an attempt to prove its superiority and maintain its position of natural leadership. One way was to place greater emphasis on qualities that the lower class could not claim, such as noble birth, or to adopt a style of life that stressed external elegance and good breeding along with conspicuous display. Reaction was inevitable; upper-class claims to superiority were criticized and challenged, largely on the basis that they were not functionally useful to the polis.

The net effect of the social tensions generated, the claims and the counterclaims, was that the aristocratic élite was forced to turn increasingly inward, striving to fashion an image that could not easily be emulated or challenged. The directional thrust of the changing aristocratic ideal was into the areas of intellectual, moral and aesthetic excellence; and from the middle of the sixth century B.C. on, aristocratic spokesmen incorporated these ideas into their pattern of values, even as they continued to emphasize their claims to eminence based on birth, style of life, and, of course, value to the polis.

Ω

CHAPTER THREE

The Crisis of Identity: Theognis and Pindar

THE FORFEITURE of their claim to an unchallenged, "natural" superiority had produced a kind of "crisis of identity" among aristocrats by about the middle of the sixth century B.C. To meet the challenge of diminished political and economic hegemony and to counter the rise of an alternative pattern of values which subsumed or appropriated the traditional claims of aristocratic worth or downgraded them, and which favored cooperative and egalitarian behavior over the competitive and exclusivistic, aristocrats concentrated on formulating a conception of nobility that would be immune to discredit—or imitation. This they achieved by stressing qualities of the inner spirit: superior sensibility and sensitivity, wisdom, grace, and, ultimately, "moral" goodness.

We are fortunate to have a relatively large body of evidence in the poems of Theognis and Pindar. Theognis of Megara was an aristocrat (*fl. ca.* 540 B.C.), under whose name has come down a collection of almost 1400 lines of elegiac poetry known as the *Theognidea*. Not all of these are by Theognis himself; some are evidently later additions, while others are found in the writings of various lyric-age poets such as Mimnermus, Tyrtaeus and Solon. Nevertheless, the prevailing opinion is that the majority of verses in the first book (lines 1-1230) are from the period of Theognis' own lifetime, or earlier, and that few of the lines are later than the first quarter of the fifth century.[1] Also, despite a few contradictory passages, the "tone" of the *Theognidea* is uniformly aristocratic, and it is a safe assertion that the poems faithfully reflect aristocratic views current in Greece from the middle of the sixth century B.C. down to the beginning of the fifth century.

A brief survey of Theognis' usage of the words for "good" and "bad" will demonstrate not only his totally aristocratic thought structure but also the new directions in the aristocratic self-conception. The terms *agathos-esthlos* and their opposites, *kakos-deilos,* occur in the

Theognidea with greater statistical frequency than in any other archaic author.[2] Often *agathoi-esthloi* are used by Theognis to mean the "nobles," and *kakoi-deiloi* to signify "commoners," as automatic designators of social class; there are frequent occasions, however, when the terms appear to have a strictly moral frame of reference (that is, with no overt sociopolitical implications) or where the line between moral and class usage is unclear. The reason for this semantic blurring, obvious even on a casual reading of the *Theognidea,* has already been implied. To aristocrats of the sixth century a distinction between *agathos-* "aristocrat" (defined in terms of bloodlines, wealth and position) and *agathos-* "good man" (defined in terms of correct behavior) no longer existed. In addition, as symbols of moral worth, the merit-demerit words came more and more to express qualities of internal goodness rather than external characteristics conducive to success or failure. The Theognidean *agathos* exhibited a set of excellences which were traits of character, but which also were confined to men who, by birth and breeding, belonged to a specific social group. The morally good man, in other words, was the aristocrat, and only the aristocrat could be a morally good man.[3] This shift in aristocratic usage is no less significant a clue to changing social attitudes than the one occasioned by the egalitarian spirit of the seventh and sixth centuries which had altered the epic conception of the *agathos* by narrowing its application to steadfastness in the ranks and usefulness to the community.

In the *Theognidea* there is evidence of the tensions caused by nonnoble reaction to aristocratic control of the epithets *agathos* and *esthlos.* In some revealing lines the poet talks about those who once wore their ragged goatskins to pieces and "pastured" like deer outside the city—men who knew neither "justice" nor "laws." Now, he says, addressing his friend, Cyrnus,

> these are *agathoi,* son of Polypaus, and those who were *esthloi* before are now *deiloi*
>
> (53-60).

The same thought, expanded, appears in lines 1109-12:

> Cyrnus, those who were *agathoi* once are now *kakoi;* and those who were *kakoi* before are now *agathoi.* Who could bear seeing this, the *agathoi* in lesser honor and the *kakiones* getting *timē?*

The meaning of the complaint is crystal clear. Theognis wants desperately to keep the old designations of class. He does, in fact, but he is

The Crisis of Identity: Theognis and Pindar

forced to admit that those whom he considered naturally inferior had laid claim to the epithets of worth—and had made them stick. Men, who because of their background, were naturally *kakoi*—"base," "worthless"—had become *agathoi/esthloi,* "worthy"; that is, they were calling themselves *agathoi* and were considered so in the community, because they were doing what *agathoi* do: voting, gaining wealth, holding some offices, fighting in the phalanx. These lines show that by the middle of the sixth century B.C. the attempt on the part of the nobility to maintain *agathos* and *esthlos* as exclusive descriptive epithets for the upper class had failed.

There are further revealing signs in Theognis' usage of these terms. We have seen that from the earliest times *agathos* (and, to a lesser degree, *esthlos*) was primarily a predicate of physical excellence, more specifically as this excellence pertained to warcraft. In the intervening period such words had tended to lose their basically physical connotation, to be sure, but it is somewhat startling to realize that in the whole of the *Theognidea,* where the words *agathos* and *esthlos* occur so frequently, and where the sentiment is uniformly aristocratic, the old sense of "brave" is simply not found. As we see it in the Theognidean corpus the ideal of the aristocratic gentleman gives little importance to the old qualities of physical courage or to skill in war. Theognis' retreat from the traditional preoccupation with war and its glory is indicative of the inward-turning character of the evolving aristocratic ideal. The utterly unwarlike wish:

> May peace and wealth embrace the polis, so that I might revel with others—I do not love evil war. And do not listen hard to the loudly-shouting herald—for we are not fighting for our own native land
> (885-88)

is merely underscored by the disclaimer:

> But it would be a disgraceful thing *(aischron)* not to mount swift-footed steeds and look tearful war in the face.
> (889-90).

The fact that *agathos-esthlos* never occur with the meaning "brave" in the *Theognidea* is perhaps the logical culmination of the "softening" observed in near contemporaries, like Anacreon.[4] A drinking song, attributed to Anacreon, opens:

> Him I do not love who, drinking wine over a full bowl, speaks of strife and tearful war; but rather one who, mixing the glorious

gifts of the Muses and of Aphrodite, remembers our lovely feasting.

(Fr. 96D)

Other mentions by Anacreon of war have a melancholy and reluctant tone. Once he refers to someone who "fell in love with the bloody spear-point" (fr. 382 Page). In another he says: "He that wishes to fight, let him fight, for he may" (fr. 429 Page.)[5]

When we inquire more deeply into Theognis' conception of the "good" man we find further confirmation of the new dimension in aristocratic thought. In Theognis the claim of pre-eminence on the basis of noble birth appears more explicit than in previous authors. In lines 183-192 he complains to his companion Cyrnus that although men desire their stock animals to be "well-born" *(eugeneis)*, an *esthlos* man will, for the sake of money, marry "the *kakē* daughter of a *kakos* man." The result, he says, is that "wealth has corrupted race." The same note is sounded in the following lines (193-96), where a man knowingly marries a *kakopatris,* "persuaded by wealth." In other passages the doctrine that good and bad qualities are determined by birth, a concept destined to be a favorite one of aristocrats, is, for the first time in Greek literature, plainly spelled out:

> It is easier to beget and to rear a man than to put good wits in him. No one yet has devised a way to make a fool *(aphrōn)* into a man of good sense *(sōphrōn)* or an *esthlos* from a *kakos* . . . but by teaching never will you make the *kakos* man an *agathos*

(429-38).[6]

Theognis' attitudes towards wealth also reveal a shift in the aristocratic value system. At first glance the many references to wealth in the *Theognidea* seem confused and contradictory. Some of them are the traditional gnomic commonplaces that had become part and parcel of early Greek ethical thought, such as the prescription that wealth was a good thing to have, but only if it was acquired honorably, or the observation that poverty is evil. But alongside these typical statements are others which show that different ideas concerning wealth were becoming part of the aristocratic scheme. Historically, of course, wealth was a distinguishing mark of the nobleman. In Homer, for example, there was no hint that wealth was not an automatic sign of merit; it was good, it was necessary, and it was an obvious by-product of the martial skill of the Homeric *agathos;* and, in general, throughout most of the archaic period wealth was considered to be a positive good and poverty an unmitigated evil (along with the strictures noted above). All the evidence, moreover, indicates that down to about 600 B.C. nobility of birth and the possession of wealth were inseparably linked. The few statements in the literature that can be construed as negative attitudes towards wealth come from those who represent a non-aristocrat viewpoint. Most noteworthy are the disclaimer of Charon the "carpenter" in Archilochus, who says that he cares not for the wealth of golden Gyges, and statements of Solon, who not only makes a dramatic distinction between wealth and *aretē,* but also makes it clear that aristocrats were synonymous with the wealthy. There is a two-line fragment of Alcaeus that does, however, seem to contradict the view that only aristocrats had wealth. The aristocratic Alcaeus, purporting to quote a certain Spartan named Aristodamos, says:

> Money makes the man; no poor man *(penichros)* is good *(eslos)* or honored *(timios).*
>
> (Fr. 360 L-P; cf. fr. 364)

This seems to be a complaint of sorts, in which Alcaeus states that without wealth a man had little social and political status, which in turn would appear to imply that there were in Lesbos non-nobles who had money and nobles who were impoverished and who had lost some of their social standing. If this is so, we may suspect that by around 600 B.C. the complacent truism that wealth was the obvious companion of the man of good birth and that poverty was the natural state of the non-noble had begun to lose its force. The corrective that must immediately be applied is that Alcaeus' isolated statement can in no way be construed as evidence of a dramatic or universal shift in the socioeconomic *status quo.* For an aristocrat like Alcaeus even a few examples of non-nobles rising in wealth to challenge the aristocratic assumption would be provocation enough to take up his pen.

The main, and only reasonable, conclusion to be drawn is that at this point in the archaic period (around the early 500's) wealth was ceasing to be an exclusive attribute of those who claimed eminence in the community. We must also understand clearly what the distinction between "wealth" and "poverty" actually meant to the ancient Greeks. It has already been noted that the gap between the wealthiest and poorest citizen was not absolutely great. And, for the Greeks of the Archaic and Classical periods a wealthy man *(plousios)* was one who could live comfortably, independently, and with leisure on his "income." A poor man *(penēs)* was constrained to toil for his livelihood. A *penēs* was not a pauper; he was typically a small farmer, tradesman or artisan (who might even have a slave or two) whose time was spent in physical work.[7] The new opportunities and the general increase in prosperity that attended the economic expansion of the seventh and sixth centuries will have seen the rise of men, not members of the landowning nobility, to the category of the "wealthy," as the Greeks understood it. This (never very large) group is sometimes referred to by modern historians as "nouveaux riches," but that term, with its misleading historical connotations, exaggerates the rather modest, if crucial, rise in absolute economic status that so troubled aristocrats like Theognis.[8] So, the apparently untypical attitudes towards wealth in the *Theognidea* became easier to understand. We have already noted a negative tone in Theognis' statements on wealth. He complains that the lure of wealth will cause a "mixing up" of the race when *agathos* and *kakos* marry (183-92) and he realizes that the threat of poverty will force an *agathos* to marry a *kakopatris* (193-96). It is not surprising, then, to find that very seldom in the *Theognidea* does wealth emerge as an unmixed good. To be sure he feels that it is fitting for the *agathos* to be rich and the *kakos* to be poor:

> For in truth, it is right that the *agathoi* have wealth, while poverty is proper for a *kakos* man to bear
>
> (525-26).[9]

Also, Theognis never admits that poverty is anything but a total evil. This is a conventional Greek attitude, of course; nowhere in the literature of this period can we find even a hint that poverty should be regarded as something else than catastrophic.[10] Nevertheless, a Hipponax could at least mock his own poverty, while in the *Theognidea* it is painted in the most lurid terms:

> Poverty depresses an *agathos* man more than all else, even more than gray old age, Cyrnus, and disease
>
> (173-74)

and a man should do anything to avoid it (175-80). Even death, he tells Cyrnus, is preferable for a poor man than to live "worn away by harsh poverty" (181-82). The passages on poverty in the collection have an especially bitter ring that seems to go beyond the standard commonplaces. We may conclude that for someone like Theognis the prospect

The Crisis of Identity: Theognis and Pindar

of being poor was doubly unbearable, because it represented for him a perversion of the natural order. In a revealing personal passage he says:

> If I had wealth, Simonides, equal to my character *(ēthē)* I would not be distressed being with the *agathoi*. But now it passes by me, whom it knew, and I am speechless from want . . . The Cargo-carriers *(phortēgoi)* are in command, and the *kakoi* are above the *agathoi*
> (667-79).

His chagrin at this state of affairs is expressed in these lines:

> Many ignorant men have wealth; but those who seek the beautiful *(ta kala)* are worn away by harsh poverty
> (683-84).

Other testimony in Theognis helps to sharpen the picture of frustrated and impotent anger. Whereas for a peasant like Hesiod wealth was acquired by hard, manual labor, Theognis concludes that wealth is bestowed by chance or by the gods—and it is given to the *kakoi* often:

> Fate *(daimōn)* gives wealth even to the man who is completely worthless *(pankakos)*, but to few men is given the measure of *aretē*
> (149-50).

The theme of a capricious fate rewarding those who are his moral inferiors is sounded again and again in Theognis; these pathetic lines sum up his attitude:

> O Wealth, fairest and most desirable of all the gods, with your help even one who is *kakos* becomes an *anēr esthlos*
> (1117-18).[11]

In many of the passages on wealth there is a strong moral note; poverty *forces* men to do things that are ethically wrong. Just as we have seen it compelling an *agathos* to marry a base-born woman for the sake of gain, so "harsh poverty"

> teaches me, against my will, by force, many shameless things *(aischra)* although I understand what is good *(esthla)* and noble *(kala)* among men
> (651-52).[12]

Out of the mélange of statements on wealth in the aristocratic corpus we know as the *Theognidea* a fairly coherent thematic line emerges—not so much a *new* attitude *vis à vis* earlier authors but an exaggeration and a shifting of attitude: the dangers of greed, which is often associated with the *kakoi;*[13] poverty leads to a moral dissolution; wealth has nothing to do with merit, but without it one is nothing; wealth can transform a *kakos* into an *agathos*. Most tellingly, the overwhelming impression of the passages on wealth and poverty is that those who have it are the *kakoi* and that those who are poor are the *agathoi*. An illustration of Theognis' tendency to connect wealth with the *kakoi*, and to see social and economic changes as proof of the moral inferiority of the lower classes is provided by a comparison with Solon. Solon, among whose concerns was the greed of the aristocrats, also cautions the *dēmos* against the desire for undue wealth. In one fragment he warns them in general terms:

> For surfeit *(koros)* breeds insolence *(hybris)* when great prosperity attends . . .
>
> (Fr. 5.9D)

In Theognis one word is changed to give the line a definite class bias:

> For *koros* breeds *hybris* when prosperity attends a *kakos* . . .
>
> (154).

The implications of this altered perspective as it reflects on a changing social and economic climate are great, if difficult to ascertain; but one thing is quite certain – the simple possession of wealth could no longer be regarded as proof of social superiority, and accordingly, could not figure decisively in the new aristocratic ideal.[14]

The reason for the strongly ethical tone of Theognis' statements on wealth emerges when we consider that Theognis is searching for qualities that make the *agathoi* an exclusive group – qualities that had not already been usurped by people lower on the social scale. Since superior military value or wealth no longer sharply distinguished the nobles from the non-nobles, and because the one certain mark of exclusiveness, birth, was being tainted by intermarriage, a more inwardly-directed set of values had to be paraded forth; and even, paradoxically, a sort of conscious reversal of the older standards. Thus the possession and acquisition of wealth, once an external sign of aristocratic *aretē*, can now be contraposed to *aretē*. In a rather odd passage, reminiscent of Tyrtaeus' fr. 9, but in a perverse sense, he says:

The Crisis of Identity: Theognis and Pindar 85

> To the mass *(plēthos)* of men this has become the single *aretē*, to be rich
>
> (699-700).

He then enumerates other *aretai:* wisdom, cunning, knowledge, rhetorical ability, swiftness of foot, saying that these are nothing compared to wealth. He ends (717-18):

> But all men must commit this maxim to memory: In every situation wealth has the most power.

Tyrtaeus, he implies, recognized manly courage as the "single *aretē*," but this age has as its "sole virtue" the acquisition of wealth. Such a strongly negative attitude points to a radical reshaping of aristocratic priorities.[15]

Some time has been spent examining Theognis' attitudes about wealth because the downgrading of wealth as a differentiating social criterion is a startling reversal of traditional aristocratic values. The divorce of wealth from birth was, without doubt, the most damaging blow to aristocratic pretensions to superiority. Inseparable for generations, their combined force as controlling social mechanisms was unassailable. When acquisition of some wealth apart from noble birth became possible, and when occasionally people of good family made marital alliances with non-aristocrats for economic advantage, a powerful psychological edge was lost. I hasten to add that the combination remained generally effective throughout Greek history simply because families of prominent lineage continued, as a rule, to be the largest landholders. Simonides of Ceos *(ca.* 556-468 B.C.), when asked who the well-born *(eugeneis)* were, is said to have replied, "those who are rich *(plousioi)* of old"; and in the fourth century Aristotle could still describe aristocratic governments as those that chose officials not only according to wealth *(ploutindēn)* but also according to excellence of birth *(aristindēn)*. Nevertheless, once the twin supports of the traditional power structure became separable, each lost something of its aura. Thus, by about 410 B.C. Euripides could generalize that wealth *(chrēmata)* was the most honored thing and confers the most power *(dynamis)*, while a poor man of noble birth *(penēs eugenēs anēr)* was of no account *(ouden)*.[16]

Theognis' statements on politics are as revealing as his attitudes towards wealth and birth. Political power (or its erosion) is no less a matter of perception than a tangible reality. Like the possession of wealth, political leadership had traditionally been the preserve of aristocrats.

During most of the archaic period in Greece politics were dominated by men of noble families; in almost all the Greek states magisterial offices were in fact, if not in theory, held exclusively by those in the upper class. We should expect political prominence to play an important and self-evident role in the aristocratic ideal, but, interestingly, the *Theognidea* is ambiguous about this. At times the corpus appears to presuppose that the *agathoi* wield political power. Cyrnus is advised not to associate with the *kakoi*, but to eat, drink and sit with the *agathoi*, and to please them "whose power *(dynamis)* is great" (31-34; cf. 411-12). Theognis understands the use of power in the hands of a strong man:

> Step on the empty-headed *dēmos;* strike them with a goad that's sharp, and place a heavy yoke on them

because nowhere else is there a

> *dēmos* that loves a despot so
>
> (847-50).

Elsewhere he reflects the typical attitudes of an aristocratic statesman:

> I shall put in order my native land, my shining polis, turning neither to the *dēmos* nor heeding unjust men
>
> (947-48).

These lines, whether by the "real" Theognis or not, express the perfectly predictable aristocratic outlook of men who felt they had a natural right to rule. They are, however, the only passages in the *Theognidea* which indicate that the *agathoi* possessed political power.[17] All other politically oriented passages seem to imply that the lower class also wielded political power:

> And now the evils of the *agathoi* have become good for the *kakoi;* and they rule with perverse laws
>
> (289-90).

The complaint that "the cargo-carriers are in command, and the *kakoi* are above the *agathoi*" (679) has already been quoted.[18] Theognis is no less bitter at what appears to him to be a loss of power and prestige among members of his class. Lines 233-34,

An *esthlos* man, Cyrnus, who is a citadel and a tower to an empty-headed *dēmos*, receives a tiny portion of honor *(timē)*,

find other echoes: "Reputation *(doxa)* often attends the fool, and one who is *kakos* gets *timē*" (665-66); "the *agathoi* are more dishonored, the *kakiones* get *timē*" (1111-12). Related to this sense of impotence and symptomatic of the inward-turning trend in aristocratic values is the almost total absence in the *Theognidea* of appeal to patriotism and duty to the polis.[19]

The evidence of the Theognid poems makes one conclusion inevitable: the traditional assertions of superiority made by the upper class had become less effective, because by the last half of the sixth century B.C. non-aristocrats had, with some success, appropriated all or most of the indicators of civic excellence. Accordingly, we look for the ideal of the *anēr agathos* of Theognis and other aristocrats of the period to be expressed in terms of inner worth; his virtues will be "quiet" ones, and the focus will be increasingly ethical-moral.

In the ideal of the good man as seen in the *Theognidea* a prominent place is given to friendship and its attendant virtues, loyalty and trustworthiness. These notions have a strong social flavor; an *agathos* is a true friend and worthy of trust, a *kakos* cannot be trusted. Corollary to this is the constant advice to associate only with *agathoi* and to shun the *kakoi,* since the former are beneficial, the latter are harmful. The "good" are the repositories of all sound advice and are therefore the teachers from whom one should learn. These ideas give a kind of didactic organization to the collection. At the outset we hear (27-28):

Because I am well-disposed towards you, I shall give you the same advice, Cyrnus, that I learned from the *agathoi* while still a child,

and,

... do not associate with *kakoi andres* but always hold close to the *agathoi*

(31-32).[20]

To love one's friends and hate one's enemies had been a norm of Greek ethical thought from earliest times (e.g. *Odyssey* 6.184; Solon 1.5-6D, etc.). This standard is amply reflected in the *Theognidea* (e.g. 337-38, 561-62, 1087-90). But for Theognis friendship has a *moral* dimension unparalleled in earlier writings. He complains that he cannot

88   CHAPTER THREE

find anyone who is as faithful a comrade *(pistos hetairos)* and free of trickery *(dolos)* as himself (415-16). He boasts that he never betrayed a friend who was a *pistos hetairos* — adding significantly that there is nothing slavish *(doulion)* in his soul (529-30). Betrayal by friends, he tells Cyrnus, is almost as dreadful as death (811-12). Lines 87-92 may be taken as a summary statement of Theognis' insistence on honesty and loyalty as preconditions for friendship:

> Do not love me with words (and yet keep your mind and heart otherwise) if you are my friend and your mind within is *pistos*. But be a friend with a pure mind, or reject me and hate me in open quarrel. Whoever has a split mind, with one tongue, Cyrnus, is a dangerous companion (better as an enemy than as a friend).[21]

Such fear and distrust is a change from an earlier ideal of friendship which simply assumed that friends were loyal. We must not be overly surprised, then, if Theognis advises his heart to show a "shifting nature towards all friends," and, like the octopus, who can change his shape at will, to adapt one's feelings to suit (213-17; cf. 73-76). The use of cunning and guile towards enemies (as in 363-64) is one thing, but to adopt such a stance with friends is a sign that the moral universe of aristocrats was in disarray. The factionalism and consequent shifting of loyalties among the upper class had blurred the sharp outlines of an older, simpler ideal. Loyalty is now contingent on political conditions:

> In times of harsh discord *(dichostasiē)*, Cyrnus, a faithful *(pistos)* man is worthy of being valued equally with gold and silver. Few comrades will you find, son of Polypaus, who remain *pistoi* in difficult circumstances
>
> (77-80; cf. 209-10).

The atmosphere is heavy with distrust:

> If someone praises you as long as he sees you, and behind your back employs an evil tongue, such a comrade *(hetairos)* is no very good friend . . .
>
> (93-95).
> No one wants to be a friend when evil comes to a man, Cyrnus, not even if he is born of the same womb
>
> (299-300; cf. 575-76).

True moral probity transcends the "party-principle" basis of judging friends and enemies.

The Crisis of Identity: Theognis and Pindar

> I shall blame no enemy when he is acting as a good man *(esthlos)*,
> nor shall I praise a friend if he is acting basely *(deilos)*
> (1079-80; cf. 323-28).

Clearly, Theognis seeks to define the true friend in terms of inner values. Such a standard is difficult to attain; for those outside the narrow circle of the *agathoi* it is impossible:

> Let no one of men persuade you to be friends with a *kakos* man, Cyrnus; what advantage is it to have a base man *(deilos anēr)* as a friend? He would not save you from hard trouble and ruin, nor would he wish to share with you any good thing he had
> (101-104).[22]

Intimately connected to this is a consequent spiritualizing of the homosexual relationship, which implied in the strongest terms that true, morally-defined, friendship of this sort was beyond the ken of non-nobles. When Theognis gives to his friend Cyrnus proper advice and counsel calculated to make Cyrnus a better man (as befits the role of the older and wiser partner in an erotic relationship) he is again equating the standards of a social class with the norms of correct ethical behavior.

Most of the advice to Cyrnus, however, concerns matters of manners and style: how to conduct oneself in company, how to behave towards friends and elders or in particular situations, etc.[23] These maxims show how important external life-style had become; and the fact that they have a somewhat stronger ethical tone in the *Theognidea* merely underscores the centrality of proper "form" to the new ideal.

Another quality, closely tied to Theognis' notion of the trustworthy friend, and one that represents a further shift in the aristocratic ethic, is the ability to "endure," which, for Theognis, means the proper attitude in all sets of circumstances. There are, he tells Cyrnus, few "trusty companions"

> of the sort, who, being of the same mind as you, would endure to share equally in your good fortune or bad
> (79-81).

But an *agathos* man

> endures whether he is set in good fortune or bad
> (319-20).

The mind of the *deilos* man cannot adapt itself to good or bad fortune, but "the *agathos* must resolve to bear this or that" (397-98). This theme is sounded again and again:

> the *esthlos* endures when he suffers misfortune . . . while the *deilos* does not know how to keep heart and be patient either in good fortune or bad
>
> (441-44).[24]

The notion of endurance *(tlēmosynē)* is found in earlier Greek thought, but there it is a much more positive, action-oriented doctrine (e.g. Odysseus. Archilochus in a poem on *tlēmosynē* (fr. 7D) calls it "tough" *(kraterē)* and advises his friend to "endure, putting away womanish grief" (cf. fr. 67aD). In Theognis' ethical scheme, on the other hand, endurance occupies a central position, it is closely connected with social class, applies equally in good or bad circumstances, and, most importantly, it is a passive, even negative quality.[25]

Other internal values are present in the ideal of the *agathos* in Theognis. The virtue of *sōphrosynē,* "prudence," "moderation," that was to play so great a role in later Greek ethical thought has a prominent place in the Theognidean ideal. In the fifth century *sōphrōn* and *sōphrosynē* become normative terms, used by the upper class to describe themselves and what they considered one of their essential characteristics; and it is interesting that Theognis is the first of our sources to provide *sōphrosynē* with a political context.[26] For Theognis, as we have already seen in some lines quoted above (429-38), *sōphrōn,* "sound-minded," is often opposed to words like "foolish," "witless" (e.g. 453-54, 483, 497-98), traits which Theognis regarded as natural to the aristocrat and the lower-class man respectively. Theognis saw these qualities in the context of class conflict. Discussing swift and unexpected changes of fortune, he says that the poor man can suddenly become rich, the rich man can lose all,

> The *sōphrōn* can err and good fame *(doxa)* can come to the fool *(aphrōn),* and even one who is *kakos* can get *timē*
>
> (661-66).

In another striking example of the new "social" valuation placed by aristocrats on *sōphrosynē* Theognis complains that the goddesses Pistis (Good Faith), Sophrosyne, the Charites (Graces) have abandoned earth for Olympus, so that no longer are "just *(dikaioi)* oaths in good faith *(pistoi)* among men," nor do men recognize "laws and reverence."

The Crisis of Identity: Theognis and Pindar

Sōphrosynē joins the familiar qualities of *pistis* and *charis* (conservators of the old standards) now threatened by "the crooked speech of *adikoi* men" (1135-50).[27]

The essentially cautious quality of moderation, upon which Theognis seized so eagerly as a distinguishing mark of the good man, finds further expression in the notion of the "mean." Before Theognis references to the "middle" are found in a non-aristocratic context; traditionally the aristocratic maxim had been "always to excel."[28] Now we read:

> Do not be overgrieved *(mēden agan aschalle)* when the citizens are in disorder, Cyrnus, but walk the middle path as I do
>
> (219-20),

and, also to Cyrnus:

> Cautious like me, walk the middle way
>
> (331).

This idea of the mean is ethical as well as political; here he connects it with *aretē:*

> Be not overeager *(mēden agan speudein);* the mean is best in everything. In this way, Cyrnus, you will have *aretē* — which is a hard thing to get
>
> (335-36).

Of course, like *sōphrosynē,* the mean is the property of the *agathoi.* The *kakoi,* he says, are unrestrained,

> but the *agathoi* know how to keep the mean in everything
>
> (614; cf. 366).

In one couplet he connects the notions of the mean and of endurance as characteristics of the *agathos:*

> Do not be sick at heart too much *(mēden agan asō)* in hardship, nor rejoice too much in good fortune, for it is the mark of an *anēr agathos* to bear all things
>
> (657-58; cf. 591-94).

The thematic line of caution and moderation which is prominent in the Theognis-collection puts us immediately in mind of the "soft" escapism—the concentration on style and manner, love and conviviality, a retreat from the martial spirit, a sense of detachment—that was noted in the poetry of Anacreon, Ibycus and others, writing around and after 550 B.C. There is scarcely a mention of the traditional values of achievement and valor in the *Theognidea*. Only once are the highly charged words *aretē* and *kleos* used in the Homeric (or Tyrtaean) sense of "valor," "courage," and the "glory" which *aretē* confers:

> The great glory *(mega kleos)* of courage *(aretē)* will never perish; for a spearman saves both his land and his town
>
> (867-68).

Another time *kleos* is won by poetry (245). Otherwise the *esthlos anēr* wins very little honor *(timē,* line 234), while the fool can win fame *(doxa)* and the *kakos* can win *timē* (665-66).

Another area of distinction separating the *agathos* and the *kakos* is superior mental ability and judgment. We have seen that Theognis considered the *agathoi* to be the model of proper teaching; consequently, good judgment *(gnōmē)* and other intellectual qualities are given great importance in the Theognidean scheme of values:

> A man has in himself nothing better than *gnōmē* nor more painful than its lack *(agnōmosynē)*
>
> (895-96).

> *Gnōmē*, Cyrnus, is the best thing the gods give to mortals. *Gnōmē* embraces the bounds of everything
>
> (1171-72).

> A better companion than any man, Cyrnus, seems to be one who has *gnōme* and power
>
> (411-12).

Intelligence, of course, is something found in *agathoi*, not in other men, and is conjoined to other marks of the upper-class character:

> It is well to be summoned to feast and to sit beside an *esthlos* man who understands all wisdom *(sophiē)*
>
> (563-64).

> *Gnōmē* and a sense of right *(aidōs)* belong to the *agathoi,* and to tell the truth, these are few among many
>
> (635-36).

The Crisis of Identity: Theognis and Pindar

Most noteworthy is Theognis' linking of *gnōmē, sōphrosynē* and endurance, which the *kakoi* do not possess:

> Cyrnus, an *agathos* man has *gnōmē* which remains constant, and he endures, whether in good fortune or bad; but if a god gives a living and wealth to a *kakos* man in his witlessness *(aphrainōn)* he cannot restrain his badness
>
> (319-22).

Since these qualities, like good birth, are inborn, they cannot be acquired, and so are the exclusive property of the aristocrat:

> Mind and tongue are good, but they are inborn *(pephyken)* in few men who have stewardship over both of them
>
> (1185-86).

> It is easier to beget and to rear a man than to put good wits *(phrenai esthlai)* in him. No one has yet devised a way to make an *aphrōn* into a *sōphrōn* or an *esthlos* from a *kakos*
>
> (429-31).

> The *deiloi* are emptier in their minds through their badness *(kakotēs)*, but the deeds of the *agathoi* are always more straightforward
>
> (1025-26).

These ideas are easily extended into the political realm; twice he calls the *demōs* "empty-headed."[29]

Naturally Theognis claims the virtue of justice for the *agathos*. Poets had been urging their listeners to be just since the days of Hesiod, but Theognis denies this quality to the non-nobles, making the adjectives for "just" and "unjust" *(dikaios-adikos)* almost synonymous with *agathos* and *kakos:*

> It is proper for the *kakos* man to think ill of justice
>
> (279).

Elsewhere he says that under the rule of the *kakoi*

> Shame *(aidōs)* is destroyed; shamelessness and violence *(hybris)* have conquered *dikē* and rule throughout the land
>
> (291-92).[30]

Lines 147-48 of the collection repeat a maxim of Phocylides:

> In justice *(dikaiosynē)* is summed up all *aretē,*

adding,

> and every man is *agathos*, Cyrnus, if he is *dikaios*.

The distich has engendered a great deal of discussion; scholars have disputed its genuineness, appropriateness to the *Theognidea* and meaning. Jaeger's explanation that even if Theognis took over this thought "from a commoner like Phocylides, he could not help adopting it as the motto of his own party," is convincing.[31] For Theognis and for those who thought like him during this period, *agathos* still meant a member of the old nobility of wealth, birth (and success), but as these factors became less persuasive *agathos* had come also to mean someone who incorporated in himself higher qualities of mind and spirit. Thus the equating of *agathos* and *dikaios*, or, more precisely, the statement that a man who is *dikaios* must also be *agathos*, given the inability of non-aristocrats to possess these inner qualities, is perfectly in accord with Theognis' changed ideal of the good man. The degree of divergence from the older conception of the aristocrat is summed up in the lines which follow (149-50), where the poet says that the god gives wealth even to the thoroughly bad man *(pankakos)* but

> to few men *(oligoi)* comes the measure *(moira)* of *aretē*.

And it is in the somewhat spiritualized conceptualization of *aretē*, most powerful of words available to the Greeks to express human worth, that Theognis best reveals the change in aristocratic attitudes. No longer in the easily apprehended realm of manly valor, *aretē* must still be the exclusive property of men like himself. It can be equated with the abstract notion of justice (confined to the *agathoi*), or, similarly, may be expressed as neither doing nor suffering "shameful deeds" (*erga aischra*, 1177-78; cf. 29-30). Although wealth can come to the "totally *kakos* man," and to the "mass of men" being rich is the "only *aretē*" (699-700), true *aretē* is for the few (*oligoi*, 150). "Concern yourself with *aretē*," he advises,

> and let the right *(ta dikaia)* be dear to you. Do not let shameful gain *(kerdos aischron)* overcome you
>
> > (465-66).

The happy *(olbios)* man, honored by all, is one who combines *aretē* and beauty *(kallos)*; this, too, is granted only to the few (*pauroi*, 933-35).

Aretē is joined to wisdom *(sophiē)* as his highest goal (789-90); the way to *aretē* is through moderation (335-46).[32]

The collection known as the *Theognidea* has revealed an evolving conception of the *agathos,* whose positive attributes are mainly moral and intellectual. The *agathos* is a trusty friend, he endures, he has *sōphrosynē* and superior wisdom, he is just. These "quiet" virtues are more distinctly underscored by the omission of the traditional excellences of the *agathos.* Physical prowess (in battle or in athletics), wealth, political hegemony, public achievement and recognition are hardly evident. Those against whom the *agathoi* are ranged, the *kakoi/ deiloi,* are given character traits that are the opposite of the moral/ aesthetic excellences of the *agathoi* — they are not trusty or loyal, they are intellectually inferior, they lack judgment, moderation and endurance; in addition they are greedy, unjust and violent.

Such an ideal can hardly be called an ideal, stated as it was in essentially defensive terms. But the *Theognidea,* full of "a bitter and brooding resentment over the course of events," reflects a period of crisis of aristocratic self-identity, a transition from an older, no longer viable set of values to a quest for newer qualities that defined the aristocrat as an innately superior being.[33]

◊

How that crisis was resolved by the noble groups in Greek society is a splendid example of dynamic change in the cultural pattern of an upper class. We are fortunate to have a large number of choral songs, composed by the Boeotian poet, Pindar, who was born in the waning days of the archaic age and who lived to see the flowering of the high classical period (518-438 B.C.). His surviving poems are mainly victory odes *(epinikia)* written in honor of the men and boys who were winners in the various contests held at the major pan-Hellenic festivals. Most of the victors were from noble families; some of them were the most powerful men in their cities.

In most respects the social attitudes of Pindar were precisely those of Theognis; the major difference is that the *Theognidea* presents a picture of an aristocracy striving to maintain its superiority in the face of challenge, and the tone is often bitter and defeatist. Pindar celebrates his aristocrats in their moments of triumph; his odes reflect a serene confidence in the values of the upper class. Soured at what he felt to be a loss of prestige and authority among the "good," Theognis concentrated on inner values. These internal qualities are present in Pindar's poetry too, but mostly he dwelled on the successes and achievements of the nobility. In fact, it is the combination of internal qualities of character and visible, external success that is the hallmark of Pindar's conception of aristocratic excellence. This conception, which represents a different (and somewhat later) stage of the developing aristocratic self-portrait, can perhaps be best understood by comparing the outlooks of each poet.

As we might expect, Pindar's employment of the words *agathos/esthlos* is very similar to the usage found in the *Theognidea*. For Pindar, as for Theognis, *agathos* was a class word; and when Pindar uses the expression *agathos anēr*, "good man," he means aristocrat. Accordingly, the *agathoi-esthloi* form a group set apart and above the rest of the citizenry; more specifically, this group is the fittest to rule, as Pindar says in his first ode (498 B.C.):[34]

> In the hands of the *agathoi* lies the noble governance of cities, passed from father to son.
> (*Pyth.* 10.71-72)

The *agathoi* are also wiser. In a poem written for the tyrant of Syracuse he informs his patron that the gods give "two woes for every good," and then continues:

> Fools cannot bear this with grace, but *agathoi* can, turning the bright side out.
> (*Pyth.* 3.82-83)

In his usage of these words Pindar is remarkably consistent with the outlook of Theognis, and we can safely assume that the two poets expressed attitudes which were held in common by most Greek aristocrats.[35] Theognis, however, was obsessed by the opposite of the *agathoi/esthloi*, those he called *kakoi* and *deiloi*. *Deilos* is not found at all in the poems of Pindar and *kakos* is never used of persons.[36] One of the noteworthy aspects of Pindar's depiction of aristocrats is an almost total lack of overt class tension — he expresses the superiority of the *agathoi* as a group simply by excluding the *kakoi* from consideration. When he does approach social questions he finds other ways to describe those who cannot compare with his noble victors. In *Pythian* 11 he says:

> For prosperity gets an envy that matches it, but he who breathes along the ground grumbles invisible.
>
> (Lines 29-30)

He means that the successful achiever is envied, but it is better to be great and envied than to be obscure. In another ode Pindar says that deceit and envy press down upon what is brilliant and raise up

> a rotten glory of the invisible.
>
> (*Nem.* 8.32-34)

Those who do not count, that is, those who are not aristocratic victors are dismissed as "invisible."[37] Pindar's avoidance of class terminology is also evidenced by the absence of "technical" terms, like *eugenēs,* that denote noble birth; he is content to bestow on his aristocrats the simple epithet "good."

This brief sketch of Pindar's word usage amply demonstrates his aristocratic bias, but the positive quality of the Pindaric ideal is better seen by a more detailed examination of his attitudes towards some of the problems that had concerned other thinkers of the archaic period. For example, despite the lack of a technical vocabulary of birth, the belief that excellence depends on birth is stronger in Pindar than in any other poet of the archaic period. A comparison with Theognis in this respect reveals the essential difference in their outlooks. Theognis had made noble birth one of the prerequisites of the "good" man, but in a somewhat defensive or negative manner, lamenting that the purer stock of the *agathoi* was adulterated by intermarriage. In Pindar the notion of noble birth becomes a more elevated concept. For him all excellence is inborn, innate; there is a direct line of spiritual descent from the gods through the legendary heroes of the past to the aristocratic victor, which is literal proof that only by "inborn nature" *(phyā)* can a man be said to possess any excellence. In other words, Pindar does not defend the idea that superior qualities are transmitted by birth, he simply *assumes* it. Theognis, we recall, had maintained that no one can make a man good or wise by teaching (429-38); in Pindar this doctrine is expressed with loftier conviction:

> what is given by nature *(phyā)* is best.
>
> (*Ol.* 9.100)

He follows this by saying that many men strive to win fame by means of "learned skills," but this is "apart from god" and should be quelled in silence (lines 100-04). The same ideas are found in *Olympian* 2:

> The wise man knows many things by nature *(phyā)*, but those who are taught are boisterous and noisy
>
> (lines 86-87)

and in *Nemean* 3:

> A man is a man of weight who has inborn *(syngenēs)* glory, but a man who must be taught is an obscure man.
>
> (Lines 40-41)

Pindar sounds the theme of innate excellence again and again — not merely the pale notion of aristocratic superiority based on high birth, but an almost mystical conviction that the glory of the victor in his brief moment of triumph is the result of qualities inherited from legendary heroes through generations.[38] From a social point of view this conception may be regarded as the supreme rationale for superiority of birth. With absolute confidence Pindar makes a leap backwards in time, linking victors, heroes and gods in the expression of a single, spiritualized ideal.

This important and central conviction was present to the poet's mind in his earliest ode:

> Happy is Lacedaemon; blessed is Thessaly; and in both rules a race descended from one father, Heracles best in battle.
>
> (*Pyth.* 10.1-3)

And in one of his latest odes, *Nemean* 11, the honoree is glorified as being descended on his mother's side from the hero Melanippus, and on his father's side from the hero Pisander, a companion of Orestes (lines 33ff.). In *Nemean* 3 he connects Zeus, the sons of Aeacus, the victor and his country:

> Thereon is fixed the far-shining brilliance of the Aeacids, O Zeus: for their blood is yours, and the contest is yours, which my song casts at, sounding the country's joy with the voice of youths.
>
> (Lines 64-66)

When we turn to Pindar's treatment of the victory itself, we see that, like his conception of *phyā,* it has become a sign of something far greater than physical excellence and the achievement it wins. Through his victory the honoree demonstrates his ability and courage; but, in addition, the deed itself is proof of his kinship with the ancient heroes of legend. The exploits of the heroes of old are symbolically reenacted in the trials and eventual triumphs of the contestants in the games. It is difficult for us today to imagine the potency of that symbol as a means of expressing the *absolute* difference between those who thought of themselves as "the good" and the rest of society, no matter how much the social realities of the "age of revolution" had blurred class distinctions or how much those below the narrow stratum of the élite had achieved a measure of success on their own. It is no exaggeration, I think, to call Pindar's harmonious grouping of all the "positive-functioned traits" of Hellenic culture in his poetic celebrations of contest victors a triumph of propaganda. The result of this brilliant focussing was an exclusivism of the purest sort. It is no wonder that Pindar was welcome in every corner of the Greek world or that the demand for his odes remained constantly high for over fifty years.

Pindar's poems are difficult and obscure; they defy rational analysis, leaping from one topic to another, in a series of abrupt stops and starts, a complex jumble of colorful images, myths, obscure allusions, ethical commonplaces, all expressed in richly ornate language and complicated rhythms. The effect on the listener of the odes is impressionistic, not logical; yet the confusion of image, ancient myth and present occasion have a single unifying core — the symbol of victory itself — which stands for the entire spectrum of aristocratic values. Pindar's non-diachronic technique of melding myth and history, the actions of gods and legendary heroes, the achievements of the victor's family and of the victor himself, conveys an effect of timelessness, as if all the concrete examples were simultaneous proofs of the validity of the underlying social values.

Those values, presented as universally agreed-upon statements of truth, are, of course, predominantly the values of the topmost group. The great athletic festivals themselves were the institutionalized expressions of the pursuits of aristocrats — controlled by the wealthy and reflecting their style of life. They were, first of all, religious celebrations. Dominance of religious cults and offices, temples, shrines, and dedications by aristocrats identified them as the legitimate transmitters and interpreters of religious norms; and those norms coincided, naturally, with the values of the Greek élite. Pindar's odes served to make the identification even more explicit. The games were also musical festivals, reflecting, again, the refined aesthetic sensibilities of the narrow group: recitations of Homer, choral lyric and dance — not the music of the "people." Participation in the games was the almost exclusive domain of the upper class. Not only were the contestants men and boys whose families could afford the considerable expense in time and wealth for training, but even the spectators needed wealth and leisure to travel the long distances to the games. The major festivals, as Andrewes says, can justifiably be called "an international aristocratic world," in which nobles from all parts of the Greek world received mutual reinforcement of their values, and reflected outward to the non-noble majority the seeming permanence of their cultural assumptions.[39]

If we want a visual counterpart to the odes of Pindar as witness to the expression of exclusivistic class superiority, then, out of all the surviving dedicatory monuments, we need only look at the magnificent bronze charioteer of Delphi, commemorating the chariot victory of the brother of the tyrant of Syracuse in the 470's. Serene, aloof, supremely self-confident, the driver parades his horses before the assembled throng, reminding us, by the way, that the horse and chariot, functionally useless, was the ideal symbol of the wealth, luxury, pride and ostentatious display of the Greek aristocracy.

Not the least of Pindar's achievements was his ability to evoke a simple and direct line of descent from mythical hero to modern patron, as if there had been no intervening questioning of the primacy of the particular *aretē* of physical prowess. From the time of Archilochus there had been a line of thought which seriously challenged this simplistic notion. Like Tyrtaeus before him, Xenophanes had questioned the relationship of the Olympic victor to the good of the community; the polis, he had said, is not in a greater state of Eunomia for this (fr. 2.19D).[40] One of Solon's chief concerns had been that the rich and powerful nobles were going their own selfish ways, and were not concerned with "our city" and its well-being. Theognis, who had drawn away from the old aristocratic ideal, spoke hardly at all of physical skill or individual glory; at the same time he neglected the city-state ethos of service to the community. In his representation of the aristocrat, however, Pindar combines all these elements; by means of the single symbol of victory in the games he links the heroic past with the present, the individual interest of his noble victors to the prosperity and glory of their *poleis*.

Thus, in *Olympian* 4.11-12 the victor is "eager to win glory for Camarina." Another victor is "an ornament to Athens" (*Nemean* 2.8). In *Nemean* 3 Aristocleides of Aegina has brought this island into glorious praise.

(Line 68)

The youthful Strepsiades is praised for his victory in the Isthmian games, and the poet commends his strength, beauty and courage. By his victory he has shared his glory with his uncle, Strepsiades, who died in battle. Pindar then says that whoever defends his fatherland provides

> the greatest glory to the race of his townsmen, both in life and in death.
>
> (*Isth.* 7.29-30)

In Pindar we observe no trace of the conflict between individual achievement, so prized by the nobles, and service to the community, the constant theme of those not committed to the aristocratic tradition. Rather, as one critic notes,

> The tales of the gods, the myths of the heroes, the achievement of the victor, the greatness of his city — Pindar ties them all together and makes the union a triumph of aristocratic achievement.[41]

Nevertheless, in one important area there is a decided similarity of attitude between the two poets. During the crucial period between 500 and 480, when all Greece was threatened by the Persian Empire and the spirit of Greek patriotism was running high, Pindar reveals a reluctance to celebrate Hellenic resistance to the invader, exhibiting instead what Ehrenberg calls a "neutralism, a form of pacifism which was practically defeatism or at least blindness."[42]

Other differences appear when we compare Pindar's attitudes toward wealth with those of Theognis and Solon, both of whom (but for different reasons) were fearful of its effects. Theognis, especially, had seen in the desire for wealth and its levelling tendencies a danger to his own class. Pindar displays none of this fear. Some wealth was a necessary precondition for participation in athletic contests, and substantial wealth was needed for horse and mule racing. Pindar did not have any poor clients; his own fee, the cost of a chorus and the attendant victory celebration were heavy expenses. Therefore it is only natural that Pindar would praise the wealth of his patrons, who were among the richest men of their states. Even so, Pindar's attitude is substantively different from that of Theognis. For Pindar wealth is a sign and a proof of the nobility of the victors, and possession of wealth is companion to their merit. Thus, he says that the race of Iamids has been famous in Hellas, and

> prosperity *(olbos)* followed together, and by prizing achievements *(aretai)* they have passed along a road conspicuous.

Numerous passages reflect the high premium Pindar places on wealth. In *Nemean* 9.46-47 wealth is regarded as one of the ultimate prizes:

> For if a man win conspicuous glory together with many possessions there is no other height for a man to touch with his feet.

Hiero and his brothers won honor *(timā)* from the hands of the gods

> such as no one of the Greeks has culled, a lordly crown of wealth.
> (*Pyth.* 1.48-50)

In the same ode (line 46) Pindar prays for prosperity *(olbos)* for Hiero which is seen to consist of two things: "a giving of wealth" and "forgetfulness of pain." Elsewhere the ultimate in human felicity is represented as a combination of wealth, beauty and might in the games (*Nem.* 11. 13-14). Success and praise are considered the "two flowers of life" along with *olbos* (*Isth.* 5.13-14). In *Nemean* 5.19 Pindar says that wealth *(olbos)*, might of hands, and mail-clad war are subjects for his verses. Even in his own case Pindar connects wealth with fame:

> If God were to give me luxurious wealth I have hope to gain lofty fame in the future.
> (*Pyth.* 3.110-11)

The admonition that only wealth with "virtue" is acceptable, a recurring theme since Hesiod, is a commonplace in Pindar also; but even with this stricture the possession of wealth emerges as something glorious. In *Olympian* 2 he states:

> wealth *(ploutos)* adorned with virtues *(aretai)* brings opportunity for this and that, providing a deep concern for achievement, is a shining star, the truest light for a man.
> (Lines 53-56)

The Crisis of Identity: Theognis and Pindar

Pythian 5 opens with a similar thought:

> Wide is the might of wealth *(ploutos)* given of fate, when some mortal man brings it home mingled with unspotted virtue *(aretā)* a ministrant providing many friends.
> (Lines 1-4)

The accent in these passages is clearly more on the goodness of wealth than on the warming that it must be coupled with *aretē*.

Theognis' deep suspicion of wealth and the possible evils which attend it is only palely mirrored in Pindar. In *Isthmian* 3.1-3 he says that if a man has good fortune

> either with games that bring good fame or by the might of wealth *(ploutos)*, and checks odious surfeit *(koros)* in his heart, he is worthy to be mingled in the praise of townsmen.

Here wealth is linked to victory in the games as a high aspiration, and the admonition to "repress *koros*," while meant to be heeded carefully, is not a dire warning but a caution not to allow success to go to one's head. Similar is his praise of the victor Xenocrates in *Pythian* 6, who

> tends his wealth with judgment, nor plucks his youth with injustice or arrogance but culls wisdom in the haunts of the Pierides.
> (Lines 47-49)

In like manner, the youthful Aristomenes in *Pythian* 8, exalted by his victory:

> has a care which is mightier than wealth.
> (Line 92)[43]

The idea of friendship was important in the Theognidean image of the good man; Pindar, too, values friendship highly and includes many examples of it in his odes.[44] The combined evidence of the two poets shows how important was the notion of the faithful and trustworthy friend in the evolution of the aristocratic ideal. This fits well the picture of an aristocratic circle drawing ever inward and increasingly conscious of the mutual ties that bound nobles even from different cities in a common interest. There is one significant difference, however, between the two. There is not in Pindar, as there is in Theognis, the same moralizing about friendship and the agonizing over the faithless friend. Theognis' attitude may well reflect factional differences among the nobles of sixth-century Megara, just as many of the poems of the aristocratic Alcaeus mirrored the internal squabblings of the Lesbian nobility. There is little trace of this in Pindar; he emphasizes instead the positive aspects of friendship; and this perhaps reflects a more pan-Hellenic conception of aristocratic friendship and a more universal appreciation of the bonds between nobles throughout the Greek world. A passionate interest in local problems gives way in Pindar to the realization that aristocrats in Sicily share the same outlook as those in Africa and Asia. With friendship, as with other aspects of the evolving ideal, Pindar seems to have a sense of the essential unity of the aristocratic ethos.

Theognis' *agathos* was superior ethically and intellectually. These qualities also have an important place in Pindar's ideal, and one of the prominent terms of approbation in Pindar is *sophos,* "wise." Often *sophos* in Pindar refers to the poet, but others are also *sophoi* in this sense. Thus the Aeginetans are

> wise stewards of the Muses and of athletic contests.
>
> (Fr. 1.6 Bowra)

A victor's fellow-townsmen are called "wise," i.e. skilled in song *(Pyth.* 4.295).

However, the adjective is not confined to describing skill in poetry and song. Apollo, Jason and the Muses are called "wise." The seven sons of Helios have "wisest understanding" (*Ol.* 7.71-72); and a client, Xenocrates, is called "wise," that is, understanding (*Isth.* 2.12). Further, the quality of being *sophos* is a gift from the gods, and it is by *phyā*, not by learning, that a man is *sophos*.[45] The high praise inherent in the word is indicated by its being associated with other terms of merit; for example, *Olympian* 9.27-28:

> ... men become *agathoi* and *sophoi* by the gods ...

In *Olympian* 14.7, *sophos* is coupled with "beautiful" and "famous"; these qualities proceed from the Muses. Elsewhere Pindar says that thanks to the gods men are *sophoi,* physically capable and eloquent (*Pythian* 1.42).[46]

In view of these passages, it is not surprising that the *sophoi* are sometimes treated as an exclusive group who alone understand his

The Crisis of Identity: Theognis and Pindar

meaning. In *Pythian* 9.77-78 "a few things among many, deftly adorned" appeal to the *sophoi* in poetry. Twice the *sophoi* are directly equated with the nobles. In a victory ode for Arcesilas of Cyrene, Pindar says:

> The *sophoi* bear more gracefully the power given them by the gods
> (*Pyth.* 5.12-13)

and in *Pythian* 2.87-88, the *sophoi* are the rulers of the city as opposed to the "noisy host."[47]

Thus, Pindar, like Theognis, makes wisdom an important attribute of the *agathos,* but he does this less contentiously and more confidently than Theognis. The latter neglected physical prowess in favor of mental qualities, but Pindar displays no sense of tension between physical and mental *aretai.* Physical and intellectual ability, recognition among one's peers and in the polis are all combined harmoniously in Pindar – the noble victor has all these qualities equally.

Pindar's confidence in the inherent superiority of the *agathos* is seen very clearly when we compare the ideas of patience and endurance in Theognis and Pindar. In the *Theognidea* the virtue of "endurance" emerges as something rather passive and withdrawn. Pindar, on the contrary, always expresses this notion in the context of confidence. The verb which means "endure" *(tolmān)* is not, in Pindar, simply a passive ability to hold out, but is a much more positive quality of "courage" and "daring" (always in a good sense) directed toward achieving an end (which is always victory or triumph). Thus, in *Olympian* 9.82 the poet prays for *tolmā* and *dynamis* (power). The victor wins the "greatest of prizes" with *tolmā* and "might" (*Pyth.* 10.24). Melissus of Thebes is

> like in soul to the boldness *(tolmā)* of loud-roaring, wild lions.
> (*Isth.* 4.45-46)[48]

The quality of moderation (*sōphrosynē,* etc.), so prevalent in Theognis, has a correspondingly high place in the Pindaric value scheme. Conservative Thebes is praised for having "prudent law and order" (*sōphrōn eunomia, Paean* 1.10). In this, as in other "sensitive" areas, Pindar differs essentially from Theognis. North points out that although Pindar uses *sōphrōn* only five times, and the noun *sōphrosynē* never specifically occurs, four of the five instances of *sōphrōn* are in political contexts; and interwoven throughout the poems are many examples of *sōphrosynē* and praise of the "mean" which are connected with his aristocratic victors and their families.⁴⁹ What Theognis felt constrained to emphasize, Pindar, in his confident manner, need only allude to.

As we might expect, Pindar placed great emphasis on manner and style. Those whom he celebrated knew how to conduct themselves correctly on social occasions, saying and doing the "proper" thing. His victors and their circle enjoyed the good things in life: feasting, singing, dancing. As aristocrats they appreciated the fine points of horsemanship and understood the intricacies of athletic training, for they had the leisure and means for these upper-class pursuits. They alone were able to understand the importance of song and to appreciate their poet (hence *they* were the "wise"). They cultivated luxury without excess; above all, they were imbued with a sense of grace and charm and beauty. For Pindar the maintenance of a splendid appearance, whether in one's own person and accoutrements, in the grand pomp of the games, in the rich costumes of the choral dancers, in the lavish hospitality of patrons, or in the flashing brilliance of the odes themselves, was evidence not only of wealth and cultured leisure, but also of nobility and character. Hardly any ode is lacking in praise of a combination of these interests and attributes, and it would be tedious to enumerate the passages. But one aspect of Pindar's ideal should be discussed in some detail, since it illustrates the major position that the notion of physical beauty had come to hold in the aristocratic self-conception.

Throughout Greek aristocratic culture, as we have seen, external appearance was of considerable importance. Often the notion of physical beauty *(kallos)* was connected with *aretē*. As early as Homer the adjective for beautiful *(kalos)* was frequently combined with other words denoting size, stature or skill. The noun *kallos* is found in similar combinations. Beauty was an important aspect of the Homeric ideal and a desirable attribute of the heroic warrior (and of his women), and its possession contributed to a person's *aretē*. In the Hesiodic poems, on the other hand, physical beauty was in no way connected with human worth.⁵⁰ During the course of the archaic period the ideal of personal physical beauty came more and more to be associated with the aristocratic groups, and played an increasingly important part in the cultural pattern of the upper classes in Greece. The emphasis on beauty is, of course, connected with the general rise of aristocratic refinement during the archaic period. We recall Thucydides' statement that the nobility in Athens had only recently left off wearing linen chitons and fastening their long hair with golden "grasshoppers." Long hair and luxurious dress as marks of the well-born are abundantly illustrated on

Attic vase paintings of the period, many of which contain variations of the erotic inscription *ho pais kalos* (beautiful youth). The period of greatest popularity of this formula appears to have been from the middle of the sixth century B.C. through the last quarter of the fifth, and the majority of identifiable *paides* were from the highest echelon of Athenian society.[51] In the *Theognidea* the motif of *pais kalos* figures prominently, and there is even an explicit linking of *kallos* and *aretē:*

> Upon few of mankind do *aretē* and *kallos* attend; happy the man who has a share of both
>
> (933-34).[52]

The aristocratic preoccupation with physical beauty is further illustrated in drinking songs that have survived. For example, in a sixth-century song "to be *kalos* in body" is rated as the second "best" next to good health.

But it is in Pindar most of all that beauty is made an integral part of aristocratic *aretē*. Thus in *Olympian* 8 a winner in the wrestling contest is said to have been "*kalos* to look upon, not betraying his beauty" in victorious competition (lines 19-20). Similarly, the victor of *Isthmian* 7 is "wondrous in strength and shapely to see; and he carries *aretā* that does not shame his nature" (line 22). This intimate connection between deeds and beauty is seen at *Olympian* 9.94, where the victor is "in his youthful prime, and *kalos*, having achieved the fairest deeds *(kallista).*" In his invocation to the Graces in *Olympian* 14 Pindar links beauty, wisdom and fame together, saying that it is due them if any man is *sophos* or *kalos*, or famous (lines 5-7). This nexus is proclaimed most emphatically in *Nemean* 3.19-20: where "the son of Aristophanes, being *kalos* and doing deeds that fit his beauty, has attained to the heights of manliness . . ."[53]

We may now examine more closely the few passages in which Pindar expresses his social and political views more directly. We have seen that Pindar considered the *agathoi* a separate group, superior to the rest of the population. On the other hand, there is little indication of a group opposed to the *agathoi;* Pindar does not speak of the *kakoi-deiloi.* there is some evidence that he considered the non-aristocrats as *aphantoi*, "invisible," but the number of such allusions is small. Just as there are no mentions of the "lower classes," so there is no mention of lower-class life, the life of toil for one's bread. The one exception, as Fränkel points out, has a "contemptuous" tone. In *Isthmian* 1.47-51 he compares "every man" *(pas tis)* who "strains, defending his belly *(gastēr)* from weary hunger," to the victor in the games or in war whose prize of "graceful fame" *(kydos habron)* and praise from citizens and strangers is the loftiest gain *(kerdos hypsiston)*.[54] In such subtle ways Pindar does display political attitudes that are typically aristocratic. Another is his distrust of "mass opinion." In *Nemean* 7 he speaks of Homer's "falsehood," "winged skill" and wisdom *(sophia)*, which

> deceives, leading astray with tales.

He says further:

> the greatest mass of men *(homilos ho pleistos)* has a heart which is blind.
>
> (Lines 22-24)

Another passage which reveals something of his political and social attitudes is found in *Pythian* 2:

> But in every form of state the man of straight speech excels — in a tyranny, or when the noisy host, or when the wise watch over the polis.
>
> (Lines 86-88)

In enumerating all the possible forms of government, rule by one man, rule of the many, and rule of the few, Pindar reveals that he considered oligarchical rule the best, for he calls them *"hoi sophoi,"* a term of high approbation. Democracy is characterized as the "noisy host" *(ho labros stratos)*, and this descriptive phrase fits in with his suspicions about "mass opinion."

The instances in which Pindar comes closest to making a definite political commitment appear in *Pythian* 10.71-72 (above, page 96), where he upholds the principle that rule of the hereditary *agathoi* is best, and in *Pythian* 11.52-53:

> I have found that of the orders in the polis the middle *(ta mesa)* flowers in the longest prosperity, and I condemn the lot of tyrannies.

Some have seen in Pindar's praise of the "middle estates" a leaning toward government by the middle class. But, like all aristocrats, Pindar most hated and distrusted control by one man. For him the "middle" was the mean between a tyrant's rule and the rule of the many—namely rule by a small group of aristocrats, those whom he would character-

The Crisis of Identity: Theognis and Pindar

ize as the "good" or the "wise." In Pindar's conception of political schemes this would represent the same ideal of moderation as Theognis' "middle." We must remember that for an aristocrat the political extremes were democracy and rule by a single powerful figure, and that power in the hands of the wise and cultured few was the ideal constitution. Although aristocratic hegemony was in decline in many parts of Greece, it was possible for Pindar to "ignore" this ugly fact because his main contact was with the conservators of the old way of life, the Sicilian tyrants, the lords of Thessaly, the king of Cyrene, the landowners of Thebes, or with men in other states who were rich and powerful even if they no longer controlled absolutely. Pindar's easy confidence in the superiority of the social group which he celebrated on a pan-Hellenic level enabled him to be detached from the localized class tensions which obsessed Theognis.[55] And yet, the very lack of vehemence in Pindar's poetry paradoxically foreshadows the beginnings of a new political attitude, in which the archaic age's feeling of loyalty to one's community (by all the groups within the community) yields to a class loyalty which transcends the bounds of the individual polis. In its developed form this is to become a destructive force in the various Greek states, when ". . . common sentiment between the upper classes of different cities had an influence which tended to outweigh the common sentiment shared by all classes in their joint citizenship of a single *polis.*"[56]

◊

We may say in summary that Pindar's ideal was a positive and confident definition of the "good man" as opposed to a negative and defeatist definition. Theognis had retreated from an external conception of the *agathos* to a different one, based on superior intellectual, ethical and aesthetic qualities. Pindar incorporated these inner qualities into his standard of aristocratic excellence; but, in addition, he gave new vigor to the old Homeric notions of valor, skill and personal glory, ignoring the seventh- and sixth-century controversy over the validity of these *aretai.* He also included in his ideal the most forceful of the archaic concepts, that of service and usefulness to the polis (although he was careful not to *define* the *agathos* as the "useful" man).

Pindar was able to accomplish this because he chose as his unifying symbol victory in the national games, which allowed him, first of all, to concentrate on a small group of men who had the wealth and the inclination to compete. Thus he could ignore all the rest except as applauding spectators, whom he could, therefore, treat with dignity as "townsmen" or citizens," and only occasionally as the "noisy host." Second, by means of this unifying theme, Pindar was able to posit a direct relationship among god, hero, victor, family and city. The *agathos* is superior because he is a descendant of the ancient heroes; he proves this superiority in the *deed* by being victorious. The victory not only proves superiority, but, according to Pindar, the victory is due to *innate* superiority. In other words, there is an unbreakable circularity of cause and effect. The glory of the victor becomes the glory of his family, which becomes the glory of the collective aristocracy, whose inherited pattern of values makes possible the achievement of individual victory in the first place. Finally, by linking the valor and skill necessary to win in competition with the valor and skill necessary in war, and by combining the victor, the ancient hero and the city, Pindar could make the victor the benefactor of his city in peace, as the hero had been its champion in war. All this is done with careful avoidance of overt involvement in political or social questions.

The ultimate unity of Pindaric thought is a unity of all value. Every element in his poetry is directed towards that which, in his conceptual framework, is good, noble, glorious, pure, pious; all else is excluded from mention. To partake of any aspect of the good is to partake of the whole, for the good is an indissoluble unity. *Aretē* (achievement, manly worth) can be expressed or acquired in a number of ways, but it cannot be divided, because any separate manifestation of *aretē* (skill, courage, daring, endurance, beauty, wealth, power, civic contribution) is living proof of a single mode of transcendent excellence that was available only to those who incorporated in themselves its separate (but inseparable) components.[57]

In some ways, of course, Pindar's scheme was as self-deceiving as was that of Theognis. The latter retreated from the harsh realities of aristocratic decline into a world of inner excellence; and to some extent this is what Pindar did also. Pindar chose to ignore the political and social changes by creating a world of aristocratic splendor which placed the nobles on an Olympian plane, apart and above the rest of mortals. He found his chief inspiration in the epic virtues which had long since ceased to be of practical importance. That he was able to do this attests to the continuing attractiveness of those ancient ideals. Also, we must not forget that he was most welcome in those places where the aristocratic outlook still had some real force. Despite this, it must be recognized, as one scholar says, that the heroics of Pindar no longer enjoyed a suitable milieu. The practical ideals for which the poet stood were no longer practicable, and we recognize his protest in the spiritualization of those virtues which had originally been so eminently practical and concrete.[58]

Pindar's creation was a *tour de force*, essentially a conscious idealization of the aristocrat, compounded partly of the antique and outmoded notions of epic *aretē* and partly of inner-directed attitudes like those of Theognis which stressed ethical and intellectual superiority. In his choral odes "the archaic ideal was expressed in impeccable purity," while Pindar "remained untouched by the revolution in ideas that was going on around him. As one born out of due time, he lived on into an age that became more and more alien to him."[59]

Ω

CHAPTER FOUR

The Aristocratic Ideal in the Classical Period

THE POEMS of Theognis and Pindar are a coherent formulation of aristocratic values during the last half of the sixth and the early years of the fifth centuries B.C. A brief consideration of other evidence available to us will provide some supplementary detail, and may serve to illustrate more precisely the form that the aristocratic ideal was to have in the Classical Period.

Simonides of Ceos (556-468 B.C.) provides an interesting contrast in values. A generation older than Pindar and a sometimes bitter rival of his in the composition of victory songs, Simonides had the reputation in later antiquity of a wise and philosophical poet. The few remains of his epinicians (in the development of which he was an important figure), while they lack the craggy grandeur of Pindar, show grace and originality. But it was as a writer of dithyrambs and epigrams that he was chiefly famed. Later generations hailed him as the laureate of the wars between the Greeks and the Persians; the poems and epigrams he wrote about this great struggle display a consciousness of pan-Hellenic unity and a remarkable affection for democratic Athens and her leaders who formulated policy during the war years. As a consequence his outlook is rather different from the defensive aristocratic posture of Theognis and the almost mystical ideal of Pindar. In his usage of the key terms of merit and demerit, for example, Simonides betrays none of the bias of the other two; he was not anti-democratic and therefore felt no need to equate *agathos/esthlos* and *kakos* with social classes. He shared with Theognis and Pindar the late archaic inclination for ethical/intellectual speculation, and in his poems there is great emphasis on internal moral qualities. In fact, he appears to have approached a conception of individual "goodness" which was more "progressive" than that of other poets of the period. But, unlike Theognis and Pindar, he did not make the possession of internal morality the exclusive preserve of aristocrats. Concerned to define true individual worth, Simonides sees goodness as existing in *intent* to act properly rather than in external success or in the mere appearance. For this reason the possibility of goodness is available to all men, not merely to a class. This philosophy is expressed in a famous poem addressed to a Thessalian dynast, Scopas.[1] Having said that the "all-blameless man" cannot exist he goes on:

> But I praise and love all, whosoever does nothing shameful *(aischron)* of his own free will.
>
> (fr. 4.19-21D)

Among the many noteworthy elements of this poem two stand out. First, is the universality of application. Simonides speaks of "every man" (10) and "as many of us who enjoy the fruits of the spacious earth" (16-17). Second, he sets his sights low. Perfection is not possible, intent not to commit *aischron* is sufficient for praise. He ends the poem with these lines (28-29):

> Everything is noble *(kala)* in which no evil *(aischra)* is mixed.[2]

The essential difference in his outlook is also vividly demonstrated in the poems that celebrate the collective triumph of the Greeks over the barbarians. A famous eulogy commemorating those who fell at Thermopylae evidences a spirit that is not found in Theognis and Pindar but which is reminiscent of the communal ideal of Tyrtaeus and Callinus:

> Of those who died at Thermopylae full of glory *(eukleēs)* is their fortune, and noble their fate. For a tomb they have an altar, for lamentation remembrance, for pity praise. Such a funeral neither decay nor time, the all-conqueror, shall dim. This shrine of *agathoi* men has gotten for its guardian the goodly fame *(eudoxia)* of Hellas. Leonidas, king of Sparta, is witness, who has left behind a fair ornament of *aretā* and everlasting glory *(kleos)*.
>
> (Fr. 5D)

What we have here resembles the Tyrtaean concepts of the *agathos* and *aretē*. There is, however, an important development of the older ideal — the service praised is not on behalf of a single state, but for Hellas, and the glory which the men are awarded comes from all of Greece. The piece is full of words and images of glory and fame which are almost totally lacking in the Theognidean corpus — not the traditional competitive, agonistic fame, but rather a collective fame won in a cooperative exercise. Ehrenberg calls this the "new patriotism" celebrating a "new consciousness" of the Greeks.[3] Such a patriotism is not found in Pindar, whose own pan-Hellenism was directed to the common bonds that yoked the aristocratic class in various parts of the Greek world. Although Pindar was at the height of his literary career during the period of the Persian wars his attitude is ambivalent; it is the older Simonides who captures the new spirit of collective exuberance and pride — and Pindar's "pacifism" in the wars of independence seems to have been shared by other aristocrats. The reason for Pindar's almost total silence about the most perilous and exciting events the Greek world had experienced in centuries is simple to understand. A number of Greek states not only did not join in the struggle against the Persians but even aided them against other Greeks. Among these were Pindar's first patrons, the dynasts of Thessaly, Macedon, and his own polis, Thebes, which actually fought on the Persian side at the battle of Plataea in 479. In fact, many aristocrats, their loyalties directed to their own "trans-national" class, resentful of their declining hegemony and fearful of the unstable fledgling democracies, favored the autocratic rule of Median princes and satraps. A new verb, "to Medize" *(mēdizō)* came into the language to describe states and individuals who sided with Persia. Apollo's oracle at Delphi leaned towards mighty Persia, advising the Greeks to surrender. These anti-war lines occur in the *Theognidea:*

> But let Apollo keep straight our tongue and mind, and may lyre and pipe sound a holy song. And conciliating the gods with libations, let us drink, saying graceful things to one another, and not fear war with the Persians. Let it be so. And it were better to spend our lives with cheerful heart in merry feasting far from cares . . .
>
> (759-67).[4]

Simonides was not a democratic partisan; neither was he concerned to represent the attitudes of the "common man." Like Pindar and the other aristocratic poets he felt at home in the tyrants' courts; the victors whom he praised were the same nobles who provided Pindar's inspiration. But he was not a spokesman for the aristocracy. In his old age he was stirred by the events that were happening in Greece and his poetry reflects his sense of admiration for what men — all men — could accomplish with good will and determination. His poems are full of the dominant theme of archaic Greece's great preoccupation, service to the commonality. He was in tune with the times and understood that the men who beat back the Persian threat had rendered spiritually obsolete the older heroic conception. The victories which caught the aging poet's imagination were the sum of the collective efforts of many "unheroic" men. Even in the poem to Scopas, which has been interpreted by many as containing a strictly moral definition of the *agathos*, he appears to be content with the average citizen of good intent:

> Nor am I a fault-finder . . . sufficient for me is the man who is not *kakos*, nor too helpless, but knows at least the justice *(dikā)* which aids the polis, a sound man. Him I will not blame.
>
> (Fr. 4.22-27D)[5]

Implicit in Simonides' version of the morally acceptable man is an awareness of his civic responsibility. Elsewhere he says that "the polis teaches a man" (fr. 53D). The same notion that the individual's worth is intimately connected with the community is apparent in another fragment:

> No one has gotten *aretā* without the gods, neither polis nor mortal man.
>
> (Fr. 10.1-2D)

For Simonides individual and polis are an inseparable unit.

It has often been said that despite the difference in their ages (forty years) Simonides seems more "modern" than Pindar. The reason is that Pindar looked backwards, seeking the inspiration for his aristocratic ideal mainly in the old epic values, blending these with qualities of brilliance and achievement that were unique to men of noble blood. Simonides found his inspiration in the deeds of the hoplites of Thermopylae, Marathon and Plataea and the rowers of Salamis. Aristocratic apologists concentrated on what was exclusive to their class, Simonides found merit in the qualities and potential for good that were common to all men.[6]

Bacchylides of Ceos, Simonides' nephew, was born about the same time as Pindar; like Simonides, he was a rival of Pindar in the writing of victory songs. Although he lacked the breadth of intellect and moral insight of his uncle, their sociopolitical views appear similar in most respects. The spectrum of Bacchylides' ethical and social attitudes reflects the standards of the late archaic period. These lines, from a dithyramb, may be taken as typical:

> But it is possible for all men to attain to straightforward Dika, the attendant of holy Eunomia and wise Themis. And happy they whose

The Aristocratic Ideal in the Classical Period

> children have made her a dweller in the home. But unabashed Hybris, flourishing on shifty gain and unrestricted foolishness *(aphrosynē)*, who quickly gives a man wealth and power that belong to someone else, sends him down to deep destruction . . .
> (Fr. 15.53-61 Snell)[7]

All men can attain to justice; *hybris*, greed, unrighteous power, lead to destruction. This kind of universalized philosophy for "Everyman" is found in a victory ode:

> To have a happy destiny from the gods is best for men, but Chance, coming with heavy weight, crushes the *esthlos*, and, bringing prosperity, makes the *kakos* eminent. Different are the forms of *timā* and myriad the *aretai* of men, but one stands out from all: whosoever guides what lays at hand with a mind that is just.
> (Ode XIV. 1-11 Snell)[8]

Esthlos and *kakos* here have no social class significance, but neither do they have a deeper moral force. Rather we should understand them as meaning "capable," "of worth" and the opposite. What is of great interest in these lines is that by now the notion that the best *aretē* is justice has become something of a commonplace in ethical thought, and can be considered valid on a universal scale. In almost every respect the system of ethical values that Bacchylides expounds is sufficiently generalized to be applied to the whole of Greek society, noble and non-noble alike; and even when he honors aristocratic victors he does not claim any exclusive excellence for aristocrats. In an ode celebrating an Athenian youth's win in the foot race at the Isthmian games he lists the various ways one can gain "conspicuous fame" *(doxa)*. A man may be "wise" *(sophos)* or "have obtained *timā* from the Graces" or be versed in divination. In terms of the ideal expressed by Pindar and Theognis these particular skills and attributes would be the province of aristocratic gentlemen. He then goes on to say that some men pursue wealth, others expend their spirits in farming or herding. Here activities that cannot be considered exclusively aristocratic are listed. All this is prelude to the thought that we do not know what the future will bring. The next lines are:

> The finest thing of all is to be an *esthlos* man envied by many. I know also the great power of wealth, which makes the useless man *(achreios)* useful *(chrēstos)*.
> (Ode X.47-51)

As in Ode XIV, just quoted, *esthlos anēr* does not signify "aristocrat," but has the general meaning of "worthy" or "estimable" because of achievement. In other words, although life is unsure, the moment of triumph in which one is called *esthlos* is fate's fairest gift. And this is naturally expressed in terms of approbation (or, in an agonistic situation, "envy") by society at large. Bacchylides' statement that money has the power to make a useless man seem useful is not an attack on wealth or the wealthy, but merely the recognition of the fact that wealth without achievement can make a man honored in the community.[9] Implicitly he rejects this narrowest conception of excellence in favor of a broader vision of *aretē*.[10] A similar pattern of thought is found in another victory song (Ode I.159-84):

> I say, and I shall say, that it is *aretā* which has the greatest glory *(kydos)*. Wealth attends even the *deiloi* of men . . .

Bacchylides then praises piety, good health and moderate means; if a man has these,

> He rivals the most important of men *(prōtois)*. Delight follows every human life (apart from disease and helpless poverty) . . .

Then follow some familiar gnomes: that abundance is no guarantee of pleasure, mortal hopes are transitory; a man who is stirred by empty cares

> gets honor *(timā)* for only as long as he lives; but *aretā*, toilsome as it is, when completed rightly, leaves a man an envied monument of glory *(eukleia)*.

As Lesky says, this is "very every day philosophy that he imparts . . .," and it might be said, perhaps, that the same sentiments are found in Theognis and Pindar. Nevertheless, in "this inherited cloak of philosophy that he never makes his own," there is lacking the persistent sense of social exclusiveness found in the aristocratic apologists.[11] Just as Simonides allowed to every man the possibility of moral worth, Bacchylides conceives general excellence to be something attainable by all, and not a quality belonging exclusively to a particular class. It has been recently demonstrated that while Pindar, in his epinicians, "insists relentlessly on the genealogical principle," Bacchylides exhibits an "overwhelming difference" in his treatment of the same theme, referring only rarely to birth and descent.[12]

The Aristocratic Ideal in the Classical Period

It is because Simonides and Bacchylides were not spokesmen for a class, even though they wrote poetry commissioned by aristocrats, that their evidence is such a valuable counterbalance. They are further proof that at the end of the archaic period the aristocratic pretensions to superiority on the basis of higher ethical and moral standards of behavior were not universally accepted. By allowing such standards to be the property of all men of proper intent (Simonides) or by presenting them as a kind of common coin (Bacchylides) they implicitly negate the exclusivism of those who insisted that only by birth and breeding could a man legitimately aspire to moral and intellectual excellence.

There has survived another body of poetry quite different in form from the epinicians of Pindar and the elegiacs of Theognis, but which echoes faithfully the social attitudes observed in their writings. This collection of about thirty short poems has come down under the title of *scolia,* or "drinking songs," mostly Athenian and composed during the last part of the sixth and the first part of the fifth centuries B.C.[13] Sung at informal gatherings of nobles, and embracing a number of subjects, their tone and content express the sentiments of their anonymous composers. They show that most of the tenets of the aristocratic ideal that had evolved during the preceding centuries continued to flourish into the fifth century, largely unchanged, but, by this time, somewhat stylized.

The aristocratic insistence on reserving the epithet *agathos* as an exclusive self-designation persists in the *scolia*. A couplet commemorating an early opponent of the Pisistratids goes:

> If it is proper to pour wine for *agathoi* men, pour a drink for Cedon, attendant, do not forget.
>
> (Fr. 906 Page)

Here the aristocratic Cedon is directly equated with "good men." Another *scolion* laments the loss of members of the Alcmeonid clan in a battle against the tyrants on Mount Leipsydrion in Attica:

> Alas, Leipsydrion, betrayer of comrades. What sort of men have you destroyed, *agathoi* at fighting and *eupatridai,* who showed at that time from what fathers they were sprung.
>
> (Fr. 907 Page)

The nobles "good at fighting" are given the by now familiar aristocratic epithet "sons of noble fathers." The primary emphasis of the quatrain is on the noble ancestry of the men, which is seen as the basis of their bravery. An early love song, not in the collection of *scolia,* but surely of aristocratic origin, combines the themes of homosexuality, noble lineage, proper style and bravery:

> O youths, who have the Graces *(Charites)* and are of *esthloi* fathers, do not begrudge to share your youth with *agathoi.* For in the *poleis* of the Chalcidians Love, the looser of limbs, flourishes along with manliness *(andreia)* . . .
>
> (Fr. 873 Page)

The aristocratic obsession with friendship and loyalty is the subject of several songs:

> Would that it were possible to open each man's chest, just as he really was, and look at his mind and close it up again, and think he was a friend with guileless heart.
>
> (Fr. 889 Page)

> Whoever does not betray a friend has, to my mind, great *timē* among both mortals and the gods.[14]
>
> (Fr. 908 Page)

The second poem, by making faithfulness in friendship a source of glory, shows not only the great importance attached to the virtue of personal loyalty in the aristocratic scheme, but also to what degree the ideal had turned from the standard of external success as the basis of *timē,* to internal considerations. The social aspect of the aristocratic concept of friendship is seen in the following couplet:

> Having learned the tale of Admetus, comrade, love the *agathoi,* but keep away from the *deiloi,* knowing that in the *deiloi* there is little *charis.*
>
> (Fr. 897 Page)

As in Theognis, *agathoi/deiloi* are used as social catchwords, right knowledge is made the province of *agathoi* and proper style is denied to the *deiloi.* The correct mode of behavior expected of an aristocratic friend is given in two lines that might have come from the pens of Alcaeus, Anacreon or Theognis:

> Drink with me, be young with me, love with me, be crowned with me. Be mad with me when I am mad, restrained *(sōphronein)* when I am restrained.[15]
>
> (Fr. 902 Page)

The Aristocratic Ideal in the Classical Period

Succinctly listed in another *scolion* are the qualities of life that commended themselves most to young nobles of this time:

> The best thing for a mortal man is to have good health, second to be born *kalos* in body, third to be wealthy without deceit, and the fourth to be young with friends.
>
> (Fr. 890 Page)

The high priority placed on personal beauty in the ideal had by this time become a convention, as, in fact, had the rest of the qualities mentioned in the song. An earlier age would have rated all these things highly, of course, but the omission of personal glory achieved by some great effort or by service to the polis reveals the inward and non-assertive character of the evolving aristocratic ideal. The slight and the frivolous are often the main subjects of interest:

> Would that I were a pretty *(kalē)* lyre made of ivory and *kaloi paides* take me to the dance of Dionysos
>
> (fr. 900 Page),

eclipsing the older calls to glory and achievement.[16] With very few exceptions the collection is devoid of martial themes or exhortations to political activity. At a time when great events were stirring the hearts of men throughout the Greek world and patriotic pride was especially high in Athens the *scolia* concentrated on the good life—song, boys, feasting —all implying the superiority of the values professed by the aristocrats. If these *scolia* are typical of aristocratic songs of the late 500's and the early 400's then they provide a perfect illustration of the psychological outlook of the aristocratic class. When noble youths raised their cups and sang,

> A mortal man does not need to have much, but to make love and eat
> — but you are too sparing
>
> (fr. 913 Page),

the impression given is of an outlook far removed from the practical cares and anxieties of their peasant countrymen and from the ideal of glory (personal or communal) that we think of as being so integral to Hellenic culture.

A much different point of view is found in a *scolion* attributed to a Cretan aristocrat named Hybrias. Like the others quoted above its date is uncertain, perhaps late sixth century. In conservative, oligarchical Crete, untouched by new currents of social change, aristocratic superiority is a matter of blunt fact:

> My great wealth is my spear, my sword and my fine shield, my skin's defence. With this I plow, with this I reap, with this I tread the sweet wine from the vines, with this I am called master *(despotās)* of the "serfs" *(mnoia)*. They who dare not have spear and sword and fine shield, skin's defence, all fall at my knees, bow down and call me *despotās* and great *basileus*.
>
> (Fr. 909 Page)

Opponents of the Athenian democracy were later to term the intense interest in civic affairs by the rank and file *polypragmosynē* (meddlesomeness) and their own withdrawal into the "quiet" life *apragmosynē* (retirement from public affairs). The aristocratic tendency to retreat, already evident in the late archaic period, was to become more pronounced as the fifth century progressed. The upper class defiantly adopted it as a symbol of their superiority, while non-aristocrats branded it as anti-social. In the famous Funeral Oration, reportedly delivered by Pericles shortly after the outbreak of the Peloponnesian War, Thucydides has the Athenian statesman give the classic democratic rebuttal to this attitude:

> Here each individual is interested not only in his own affairs but in the affairs of the state as well: even those who are mostly occupied with their own business are extremely well-informed on general politics – this is a peculiarity of ours: we do not say that a man who takes no interest in politics is a man who minds his own business *(apragmōn)*, we say that he is useless *(achreios)*.[17]

The fifth century was, as we have intimated, a period of crisis for the aristocracy. During the course of the century, in many of the *poleis* of the Greek world, especially in Athens, the largest and the most powerful, the balance of political power had shifted to the *dēmos*. Space and the nature of our study permit only a brief account of political and constitutional developments. We may begin by stating some general considerations. First, "We do not know when or in which states or by what stages the demos as a whole first gained the constitutional power of decision in a Greek city."[18] The process varied in time and in degree from state to state; broadly speaking, however, the evolution took place during the turbulent sixth century, in face of the deep resentment and active resistance of the dominant élite of birth and wealth. By 500 B.C. "rule by hereditary aristocracies had become rare in the Greek world,"[19]

The Aristocratic Ideal in the Classical Period

having been replaced by governments with a broader base of participation – typically ones in which the *whole* of the citizenry, the *dēmos* (freeborn, adult males with kin-group membership), enjoyed equal protection under law and formed a sovereign assembly whose decision on communal matters was final. Second, "citizen" *(politēs)* was "defined" along a narrower or broader spectrum of property ownership. In some *poleis* (like Athens) even those with no land had citizen rights, while in others ownership of land was prerequisite even for assembly membership. The same criterion of property ownership dictated the extent of wider civic participation – as in the holding of political and judicial offices and in military status – so that during the fifth century power could be said to be in the hands of "the few" or "the many." Thus, both explicitly and implicitly "rule by the few" *(oligarchia)* and "rule by the *dēmos*" *(dēmokratia)* stated, politically, the range of economic control in a polis. In a "broad-based" oligarchy, for example, the whole of the hoplite class (defined in terms of landholding) will have been full citizens; other polities would extend to the left or right of this centrist pattern. Third, in all *poleis,* oligarchic or democratic, despite the loosening of its exclusive hold on the machinery of government, the ancient aristocracy maintained its unique position of leadership, providing the bulk of prominent politicians and exerting a constant (if uneven) pull towards more oligarchical rule. Although Athens exemplifies the movement towards the extreme form of democracy, she can serve as a model of the constitutional evolution of most Greek states during this period.

As we saw (above, pp. 68-69), the reforms of Solon did not solve Athens' political and economic problems. The difficulties of the poor remained, and infighting among aristocratic factions continued; the result was a period of civic disorder, culminating in the emergence of a *tyrannos,* Pisistratus, in 546 B.C. Although he was an aristocrat (a kinsman of Solon, in fact) Pisistratus' rule favored the *dēmos,* which had supported him, and tended to neutralize the powerful aristocratic houses: by centralizing the powers of government, giving loans to small farmers, initiating large public works, strengthening the state cult of Athena (over local, hence aristocratic, hero cults), enlarging the Panathenaic festival, and increasing the scope of Athens' interests abroad. He was succeeded at his death by his sons, one of whom was assassinated by a pair of aristocratic lovers, and the other exiled when rival aristocrats, led by the Alcmeonid Cleisthenes, called in the Apartans (always eager to bring down tyrants) who ended the dynasty in 510.

After two years of renewed aristocratic quarreling Cleisthenes and his faction won out over his conservative opponent Isagoras, by offering to the people a revolutionary political program which transformed Athens into a democratic state.

Space allows only the briefest sketch of Cleisthenes' complex legislation, by which, as Herodotus says, "he took the *dēmos* into partnership" (5.66). The essential step was the replacement of the four ancient Ionian tribes by ten new and totally artificial "tribes," into which citizens from the whole of Attica were redistributed in such a way that each tribe contained a geographical cross-section of the population. Thus at one stroke the old allegiances to region and to the aristocratic lineages which held local political power were broken up. The ten tribes also mustered as hoplite regiments and formed the framework of a new democratic council *(boulē)* of 500 members (50 from each tribe) selected annually by lot. The basic building blocks of the new tribes were the 170 or so existing "demes" (villages or urban neighborhoods) which had their own governmental apparatus. By making the deme the focus of a citizen's daily life (one's deme became part of one's name) Cleisthenes preserved the vitality of the local tribal principle, at the same time reducing the extent of control of powerful local families. Henceforth the Athenian's political activity centered on his residential "home rule" deme and the central state, freed from dependency on coalitions of regional "big men."

Of the many striking features of this remarkable restructuring of an ancient government, the most striking is that it was a deliberate act, by one of the most powerful aristocrats, consciously intended to give power to the majority and take it away from the old ruling families. The event is proof of the increased power of the non-aristocratic majority. After 508 B.C. the would-be leader had to accommodate himself to the interests of the sovereign people. Athens' internal politics after Cleisthenes is the record of steady (if uneven) growth of democratic government, punctuated by the continued jockeying for leadership by prominent nobles, some favoring, some opposing, the rapid rate of democratization, but all constrained to woo the *dēmos*. Those politicians with oligarchical tendencies inclined towards Sparta and were reluctant witnesses to the widening rift between the two powers, which solidified after the Persian Wars. Democratic leaders pushed for Athenian expansion and were committed to an Athenian "empire" overseas, made possible by a strong navy, manned by rowers who were from the lowest socioeconomic stratum. By the late 460's the "radical" demo-

The Aristocratic Ideal in the Classical Period

crats had prevailed; under Ephialtes, and later Pericles, sweeping popular reforms were enacted which further reduced the authority of the old aristocratic institutions and placed their powers firmly in the hands of the majority. Both in Athens and elsewhere by the middle of the fifth century there had evolved a consciously expressed democratic ideology, based on the fundamental premise that every citizen, regardless of status, was equally useful to the community. As the old, exclusive organs of government, by which a few could make policy binding on the many, were dissolved or rendered impotent, and as decision-making at every level and on every matter became the prerogative of the entire citizenry, an aggressive spirit of total equality surfaced.

The most eloquent exposition of the Athenian democratic system is preserved in Pericles' Funeral Oration of 431 B.C.

> Our constitution *(politeia)* is called a *dēmokratia* because power is in the hands not of a minority *(oligoi)* but of the whole people *(pleiones)*. When it is a question of settling private disputes, everyone is equal before the law; when it is a question of putting one person before another in positions of public responsibility, what counts is not membershp in a particular class *(meros)*, but the actual ability *(aretē)* which the man possesses. No one, so long as he has it in him to be of service to the polis, is kept in political obscurity because of poverty ...
>
> Our love of what is beautiful does not lead to extravagance; our love of the things of the mind does not make us soft. We regard wealth as something to be properly used, rather than as something to boast about. As for poverty, no one need be ashamed to admit it: the real shame is in not taking practical measures to escape from it ....
>
> Taking everything together then, I declare that our polis is an education *(paideusis)* to Greece, and I declare that in my opinion each single one of our citizens, in all the manifold aspects of life, is able to show himself the rightful lord and owner of his own person, and do this, moreover, with exceptional grace *(charis)* and exceptional versatility ....
>
> (Thucy. 2.37.1; 40.1; 41.1;
> adapted from the Warner trans.)

Even in these brief excerpts the main aspects of the democratic ideology, in contradistinction to the aristocratic ideal, are evident: positive equality (as opposed to the earlier, less inclusive, notion of equal protection under law), service to the polis as the sole basis of approbation, preference of ability over privilege, and, not insignificantly, slighting reference to aristocratic life-style. The condition of political equality inevitably fosters the idea of social equality, and the dilemma of the aristocrat in the fifth century was the maintenance of a sense of class superiority in a society which now consciously opposed manifestations of class superiority. The dilemma was heightened by the very nature of Greek ethical thought. Since the early archaic period the ultimate justification for calling oneself *agathos* had been expressed in terms of service and usefulness to the community, in accordance, naturally, with the demands of the society at any particular time. In a democracy one could be *agathos* only insofar as he fostered the interests of the *democratic* state; thus the traditional upper class indicators of exclusiveness and superiority were in jeopardy. Adkins neatly summarizes the problem which confronted the aristocrat:

> If one is a democrat in a democratic society, and finds those who are traditionally held to be the 'best' citizens — i.e. men of wealth and good family — not to one's taste, the manner in which one will redefine the term *agathos* is clear. The cry must be 'It isn't what a man is that matters, but what he does.'[20]

Accordingly, it became important in the fifth century to devise subtle means of suggesting superiority without antagonizing middle and lower class democratic sensibilities. In general, those who wanted positive recognition of their status as aristocrats managed to impress on the public consciousness the traditional claims to excellence. Some fifth-century aristocrats resolved the problem with little strain, making themselves champions of the *dēmos,* identifying themselves with the aspirations of the common people and the ideals of the democratic institutions, while all nobles in public life could exploit their ancestry and wealth by referring to the services of their forebears on behalf of the state or to their own public expenditures as trierarch or choregos.[21] The aristocratic ideal, then, lived on through the fifth century, adapted to the pressures which democracy placed on the open expression of class superiority.

Other new directions in the evolving aristocratic ideal are connected to the changes in political life. As automatic hegemony in the sphere of political activity diminished, the aristocratic tendency to claim higher intellectual and moral worth, observed in the late archaic period, becomes more pronounced, while at the same time manifestations of a distinctive life-style become even more obvious. This section will treat the main elements of the self-image of the upper class in the fifth century B.C.: subtle evocation of noble lineage and ancestral wealth, and pretensions to innate qualities of mental and moral excellence possessed only by this group. The final chapter will deal with the style of life peculiar to the noble class.

As in the previous chapters an examination of social terminology will illuminate trends in the aristocratic class' conception of itself and of the lower classes. We are immediately struck by the fact that in the course of the fifth century sociopolitical vocabulary became much richer and more varied. A larger number of such terms is found, many apparently for the first time, and these have greater social impact. They are, for example, more vividly descriptive and emotional, attesting to a deepening awareness of social and economic distinctions. Words indicating noble birth and pride of ancestry had been evident in Greek literature since the early seventh century. In the fifth century expressions of birth appear more often, with some increase in variety.[22] More significant is the appearance of a larger number of "valuative" words employed by aristocrats to describe themselves and others. Epithets like *eugeneis* and *gennaioi* had, through long usage, achieved by this time a quasi-technical status, but other terms reveal a much higher level of class consciousness. The common use, for example, of *hoi oligoi* (the few) as a self-appellation of aristocrats signals the desire for an appearance of exclusiveness. The opposite term, *hoi polloi* (the many) was almost always used disparagingly, as was very often the case with *ho ochlos* (the mob) or *to plēthos* (the mass). Other words had an even greater value significance. Fifth-century aristocrats called themselves *gnōrimoi* (well-known, notable), *epieikeis* (capable), *epiphaneis* (conspicuous), *charientes* (elegant, accomplished).[23] *Agathoi* and *esthloi* continued to be used as class terms, although by the fifth century these had become more generalized in meaning and application and hence less exclusive; the superlatives *aristoi* and *beltistoi*, which were very seldom found as social terms in the archaic period, became more favored epithets.

Most such terms of self-designation stress both the ability and the visibility of the upper class and illustrate an important dimension in aristocratic thinking during the classical period. With the triumph of "government by popular consent" in the fifth century it became even more imperative for those who wished to lead to convince the majority of their value to the community. Whereas in the earliest period aristocrats had ruled by virtue of automatic prestige, exercising a natural control over their communities, under the impact of popular challenge to this self-assumed hegemony the nobility began to insist on its pre-eminence in birth, manners and character. But during the classical period when control by popular assemblies became more widespread it was necessary to create a broader image of superiority of talent and innate ability. It was for this reason that so many of the epithets chosen by aristocrats to describe themselves during the fifth century self-consciously affirm that the upper class was "fittest" to hold positions of political and social eminence.

Other items in the arsenal of aristocratic vocabulary were designed to reinforce this impression. For example, the terms *hoi dynamenoi, hoi dynatoi* (the able, the powerful — sometimes found in the superlative form, *hoi cynatōtatoi*) were commonly applied to the oligarchical factions of the various Greek states to underline the capability and the political potency of the aristocratic class.

Still another group of descriptive terms proliferated in the fifth century, accenting the fact that the upper class possessed the requisite material means to allow leisure for political activity. Words describing the wealthy class during the archaic period, like *plousioi* and *olbioi*, were fairly neutral in meaning, with little inference of value judgment. Fifth-century expressions describing possession of wealth or its lack were more heavily laden with ethical implications: e.g. *hoi euporoi* (those who have the means), *hoi ta chrēmata* (or *tas ousias*) *echontes* (those who possess goods, those who possess the means). The fact that a number of valuative epithets denoting the opposite condition come into use, shows how important this aspect of the aristocratic self-conception was. Thus the neutral term *hoi penētes* (the poor) was often joined in context with the disparaging "the many," while others, like *hoi aporoi* (those without means), *hoi ouk echontes* (those who do not have) reveal a similar bias. The pejorative intent of such a clear-cut delineation of economic competence is seen in new words like *misthioi* and *misthophoroi* (wage earners), applied to the common people.

Most revealing are the words used by aristocratic writers to describe the lower class which have definite overtones of moral inferiority. Some of them survive from the archaic period — *kakoi, deiloi* — others, like *hoi cheirous* (the inferior), seldom used earlier with social significance, now become common descriptions of the lower class. A good example of this process is the frequent use of the words *ponēroi* and *mochthēroi* as synonyms for the lower class. Both words derive from roots indicating difficult labor, toil or suffering, and had a neutral sense until the fifth century, at which time they became ethical/social terms describing

The Aristocratic Ideal in the Classical Period 129

persons who, because they had to work hard, were politically and socially inferior, "knavish."[24]

The depth and intensity of the battle of semantics, in which old words were given social, political and moral nuances and new terms were coined which were colorfully emotive is symbolized in the fifth-century usage of *dēmos* and *kaloskagathos*. *Dēmos* was not a descriptive term; as ancient as the language itself, it had, until the end of the archaic period, little social or class significance and very little sense of a political division within the polis. But in fifth-century aristocratic usage it served as an equivalent to "the mob," "the commons," as opposed to the "better" class of people. It was also during the fifth century that adjectives and nouns were formed from the originally pallid *dēmos* – *dēmotikos, dēmokratikos, dēmokratia* – which, in the mouths of the nobles, were often used as pejorative terms. *Kaloskagathos* (beautiful and good) made its appearance only in the fifth century and shows clearly the psychological "mood" of the aristocratic class during this period, for it evoked a powerful range of responses, combining the ancient (but now disputed) aristocratic self-epithet with one that by universal consent was confined to the noble group. *Kalos* signified not only external physical beauty but also the whole range of elegance in style and appearance, fine manners and proper comportment, with overtones, in addition, of the aristocratic practice of pederasty. If we translate it as "gentleman" in the sense that it was used in England during the eighteenth and nineteenth centuries we can fairly closely approximate its meaning.[25]

The preceding sketch of sociopolitical vocabulary makes clear the main intent of the self-image projected by aristocrats in the fifth century: because of their superior natural ability and qualities of mind and spirit, together with their greater economic competence, aristocrats were more fit than others to assume leading roles in the machinery of government. A closer examination of the writings of fifth-century intellectuals will reveal these attitudes in greater detail. It must be borne in mind that the literature that has survived from this period (as from the earlier periods) is largely the expression of an intellectual and social élite, often antagonistic to the claims of the classes below them, even in a democratic state like Athens. Less has come down to us of the democratic opposition to the "propaganda" of aristocratic reactionaries. When, for example, we find those who would term themselves "the rich," referred to as "the fat" *(hoi pacheis),* we can assume that this was a popular counter-epithet meant to disparage, but too little of this kind of thing survives to indicate the extent or manner of lower class rejection of aristocratic terminology.[26] The one-sidedness of our information makes it difficult to identify fully the complete spectrum of social attitudes; nevertheless, enough has survived to demonstrate the existence of an anti-aristocratic, pro-democratic body of opinion.

The intellectual foundations of the democratic ideology were laid by certain fifth-century thinkers, known collectively as the "sophists." The so-called "sophistic movement," a free-wheeling, radical reexamination of man in relation to his environment — described by Fränkel as "the emancipation of the intellect from any and every shackle laid upon it"[27] — took place after the middle of the century in Athens, by then the acknowledged intellectual center of Greece, which magnetically drew thinkers from all over the Hellenic world. So complex a mélange of ideas as the sophistic movement is not easily summarized, especially since the sophists were individual thinkers, not a systematic school. Nevertheless, certain fundamental attitudes were shared by all the sophistic teachers, among which were a strong bias towards the practical and the possible (grounded in the realm of common-sense reality) and a thoroughgoing scepticism which negated the possibility of absolute knowledge. The most controversial result of sophistical speculation was the dichotomy they perceived between "law" or "custom" *(nomos)*, the result of pure convention, and "nature" *(physis)*, an impersonal force, the real state of things. The application of the *nomos-physis* antithesis to human society led to the bold idea that law and custom were man-made conventions relative to the natural human state. All laws and all "moral" values, including even justice, were creations of human intellect. The state itself was an invention of man, a social contract, evolved over time for mutual security, support and benefit. Such an "anthropological" view of humankind and its institutions, which sees all men as genetically similar and possessing a common set of drives, leads easily to the idea that society is necessarily a cooperative endeavor, in which everyone had an equal stake (and share). The primary objective of political organization is the cohesion and stability of the group; hence, all group members, regardless of status, are essentially equal.

These principles, arrived at by means of strict rational enquiry, naturally favored the fact of Athenian democracy, and the "liberal" teachings of the sophists were diffused into the general intellectual climate of fifth-century Athens. The "twin articles of faith" of the liberal theorists — first, that men are biologically equal and demand a relationship in law and justice that conforms to this equality, and second, that men possess a fundamental good will that would be dangerously thwarted by any principle which advocated superior force — were, as we have seen, quite antithetical to the traditional presuppositions of the upper class.[28] The reaction against such reasoning was fierce, especially because the sophistic notion that egalitarian democracy, for all its faults, was "a natural and historical condition," responded to the deep-rooted sense of egalitarianism inherited from the Greek tribal past.

Two quotations from the political theorists will give us a sense of their pro-democratic, egalitarian point of view. Democritus of Abdera (in Thrace), known not only as a scientist but as a political philosopher, was active in Athens in the second half of the fifth century. Among his political maxims this one stands out:

> Poverty under democracy is as much to be preferred to so-called prosperity under an autocracy as freedom to slavery.
>
> (B 251)

Antiphon, the fifth-century sophist, has this to say about noble birth:

> We revere and honour those born of noble fathers, but those who are not born of noble houses we neither revere nor honour. In this we are, in our relations with one another, like barbarians, since we are all by nature born the same in every way, both barbarians and Hellenes....
>
> (B 44)[29]

At this point we can attempt a more developed analysis of the configuration of the aristocratic ideal in the fifth century B.C. The centrality of the notion that aristocrats were *by nature* better suited than others to lead is evident from our examination of terminology, and it is to be expected that the noble class would concentrate its greatest energy in proving this contention. Theognis, we recall, had expressed the idea as a kind of forlorn hope and Pindar had proclaimed it with myopic optimism, saying that the *agathoi* were fittest by birth to rule, and proving it by connecting the *agathoi* of his day with the ancient heroes of their *poleis.* Pindar's somewhat simplistic appeal to inborn superiority was not without force during the fifth century, and from time to time we find this idea expressed in the literature, put in the mouths of aristocratic spokesman.[30] In the *Ajax* of Sophocles, Menelaus, confronting Ajax' brother Teucer, says:

And yet, it is the mark of a *kakos* man when one who is an ordinary citizen *(dēmotēs)* thinks it right not to heed those who have been set over him.

(1071-72)

Implicit in Menelaus' statement is the value judgment that men are naturally divided into rulers or the ruled, a notion that is made explicit in 666ff., where submission to leaders *(archontes)* is analogous to natural law, as when winter yields to summer. To be sure, this sort of sentiment could be accepted by everyone since the appeal is not overtly to rule by an upper class but merely by those who have been set above. Menelaus, in fact, continues to speak in terms of the safety of the polis and the need to respect the laws. After Menelaus' speech the chorus agrees that his were "wise words" (1091-92). Still, Teucer recognizes the social implications quite clearly; he retorts that it is no wonder that a man "who was nothing in birth" would commit wrong when "those who claim to have been born *eugeneis*" err so in their speech. Teucer's point is that Menelaus was in no way the rightful lord of the Salaminians:

You came as lord of Sparta, not as ruler over us; you had no more right of rule over them than he over you.

(1102-04)

Teucer makes the clear distinction between a ruler who commands by right (i.e. by consent of the people, in democratic terms) and one who assumes it by the claim of birth or heritage (1093-1108).

This exchange is significant in that it expresses the polarization between the claims of democracy, in which all men are (at least theoretically)equal and the aristocratic conviction of a group fittest to rule by "nature."[31] An excellent example of such tension is found in an anecdote related by the historian Herodotus. He says that when the tyrant of Samos, Polycrates, died (*ca.* 522 B.C.), his apparent successor, a man named Maiandrios, assembled the citizens and proclaimed that he wished not to be tyrant but wanted to give the Samians their freedom. His democratic gesture was met by the retort of a Samian aristocrat, who immediately rose in the assembly and said: "But you are not fit *(axios)* to rule anyway, since you were badly born *(gegonōs kakōs)* and a plague," and demanded instead that Maiandrios give an accounting of public monies (3.142). The point of interest to us is not that the nobleman, Telesarchus, was not anxious to see a democracy in Samos, but that he also gave voice to his resentment that a man of low birth could presume to hold or relinquish power.

A similar attitude is found in the *Oedipus Tyrannus* of Sophocles, from a different vantage point. Although the passage in question (1062ff.) is primarily concerned with the dramatic irony of Oedipus' real parentage, the situation may be taken as sufficiently representative. Thinking that he may be the son of a slave, Oedipus is determined to discover the truth. Jocasta, fearing the real truth and trying to dissuade Oedipus from further enquiry, appears to Oedipus to be upset at his low birth. Throughout the scene the reaction of Oedipus is that regardless of his low birth, or the shame that his high-born queen may feel, he is still the same man and (by implication) worthy to rule. Here again, the polarity in fifth-century political thought is revealed. On the one hand was the jealously guarded democratic tenet that low birth was not a deterrent to high position or prestige; on the other, the aristocratic idea that low birth was an automatic disqualification.

There are instances of this aristocratic conceit in the plays of Aristophanes. In the *Knights* the ignorant Sausage Seller is being interviewed as a possible successor to the democratic politician Cleon as the leader of the Athenians. Surprised at being considered for the post he demurs that his position makes him unqualified, but Demosthenes insists that the very baseness of his life makes him the perfect replacement for Cleon. When the Sausage Seller continues to say that he is unworthy Demosthenes asks:

>   You are not of the *kaloik' agathoi* are you?
> S.S. No, by the gods, but sprung from knaves *(ponēroi)*.
> De. Oh, blessed man, the perfect background for public life!
>   (*Knights* 185-87)

Here, in exaggerated form, is the aristocratic feeling that in the extreme democracy high birth was a distinct disadvantage for high position. These passages also obliquely demonstrate that during the classical period aristocrats made specific claims to public leadership on the basis of innate superiority and that this claim was resisted by the mass of public opinion. They show, in addition, that noble birth, *eugeneia,* one of the chief emblems of superiority during the archaic period, continued to hold a certain pride of place, but not the foremost by any means; public sentiment was so suspicious of it that it could function as only one of the indexes of upper-class superiority. The problem for the aristocrat was that as *eugeneia* became more important in the aristocratic self-conception it clashed head on with democratic ideas of equality. The consequence of the tension was that *within the context of democratic politics* noble birth could not be used as a primary justification of superiority, and yet it could not be omitted without abandoning a fundamental precept of the aristocratic ideal. The obvious solution to the paradox was to align *eugeneia* with other qualities, giving it an emphasis, but not an absolute one. This raises another difficulty: *eugeneia*, if coupled with other, more active qualities, will inevitably appear extraneous and accidental, hence, more vulnerable to attack. Thus the objective accident of *eugeneia* had to be made to appear an intimate part of the nexus of aristocratic personal qualities, integral to it and not an isolated phenomenon. It was this kind of necessity that motivated the coinage of a term like *kaloskagathos*, which subsumed the idea of *eugeneia*.

In contexts other than purely political the argument from birth is more frequently found. In these instances the resort to *eugeneia* is not the bald assertion of automatic superiority but a (more or less implicit) plea that good lineage makes a man a better man. It was least assailable when it was linked to the good of the polis and stated subtly, as in the *Knights* (565 ff.) where the youthful knights praise "our fathers" who made the polis great and protected her against the foe. The appeal to the great deeds of ancestors as a justification for the goodness of the present generation was a potent one, frequently resorted to by the upper class. And, in general, precisely because *eugeneia* was not advanced as a simple justification of superiority but as an index to a higher mode of ethical behavior, it was not as vulnerable to challenge. When Antigone says to Ismene, concerning Creon's order denying burial to their brother, "You will soon show whether you are *eugenēs* or the *kakē* daughter of *esthloi*" (Sophocles, *Antigone* 37-38), she is using noble birth as a criterion of moral courage. Should Ismene prove morally weak, however, she would, in essence, belie her heritage; thus *eugeneia* is not made a *guarantee* of better conduct but a *spur* to better conduct. Such an attitude is really a form of *noblesse oblige,* which could be appealed to by aristocrats with little fear that society at large would oppose or contradict, especially because its basis was the tradition of heroic behavior, long enshrined in the Greek consciousness. As Ajax says, before he commits suicide:

> But either to live nobly or to die nobly *(kalōs)* is the duty of the *eugenēs*.
>
> (*Ajax* 479-80)

A similar attitude is reflected by Philoctetes who, grateful to Neoptolemus for his kindness, praises the youth by telling him that "your nature *(physis)* is *eugenēs* as you are from *eugeneis*" (Sophocles, *Philoctetes* 874), but when he felt betrayed by Neoptolemus he reverses the praise: "Most shameful *(aischistos)* born of an *aristos* father" (1284).

The opposite claim did not find general acceptance. When Agamemnon berates Teucer in Sophocles' *Ajax* (1226 ff.) for attempting to bury the body of Ajax against his orders, he concentrates on Teucer's slave parentage and the temerity of a "nobody" in challenging the will of a king; but Teucer easily counters by citing his own courageous service at the side of Ajax:

Such were the deeds he did, and I at his side, the slave, born of a barbarian mother.

(1288-89)

This was, nevertheless, a touchy issue for the fifth century; and even when, as here, the appeal to real excellence overrides low birth the absolutist claim that true worth was inextricably connected with noble birth still had force and had to be combatted on its own terms. Teucer continues by criticizing Agamemnon's own parentage (in semi-moral terms: Pelop's Phrygian descent, Atreus' monstrous crime, his mother's infidelity), boasting in turn of his descent from Telamon and a royal mother. He can, then, call himself *"aristos* son of two *aristoi"* (1304). Oedipus' response to Jocasta's apparent misgivings about his low birth is similar. He is determined to learn his background "even if it is paltry *(smikros)*" and even though Jocasta may "be ashamed *(aischynomai)* at my base birth *(dysgeneia)*." As "fortune's child" he is secure:

So sprung, I would never prove to be other than I am; so shall I learn my birth.

(1076-85)

Of the fifth-century dramatists Euripides was the most concerned with conflicting social attitudes, and he expresses the problems and tensions of class from many vantage points. The aristocratic doctrine that their class was morally superior by virtue of birth is stated explicitly several times in his plays. In the *Iphigeneia at Aulis,* for example, Agamemnon, faced with the terrible prospect of having to sacrifice his daughter to ensure a sailing of the Greeks for Troy, laments:

Low birth *(dysgeneia)* has such advantages—for it is easy for them to weep and to speak out everything. And one who is *gennaios* by birth has the same suffering, but dignity rules over our lives, and we are slaves to the mob *(ochlos)*.[32]

(446-50)

This is a clear statement that dignity and restraint are natural (and exclusive) attributes of the aristocratic class.

It must be noted that these passages on *eugeneia* are concerned with ethical/moral superiority; the traditional "success" standard is not in question, since by this time no one, aristocrats included, could reasonably assert that birth (or upbringing) were guarantees of success in war, business or politics; and in democratic Athens it was politically dangerous to claim *tout court* that birth or background made one fitter to direct the destiny of the state in peace or war. These passages also point up one of the thorniest social issues of the age: To what extent was the possession of the "quiet" virtues attributable to birth and upbringing alone or to qualities of character quite independent of these? The discussion thus far indicates that the aristocracy had the natural edge in the argument; those who disagreed could only claim possession. Thus the slave messenger in Euripides' *Helen* says:

For he is *kakos* who does not reverence his master's fortunes, and rejoice with him and sorrow with him in his evils. Indeed, may I, even if I was born a slave, be numbered among the noble slaves *(gennaioi douloi)*, not having the name of free, but the mind. For this is better than being one person to bear two evils — to have a *kakē* mind, and, as a slave, to do the bidding of others.[33]

(726-33)

The "noble slave" type of argument may have been an attempt to bypass the difficulties of debate on the social level and to put the question of personal excellence on a more general plane. In the *Hecuba* of Euripides the queen has just been informed of the sacrificial slaying of her daughter Polyxena by Achilles' son, Neoptolemus. Hecuba's philosophical musings deal with the relationship between natural goodness, lineage and upbringing, but in purely moral terms, skirting explicit mention of any underlying issue of social class. Hecuba says that it is strange that bad *(kakē)* soil can bear good crops and good *(chrēstē)* soil bad crops, depending on circumstances, but always among men the *ponēros* is nothing but *kakos,* and the *esthlos* is *esthlos,* nor is his nature *(physis)* destroyed by misfortune, but he is always worthy *(chrēstos).* Then is it his parentage *(hoi tekontes)* or his upbringing *(trophai)* that makes the difference? In truth, being brought up nobly *(kalōs)* gives the lesson of what is *esthlon;* and if someone has learned this well, he knows what is *aischron,* too, because he has learned according to the standard of the *kalon.*

(592-602)

This is an equally clear statement that blood does not determine good or bad behavior, but that education and training do. Neoptolemus has acted basely, Polyxena has died nobly (546-82). Neither *eugeneia* nor *dysgeneia* are at question since the bloodlines of both characters are excellent, and this gives the playwright an opportunity to set forth egalitarian social philosophy in a non-polemical context. We note, too, that the terms of merit and demerit, all of which were social catchwords in the mouths of aristocrats, have been generalized into a transcendent moral vocabulary, applicable without reference to social standing.

It is in the *Electra* of Euripides (413 B.C.) that we see the clearest exposition of the social problem. Clytaimnestra had forced her daughter Electra to marry a Mycenaean peasant, to insure that there would be no high-born heir to pose a danger to Clytaemnestra and her paramour Aegisthus. But the peasant, out of deep respect for his princess, had not consummated the marriage. The dramatic crux of the relationship between the peasant and Electra rests on the disparity of their stations and the *natural* high-souled quality of the peasant. The peasant establishes his condition in the prologue:

... sprung from Mycenaean ancestors — in this I am not ashamed. For illustrious we are in birth *(genos)* but poor in goods, whereby *eugeneia* is destroyed.

(*Electra* 35-38)

Such a description would fit (as it doubtless was intended to) the majority of the Athenian spectators, freeborn but with little wealth. The problem of the peasant husband's justification of his worth despite lack of high station would have been of great interest to the audience. The justification is given, appropriately enough, by Orestes, Electra's brother, who has just learned of the peasant's reverent and chaste care of his sister. He is ushered into the humble cottage by the peasant, who says proudly:

For even if I was born poor, in no way will I show a nature low-born *(ēthos dysgenes)*.

(Electra 362-63)

Orestes' statement is worthy of being quoted at some length. He begins:

> There is no sure gauge for manliness *(euandria)*; for the natures *(physeis)* of mortals have much confusion. I have seen the son of a *gennaios* father turn out to be nothing, and *chrēsta* children come from *kakoi;* starvation in the soul of a rich man, and great wisdom *(gnōmē)* in a poor body.
>
> *(Electra* 367-72)

Here Orestes contradicts the aristocratic assertion that while an evil man may come of noble parents, no good man can come of *kakoi* parents. Earlier in the play, in a dialogue between Electra and Orestes, Electra terms her peasant husband "born *sōphrōn*" (self-controlled, prudent) because he has not slept with her. Orestes replies:

> A noble man *(gennaios anēr)* you have named him; he should be rewarded.
>
> (261-62)

By having the highborn pair confer on the peasant the important qualities of *sōphrosynē* and *gnōmē* (long claimed as exclusively aristocratic traits), Euripides makes a direct attack on the aristocratic position. An even more explicit statement (clearly traceable to the "anthropological" arguments of the liberal sophists) that noble birth was an accident, and therefore no warrant for claiming exclusive excellence, is found in Euripides' *Alexandros:*

> It is an excessive statement if we praise *eugeneia* in mortals. For long ago, when first we came to be, and earth, our mother, brought mortals forth, the land impressed a like appearance on us all. We have no peculiar trait *(idion);* high birth *(to eugenes)* and low birth *(to dysgenes)* are a single stock *(gona);* but time, through custom *(nomos),* has made it a thing of pride.
>
> (Fr. 52.1-8 Nauck)

The preceding discussion has traced the general outlines of the ideological controversy of the second half of the fifth century. Aristocrats could not press too hard the proposition that noble birth *(eugeneia)* made them naturally fit to assume political leadership; direct appeals to *eugeneia* as authorization for political hegemony are infrequent because of the sensitivity of public opinion to bald assertions of this type. More persuasive (and therefore more frequent) is the claim to social priority based on the beneficial deeds of noble forebears. The most complex area of disputation was the extent to which birth and ancestry could be said to determine individual traits of character. The aristocratic presumption that good character was somehow the result of noble birth had a broader latitude of acceptance – such was the force of tradition, coupled to the "by nature" argument, which could be used to support aristocratic superiority as well as democratic equality. Nevertheless, aristocratic insistence that noble birth was an indispensable factor of ethical/moral worth (or its corollary, that low birth automatically precluded internal excellence) was not allowed to go unchallenged. Although it was an essential ingredient in the aristocratic self-conception, ancestry could not stand alone as the determinant of class superiority, whether in questions of political leadership or of social preeminence. Other qualities had to be joined with *eugeneia* in order to make a commanding case. The true role of *eugeneia* in aristocratic propaganda of the fifth century was the subtly stated assumption that nobility of birth was somehow the *basis* of the aristocracy's mental and moral superiority over the other groups in the democracy. *Eugeneia,* then, was fundamental and indispensable because it could appear as the wellspring of those qualities of mind and spirit that made a nobleman a superior person. Intellectual and moral proclivities are traced back to character, which, in the final analysis, is determined genetically.

◊

Keeping in mind this extremely sophisticated, almost subliminal, justification, we can now turn to the more obvious aspects of the upper-class cultural pattern which functioned to demonstrate the depth of the gulf that separated aristocrats from the other orders of Greek society. The pattern may be described as a mosaic of interconnected elements – wealth, moral/intellectual superiority, style of life, education and upbringing – the central and seminal feature of the pattern being noble birth, *eugeneia.*

In the *Electra* of Euripides it was seen that the question of wealth was intimately bound up with nobility of birth. Possession or lack of wealth was a major index of individual worth during the fifth century and was very important in the aristocratic self-image. The reasons for this are obvious; first of all, historically the upper class was composed of families rich in land, and the traditional identification of an aristocracy of birth with the large property holders held true throughout the classical period. There were impoverished nobles and wealthy non-nobles, but for the most part the old landed aristocracy, even after trade and commerce became important sources of income, remained the rich.[34] This fact took on far greater significance in democratic states where large numbers of men of little means had begun to enjoy unprecedented political power, with the result that the needs and demands of the poor were much more apparent. Additionally, for the ancient Greeks (as for many people today) the problems of wealth and poverty were regarded as moral issues as much as purely economic ones. The rich took the position that poverty was a disgraceful condition which diminished the worth of a man and even led to anti-social behavior, whereas the poor maintained that poverty strengthened the will and was an effective inducement to good.[35] In general, however, those who had money held the moral advantage. Even in Pericles' praise of the democracy the bias against poverty is evident. No one should feel shame *(aischron)* in admitting poverty, he says; the more shameful thing *(aischion)* is not to do something to escape it (Thuc. 2.40.1).

These attitudes help to explain why, in an openly partisan attack on the democracy (the so-called *Constitution of the Athenians,* attributed in antiquity to Xenophon), the author could indiscriminately link terms connoting birth, economic status, intellectual ability and moral capacity, everywhere equating the upper class with the rich and useful elements and the lower class with the poor and depraved.[36] In the aristocratic assumption of superiority the intimate connection between wealth and worth was almost axiomatic. Thus, in the *Ion* of Euripides, king Xuthus assures the young prince Ion that his fortune is secure:

> You will not be called either of the twin diseases, ill-born *(dysgenēs)* and poor *(penēs)* together, but *eugenēs* and a man of great wealth.
> (579-81)

Birth, wealth and competency to lead are all connected in a fragment from Eupolis' *Demoi* (412 B.C.?). The chorus of old citizens, complaining of the bad leadership of contemporary Athens, say that in the old days

> We had our generals *(stratēgoi)* from the greatest houses, first *(prōtoi)* in wealth and birth *(ploutos, genos)* to whom we prayed as if to gods — and indeed they were!
> (Fr. 103.4-6)

The Aristocratic Ideal in Classical Greece 141

In an anti-democratic polemic delivered by the Theban herald in Euripides' *Suppliants,* the argument is that ordinary people lack the mental and moral capacity to rule themselves. Democracy is rule by the mob *(ochlos),* which is easily twisted by unscrupulous demagogues; the *dēmos* cannot reason clearly and, therefore, cannot run the polis. Moreover,

> A peasant *(gaponos),* a poor man *(penēs),* even if he were not ignorant, would not be able, because of his toil, to oversee the common interest.
>
> (420-22)

The "Old Oligarch" (as the author of pseudo-Xenophon *Constitution of the Athenians* is called) directly blames the poverty of the *dēmos* for their inclination to commit shameful acts *(aischra),* adding parenthetically that lack of money is also a reason for their ignorance (1.5). Such was the importance of wealth as an index of personal value that at times it is made to supersede even the powerful commendation of birth, as is apparent from this exchange between Jocasta and Polyneices in Euripides' *Phoenissae:*

> Jo. Did not your *eugeneia* lift you to a high station?
> Poi. To have nothing is an evil; my *genos* did not feed me.
>
> (404-405)

In the same play Polyneices makes a statement with which the majority of the audience would doubtless have agreed:

> An ancient saying, but nevertheless I will speak it — wealth is the thing most honored by men, and of things on earth has the most power. And in quest of it I come with a countless host of spearmen; for a *eugenēs* man who is *penēs* is nothing.[37]
>
> (438-42)

The question of wealth was also central to theoretical discussions of forms of government. In his defense of democracy in the *Suppliants* of Euripides Theseus speaks only of rich and poor (406-408, 433-37). The famous passage in the *Suppliants* on the classes which make up the polis is most instructive in this regard. Theseus divides the state into three groups: the rich *(hoi olbioi),* who are "useless," and "ever greedy for more"; the poor *(hoi ouk echontes),* full of envy and easily controlled by base leaders *(ponēroi prostatai);* and those "in the middle" who save *poleis* and keep the order ordained by the polis (238-45). The class division is purely economic, but at the same time wealth or its lack is made a function of ethical behavior. Thucydides puts a defense of democracy in the mouth of a Sicilian demagogue *(dēmou prostatēs)*, Athenagoras (6.39), which also demonstrates how important economic status was in the Greek conception of political competency. Athenagoras begins by repeating the oligarchic credo:

> There are people who will say that *dēmokratia* is neither an intelligent nor a fair system, and that those who have the money *(hoi echontes ta chrēmata)* are also the best fitted to rule *(archein arista beltious)*....
>
> (Adapted from the Warner translation)

It is important to note the weakness of the Sicilian's rebuttal of this doctrine. The *dēmos*, he says, is the name for the *whole* people, *oligarchia* is only a portion; the rich *(hoi plousioi)* are the best guardians of wealth, the wise *(hoi xynetoi)* are best at counsel, and the many *(hoi polloi)* are the best at listening and judging. He concludes by saying that in a *dēmokratia* all the groups share equally while in an *oligarchia* the many *(hoi polloi)* are given a share of the dangers but get little or none of the benefits. Athenagoras has simply skirted the issue without really addressing himself to the aristocratic claim of superiority based on wealth.[38]

The passages we have examined show quite plainly that in the debate over economic status as a determinant of civic worth the wealthy had a definite edge. The practical Greeks never seriously questioned the advantages of wealth over poverty for individual well-being, but, more importantly, both sides were in increasing agreement that wealth was the real basis of grouping within the political structure of the state. Our fifth and fourth century sources are, in fact, virtually unanimous on two points: first, that "class struggle" was perceived in economic terms, i.e. as the contest between the propertied classes and the poor; and second, that forms of government themselves, quite aside from any ideological trappings they may have acquired, were based on wealth and its lack. Oligarchy was rule by the few wealthy, democracy by the many poor.[39] For propaganda purposes, the realization that wealth was the criterion for rule gave a clear advantage to the elitist position: oligarchs could proclaim that poverty made men inferior or valueless to the polis, at the same time listing the benefits that the rich conferred on the polis through liturgies and taxes.[40] The only effective line of argument for the poor was to accuse the wealthy of arrogance and greed, and assert that poverty actually strengthened a person's character.

◊

We have examined in some detail the importance of wealth in the aristocratic scheme of values; we have also seen that those who were distinguished by noble ancestry were permitted to claim that their lineage was, somehow, an effective inducement to a high standard of ethical behavior. When we probed more deeply into this attitude we found that aristocratic propaganda of the fifth century often went much further, maintaining not simply that noble birth required one to act in a certain way or that it created a predisposition to admirable and praiseworthy characteristics, but that moral and intellectual excellence were inborn qualities possessed only by the nobility. Naturally, if aristocrats could persuade the general populace that this was indeed true, then they possessed a valuable means of retaining the social and political deference of the lower class, even in democratic states. It is easy to understand, therefore, the intensity of the debate among thinking men of the time.

Intelligence, moral rectitude and aesthetic sensibility had become integral to the aristocratic self-conception by the end of the sixth century. During the fifth century those ideas received more systematic articulation, and an even greater intensification of the premium placed on the "quieter" aspects of human nature can be observed (a process which accelerated and reinforced the already apparent inward-turning tendencies of the upper class). By the latter part of the century the claims of mental and moral superiority were central elements in the nobility's defense of its primacy, and aristocratic self-justification increasingly and explicitly asserted that those who were not members of their class were incapable of high ethical behavior or refinement of thought and feeling.

These pretensions were closely linked to the other aristocratic claims of superiority based on noble birth, wealth, education and style of life. The obscure and fragmentary sayings of the Ionian philosopher Heraclitus (*fl. ca.* 500 B.C.) provide an early illustration of these ideas:

> For *hoi aristoi* choose one thing in place of all else, everlasting glory among mortals; but *hoi polloi* are glutted like cattle.
> (B 2)

> Although the logos is common, *hoi polloi* live as though they had private understanding.
>
> (B 29)
>
> One man is worth a thousand if he is *aristos*.
>
> (B 49)
>
> For what mind or understanding do they have? They believe the poets of the *dēmoi* and use as their teacher the crowd *(homilos)* not knowing that *hoi polloi* are *kakoi*, and the *agathoi* are *oligoi*.
>
> (B 104)

By the last quarter of the century we see the network of attitudes more fully worked out in the Theban herald's speech against democracy in the *Suppliants* of Euripides in which are expressed ideas that recur again and again in anti-democratic arguments: Thebes is ruled by one man, not by the fickle mob *(ochlos)*, seduced by a self-serving, glib demagogue; the *dēmos* cannot reason straight (410-18).

> It is a pestilence *(nosōdes)* to the better sort *(ameinones)* when a base man *(ponēros)* gets honor, charming the *dēmos* with his tongue, having been a nobody before.
>
> (423-25)

In the famous political debate of the Persian princes in the *Histories* of Herodotus the arguments are also moral/intellectual. Speaking in favor of oligarchy and against democracy Megabyzus calls the populace "useless," "witless," "violent," "undisciplined," "without knowledge."

> For how could it know anything when it is untaught, and perceives neither what is *kalon* nor what is fitting; and rushes headlong into affairs without thought, like a river in winter time?
>
> (Herodotus 3.81)

The oligarchs are called by Megabyzus simply *andres aristoi*, as if there could be no argument about their mental and moral superiority.[41]

The Old Oligarch also makes the moral and mental pre-eminence of the upper class the basis of his attack on the democracy. As in the passages previously cited noble birth is not directly named as a proof of aristocratic superiority. The only birth word that appears in the Old Oligarch's political broadside is *gennaios*, found but three times and given no special prominence. The author's principal argument is that the Athenian upper class enjoyed, innately and by virtue of its life-style, higher ethical and intellectual standards than the mass of citizens:

The Aristocratic Ideal in Classical Greece 145

> Throughout the world the best element *(to beltiston)* is opposed to democracy. For among the best people *(hoi beltistoi)* there is the least amount of licentiousness *(akolasia)* and injustice *(adikia)*, but a very keen sense of probity *(ta chrēsta)*; among the *dēmos* there is a great deal of ignorance *(amathia)*, disorder *(ataxia)* and depravity *(ponēria)*, for poverty makes them more prone to disgraceful acts *(aischra)* — their lack of education *(apaideusia)*, too, and ignorance *(amathia)*, which in some men is due to lack of money.
> (Pseudo Xen. *Ath. Pol.* 1.5)

Later in the same chapter it is explained why the *dēmos* likes a knavish *(ponēros)* leader: it is because his *amathia* and *ponēria* are more profitable to them than the *aretē* and *sophia* of a worthy *(chrēstos)* man (1.7). For the Old Oligarch ignorance and moral turpitude are emblematic of the lower class, wisdom and "virtue" the hallmark of the aristocrat. It is further stated that good government *(eunomia)* is dangerous to the *dēmos* because in such a constitution laws are made by the most clever *(dexiōtatoi)*, the *chrēstoi* punish the *ponēroi*, the *chrēstoi* do the deliberating and do not allow the "madmen" to take part in Council or even to speak in assembly (1.9). The obvious implication is that the upper class possesses a moral and intellectual integrity which the lower class does not, and which it fears. An even more explicit statement of this notion occurs in 2.19 where it is said that the *dēmos* knows which of the citizens are *chrēstoi* and which are *ponēroi*, and that they prefer the *ponēroi* if such are useful to them, and hate the *chrēstoi*:

> For they do not think that the *aretē* of these [*chrēstoi*] was inborn *(pephykenai)* in them for their own [the *dēmos'*] benefit but for their harm.

Here the idea that *aretē* is an inborn quality of the aristocracy is stated as a simple article of faith. Its complement, that the *dēmos* finds this innate *aretē* inimical, means that *aretē* is by nature lacking in the lower class. Assertions of this kind permit the statement (logically absurd, but perfectly consistent with aristocratic doctrine) which follows, to the effect that whoever is not (by birth) a member of the *dēmos* and yet prefers to dwell in "a polis which is democratically rather than oligarchically ruled has prepared himself to be unjust *(adikein)*, and knows that it is easier for a *kakos* to hide in a democratically ruled polis rather than in one that is oligarchical" (2.20)

The comedies of Aristophanes abound in examples of the aristocratic assumption of mental and moral superiority. In a passage from the *Knights,* previously cited, the Sausage Seller confesses that, in addition to his low birth, he is also ignorant:

> But I don't know literature *(mousikē),* except for my letters, and these few and badly.

Demosthenes retorts that it is a pity he knows even this much,

> For *dēmagōgia* is not for the literary man, nor for one who is *chrēstos* in his habits, but for the ignorant *(amathēs)* and the disgusting *(bdelyros).*
>
> (188-93)

How important these criteria were is seen in the constant employment by aristocrats of epithets connoting mental and moral capacity. The upper class man is invariably *chrēstos, sōphrōn, dikaios;* others are *ponēroi, amatheis,* and so on. The nobility of birth and wealth simply assumed for its own the entire realm of positive traits of mind and spirit. This process, already advanced during the archaic period, became more widespread during the classical period, and, in addition, was extended more fully to cover all aspects of the "interior" life, private as well as public. The all-embracing quality of the aristocratic point of view is exceptionally well illustrated by a chorus in the *Frogs* of Aristophanes. There they complain that the city behaves towards the *kaloi te kagathoi* of its citizens as it does towards its ancient coinage of silver. Those perfect, most beautiful, unadulterated coins, they sing, the Athenians do not use; instead they prefer the *ponēroi* bronzes, newly minted and of *kakistos* stamping. Just so, the city prefers as its leaders those who are "bronze and strangers and outlanders, and *ponēroi* sons of *ponēroi*" (730-31), and treats with contempt those

> whom we know are *eugeneis* and *sōphrones* men, and *dikaioi* and *kaloi te kagathoi,* who were nurtured in *palaistrai* and *choroi* and *mousikē.*
>
> (727-29)

At the end, the "foolish" *(anoētoi)* citizens are urged to change their ways and to use again the *chrēstoi* (734-35). In this familiar litany of fifth-century aristocratic terminology, birth, intellectual and moral qualities, and style of life are all combined to present a composite image of aristocrats and their non-noble opponents.

The Aristocratic Ideal in Classical Greece 147

Aristocratic contentions of this sort had great force and power, and democratic apologists found themselves hard-pressed to combat them. The only line of counterclaim available to the non-nobles was, in fact, simply to declare that they themselves possessed the same virtues and qualities; but almost always their arguments are accompanied by statements to the effect that despite their poverty and lack of high birth they were nevertheless good citizens and good men. So, a character in the *Diktys* of Euripides says:

> I can say little good about *eugeneia*. In my eyes the good man *(esthlos)* is *eugenēs*, and the unjust man *(ou dikaios)*, is base-born *(dysgenēs)*, even though his father be greater than Zeus.
> (Fr. 336 Nauck)

Peleus, in Euripides' *Andromache,* asserts that

> it is better for mortals to have a poor and useful man *(penēs chrēstos)* than a bad and rich man *(kakos kai plousios)* for marriage-kin or friend.
> (639-41)[42]

Otherwise, non-aristocrats had to be content with the standard complaints about the greed and arrogance of the rich and powerful. A good example of the difficulties of this counter-argument is provided by the *Ploutos,* the last of Aristophanes' comedies, produced in 388 B.C. A constant, underlying current of the play is the non-noble dilemma of having to demonstrate that the poorer class in Athens was neither morally inferior nor socially useless. The theme of the *Ploutos,* that wealth is blind and therefore honors the wrong people, is an old one in Greek thought. It had a special timeliness in the late fifth and early fourth centuries when the gulf between rich and poor was widening and when money as an index of civic usefulness had become a central issue. Those who had no wealth were constrained to defend their worth by appealing to their own transcendent qualities of goodness. Thus the old Athenian, Chremylus, laments:

> Even though I am a pious *(theosebēs)* and *dikaios* man, I have been unlucky and poor *(penēs)* . . . while others, temple breakers, politicians, informers and knaves *(ponēroi)* grew rich.
> (*Ploutos* 28-31)

Chremylus' plan to restore Ploutos' sight has as its purpose to make "only the *chrēstoi*, and the bright *(dexioi)* and the *sōphrones* rich" (386-88). Throughout the play it is the poor who are characterized as *dikaioi, chrēstoi, agathoi*, while the rich are called *ponēroi, atheoi*.[43] Even more striking, at one point the goddess Penia (Poverty) argues that her people are really better *(beltiones)* than Wealth's (557ff.): they are better in *gnōmē* and in appearance, have *sōphrosynē*, are orderly, while Wealth's are fat and hybristic.[44]

Two special points of interest emerge from Aristophanes' treatment of social problems in the *Ploutos*. First, those who are not members of the wealthy upper class, unable to resign themselves to a position of social inferiority, could only assert that they themselves possessed the qualities proclaimed by aristocrats as exclusively their own; second, the aristocracy of birth is not attacked directly, but unscrupulous politicians, informers, and the like. Quite clearly, even if the animus of the non-nobles was directed against the nobility for its wealth and its pretensions to a higher mode of intellectual and ethical behavior we have little evidence that anti-aristocratic sentiments were extensively exploited or that leaders of the *dēmos* were willing (or able) to initiate serious class conflict. Thucydides puts a speech in the mouth of Cleon, Pericles' successor as the leading man in Athens, which illustrates, I think, the limit to which a popular leader in the fifth century could go in publicly asserting the superiority of lower-class values. The scene is the dramatic debate in the Athenian assembly over the punishment of a recalcitrant "ally," Mytilene. He says that

> ignorance *(amathia)* combined with *sōphrosynē* is more helpful than this kind of cleverness that gets out of hand *(dexiotēs meta akolasias)*, and that as a general rule *poleis* are better governed by the man in the street *(hoi phauloteroi)* than by intellectuals *(hoi xynetōteroi)*. These are the sort of people who want to appear wiser *(sophōteroi)* than the laws . . . and who, as a result, very often bring ruin on their *poleis*. But the other kind – the people who are not so confident in their intelligence *(xynesis)* – are prepared to admit that they are less wise *(amathesteroi)* than the laws, and that they lack the ability to pull to pieces a speech made by a good speaker; they are unbiased judges, and not people taking part in some kind of competition *(agōnistai)*; so things usually go well when they are in control.
>
> (Thuc. 3.37.3-5 adapted from the Warner trans.)

The Aristocratic Ideal in Classical Greece 149

We may be sure that Thucydides, who disliked Cleon intensely, intended this attack against the ruling intellectual élite to be taken as an example of the demagogue at his most demagogic (Cleon was the "most violent of the citizens," 3.36.6), but as a polemic against the upper class or as an attempt to demonstrate the superiority of the common citizen it is certainly mild. The *dēmos' amathia* is combined with *sōphrosynē*, the intellectuals' cleverness is coupled with "intemperateness," *akolasia,* the opposite of *sōphrosynē*. In praising ignorance Cleon has simply made a "virtue" out of the defect for which the *dēmos* is most commonly attacked. His essential message is that the *dēmos* is *sōphrōn*, moderate and law-abiding, the nobles are arrogant, self-serving and ruinously competitive; the *dēmos,* in other words, is the true possessor of the qualities claimed by the upper class.[45]

Even the old jurymen, die-hard democrats all, in Aristophanes' *Wasps,* are not virulent in their resentment of the rich and powerful. Their dislike is expressed in terms of apprehensions that individual members of the upper class may be aiming at a tyranny, alliance with Sparta, destruction of the democracy, exploitation of wealth for private ends, but with complete confidence that the ruling majority is in control of the situation. There is a fierce determination to preserve the rule of the *dēmos* with all its advantages to the non-rich and non-powerful of the citizens, but there are few indications of an attempt to establish a "proletarian" ethic.

It seems, in fact, that it was almost impossible for the non-nobles in Greek society to list ethically positive qualities of mind and spirit that were exclusively their own, because for so long the aristocracy, with its greater ability for self-expression, had simply claimed them as the property of their class. This attitude was both a conviction deeply held, hence implicit in all aristocratic writers, and self-consciously propagandistic, intended to persuade the *dēmos* that those born noble possessed superior mental and moral capabilities. The cumulative psychological effect of the "automatic reflex" and vigorous public propaganda must have been numbing.[46] As a consequence, any lower-class challenge to aristocratic assumptions of ethical/intellectual superiority in the fifth century was essentially negative and passive: either to insist that they too were wise, just, moderate, pious, and so on, or to assign to the upper class (or segments thereof) the same bad qualities they were accused of. The only "positive" claims to excellence in this sphere are statements like those in the *Ploutos,* that Penia strengthens character or, like Cleon in Thucydides, that *amathia* is more beneficial to the common good than *xynesis*.[47]

The most carefully worked out justification during the fifth century of the lower class' equality in goodness of mind and character is found in the *Electra* of Euripides. There Orestes, in his praise of the peasant husband of Electra, asks by what test the worth of a man *(euandria)* is determined. He considers the various criteria of birth, wealth (and poverty), and the ability to bear arms. These, he concludes, are improper and indeterminate. He continues:

> For this man is not great *(megas)* among the Argives, nor puffed up by the reputation of a noble house, but, although he is numbered among *hoi polloi,* he has been found to be *aristos.*
>
> (*Electra* 373-82)

Although the peasant fails the conventional test of the aristocratic conception he is still somehow *aristos.* The true measure of worth is given in the lines immediately following:

> Will you not cease to be foolish *(aphroneō)*, you who wander about full of empty notions — judge mortals by their intercourse *(homilia)*, and by their characters *(ēthē)* judge men *eugeneis.* For such men administer well their *poleis* and their homes; but hulks of flesh, devoid of mind are statues in the market place. Neither does the strong arm endure the spear better than the weak — this lies in one's nature *(physis)* and in his courageous spirit *(eupsychia)*.
>
> (383-90)

The passage is instructive for several reasons. First, it shows how potent still were the external valuations — birth, wealth, prowess, success — throughout the whole of the fifth century. Second, Euripides does not say that the traditional standards have no validity at all, simply that they are inadequate to explain the fact that the peasant, despite his lack of the obvious qualifications, was a truly worthy man. Third, what is put in place of the visible criteria is a series of very vague standards of measurement: *homilia* and *ēthos*, which seem here to mean correct ethical conduct in daily life and soundness of character; *physis*, which is one's inborn nature; *eupsychia,* which is the spirit of courage. Not only is the measuring device internal rather than external, but also the very qualities that prove Electra's husband to be truly "noble" (i.e. that he is *gennaios, sōphrōn, aristos* and has *euandria*) are internal and spiritual: in this particular case his self-restraint and reverence for Electra.

Arnheim's comments on *Electra* 367-85 bear some consideration here.[48] The passage is an expression of the "increasing doubts about the primacy of birth as the determining factor in human merit"; Orestes' tribute "is an eloquent assault on aristocratic notions ... All the traditional criteria of human worth are here unceremoniously rejected ..." Nevertheless, "what Euripides is *not* saying is that all men are equally good. The problem for him is one of criteria and measurement, and although he suggests some criteria in the last lines quoted, he clearly regards the problem as insoluble ..." Therefore, according to Arnheim, the passage gives "an exaggeratedly radical impression of Euripides' social values." Euripides hedges somewhat here, because to claim that one who is poor and of ignoble birth is at the same time *gennaios* and *aristos* is impossible. That is why the poor peasant is given a noble pedigree and is not permitted to consummate the marriage.

> Not even Euripides can bring himself to allow a peasant to be his heroine's real husband. Euripides' ambivalent attitude is a good reflection of the dilemma confronting his age. The traditional aristocratic canons were now unacceptable, but what was there to replace them?

Arnheim is partly correct in his assessment. There is no question that Euripides and other champions of democratic equality were convinced that social and ethical goodness was possible for those who lacked noble birth. They expressed the conviction frequently, as we have seen. The problem was, as Arnheim says, one of criteria — non-aristocratic justification of social equality always came up against some version of the deeply ingrained equation of goodness with birth and wealth. The intellectual difficulty was to demonstrate that noble lineage and all that went with it were merely accidents, not fundamental determinants, a point not easy to make in a hierarchically conceived society.

Euripides presents us with another exemplar of the "naturally" good man in the *Orestes*. The scene is the Argive assembly, debating the murder by Orestes of his mother:

> Another man, standing up, spoke in opposition to this man; in outward form not handsome to look on, but a manly man *(andreios anēr)*, seldom found in town or the circle of the market place, a peasant *(autourgos)*, the sort who alone save the land, yet wise *(xynetos)* when he wanted to grapple with words, uncorrupted, a man trained in the blameless life.

The peasant speaks for the acquittal of Orestes, on the grounds that he had acted correctly according to the traditional social and religious norms,

> and to the *chrēstoi* he seemed to speak well, and no one spoke after him.
>
> (*Orestes* 917-31)

The peasant lacks the obvious qualifications by which the contemporary upper class defined a man as good — birth, good looks, social polish, wealth, education. He is, nevertheless "manly," has an untutored wisdom, is blameless in character and conduct.[49]

These examples show that the ultimate basis for non-noble justification of individual goodness had to be an appeal to *behavior,* with no reference to external or accidental factors. The *source* of this behavior was necessarily unidentifiable; the non-noble could only insist that somehow or other he possessed the qualities of mind and spirit admired by the society, either despite or because of the lack of the criteria flaunted by the upper class. The principle was stated by a messenger in the fragmentary *Melanippe* of Euripides:

> I do not know how one should inquire *(skopein)* into *eugeneia*. For I say that those who are *andreioi* and *dikaioi* by *physis* are more noble *(eugenesteroi),* even if they are slaves, than those who are empty show.
>
> (Fr. 495.40-43 Nauck)

The same idea is voiced by Electra, speaking over the corpse of Aegisthus:

> This wealth is nothing, a companion for a brief time only, for it is *physis* which is constant, not possessions *(ta chrēmata).*
>
> (*Electra* 940-41)

It is true, as North says, that "With regard to the origin of virtue, including sophrosyne, Euripides is firmly of the opinion that *physis* plays the chief role";[50] in fact, there was no other source from which to draw if one wished to make a case for lower-class excellence. Otherwise the paradoxical assertion must do, as did the messenger in the *Orestes,* who calls himself (870)

> a *penēs* man, but *gennaios* in the way I treat my friends.

But the posture, inevitably, was a defensive one. Peleus, in the *Andromache* of Euripides, defends the native intelligence of the common man against the pretensions of the mighty, who

> sitting haughty *(semnoi)* in authority, being nothing, despise the *dēmos* in the polis, who are wiser *(sophōteroi)* a thousandfold than they . . .
>
> (669-701)

Even a simple emotion like parental love must be given explicit utterance, as Heracles does:

> In all respects are men alike. They love their children, both the better sort *(ameinones)* and those who are nothing. They differ in wealth — these have it, those do not — but every sort loves its children.
>
> (*Hercules Furens* 633-36)

◊

Aristocratic self-justification had turned increasingly inward since the late archaic period, but the internal excellences claimed by aristocrats rested, in the final analysis, on external conditions. An aristocrat proclaimed himself better on the grounds that his character or "nature" were better; but a superior nature was eventually (and inevitably) traced back to tangibles: noble birth, wealth, education, a particular life-style. As we saw from the passages above, the non-aristocratic claim was that much vaguer, hence, less compelling. From earliest times the Greek mind had been conditioned to adjudge merit according to the yardstick of success, achievement, appearance; and even though a long tradition of thought existed (and found eloquent expression in the fifth century) which challenged the standard of external social measurement, it was still powerful enough at the end of the fifth century to make an appeal to worth founded simply on intent or *physis* or proper behavior not universally persuasive.[51]

In short, appeals to birth, wealth and "inherited" excellence of mind and character gave aristocrats a decided advantage in their attempts to show that they were better suited to rule and to maintain themselves as leaders of the society. This need for visible demonstration of superiority accounts, I believe, for the very great emphasis placed on a style of life that appeared unmistakably the property of the noble class.

Ω

CHAPTER FIVE
Aristocratic Life-Style in the Fifth Century

LIFE-STYLE may be characterized as the visible manifestation of the cultural "personality" of an individual or group within a society. It reveals, often in small and trivial ways, the basic psychological needs of its practitioners, and is, therefore, an excellent sociometric indicator. We saw how, in response to the pressures generated by rapid and radical social change, the Greek nobility of the archaic period evolved a style of life which was distinctively "aristocratic." We might expect that in the classical period, at least in those states whose constitutions were democratic and whose sociopolitical norms were professedly egalitarian, an aristocratic life-style would be deemphasized; but quite the reverse seems to have been true. The reasons for this apparent paradox are not difficult to perceive. In societies that emphasize equality it is even more imperative for those who would be prominent to project an image of uniqueness that is unambiguous. Non-aristocrats had increasingly laid claim to or had challenged the exclusively aristocratic patents of excellence, including even the "quiet" virtues; consequently the need for visible proof of superiority was the more compelling. In addition, the traditional success standard still had much force. When a distinctive lifestyle can be tied to other claims of superiority, especially in a culture that was essentially competitive and where the ability to carry anything off with verve and brilliance commanded respect, it can have a powerful psychological effect.

There are dangers, too. Style of life is subject to attack by moralists when it offends the wider cultural norms, and it is susceptible to some degree of imitation. But these problems can be circumvented by careful avoidance of extremes of behavior which provoke popular censure on the one hand, and, on the other hand, by jealously limiting the possibilities of social mimicry. The greatest advantage, in fact, of the upper class life-style lay in its inimitability. Because it depends (by definition) on birth, wealth and an inherited set of attitudes, in short, on existing membership in a class, it is the ultimate and indisputable area of social differentiation. It is for this reason that fifth-century Athens, the most belligerently egalitarian polis in the Greek world, evolved something resembling a cult of aristocratic exclusiveness that permeated every aspect of social behavior. The aristocratic style of life must have had an especially vivid impact in the compact polis, with its small number of inhabitants. Even in populous Attica, which in the mid-fifth century had perhaps 40,000 citizens (native-born, free males over eighteen), the tiny group of men of noble lineage and landed wealth will have stood out sharply against the much larger, essentially undifferentiated mass of non-aristocrats — all the more so because of their efforts to appear as a visibly distinctive minority.

In his essay on the democracy at Athens the Old Oligarch makes frequent reference to the social and political levelling which is the consequence of a democratic constitution. Anyone, he says, can hold office, and anyone who wishes can speak in assembly (1.2). In an even more pointed comment on equality he notes that it would be better if they did not allow every citizen to speak or be a member of the Council *(boulē)* equally *(ex isēs)*, but only the "cleverest" men *(dexiōtatoi)* and the *andres aristoi;* but democracy best suits and strengthens itself when the *ponēroi* are allowed to speak (1.6). As an example of the extreme lack of distinction in Athens (an excellent example, too, of cultural mimicry) the Old Oligarch points out that it is impossible to distinguish free citizens from slaves, resident aliens *(metics)* and freedmen, "for the *dēmos* is no better dressed than the slaves and the metics, and no better in appearance either" (1.10).

As we have already seen, the Old Oligarch (1.5) maintained that it was the *dēmos'* lack of education and their poverty which led them to prefer a levelling of social differentiation. Education or its lack, was, in fact, one of the essential elements adduced to make clear the distinction between aristocrats and non-aristocrats, and the Old Oligarch seizes upon this eagerly:

> The *dēmos* has broken down respect for preoccupation with gymnastics and *mousikē*, thinking this not to be *kalon*, knowing that they are not able to pursue these occupations
>
> (1.13).[1]

Our sources make it abundantly clear that education beyond the elementary stage, predominantly athletic training *(gymnastika)* and instruction in the "arts" *(mousikē)* were, practically speaking, available

Aristocratic Life-Style in the Fifth Century

only to young men who had leisure and money — the upper stratum — and that the possession of this kind of education identified the aristocrat.

> The noble was instructed and trained in the palaestra, in sports, dancing and music; these were the usual forms of education in earlier times. The gymnastic and musical education, with its emphasis on the 'agonal' feelings, was the inevitable accompaniment of nobility.[2]

A statement by the chorus in the *Knights* of Aristophanes shows that the wrestling-ground (or palaestra) was considered to be the special province of the upper class:

> When peace comes and we are freed from toil, do not begrudge us our long hair and our cleaning and scraping with oil.
> (579-80)

In the *Frogs* it is the *eugeneis, sōphrones, dikaioi, kaloi te kagathoi* who are "nurtured in *palaistrai, choroi* and *mousikē*" (727-29). We are immediately reminded of the Sausage Seller, who, having said that he was unworthy of high position because he knew nothing of *mousikē* and could barely write, was answered that *dēmagogia* was not "for a *mousikos* man, nor for one who was *chrēstos* in character, but for an ignorant *(amathēs)* and disgusting *(bdelyros)* man" (*Knights* 188-93).

Gymnastic training had another social effect, important to the aristocratic image. Since earliest times the spirit of competition had been ingrained in the Greek consciousness; and, traditionally, the upper class was the principal guardian of the agonal impulse.[3] Victory in the national and local games brought great glory to the winners, their families and *poleis;* and since ability to compete successfully depended on training (usually very expensive) and leisure, the upper class naturally dominated this important aspect of Greek life. In this way education could be, and was, exploited by the aristocracy to their own social advantage, simply because it was they and not the lower class who exhibited this particular *aretē*. The aura of glory won in the games was often converted into political prominence. A related advantage was that training in *gymnastika* was identified with the Dorian ideal of manliness; thus the noble youth of Athens and of other states acquired some of the exotic glamor attached to the citizens of Sparta, universally respected (if not admired) for their courage and strict discipline. As an added consequence of the prominence of physical training in higher education, the universal Greek ideal of the beautiful male body, finely exercised and cared for, became almost exclusively the property of the upper class, and was equated with moral and civic worth.[4]

"Higher" education, which was a creation of the fifth century, consisted primarily of training in public speaking, with the purpose, both avowed and implicit, of preparing young men to be political leaders. During the latter half of the fifth century the word for "speaker" *(rhētōr)* came to signify "politician." Higher education, which also included deeper study of literature, mathematics and moral philosophy, was provided by the sophists, whose brilliance and novelty made them immensely popular among the wealthy young men of Athens. The sophists, most of whom charged substantial (and sometimes enormous) fees, supplied a demand for more refined techniques of persuasion in an open and increasingly litigious society. Rhetorical education inevitably tended to widen the social gulf; the trained speaker, who of necessity belonged to the wealthy class, had a distinct practical advantage over poorer citizens in gaining public prominence and influence.

Paradoxically, for those few who enjoyed the advantage of wealth but not the old family connections, sophistic training was an entrée into power; for the first time (in Athenian history at least) a number of men who did not belong to the ancient aristocratic lineages rose to prominence in the state. Thus, from the point of view of the traditional aristocracy, sophistic teaching could be considered subversive, since the claim "to teach the art of politics and to undertake to make men good citizens" (Plato, *Protagoras* 319a) was precisely what aristocrats felt themselves exclusively fitted to do by a kind of natural instinct peculiar to their class. Despite the great variety in personality, methodology, and style, which prevents us from calling the sophistic movement a "school," all the fifth-century sophists taught rhetoric, and all shared "one epistemological standpoint . . . namely, a scepticism according to which knowledge could only be relative to the perceived subject."[5] Consequently, sophistic relativism and the *nomos/physis* argument could be employed to champion either the natural superiority of the old élite or the ideals of democratic equality. Now oligarchic and democratic leaders both had the means to express, in logically persuasive terms, competing ideologies.

The net result of the "sophistic mentality," which permeated Athenian intellectual thought in the second half of the fifth century, was a measure of moral confusion. Sophistic influence is evident in such disparate figures as Thucydides the historian, Euripides the dramatist, Critias the extreme oligarch, the medical writers. The *dēmos* itself, by

Aristocratic Life-Style in the Fifth Century

constant exposure in the assembly and law courts, developed a keen critical appreciation of persuasive eloquence, and in our sources is constantly faulted for its tendency to be swayed by clever orators. To some contemporary critics, like Aristophanes, the new intellectualism was a sign of decadence; in the *Clouds* and elsewhere he attacks it as being morally corrupting to both individuals and the state. The main victim, perhaps, was the traditional aristocratic certitude of the superiority of birth and wealth, but the democratic process also was affected. Democracy's vaunted lack of distinction, proclaimed by the catchwords *isēgoria* (the right of equal speech) and *parrhēsia* (freedom of speech), was theoretically true; in practice these rights were effectively exercised by a highly trained élite, whether of conservative oligarchs or of "champions of the people."

In point of fact, most of the recipients of formal higher education were young aristocrats. But the distinctive factor of their educational formation was the patterns of behavior they learned informally at home in association with their elders. This enculturation into the ways of the subgroup was primary — and exclusive. The study of poetry, music, mathematics, athletics, served to reinforce the basic values; training in rhetoric and ethical speculation fostered the persuasive expression of an ingrained system of beliefs. What finally mattered, though, was the elusive quality of "style" — the ultimate differentiation. The poorer classes were completely excluded from participation; wealthy non-nobles might attempt to imitate an aristocratic life-style, but such mimesis is rarely effective.

In Aristophanes' *Wasps,* the old juror Philokleon, prodded by his son Bdelykleon to enter high society, is given lessons to prepare him socially to take part in a symposium. The son asks if the old man knows how to tell "respectable" *(semnoi)* stories if he dines with men who are *polymatheis* and clever *(dexioi);* Philokleon can only come up with coarse or simple barnyard tales. Bdelykleon gives as proper examples stories relating to incidents that occurred on foreign embassies (on which only the eminent were sent), or sporting tales of athletic contests, for "that is the way the *sophoi* are accustomed to converse" (1174-96). When Bdelykleon urges his father to tell the manliest *(andreiotaton)* adventure of his youth the old man can only recall the time he stole someone's vine poles. The son, exasperated, exclaims:

> You'll be the death of me! Vine poles! Tell how you hunted boar or rabbit, or ran the torch race; give us your most youthful prank.
> (1201-04)

The best that Philokleon can do is to reply with a feeble tale about the time he "hunted down" a famous Olympic runner in the law court. The lesson then turns to the proper way to behave at a symposium; the context makes it quite clear that Philokleon had never attended a drinking party. The son tries unsuccessfully to teach the father how to recline "elegantly" *(euschēmonōs)*:

> Stretch out your knees, and, in a gymnastical way, ease yourself languidly on the cushions; then praise the table setting, look up at the ceiling, admire the tapestries.
> (1212-15)

Next follows a lesson in the singing of *scolia* (1219-49). Satisfied now with his father's progress in learning polite behavior, Bdelykleon invites him to a drinking party. The old dicast's response to the invitation typifies both the distance between the upper class, trained to "correct" behavior, and the ordinary citizen, to whom such things were foreign, and the general public's conception of aristocratic society:

> Phil. No! Drinking is bad! Wine leads to breaking down doors, beatings and blows — then a fine to pay and a hangover.
> Bd. No, not if you do it with men who are *kaloi te kagathoi*. For either they will intercede with the injured party and get you off, or you tell an urbane story, a joke from Aesop or from Sybaris that you learned at a symposium. And so, you turn the thing into a joke, and he goes off and leaves you be.
> (1252-61)

The result of the drinking party is predictable — Philokleon gets drunk and insults the other guests,

> making fun of them like a country boor *(agroikōs)* and telling inappropriate stories in a most ignorant way *(amathestata)*.
> (1320-21)[6]

As comical as these scenes are, they incisively indicate the rather deep social gulf that existed in the fifth century, directly traceable to education and to the conscious fostering of a particular manner of life. Philokleon was not from the lowest stratum of the Athenian citizen body; he was of hoplite status, an old-fashioned patriot, respectable and fairly well-off economically.

The literature of the fifth century abounds in references to aristocratic customs and manners which detail, in more specific terms, the importance of life-style to the upper class' "image" of itself as a group that was different and better. Physical appearance was an obvious, but telling, mode of differentiation. The custom of wearing the hair long, a sign of aristocratic vanity since the archaic period, continued to be in the fifth century an outward manifestation of their apartness. This somewhat obsolete fashion, along with careful attention to other aspects of personal grooming, such as frequent bathing, oiling and scraping, are treated in our sources as identifying traits of the nobility. Thus, Strepsiades contrasts the noble youth with the followers of Socrates who "never take care of their hair, nor anoint themselves with oil nor go into the bath to wash" (*Clouds* 836-37). In the *Birds* of Aristophanes a character expresses surprise to a poet (who called himself a "slave" of Homer): "What? You are a slave and you wear your hair long?" (911). The very noun *kometes* (a man with long hair) is often used as a synonym for aristocrat.[7] Frequently there is, in this identification, a sense of class tension. The chorus of young aristocrats in *Knights* 579-80, we recall, ask the audience not to "begrudge" *(phthoneō)* their long hair and oiling and scraping. In one of the speeches of the orator Lysias a youthful aristocrat defends himself:

> And, indeed, it is according to this standard [proper conduct and bravery as a soldier] that one should judge the ambition and propriety of a citizen, and not hate a man because he wears his hair long *(komaō)*; for habits like these do harm neither to private citizens nor to the public good . . . . Thus it is not fair, members of the Boulē, to like or dislike someone because of his external appearance *(opsis)*; judge him by his acts instead. For many men who speak little and who dress soberly have been the cause of much evil; others, who do not care about such things, have done many good deeds for the state.
> (16.18-19)

Sometimes the verb which means "to wear the hair long" *(komaō)* is equivalent to "act grandly." Old Philokleon at the symposium berates one of the guests:

> Tell me, why do you play the nobleman *(komās)* and pretend to be elegant *(kompsos)*?
> (*Wasps* 1316-17)[8]

The verb *komaō* could have, in popular parlance, a sinister, oligarchical intonation. Herodotus, speaking of the conspiracy of the sixth-century aristocrat, Cylon of Athens, says that he "aimed his sights *(ekomēse)* at a tyranny" (5.71). In an argument with Bdelykleon the chorus of jurors in the *Wasps* says:

> So then, isn't it quite clear to the poor that tyranny is secretly creeping over us, if you, you wicked rascal and long-haired Amynias,[9] keep us from the laws which the polis has set up . . . ?
>
> (463-67)

Even minor manifestations of aristocratic vanity bear witness to an intentional fostering of a visible differentiation between the classes. In the *Ecclesiazusae* (631-33) the wearing of seal-rings distinguishes "the more elegant gents" *(hoi semnoteroi)* from the poor citizen in his cheap sandals *(embades)*,[10] and in the *Birds* the aristocratic Poseidon (patron of the *hippeis*) expresses disdain for a barbarian god because he wore his cloak on the left side instead of the right, saying:

> O democracy, to what a pass are you bringing us if the gods elect someone like this?
>
> (1570-71)

In the scene in the *Wasps* between Philokleon and Bdelykleon, preparatory to the lessons in symposium etiquette, much attention is paid to the difference between the old man's peasant clothing and the fashionable attire his son wants him to wear to the party (1131-69). Bdelykleon urges his father to throw away his short inexpensive cloak *(tribōn)* and to don the more costly, longer mantle *(chlaina)*. It is evident that the father has never worn such a garment, for he does not even recognize it for what it is—a woolen, tasseled cloak imported from Persia. The same ignorance (and disdainful reluctance) is shown when Bdelykleon tries to persuade his father to exchange his peasant sandals *(embades)* for expensive red boots *(Lakonikai)*. Thus accoutred the old man is advised to "walk like a rich man *(plousiōs)* with a dainty, pretentious swagger," and Philokleon, having practiced a bit, asks:

> O.K., now look me over and see what rich man my walk most resembles.
>
> (1168-71)

In this exchange, as in the rest of the scene, is manifested not only the obvious, external distance between the classes, consciously engendered by distinctions in clothing and manners, but also the suspicion and distrust with which the ordinary man viewed the pretensions of the upper class.

Another pervasive popular attitude during the fifth century was that aristocratic youths were addicted to luxurious and dissolute living. Even allowing for the fact that an older generation is always inclined to view the high spirits of the young (regardless of their social standing) with a critical eye, and the fact that the poor naturally resent the ability of the rich to pamper themselves, the nature of the evidence shows clearly that this kind of behavior was considered specifically class oriented, and, further, that it was an integral element of a life-style purposely designed to create an impression of class superiority. The following exchange between Aeacus and Dionysus' slave, Xanthion, occurs in the *Frogs:*

Ae. By Zeus the savior, your master is some nobleman *(gennadas anēr).*
Xan. How could he not be a *gennadas* when all he knows is how to drink and screw?

(738-40)

In the *Wasps* it is said that drinking is "the disease of *chrēstoi andres"* (80). The popular image of the aristocrat as one who behaved in a manner divergent from the ordinary and acceptable norms of society is reinforced time and again. Demus in the *Knights* depicts them, censoriously, as beardless young dandies who hang about the perfume market engaging in pseudo-intellectual chatter which they learned in the schools of the sophists (1373-80). In a fragment of the comic poet Hermippus a character says:

But, by Zeus, it isn't right for an *agathos* man to get drunk and take hot baths — the way you do.

(Fr. 76)

A father in the *Banqueters* of Aristophanes says of his son:

But when I sent him to school he didn't learn this; instead they taught him how to drink, sing badly, keep a Syracusan table, Sybaritic feasts, Chian wine from Lakonian cups, get drunk in a pleasant and friendly way.

(Fr. 216)[11]

In addition to distinctive personal appearance and grooming, a proclivity for drinking and licentious behavior, affectations of manner and speech, there were other particular manifestations of aristocratic lifestyle that set them apart from the rest of the citizens. Nobles were addicted to the keeping and racing of horses, an expensive hobby far beyond the reach of the average citizen. Strepsiades, a fairly well-to-do Athenian citizen, is tormented by the expensive habits of his "socialite" son Pheidippides, lamenting that he is being eaten up

> by expenditures, feed bills and debts . . . while he, with his long hair, rides his horse and races a chariot — he even drives in his dreams!
> (*Clouds* 12-16)[16]

Strepsiades' reaction to his son's activities shows that such pursuits were understood to be a deliberate means of expressing differences of class. He styles himself a simple rustic *(agroikos)* who had married above his station. His wife, "a niece of Megacles, son of Megacles," was a "high class" *(semnē)*, "luxurious" *(tryphōsa)* member of the ultra-aristocratic clan of the Alcmeonids, and Strepsiades bitterly contrasts her refined and expensive upper-class habits with his own peasant way of life (41-55). When their son was born she wanted to give him a "horsy" name like Xanthippos, Charippos or Challippides; the father wanted to name him after the grandfather, Pheidonides ("Thriftson"). The wife would say to the young child:

> When you are grown up you'll drive your chariot to the Akropolis, like Megacles, in your fancy robe,

while Strepsiades would say:

> When you are driving the goats from the rocky hills, like your father, in your sheepskin coat.
> (69-72)

Another, and most distinctive, characteristic of the aristocratic lifestyle, was male homosexuality. Our sources leave little room for doubt that in the popular conception the practice of pederasty was the almost exclusive preserve of the upper class and one that was viewed with some disdain by non-aristocrats. This (perhaps exaggerated) general notion is summed up succinctly in a line from a lost comedy:

> There's no long-hair *(kometes)* who hasn't been buggered.
> (*Adespota* 12-14)

Aristophanes twice describes himself as never having made advances to young boys in the palestrai,[13] and in many of the allusions of the period to the pederastic impulse there is a strong note of disapproval.

Aristocratic Life-Style in the Fifth Century 165

Some of the favorite butts of the comic poets were nobles notorious for their chasing of boys.[14] It is impossible to say for certain that homosexuality was a consciously expressed manifestation of the aristocratic self-image, but there was certainly a strong identification. To the comedians homosexuality and effeminacy were almost synonymous with aristocracy, and even allowing for comic exaggeration this must have been the universal public opinion. Without a doubt homosexuality fitted the pattern of upper-class values in the fifth century. It had a long association with Greek aristocratic culture, hence it was "traditional"; because it was an expensive practice it had definite overtones of conspicuous display; it was connected with the Spartan ideal of manliness (which had great appeal to the oligarchical-minded Athenian upper class), and with the aesthetic ideal of the beautiful male body and the training and refining of it.[15] And, in its idealized form, the relationship between an older, experienced man and a young man who looked up to and depended on his lover, male homosexuality gave scope to the expression of qualities to which the aristocracy had long laid claim: loyalty, fidelity, moderation, intellectual and moral superiority.

Dover's researches on Greek homosexuality confirm in detail the pattern described above. The absence of homosexual allusions in Homer, Hesiod and the seventh-century iambic and elegiac poets, and the fact that the earliest scenes of homosexual courtship on Attic vase paintings occur at the time of Solon, lead Dover to conclude that homosexuality's "social acceptance and artistic exploitation" became widespread only by the end of the seventh century B.C. By the middle of the fourth century heterosexual love dominated and "was beginning to sweep homosexuality under the carpet."[16] Thus the period of greatest outward manifestation of homosexual activity coincided with the rise of aristocratic emphasis on a particular style of life, reaching its height in the late sixth and early fifth centuries, which "witnessed a more open, headstrong, sensual glorification and gratification of homosexuality than any other period of antiquity."[17]

Also, according to Dover, the contrast between the generally favorable attitude towards male-centered eroticism in Plato and the "fundamentally heterosexual" point of view of comedy was the result of class distinctions. Among the youthful rich heterosexual satisfaction was difficult because of sexual segregation in the upper class, while the poorer classes had more opportunities for male-female contact. Dover's evidence confirms the fact that homosexuality was perceived by the general populace as the province of the upper class, with the result that

> the ordinary Athenian citizen, however ready to identify himself as a man of property with his social superiors, could also pride himself that he wasted no time on homosexual love-affairs such as occupied idle young men who had more money than was good for them.[18]

The ultimate causes for homosexuality as a positive-functioned trait, the appeal of which was largely confined to the upper stratum, are complex. Dover sees the underlying basis in the need for intense personal relationships not available in the family, eventually traceable to the political fragmentation of the Greek world, in which competitiveness and the emphasis on the male warrior inhibited the full development of marital or familial intimacy. Inasmuch as these tensions manifested themselves most among the ruling élite, and because the upper class homosexual ethos was transmitted as part of the educative process, it is proper to conclude that male homosexuality in ancient Greece functioned as an identifying (and exclusive) sign of class membership, self-consciously expressed to a significant degree.[19]

One other example will show how pervasive was the awareness of life-style among Athenians and how intimately associated with public morality it had become in the minds of the citizens. In the *Clouds* of Aristophanes (produced in 423, a year before the *Wasps*) there is a long *agōn* between "Right Argument" and "Wrong Argument," who represent, in the play, the old style of education and the new sophistic teaching. Somewhat naively, perhaps, Aristophanes fixes the blame for what he sees as a disintegration of the older, conventional values on the new education, and retrospectively views the old education *(archaia paideia)* as the key to the past greatness of Athens — a mistake not unknown in modern times. It should be added that although Socrates was the focus of Aristophanes' criticism, the figure of Socrates in the *Clouds* was more likely an agglomerate of the popular conceptions (and misconceptions) of the fifth-century sophists. Additionally, and very importantly, it is necessary to realize that the bad social effects which Aristophanes traces directly to the teaching of "Wrong Argument" is really the whole network of life-style and attitudes prevalent among young men from the best families.[20] If, then, we take this exchange as a fairly coherent depiction of the older and newer cultural patterns, keeping in mind that the practitioners of the "new" style would be youths from the upper class, we have a valuable summary of the ordinary Athenian's percep-

Aristocratic Life-Style in the Fifth Century

tions of the aristocratic self-image in the last quarter of the fifth century. We are told that the old upbringing, the *archaia paideia,* fostered *ta dikaia* and *sōphrosynē.* Under its stringent regimen boys did not complain; they walked through the streets of the city in an orderly *(eutaktōs)* and modest fashion, in groups, thinly clad regardless of the weather, singing the old patriotic songs, shunning the newfangled and effeminate tunes, under threats of beatings. At school they sat modestly, hiding their genitals: no boy ever oiled himself below the navel, nor whispered in a soft voice to his lover, or prostituted himself to the gaze of others. They were not allowed to be choosy about their food, nor to giggle, nor to dangle their feet (961-83). "These are the things," says Right Argument, "from which my *paideusis* nurtured the men who fought at Marathon." But now, he continues, boys go to school all wrapped up in warm cloaks and are not able to hold their shields out straight in the shield dance (985-88). He urges the youth to hate the agora and to spurn the baths, to be modest, respectful to elders and parents, to stay away from dancing girls and whores (991-99). If these things are done the young men will be physically fit and athletic, will not waste their time in idle jesting and chatter in the agora or be constantly in court on trifling matters (1002-04). Right Argument further extols the rewards of good training in the field of Akademos, comparing that to the afflictions which result from the manner of life today. If you follow my way, he says

> You will always have a firm chest, shiny skin, big shoulders, short tongue, big rump, short penis — but if you adopt today's customs, first you'll have pale skin, small shoulders, thin chest, big tongue, small rump, big penis — and a long decree.
> (1011-1019)

Wrong Argument's prescription for education, according to Aristophanes, is nothing more than a life-style of pleasure and licence:

> Boys, women, cottabus, feasting, drinking, laughing. Is life worth living if you don't have these?
> (1073-74)

These, then, are alternative life-styles presented to the young socialite Pheidippides. Wrong Argument triumphs in the *agōn* and the youth becomes an adherent of his teaching.

◊

By the middle of the fifth century Athens and Sparta had become locked into a fateful power struggle which, for much of the rest of the century, took the form of open warfare between the two powers and their allies and dependent states. In Athens itself the "democrats" (the vast majority of the citizens and their leaders, mostly the non-rich, non-noble elements) were deeply suspicious of the "oligarchs," that minority of the civic body largely identifiable as the wealthy upper class. Increasingly disaffected by the democratic constitution, the oligarchs set themselves in conscious opposition to the democracy and twice, towards the end of the century (in 411 and 404), succeeded briefly in overthrowing the democracy and in establishing minority rule at Athens. As we have seen, the sympathies of the upper-class oligarchs were often with the enemy itself, manifested by expressed admiration for and aping of Spartan customs and manners. Not unnaturally this "laconizing" was frequently interpreted by the lower class as part of an attempt to subvert the democracy, hence the often stated feeling that those who adopted Spartan mannerisms were inimical to the state. Homosexuality, for example, was viewed as a Spartan practice, which helps to account for popular reaction against it. Even the rather innocent practice of Athenian upper-class youth to dress and style themselves in Spartan fashion was given a sinister connotation. Thus the chorus of old jurors in the *Wasps* call young Bdelykleon

> hater of the *dēmos* and a lover of monarchy, an associate of Brasidas, a wearer of woolen fringes and a cultivator of an uncut beard.
>
> (474-75)[21]

For the same reasons the aristocratic phenomenon of the drinking club *(hetairia)* was viewed with alarm. Ostensibly organized for purely social purposes, these gatherings of the well-born and wealthy were sometimes occasions for oligarchical plottings against the democracy. Thucydides relates how the *hetairiai* at Athens were the focal point of the plots to overthrow the democracy in 411.[22] In the *Knights* Cleon calls the chorus of young Knights *synōmotai* ("conspirators") and frequently this word is used as a synonym for club members.[23]

Apart from the literary illustrations of the aristocratic self-image in the fifth century B.C. there is one historical figure whose life is a paradigm of the characteristics which have been discussed in this chapter— Alcibiades, son of Clinias, distinguished by his wealth and noble lineage. It is not possible here to detail the career of this spoiled darling of the Athenian people, who was alternately seen as the hero and the villain

Aristocratic Life-Style in the Fifth Century 169

of his polis. Of interest to us is the style and manner of his life which was consciously cultivated to set him apart, distinct and unique, from his fellow citizens. As the most prominent young politician in Athens at the time of the ill-starred Sicilian adventure (415 B.C.) Alcibiades was considered the natural "leader" of the youthful aristocrats and was viewed with a mixture of admiration for his dashing personal qualities and suspicion of his unconventional life-style. Even the sober Thucydides seizes upon these aspects of his personality as being the most characteristic. Nicias, a conservative, older, general, speaking in opposition to the expedition to Sicily, accused Alcibiades of wishing to be a commander in order to further his own personal ambition. Alcibiades is too young to command, the assembly was told; he wishes "to be admired for his keeping of horses *(hippotrophia)*, and, because of the expense, hopes to profit from his command." Nicias ends his attack by counselling the Athenians not to allow Alcibiades to gain distinction at the polis' risk, but consider that "people like him harm the common interest *(ta dēmosia adikein)* and squander their own private fortune" (Thuc. 6.12.2). Thucydides himself gives the same assessment of Alcibiades' motivations, saying that he was eager to command in order to increase his wealth and fame *(doxa):*

> For he was held in esteem *(axiōma)* by the townspeople, and his enthusiasm for horse-breeding and other extravagances went beyond what his fortune could supply. This, in fact, later on had much to do with the downfall of the city of Athens. For *hoi polloi* became frightened at the quality in him which was beyond the normal and showed itself both in the lawlessness of his private life and habits and in the spirit in which he acted on all occasions. They thought he was aiming at a tyranny, and so they turned against him. Although in a public capacity his conduct of the war was excellent, his way of life made him objectionable to everyone as a person; thus they entrusted their affairs to other hands, and before long ruined the city.
> (6.15.3-4; adapted from the Warner translation)

Alcibiades' speech in reply to Nicias' criticism is a masterful defense of the style of life he typified. The very things he was accused of, he says, bring *doxa* to his ancestors *(progonoi)* and to himself and profit to the fatherland — namely the entering of an unprecedented seven chariots in the Olympic Games, which won first, second and fourth prizes. He realizes that this kind of display and other liturgies arouse envy, but:

> Indeed, this is no useless foolishness *(achrēstos anoia)*, when a man spends his own money not only to benefit himself but his polis as well. And it is not *adikon* for a man who has a high opinion of himself not to be put on a level *(isos einai)* with everyone else.
> (6.16.3-4; adapted from the Warner translation)

It would be difficult to find more convincing evidence than the (not unfriendly) treatment by Thucydides for our contention that the aristocratic style of life was deliberately cultivated to bestow on that group an aura of superiority, the ultimate purpose of which was political and social hegemony. In addition, this kind of behavior explains the alternate effect of respect and distrust aroused in the mass of the citizens by the man for whom, in exile, the polis

> yearns for and hates and wants to have.
> *(Frogs* 1425)

Alcibiades' bravado speech in favor of the expedition prevailed over the opposition of the reluctant Nicias, but the same qualities of unconventionality that charmed the people on that day made Alcibiades the chief suspect in the affair of the mutilation of the Herms just before the sailing. Although no direct proof was forthcoming that Alcibiades was guilty, allegations were made concerning previous mutilations of other statues "by young men, in childish amusement and wine" and mock celebrations of the mysteries. Alcibiades was (naturally) accused of being the leader in these profanations, Thucydides relates; further, his political opponents, wishing themselves to be foremost *(prōtoi)*, maintained that these were part of a plot to overthrow the democracy:

> evidence for which they found in the unconventional and undemocratic *(ou dēmotikē)* character of his life in general.
> (6.27-28)

In other respects, too, Alcibiades was the personification of the aristocratic mentality, which strove to impress the *dēmos* with its superior manner and style while at the same time expressing contempt for their inferior mentality and moral character. When he was in exile from Athens and plotting for his return he reportedly sent word to the most powerful *(dynatōtatoi)* leaders of the army:

> to make his views known to the best people *(hoi beltistoi)* in the army and to say that, if there were an *oligarchia* instead of the *ponēria* which had exiled him, he was ready to return . . . .
> (Thuc. 8.47.2; adapted from the Warner translation)

Thucydides records another, earlier, speech of Alcibiades, delivered when under sentence of death *in absentia*. Alcibiades was in Sparta, to which country he had deserted, and was trying to persuade the Spartans to follow his advice on how to defeat Athens. In defending his previous anti-Spartan role as a leader of the people he was at pains to show that in reality he and his fellow aristocrats were different from the Athenian *dēmos* and their democratic leaders. Because a democracy existed at Athens, he says, he had to conform to its institutions:

> However in the face of the prevailing political indiscipline *(akolasia)*, we tried to be more reasonable *(metriōteroi)*. There have been people in the past, just as there are now, who used to try to lead the masses *(ho ochlos)* into evil ways *(ponērotera)*. It is people of this sort who have banished me. ... As for *dēmokratia*, those of us with any sense at all *(hoi phronountes ti)* knew what that meant, and I just as much as any ... but nothing new can be said of a system which is a generally recognized foolishness *(anoia)*.
> (Thuc. 6.89.5-6; adapted from the Warner translation)

In every respect Alcibiades' assessment of democracy matches those which we have already examined, from Megabyzus in Herodotus (3.81) to the Old Oligarch; and the attitudinal stance is exactly the same: aristocrats are moderate and possess *sōphrosynē*, the *dēmos* is unbridled, and, being prone to immorality, is easily led by unscrupulous politicians; only aristocrats have sense, the common people (and their form of government) are foolish.[24]

The example of Alcibiades shows that aristocratic life-style entailed difficulties as well as advantages. There was, on the one hand, the need to rise above the mass, to exhibit qualities of flamboyance and unconventionality, which had the effect of making the aristocrat unique and different in a society whose professed ethos was equality, but this very visibility heightened mistrust, envy and suspicion. Nevertheless, despite the "backlash" dangers, the pursuit of a distinctive mode of living was the best means of expressing superiority; hence it was the most prominent feature of the aristocratic image during the fifth century.

It is now easy to understand why Athenian politicians who were not members of the old aristocracy were subjected to vicious attack precisely on the grounds that they did not conduct themselves in the style of aristocrats. Speaking in general terms of the successors of the aristocratic, aloof, Pericles, Thucydides notes that they failed to lead the polis properly because they were "more on a level with each other," and conducted public affairs "to suit the whims *(hēdonai)* of the *dēmos,*" whereas under Pericles Athens was "in name a *dēmokratia,* but in fact the rule of the first man" (2.65.9-10). We recall that Cleon was introduced by Thucydides as "the most violent of the citizens" (3.36.6). His "empty talk" *(kouphologia)* is mockingly contrasted to those of the citizens who were *sōphrones* (4.28.5); his boasting promise of success in the field (which was brilliantly fulfilled) is called "mad" *(maniōdēs,* 4.39.3); his leadership displayed his "ignorance" *(anepistēmosynē)* and "softness (*malakia,* 5.7.2); he died a coward's death (5.10.9); he was an evildoer and an "untrustworthy *(apistoteros)* slanderer" (5.61.1) Hyperbolus, in the one mention accorded him, was a *mochthēros anthrōpos* (8.73.3). In the same way, Cleon, Hyperbolus and other *dēmos* leaders were constantly lampooned by the writers of Old Comedy, not so much because they were ineffectual as leaders but because their attitudes, manner, and style of life were not aristocratic.[25] These men, economically very well-off, could be termed, anachronistically, "middle class entrepreneurs," but Old Comedy consistently degraded them to the level of the lowliest street vendors — loud, coarse, dishonest rascals, who lied and cheated their way to the top, aided by an ignorant *dēmos* which was easily gulled by their cheap flattery and empty promises. In every possible detail they exhibited characteristics exactly opposite to the aristocratic ideal.[26]

Antipathy towards manual labor and petty trade and commerce (the so-called "banausic" pursuits), as opposed to the acceptable occupation of agriculture, was old in Greece. The prejudice stemmed from the deep-rooted cultural conviction that to be forced to labor for another was a form of degradation, and is related to the tenacious survival of tribal egalitarianism. It applied almost as equally to the artisan who sold his own products as to the wage earner who sold his labor, for both worked to satisfy the needs of others, not their own. *Autarkeia* (self-sufficiency, independence) was the ideal; accordingly, the peasant who toiled endlessly in the sun on his own land was "freer" and, in a sense, enjoyed higher status than a smith or potter, who might actually have had a higher standard of living. What counted was not labor itself but the relations of labor, and there can be little doubt that the feeling against banausic pursuits was common to all Greeks, not just to the leisured upper class. And yet, even at times when the majority of free Greeks "enjoyed" the life of a small farmer, a substantial percentage was engaged in manual work or trade.

The fact that no counter-ideology was formulated that put high value on labor *per se* (just as there was never any real effort to put a positive valuation on poverty) was another important psychological advantage for the aristocratic value system. That the leisured life of the wealthy landowning minority represented an ideal that was universally accepted as valid (even if it was resented) demonstrates once again how powerfully persuasive the aristocratic ethos was, even in a period of democratic levelling. It is also significant that, despite the antiquity of the anti-banausic prejudice, its most vehement expression, including the intellectual formulation that the practice of these occupations led to physical and moral degeneration, comes in the period after 450 B.C. It follows that the aristocratic attempt to portray its style of life as the only "proper" one would result in a heightened emphasis of the principle that manual labor and trade were inimical to the realization of a man's potential, whether as citizen or leader. Cleon was no mere "tanner"; he was the owner of a prosperous tannery, and the same is true of other post-Periclean politicians who were not from the old, leading families. But in anti-democratic propaganda they are portrayed as artisans of the lowest class, as proof of their inferiority as leaders (in Aristophanes *Knights* 128-43 they are lumped together as "something-sellers"). If they emulated the life-style of their landowning "betters" they were subject to lampoon as social upstarts; if they chose, as they apparently did, to identify with the aspirations of the poorer elements, they were classed with them.[27]

Nevertheless, the deliberate rejection by these men of the upper class ethos and their consequent success in gaining political hegemony posed a frustrating dilemma to aristocrats, who were certainly not disposed to abandon a style and manner so integral to their claim to be superior; they had no choice but to continue to concentrate on the differences between the *kaloikagathoi* and the masses.

The hardening of attitudes was, in great part, the result of the economic situation. For a variety of reasons (not always clear to us) the differential between rich and poor increased in the last third of the fifth century. For Athens the war itself was a major cause, as has been emphasized recently by a number of scholars.[28] The Periclean policy in 431 of abandoning the countryside to the enemy effected both a sudden spurt of urbanization and the destruction of the land outside. These factors, along with a sharp increase in the volume of trade, the beginnings of a new "market" economy, and the economic dependence of Athens on its empire, produced severe dislocations not only in the economic sphere but in social attitudes as well. The polis was no longer self-sufficient; the traditional autarky of the small farmer was similarly diminished. The growing dependency on a money economy both widened the economic gap and presented the poor with the dilemma of having to resort to banausic activities, which ran counter to the received ideology. The impoverishment of the Athenian citizens in the fourth century had its visible roots in these conditions, and as the fifth century wore on to its bitter, tragic end, a true polarization of the classes had become evident. Income from the empire, redistributed in the form of state pay (pay for jurors and political offices, and for military service), took up some of the economic slack for the poorer classes, but reinforced the feeling among the wealthy that the *dēmos* was using the state revenues as its personal treasury (so the Old Oligarch). For the *dēmos* this was as it should be, just as the rich were supposed to be liberal in the outlay of their own fortunes for the public good—reflecting, once again, the persistent survival of the ancient tribal egalitarianism. The rich, for their part, felt threatened, not just by the people's demands for equitable distribution of the polis' wealth and by their increased control of political power through anti-aristocratic leaders, but also by their doctrinaire insistence on social equality and their resentment of the traditional aristocracy's style of life, criticism of which had steadily grown during the second half of the century.

The defensive reaction of the leisured class in heightened display of their assertions of superiority exacerbated the tensions. As social harmony disintegrated, and as empire slipped away in the face of impending defeat, Athenian aristocrats either withdrew from active political life or plotted revolution. W. R. Connor summarizes the inevitable choices:

> For some the best course seemed to be to withdraw from politics into private circles of like-minded friends, small informal gatherings . . . or the 'narrow circle' of cultured comrades. . . . This form of reaction was essentially apolitical; the other, however, aimed at a new kind of political arrangement in which the 'better' people would again be dominant.[29]

By 403 the democracy, twice restored, was firmly in power. The "backlash" dangers of the unbridled aristocratic life-style (of which Alcibiades' successive rises and falls provide an illustration) became a permanent fact of life. In the restored democracy citizens had to proclaim their faith in the levelling ideal of democracy and to play down expressions and manifestations of class superiority. The case of Alcibiades, son of Alcibiades, is an example of the dominant sentiment in Athens after the War.

Aristocratic Life-Style in the Fifth Century

In 395 B.C. the younger Alcibiades was brought to trial on a charge of deserting the ranks in a minor skirmish against the Spartans. In the speech, written by Lysias, the main target of attack was the *character* of the son, who was, naturally, compared in vice to his notorious father. The speech abounds in the familiar socio-political/moral terminology of fifth-century political rhetoric – except that the positive categories refer to democrats and the negative ones to oligarchs. The military court is told at the beginning that the purpose of the trial is not only to punish wrongdoers, but "to make other disorderly persons *(akosmountes)* more sensible of duty *(sōphronesteroi)*." Therefore, voting against "unknowns" *(agnōtai)* will do no good, but punishing "the most conspicuous offenders" *(hoi epiphanestatoi)* will make the citizens "better" *(beltious)* (14.12).

Many of the character defects of the defendant are related to style of life: Alcibiades should not be let off because of his birth (*dia to genos,* 14.18); he is accused of an unworthy homosexual affair while still a child, and of having a mistress when he was still a minor; he was debauched by a friend with whom he was in alliance against his own father, and was then imprisoned by the same lover; he was released by another lover, gambled away his fortune, tried to drown his own friends, seduced another man's wife, and so on and on (14.25-29). The prosecutor links the evil character of the son with that of the father, concluding:

> You must ask yourselves, gentlemen of the jury, why anyone should spare men like these – because though unfortunate in their public life they have otherwise been orderly *(kosmioi)* and restrained *(sōphronōs)*? Have not many of them consorted with prostitutes, while some have lain with their own sisters, and some have had children by their own daughters, some have performed mysteries, mutilated the Herms, dishonored all the gods, offended against the whole polis, acted unjustly and unlawfully against others and themselves, holding off from no act of daring, unversed in no deed of horror? They have suffered and done every possible act; for such is their character that they are ashamed at *ta kala* and give honor to *ta kaka*....
>
> (14.41-42)

What we have here, in the early fourth century, is one example of many attacks on individuals, in which the style of life and the norms of behavior of the upper class are discredited.

The new hero is the *sōphrōn politēs,* the "law-abiding citizen," who is above all a fervent democrat and a hater of oligarchy. Claims of superiority are muted; now the emphasis is on the citizen as an aid to the community. Service to the polis, modesty and self-effacement in public life, morality in private life, are now the ideal; and this ideal is attainable by all citizens, not only by a small group. As North says, "All the familiar aristocratic values have been thoroughly 'democratized' in fourth-century Athens."[30] Word usage has come full circle; now it is democrats who are *agathoi, sōphrones* and *chrēstoi,* while oligarchs are *kakoi, ponēroi* and *anandroi.* Thus, by the middle of the fourth century the orator Aischines can compare the "nature" *(physis)* of the man who is *dēmotikos kai sōphrōn* with that of the man who is *oligarchikos* and *phaulos:* freeborn on both sides (in order that he may not, by any misfortune of birth, be disloyal to the "laws which save the *dēmokratia*"); have a legacy of "some good work from his *progonoi* to the *dēmos* (so that he may not harm the polis by attempting to avenge the misfortunes of his family); be *sōphrōn* and *metrios* in daily life (in order that he may not take bribes to feed expensive tastes); have good judgment and ability in speaking; be brave (3.168). Every one of these qualities is possible for the ordinary citizen (except, perhaps, ability in speaking, which must be acquired by expensive education; but Aeschines, even here, explicitly places *eugnomosynē* "reasonableness," "sensibleness," above speaking ability). Naturally, an aristocrat could be all of these things too, but distinguished birth, wealth and education are not essential, while aristocratic pride and style of life are distinct hindrances. The traditional aristocratic virtues have been made available to all men of good will towards the state. In short, *agathos* and *aretē* had been redefined: ". . . it is now *agathos* to be a democrat *per se;*" and the scope of *aretē* had become restricted to a somewhat passive spirit of public fostering of equality, justice and the good of the polis, and a private demeanor of sobriety and moderation.[31]

◊

Thus the events of the final years of the fifth century forced aristocrats to yet another revaluation of the aristocratic ideal. How their class adjusted to the social changes is beyond the scope of this discussion; but the main directional thrust of the newest form of the ideal has been foreshadowed, for it had been a part of the aristocratic ideal for over a century, and it already held a central position in the aristocratic scheme

Aristocratic Life-Style in the Fifth Century 177

of values. Class superiority will be increasingly stated in terms of the inner excellences: intelligence, wisdom, moderation, personal morality. If these qualities are now successfully proclaimed by non-aristocrats (the struggle over who could be called *agathos* is over), aristocrats will have them to a greater degree, or will exhibit a higher form of these virtues or they will comprehend them in an idealized, transcendent form: they will possess and control the excellences of mind and spirit and alone will be able to understand their deeper nature and to teach them to others. Plato, of course, is to be the classic conveyer of these ideas. For him

> The philosopher-ruler contemplates the values as they actually are (*phusei*, 'in their nature') in the Forms, and cannot resist trying to reproduce them in his own soul. Thus he becomes as well ordered (*kosmios*, a significant epithet) and godlike as a man can be. . . . Then he turns, however reluctantly, to his duty as statesman and stamps these same characteristics on the citizens, who thus possess *dēmotikē aretē* – the result, not of *epistēmē* on their part, but merely of right opinion.[32]

◊

The Greek aristocratic ideal, which we have traced from its earliest manifestation at the end of the Dark Age through the fifth century B.C. was not a static model. The permanent core of its conceptual frame was the conviction that the dominant class was superior in all respects to other elements of the community and should be accorded the privileges and deference due them by reason of their superiority. Operationally, the ideal was a series of flexible "stances," which could be adapted to changing conditions and pressures. Certain aspects of the ideal remained unaltered from beginning to end; others were added as they were needed or eliminated as they proved inadequate or counter-productive to the central purpose of continued recognition of superiority. Because most of the "changes" in the ideal took the form of subtle shifts of emphasis, in response to socio-historical developments, modern observers have often accepted as true the surface impression of a pattern of aristocratic values unaltered from the time of Homer to the end of the fifth century. That impression is misleading. The remarkable staying power of the cultural attitudes of the Greek nobility over a long period of time, even in political situations where those principles were in direct opposition to the expressed values of the mass of people, was the result of an ability to conform to changing social realities.

The impression of an aristocratic ideology unaltered over time and the corresponding inability of non-aristocrats to formulate a coherent and positive counter-ideology have also led to the belief that aristocratic values were not seriously questioned and to the equation of the elitist value system with the cultural ideal of all Greeks.[33] In reality, there was, from the beginning, constant pressure from below which forced aristocrats to make defensive alterations in the images of superiority which they projected. No element of the dominant group's spectrum of values − birth, wealth, mental and moral capacity, habits, and style of living − escaped serious challenge. Although that challenge issued as a formal expression of lower class values only sporadically and inconsistently, it significantly shaped the evolution of upper class behavior until, by the end of the fifth century, the whole network of traditional claims to class superiority had become politically and socially invalid.

The underlying impulse of the erosion of class pretensions was the profoundly rooted legacy of egalitarianism from the tribal past; it was that inheritance, in fact, that was never seriously challenged. The Greek aristocratic ideal had its formation in the tribal chiefdoms of the Dark Age, and its historical development was intimately related to the emergence of the polis, the complex expression of Greek tribal life. The tribal nature of the polis, which was never perceived as anything but a community of all the citizens, insured that political, economic and social stratification within the body of fictive kinsmen could never advance to a true class system. The few wealthy, well-born and influential − those we have termed "aristocrats," "nobles," "upper class" − found themselves, from the beginning, in a constant struggle to maintain (or to regain) their positions as the "rightful" and "natural" leaders of the people. The many, who stood outside the small and jealously exclusive top layer, never permitted the élite to solidify into a true hereditary, ruling class, but forever chipped away at old assumptions and prerogatives.

Finally, the points of identification between the "aristocratic ideal" and the wider cultural ideal were not the results of the filtering down and acceptance by the many of the values of the few, but the reflection of a culture-wide homogeneity of values and attitudes which all Greeks shared. We can accept as correct Starr's conclusion that:

> Fundamentally, the Greek upper classes shared the values and ethical standards of Hellenic civilization as a whole, though they voiced and exemplified those views in a more conscious manner. . . . Those

historians who explore the lower classes and begin with the premise that their culture is essentially different from that of the elite do not stand in full accord with anthropological studies of peasantries.[34]

The aristocratic assertion that their group was the sole possessor of the qualities of mind, body and spirit that made a man good was psychologically persuasive, especially in a culture which put a premium on competition and success, because "noble" ancestry and landed wealth easily translate into political power and social prestige in small, pre-market societies. Because aristocratic claims to exclusive excellence were founded on the potent twin supports of birth and wealth, and their material consequences of a visibly grander style of life and conspicuous display — none of which could be imitated — non-aristocrats found it difficult to formulate a competing ideology, except in negative terms.

Nevertheless, the very nature of the polis had a moderating influence on social discord; the polis idea was the centripetal principle which thrust the complex of contradictory social impulses into the frame of "the common good." The nobleman may have considered himself to be above and apart from the common people, but never apart from the polis; aristocrat and non-aristocrat alike agreed that a man existed to serve the community. The disagreement was over who did this best, which element should hold which relative position. True class conflict would have destroyed the very framework within which both sides were competing — hence the restraint and the reluctance to choose radical alternatives. Both groups shared equally a fear of the *monarchos,* the single ruler (thus hatred of the *tyrannos* was a common element in both democratic and oligarchic propaganda); but, in addition, the upper class often rejected too narrow oligarchies, and the *dēmos,* to a surprising degree, had misgivings about too extreme democracies.[35]

By the dawning of the fourth century the precarious balance had become eccentric; despite the frequent appeals to *homonoia,* "concord," by fourth-century orators, attitudes had begun to rigidify, the spirit of compromise and give-and-take waned as the polis ideal ceased to be the central focus of human activity. Political theorists like Plato and Aristotle reflect the loss of the ideal and the narrowing of interests, as they construct highly rational, static political systems based on a hierarchical social order (and, anachronistically, project these attitudes backwards into the previous centuries).[36]

The Greek aristocratic ideal evolved during the period of benign tension; the ideal was pragmatic, functioning on both the conscious and unconscious levels to preserve the nobility's position at the top of the social pyramid, to create and to foster a gulf between themselves and the rest of the people. Its means, as we have seen, were fundamentally persuasive, not coercive, exploiting every natural advantage and evolving new combinations as necessary. In the process of challenge and reaction the whole of Hellenic society absorbed and benefited from the creative energies generated.

$$\Omega$$

NOTES TO THE TEXT

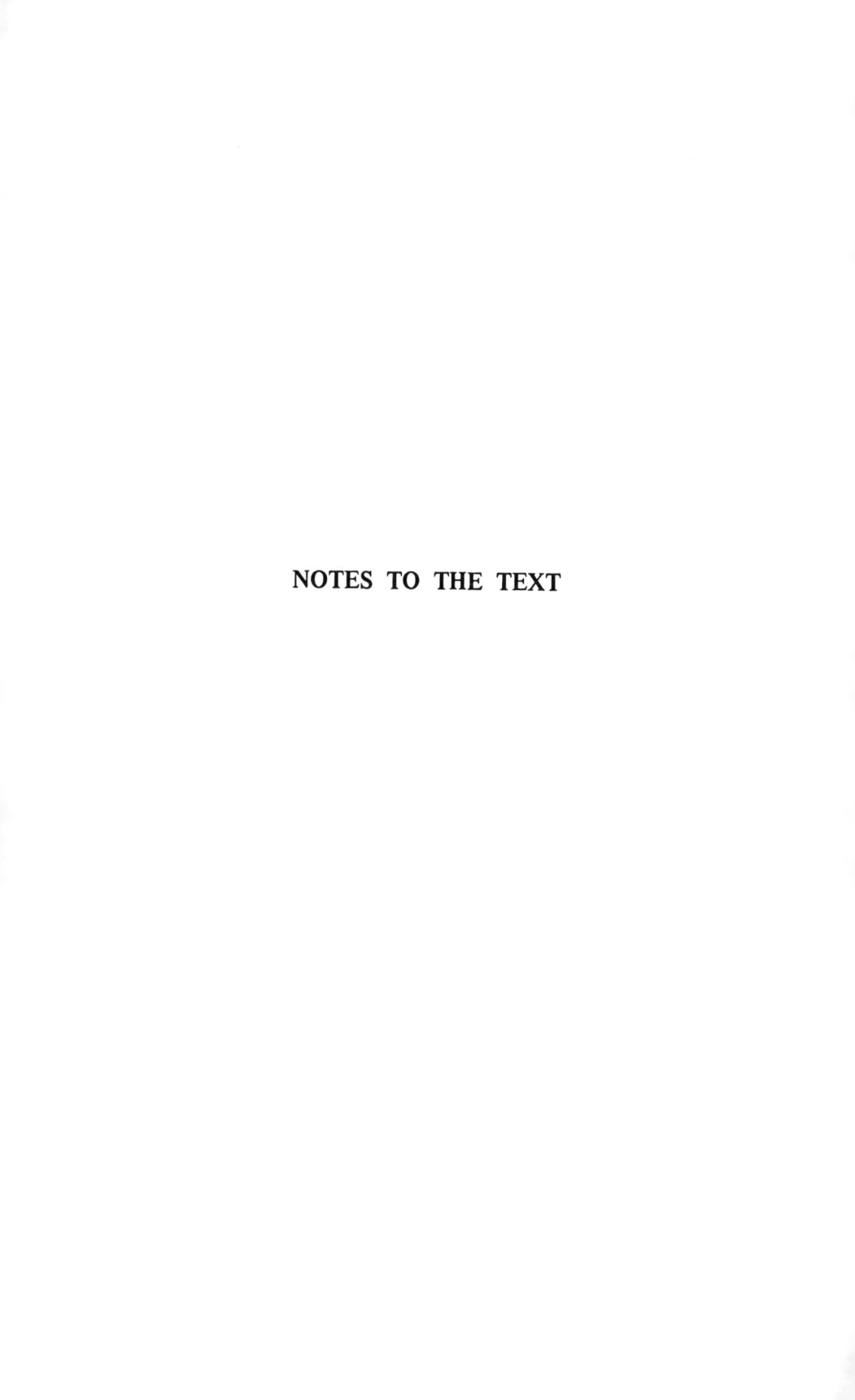

CHAPTER ONE

1. Although some scholars still maintain that Homer's "background" is Mycenaean, the decipherment of the Linear B tablets and the accumulation of archaeological research make that possibility more and more remote. Most debate centers about a Dark Age milieu, the poet's own time, or an "amalgam" theory. The question is a difficult one and will not be answered definitively in the near future. M.I. Finley, in *The World of Odysseus,* 2nd ed., rev. (New York 1965) proposed that the *Iliad* and *Odyssey* reflected the social institutions of the tenth and ninth centuries B.C. (p. 43; see his eloquent restatement in "The World of Odysseus Revisited," *PCA* 71 [1974] 13-31). M.M. Austin and P. Vidal-Naquet, *Economic and Social History of Ancient Greece: An Introduction,* trans. and rev. by M.M. Austin (Berkeley and Los Angeles 1977), in a judicious survey of the problem, reach the same conclusions (pp. 37-40). By and large it is archaeologists, who, recognizing the tripartite layering of the material background of the epics, label the social culture as an amalgam. A most forceful expression of this view is A.M. Snodgrass, "An historical Homeric society?" *JHS* 94 (1974) 114-25. The most fruitful approach, in my opinion, is the kind essayed by J.M. Redfield, *Nature and Culture in the Iliad* (Chicago 1975), who sees the historical culture embedded, of necessity, in the poems – the poem had to make sense to a contemporary audience – regardless of specific anomalies. Akin to this point of view is the insight of E.A. Havelock, *Preface to Plato* (Cambridge, Mass. 1963), that the Homeric epics constituted a "tribal encyclopedia," a paradigm of accepted contemporary norms (and of deviations from these norms), representing the "general state of mind."

Finally, that the norms of heroic behavior in the *Iliad* and *Odyssey* were the basis of the later aristocratic "code," is to me a fact beyond dispute. To what extent this (very loose) "system" of beliefs and attitudes became the property of all Hellenes, not just of the upper class, is disputable. A premise of this study is that non-aristocrats did not so much rebel against or reject this set of attitudes; rather, that as this ideal became more and more self-consciously (and defensively) the "property" of aristocratic groups, non-aristocrats formulated other values, more compatible with their own social reality.

2. On the chiefdom form and its relationship to tribal society see M.D. Sahlins, *Tribesmen* (Englewood Cliffs, NJ 1968); *idem, Stone Age Economics* (Chicago 1972); E.R. Service, *Primitive Social Organization. An Evolutionary Perspective* (New York 1965). Especially interesting are Sahlin's comments (*Tribesmen,* 32-39) on the tendency of pastoral nomads to develop "disorderly" chiefdoms, based partly on a corporate descent system (e.g. clans, lineages) and partly on "contractual" relations (e.g. clientage, blood-brotherhood), and the endemic nature of warfare in such groups (cf. the Bedouin saying: "Raids are our agriculture"). The causal role of warfare in the rise of social ranking is hotly debated by anthropologists. For our purposes it is sufficient to point out that externally directed aggression was highly regarded in Homeric society, and that those who placed high on the political, social and economic scales were outstanding fighters. Austin and Vidal-Naquet (above, note 1, 40-47) give a sound, short description of the role of the *oikos* and of other characteristics of the Homeric world. For recent, detailed accounts of Dark Age material life see A.M. Snodgrass, *The Dark Age of Greece*

(Edinburgh 1971), esp. ch. 7; V.R. d'A. Desborough, *The Greek Dark Age* (New York 1972); and J.N. Coldstream, *Geometric Greece* (New York 1977). What makes the Greek Dark Age "dark" is the lack of material evidence from which to reconstruct the society. If Homeric society is to be placed roughly between 1000 and 800, then the society, as revealed by archaeology, is one that is slowly, but with sure direction, emerging from stagnation, isolation, depopulation, nervous movement, to settled village life, rising population, increased vitality and prosperity – not uniformly, and not always steadily, of course, but the trend is evident.

3. The best exposition of this tool is found in the valuable study by A.W.H. Adkins, *Merit and Responsibility: A Study in Greek Values* (Oxford 1960) 30-31 (cited hereafter as *M&R*). See also a more recent treatment by Adkins, *Moral Values and Political Behaviour in Ancient Greece* (New York 1972) 1-9, 12-13 (cited hereafter as *MV&PB*). I disagree with many of Adkins' conclusions concerning the usage of these key words, but his methodology is sociologically sound and makes possible the extraction of valuable information from our often inadequate source material. For a complete analysis of every occurrence of these terms from Homer to Pindar see my unpublished dissertation, *Agathos-Kakos: A Study of Social Attitudes in Archaic Greece* (Northwestern University 1968). Two older studies are often very useful: J. Gerlach, *Aner Agathos* (Munich 1932) and M. Hoffman, *Die ethische Terminologie bei Homer, Hesiod und den alten Eligikern und Jambographen* (Tübingen 1914).

4. E.g. the formula *boēn agathos* (good at the war-cry) occurs 47 times in Homer. For *esthlos* see *Il.* 4.458; 15.283; 17.590.

5. E.g. *agathos: Il.* 10.559; 13.238, 284, 314; 17.632; 21.280; *Od.* 18.383. *Esthlos: Il.* 5.581; 6.444; 9.319; 11.673; 16.600; 20.383, 434; 22.158. *Kakos: Il.* 2.365; 4.299; 5.643; 6.443; 8.94, 153; 9.319; 11.408; 13.279; 16; 570; 17.180, 632; *Od.* 3.375; 4.199; 21.131.

6. The selling of slaves and the ransoming of prisoners was also a source of income for the high-ranking warrior; cf. *Il.* 21.34ff.

7. Significantly, only twice in Homer is a word for wealthy *(aphneios)* coupled with *agathos* (*Il.* 13.664; 17.576); the very epithet *agathos* subsumed the notion of a wealthy man. For a broader discussion of wealth and its uses in the Homeric world see M.I. Finley, *The World of Odysseus* (cited hereafter as *WO*) 128-30; cf. 58-59, 61-63, 66, 102. It was Finley, who, following the lead of M. Mauss and K. Polanyi, first brought to the attention of Hellenists the proposition that in prestate societies the economy is "embedded" in the social structure. S. Humphreys, "History, Economics, and Anthropology: The Work of Karl Polanyi," *History and Theory* 8 (1969) 165-212, has an excellent summary and analysis, with extensive bibliography, of the important concept of reciprocity. For a brief account of "the controversy over the ancient economy," and of Polanyi's contributions, see Austin and Vidal-Naquet (above, note 1) 3-11.

8. E.g. *Il.* 8.139-50; 11.401-10; 17.90-105. See W.K.C. Guthrie's characterization of the "emotional and mental instability" of the Homeric heroes in "The Religion and Mythology of the Greeks," published as a separate fascicle of the revised vol. II of the *CAH* (Cambridge, Eng. 1964) 42-43.

9. E.g. *Il.* 4.370-400; 8.90-96; 12.244-47; cf. *Il.* 17.325ff.

10. *M&R*, 49.

11. *Il*. 22.38-130; cf. *Il*. 6.440-46.

12. E.R. Dodds, *The Greeks and the Irrational* (Berkeley and Los Angeles 1951) 17, 28ff. On failure see Adkins, *M&R,* ch. 3. Redfield (above, note 1) 116, says that "the heroes do not distinguish personal morality from conformity," and emphasizes that the Homeric Greeks "make no distinction between propriety and morality."

13. *Il*. 3.170 (Agamemnon); *Od*. 17.416 (Antinous); 20.194 (Odysseus); 24.253 (Laertes). Cf. also *Il*. 3.158; 24.630; *Od*. 4.27. See B. Fenik, *Studies in the Odyssey,* Hermes Einzelschriften 30 (1974) 61.

14. In *Od*. 13.297ff. Athena changes Odysseus into an old man. Very significant in the transformation is his clothing – vile and filthy – which stamps him obviously as a beggar (434-38). When Athena restores his heroic appearance, in order that he might be recognized by Telemachus, clothing plays an important thematic role (16.172-76, 199-200, 209-12, 456-5). In Book 23, when the logical "proof" of his identity should have been the slaying of the suitors, Penelope still refuses to recognize him because of his rags (94-95). A few lines later Odysseus explains this strange behavior to an angry and bewildered Telemachus:

> Now because I am filthy and wearing vile clothing, for this she dishonors me and does not yet say I am her husband

15. *Il*. 2.216-19. See below, pp. 20-22. As Albin Lesky, *A History of Greek Literature,* 2nd ed., trans. by J. Willis and C. de Heer (London 1966) 111, says: "To the world of Homer the outer and the inner man were inseparably linked."

16. The description of the relatively minor hero, Thoas, may be taken as an expanded paradigm of this advice:

> skilled in the spear's throw and brave in close fight. In assembly few of the Achaians, when the young men contended in debate, could outdo him.
> (*Il*. 15.282-84)

Here, and elsewhere, I have adopted the translations of Richmond Lattimore, *The Iliad of Homer* (Chicago 1951), *The Odyssey of Homer* (New York 1965) and have so indicated in the text. Lattimore's line divisions have not been retained.

17. Cf. *Il*. 13.726-34.

18. It is obvious that mere physical beauty, unaccompanied by strength or valor, is not prized at all in the heroic scale of values. The phrase "admirable in *eidos*" (*Il*. 5.787; 8.228) becomes a term of reproach when unconnected with other excellences of body and mind. Paris is despised because he is merely beautiful, but without warlike spirit (*Il*. 3.39-57; 13.769ff.); cf. *Il*. 10. 316; 24.261-62.

19. Odysseus asks: "at least take pity on all the other Achaians who are afflicted along the host, and will honour you as a god. You may win very great glory *(kydos)* among them" (*Il*. 9.301-303, Latt.). Here the appeal is to pity and to personal glory. In his long reply (lines 308-426) Achilles does not deign even to mention Odysseus' appeal. Phoenix' cautionary tale of Meleager (529-99) implies a claim of responsibility to the larger group. Ajax' blunt response to Achilles' obduracy focuses on the hero's excessive pride and on his betrayal of friendship: "nor does he care for the friendship *(philotēs)* of his companions" (630). It is this appeal, by the way, which touches Achilles most directly (644-45). When

Patroclus sets out to fight in Achilles' armor, his exhortation to the Myrmidons is not that they should save the Greeks but rather give *timē* to Achilles and spite Agamemnon (*Il.* 16.269-74).

20. Cf. *Il.* 16.830-33; 18.265, 514-15. A similar appeal to wives, children, parents, possessions can also be made by the Greeks (*Il.* 15.662-64).

21. As the dead Hector is called "a great joy to the polis and all the *dēmos*" (*Il.* 24.706).

22. *Il.* 22.38-89, 416-36, 477-514; 24.725-75. But in 22.46-55 the possibility of Hector's death is seen as a great sorrow to the *laoi* of Troy.

23. *WO,* 125. See P.A.L. Greenhalgh, "Patriotism in the Homeric World," *Historia* 21 (1972) 528-37, who corrects the exaggerated view of some scholars that *no* sense of community responsibility can be found in the epics. Still, true patriotism and a self-transcending idea of community responsibility must wait until the emergence of the city-state.

24. An example is the treatment of the captured Trojan spy, Dolon, who was implicitly promised his life if he told the truth about the Trojan encampment, yet was cooly dispatched by Diomedes when he did (*Il.* 10.378ff.). A defeated warrior may beg for mercy, invoking "religious" sanctions, but the victor apparently feels free to listen or not (e.g. Achilles and Lycaon in *Il.* 21.74-77). The gods do have a regard for pity; they are angered at Achilles' mistreatment of Hector's body (*Il.* 24.33ff.); they are opposed to the use of poisoned arrows (*Od.* 1.262). In contrast the Cyclopes have no "assemblies for council," no "custom laws" *(themistes),* nor any reciprocal relations beyond the nuclear family (*Od.* 9.112-15). For Homer the absence of civic association and of religiously sanctioned rules for the treatment of strangers are equally the sign of uncivilized beings.

25. Compare the "proper" response by the very civilized Phaeacians to a suppliant stranger (*Od.* 7.155-66).

26. Cf. *Od.* 24.351-52: Laertes' prayer that Zeus has punished the suitors for their *hybris.* In the same way Troy's destruction is seen as a punishment from Zeus for breaching the laws of hospitality (*Il.* 13.62-32; cf. 3.351-54) and for the breaking of oaths (*Il.* 4.155-68). Homer indulges in moralizing disapproval of Heracles, who slew Iphitus when he was a guest at his table (*Od.* 21.24-28).

27. See Finley, *WO,* 63, 103-108, 133-36; Austin and Vidal-Naquet (above, note 1) 43. For representative descriptions see *Il.* 11.769-79; *Od.* 3.34-74 4.26-67; 15.72-159). *Xeniē* is "foreign policy" in its tribal form. The intertribal marriage alliance in Homer, by which "strangers" are turned into kin, had the same instrumental purpose, the increase of one or both *oikoi* (e.g. *Od.* 7.311; 14.211). Throughout the archaic and classical periods both the *xeinos* relationship and marital alliances between families from different *poleis* continued to be important mechanisms by which aristocratic *oikoi* increased their sphere of influence, often in contradiction to communal solidarity.

28. It is assumed in the epics that Greek and Trojan speak the same language just as they worship the same gods. Homer *is* aware that different peoples speak different languages; *Il.* 2.803-806; 4.436-38: Trojan allies speak mutually unintelligible languages; *Il.* 2.867: the Carians are *barbarophonoi; Od.* 19.172-77: differing tongues among the peoples of Crete. Cf. also the Homeric hymns to Apollo (162-63) and Aphrodite (113-14).

29. See C.M. Bowra, *Tradition and Design in the Iliad* (Oxford 1930) 170; W. K. Lacey, *The Family in Classical Greece* (London 1968) 37-38. Aeneas claims seven generations, Glaukos six, Antilochus five, Diomedes and Idomeneus four. The original ancestor is usually a god or a shadowy eponym.

30. G.M. Calhoun, in an important article, "Classes and Masses in Homer," *CP* (1934) 192-208, 301-16, noted that despite the wealth of genealogical material available to Homer surprisingly little attention is centered on it. It is introduced "in moderate amount and for definite reasons of art" and is focused primarily on "kings" and "kingly families" (pp. 207-208).

31. Cf. *Il.* 6.207-210; *Od.* 24.506-509.

32. *Od.* 1.386-87, 402-404; 16.383ff.

33. Eumaeus the swineherd was the son of a *basileus* in his own land, kidnapped and sold as a slave (*Od.* 15.403-84). The women Chryseis and Briseis were both well-born spear prizes of Agamemnon and Achilles (*Il.* 1.11ff.; 19.291ff.).

34. Finley, *WO*, 86ff.; C.G. Thomas, "The Roots of Homeric Kingship," *Historia* 15 (1966) 387-407.

35. *Od.* 14.199ff.

36. The one (and only) exception to this is *Il.* 2.198-206, where, in the aftermath of Agamemnon's abortive "test" of the army's morale, there is a general rush of high and low to the ships. Odysseus restores order, and whenever he came upon a "man of the *dēmos*" he struck him with the sceptre, calling him "unwarlike and weak, of no account in war or in counsel." It is possible, as Calhoun says (above, note 30) 304 that "it is not one of the heaven-born flogging common clay, but the *de facto* commanding officer stemming a rout which may at any moment bring disaster." Clearly, however, there is real significance in this isolated statement of inferiority – the man of the *dēmos* is said to lack precisely those qualities of body and mind which belong to the warrior-aristocrat.

37. E.g. *aristoi: Il.* 2.577-78; 5.780; 12.89, 197; 13.128; heroes: *Il.* 2.110, etc. 12.165; 15.230, 261; 19.34.

38. E.g. *Od.* 9.60, 63; 10.134; 12.281, 309.

39. E.g. *Il.* 1.374-77; 2.149-54, 333-35; 9.50-56; 23.539-40, 822-23; *Od.* 3.149-50; 16.375-82, 424-29. See also *Il.* 18.497-502; *Od.* 2.239-41; 3.214-15; 14.238-39.

40. Apparently, although we are not told this explicitly.

41. For an analysis of Thersites and his place in Homeric society see H.D. Rankin, "Thersites the Malcontent, A Discussion," *Symbolae Osloenses* 47 (1972) 36-60.

42. E.g. Adkins, *M&R*, 34, maintains that even Thersites accepts the epic scale of values. In *MV&PB* he says sweepingly, "the *kakoi* agree with the *agathoi* about the evaluations of Homeric society" (pp. 13-14).

43. *WO*, 19.

44. Finley's assertion (*WO*, 102) that this passage is "anachronistic" and that here Homer "permitted a contemporary note to enter, carefully restricting it, however, to a harmless simile and thus avoiding any possible contradiction in the narrative itself," is an example of the unwillingness of many modern scholars to admit the possibility of anything but acceptance of the aristocratic value system in Homeric society.

45. C.G. Starr, *The Economic and Social Growth of Early Greece: 800-500 B.C.* (New York 1977) 120; see also Starr, *The Origins of Greek Civilization: 1100-650 B.C.* (New York 1961) 123-38.

46. Translations of Hesiod are by H.G. Evelyn-White in the Loeb Classical Library (Cambridge, Mass. and London 1967), except as noted.

47. See *Works and Days* 80-89; *Theogony* 585-602. See S.C. Humphreys, *Anthropology and the Greeks* (London, Henley, Boston 1978) 216: "The story of Pandora sums up in a single image the rejection of two essential values of the Homeric world, women and gifts. A gift to Hesiod is either a bribe, a debt, a tax, or a trap. Women are a necessary evil."

48. *The Livelihood of Man*, ed. by H.W. Pearson (New York 1977) 152.

49. See E.A. Havelock, *The Liberal Temper in Greek Politics* (New Haven and London 1964) 36-40.

50. *Works and Days* 190-91.

51. *Kakos anēr* in *Works and Days* 240-41 (see above, p. 28) has no parallel in Homer and can only be taken in an ethical sense of a man (in a position of leadership) who commits injustice. Adkins insists that *kakos* here still decries the absence of "prosperity and social status," i.e. that the usage of these words is the same in Hesiod as in Homer (*MV&PB*, 30).

52. *Works and Days* 286-92. See W. Jaeger, *Paideia: The Ideals of Greek Culture*, vol. I, trans. by G. Highet (New York 1945) 70-71 and Adkins *M&R*, 71. More recently Adkins has modified his conception, and sees Hesiod and Perses as *déclassé agathoi (MV&PB*, 25ff.).

53. Examples of Hesiod's peasant values in the *Works and Days*: appreciation of simple things (40-41); praise of common sense (293-97); industriousness (238-309, 381-82, 398-413, 493-503); thrift (361-71); social cooperation (342-51); peasant view of women (60-105, 373-75, 695-705). Also, Zeus as protector of the weak (5-8); distaste for violence and strife (12-16, 161-66, 182-94, 213-16, 320-22); violence, greed, injustice of the leaders (38-39, 202-212); primacy of justice (225-35); divine retribution for injustice (217-24, 238-73, 333-34). In the strictly formal anthropological sense, a "peasant" is a rural producer who is in a relation of dependence on others in the society, who use the surplus for their own means. It is permissible, however, to employ the term more loosely to describe Hesiod and others of his economic class — small to middling independent freeholders — in a society which is in the process of structural change. Cf. Starr, *The Economic and Social Growth of Early Greece* (above, note 45) 162-67.

54. See A.M. Snodgrass, *Archaeology and the rise of the Greek state. An inaugural lecture* (Cambridge, Eng. 1977); Austin and Vidal-Naquet (above, note 1) 49-69; Starr, *Economic and Social Growth of Early Greece*, 21-117. For a general discussion of the interrelationship among economic, political and ideological structures see L.A. White, *The Evolution of Culture* (New York 1959) 308ff.

55. White (above, note 54) 220. For an exposition of this theory see G.E. Swanson, *The Birth of the Gods. The Origin of Primitive Beliefs* (Ann Arbor 1968) 153-74.

◊

CHAPTER TWO

1. For a somewhat different point of view, see Starr, *Economic and Social Growth,* 82-83, who speaks of "the great technological upsurge in the Aegean world" after 900. Although Starr admits that most of these skills were borrowed, he insists that Greek craftsmen surpassed "their Near Eastern sources in matters of technique." The most important technological advance made by the Greeks was the ability to work iron, which became common after 800 B.C. This (borrowed) technique was certainly significant for agriculture and warfare and may even qualify as a "revolutionary" step (see Polanyi, *The Livelihood of Man,* 149-50).

2. Starr, *Economic and Social Growth,* 40-41. See also Austin and Vidal-Naquet, *Economic and Social History,* 53ff., who correct the earlier, exaggerated, theories about large-scale production, manufacture and commerce.

3. White, *The Evolution of Culture,* 220, 221.

4. For recent discussions of the origin and nature of the early polis, see Starr, *Economic and Social Growth,* 31-34, 98ff., and Austin and Vidal-Naquet, *Economic and Social History,* 49-53. Still valuable are the 1937 and 1943 articles by V. Ehrenberg, reprinted in *Polis und Imperium* (Zurich 1965) 83-97, 98-104. L.H. Jeffery, *Archaic Greece. The City-States c. 700-500 B.C.* (New York 1976) gives useful summaries of the constitutional histories of the most important *poleis.*

5. For an excellent brief account of the age of tyranny in Greece see A. Andrewes, *The Greek Tyrants* (London 1956); cited hereafter as *Tyrants.*

6. The technical stages from the old style of fighting to the new hoplite tactics, the connections between the tactical revolution, the emergence of the polis and the rise of the tyrants are still matters of great controversy. A brief, plausible reconstruction of these events may be found in W.G. Forrest, *The Emergence of Greek Democracy* (New York 1966) 88-93, 104-105 (cited hereafter as *Greek Democracy*); see also Andrewes, *Tyrants,* 31-38. For a more detailed analysis of weaponry and tactics consult A.M. Snodgrass, *Arms and Armour of the Greeks* (Ithaca 1967).

7. Many historians find a causal link between the formation of the hoplite style of fighting and the rise of the tyrants — i.e. the *dēmos* which was championed by the early tyrants was the "middle class" of hoplite infantrymen (Andrewes, *Tyrants,* 34-38). Forrest, *Greek Democracy,* 105 cites "a growing sense of independence among ordinary men; an awareness of a sort among the hoplites; a shift of power inside the aristocracy itself . . ." It is impossible to know what percentage of the (male) population possessed sufficient wealth to take the field as hoplites during the archaic period. Some scholars insist that the number was small and, therefore, that the "hoplite revolution" was not in any real sense a democratizing influence — the number of *agathoi* was merely being increased. But the very essence of the phalanx is numbers and it is difficult to imagine that in times of danger any large number of able-bodied men from any polis would be ignored. In any case we must consider that more than a third of the men of fighting age were hoplites (Forrest, *Greek Democracy,* 94).

We must be careful above all not to import the modern concept of Klassenkampf into the picture. The Greek tyrant was no popular revolutionary, leading his people against an oppressive aristocracy. Tyrants, most of them aristocrats themselves, were motivated by concern for their own prestige and position. In the absence of a true "class system," class warfare is not possible. The number of recorded incidents of bloody violence between the upper and lower classes during the Archaic period is quite small, and none of these appears to have had the character of a popular uprising. See Starr, *Economic and Social Growth,* 178-80. M.T. Arnheim, *Aristocracy in Greek Society* (New York and London 1977) 121-29, asserts that the tyrants "were genuinely popular leaders of anti-aristocratic revolutionary movements" (p. 121), who capitalized on the "combination of growing hope and growing frustration" of the lower classes, and that "tyranny was not only an alternative to aristocracy. It was *the* alternative to aristocracy" (pp. 128-29).

8. Cf. fr. 6.7.15-32D. The fragments of most of the lyric poets are taken from the Teubner text of E. Diehl (ed.), *Anthologia Lyrica Graeca,* 3rd ed. (Leipzig 1949-52). The translations are mainly my own, with occasional reliance on those of J.M. Edmonds in the *Loeb Classical Library.* What follows conforms in most essentials to the perceptive analysis of the Tyrtaean poems by W. Jaeger in *Paideia,* I, 87-98. For a more complete treatment see Jaeger's "Tyrtaeus on True *Arete,"* tr. A.M. Fiske, in *Five Essays* (Montreal 1966) 103-42.

9. H. Fränkel, *Early Greek Poetry and Philosophy,* trans. by M. Hadas and J. Willis (New York and London 1973), cited hereafter as *EGPPh,* sees in Callinus' thought implications of transition from Homeric concern with personal glory, honor and shame to the polis-concept of community reaction (pp. 152-53). Snodgrass (above, note 6) 64, notes in fr. 1 (lines 5, 14) evidence of a transition from the old style of fighting to the phalanx.

10. *Paideia* I, 90. In reducing the whole complex of heroic qualities to the one essential of savage valor (*thouris alkē,* a Homeric term, see *Il.* 15.250), Tyrtaeus implies that none of the concomitant qualities so prized by the epic hero was required for a man to be *agathos* or to win *timē.* It should be stressed that the Sparta of the Tyrtaean poems is a special case, for he wrote during a period of grave external danger to the Spartan state; accordingly, these are crisis poems. Elsewhere in the fragments Tyrtaeus urges his compatriots to honor and obey their aristocratic leaders. Fränkel, *EGPPh,* 337-39, maintains that fr. 9 is not by Tyrtaeus, but belongs to the time of Xenophanes, about 100 years later.

11. Fränkel, *EGPPh,* 137, says: "Archilochus seriously balances the value of life against an exaggerated notion of honor, draws a realistic conclusion, and acts accordingly; and at once, in a tone of aggressive challenge, he proclaims to all the world what he has done." See also Jaeger, *Paideia* I, 119. Another point of view, shared by many modern scholars, is that although Archilochus may have been "un-Homeric," he was not "anti-Homeric" (G.M. Kirkwood, *Early Greek Monody* [Ithaca and London 1974] 32-33). Despite differing opinions about the degree of Archilochus' divagation from the traditional epic norms of behavior, there is almost universal agreement that he expressed new attitudes to old values.

12. E.g. *Od.* 9.27: Ithaca is "rough, but a good nurse of young men."

13. A rather large portion of the fragments has to do, in one way or the other, with the polis and its citizens: frgs. 7, 9, 19, 52, 54, 60, 64, 70, 79, 85, 88, 109D. The point that Archilochus, despite his hardbitten cynicism, was essentially a patriot, is made well by P. Green, *The Shadow of the Parthenon* (Berkeley and Los Angeles 1971) 132-69.

14. The fears of old age and death voiced by later archaic poets (see below) is another manifestation of this mood. Hesiod's obsessive religious scrupulosity (or "superstition," if you will) in *Works and Days,* so starkly different from Homer's "un-miasmic" version of divine-human relations, is mirrored in archaic art's preoccupation with fearsome beasts and monsters. On this and other manifestations of "general stress" see Starr, *Economic and Social Growth,* 170-72; also 136-37.

15. H.D. Rankin, *Archilochus of Paros* (Park Ridge, NJ 1977) 36.

16. Cited and translated by Rankin (above, note 15) 11.

17. E.g. fr. 1.54D.

18. See C. Gallavotti, "Il tiranno di Archiloco," *PP* 4 (1949) 69-71: Leophilos is a tyrant, and Archilochus is delivering a moral judgment. Cf. G.L. Huxley, *The Early Ionians* (London 1966) 60, who suggests that Leophilos was an archon in Paros or Thasos.

19. See Jaeger, *Paideia* I, 102 and note 11. Green (above, note 13) emphasizes the similarity of outlook among Hesiod, Archilochus and Thersites, whom he calls "the voice from the ranks, the snarling apostle of self-help and common sense, the deft puncturer of epic pretensions" (p. 152).

20. Hesiod, *Works and Days* 202-212. See Jaeger, *Paideia* I, 121-23; Lesky, *History of Greek Literature,* 154-56; M. Treu, *Archilochus* (Munich 1959) 230-35. Kirkwood, *Monody,* 45, says: "The fable from its beginning in Greek literature suggests earthiness, simplicity, the non-heroic, non-Homeric."

21. See above, Ch. 1, pp. 15-17.

22. E.A. Havelock, *The Greek Concept of Justice* (Cambridge, Mass. and London 1978) 196, renders *deilos* as "down and out," and *esthlos* as "noble," "distinguished." V. Ehrenberg, *Polis und Imperium,* 92, translates them as "poor man," and "the wealthy."

23. Starr, *Economic and Social Growth,* 166. See Starr's discussion of "The Agricultural World," pp. 147-67.

24. J.D. Beazley, *The Development of Attic Black-Figure* (Berkeley and Los Angeles 1951), esp. pp. 22, 38, 49-50, 61; T.B.L. Webster, *Potter and Patron in Classical Athens* (London 1972) 297-300. For grave *stēlai* and bronze figurines depicting warriors and horsemen, see Starr, *Economic and Social Growth,* 121, 132-33. Cf. Jeffery, *Archaic Greece,* 30-31, 90.

25. Translated by Rex Warner. According to A.W. Gomme in his *Commentary on Thucydides,* I (Oxford 1956) *ad loc.,* the adoption of these fashions took place in the sixth century and continued through 480 or 470 B.C.

26. H.I. Marrou, *A History of Education in Antiquity,* tr. by G. Lamb (London and New York 1956) 366, note 5, asserts that there are no homosexual allusions at all in Homer. Cf. D.M. Robinson and E.J. Fluck, *A Study of Greek Love Names* (Baltimore 1937) 18-19, who list possible oblique references to homosexuality in the epics. Some, e.g. Finley, *WO,* 138, are willing to see the absence of overt mention as another example of Homeric "expurgation," but it is hard to see why, if male homosexuality was part of the early warrior ideal, Homer would not have given it a prominent place.

27. A.W. Gouldner, *The Hellenic World. A Sociological Analysis* (New York 1965), has made the interesting suggestion that Greek pederasty was partly the result of a "crisis of intimacy" occasioned by the decline of the kinship system (reliance on relatives) — hence the need for friends. But within a highly

competitive culture there is an inevitable ambivalence in friendship, and, therefore, a need for relationships which provide a basis for trust and security. Accordingly, "pederasty must be most common among the males most deeply involved in the contest system, and thus most common among the upper classes or aristocracy" (pp. 60-62).

28. C.M. Bowra, "Xenophanes, Fragment 3," in *CQ* 35 (1941) 119-26, details other examples of luxury during this period. Bowra also maintains that the chief concern of Xenophanes was that this luxury was both useless and harmful to the polis. See also Starr, *Economic and Social Growth*, 134-35, 139-46 on aristocratic leisure activities and luxury.

29. E.g. *Il.* 6.161; *Hom. hymn* 10.2; cf. *Il.* 15.32.

30. Actually *aischros* is found only once in Homer pertaining to persons (Thersites in *Il.* 2.216); otherwise it refers to actions. *Aischistos* (the superlative), used of Thersites, seems to mean "ugliest," in which case the aesthetic reference predates Mimnermus' usage, and also shows the genesis of the important aristocratic notion that lack of physical beauty is an indication of lower class status.

31. Contrast this with Tyrtaeus, fr. 9.39-42D, where the old, brave warrior is honored by his fellow townsmen.

32. Cf. fr. 4D, where Tithonous' immortality is "an old age chillier than painful death," and fr. 6 where he prays to die in his sixtieth year without disease or care.

33. E.g. frgs. 10, 12a, 13, 14D.

34. The fragments of Anacreon and Ibycus are from D.L. Page, *Poetae Melici Graeci* (Oxford 1962).

35. Athenaeus 13.600d (8 Diehl) preserves a poem by Critias in praise of Anacreon, in which the poet is represented as completely devoted to wine, women and song. For some acute observations on Anacreon's psychology see C.M. Bowra, *Greek Lyric Poetry*, 2nd ed. (Oxford 1961) 272, 282-84 (hereafter cited as *GLP*). Anacreon was not, of course, devoid of civic sense. Like all Greeks of the period he was a man of the polis and some of his fragments attest his patriotism and awareness of the citizen's duties; but very few of the surviving poems speak of fighting and glory, and there is a very definite sense of withdrawal from the simple heroic code of prowess and valor. Cf. frgs. 382, 391, 401, 419 Page.

36. For further citations and fuller discussion of these themes see Fränkel, *EGPPh*, 291-303, and Kirkwood, *Monody*, 150-77. Thus Fränkel speaks of Anacreon's "lightly jesting tone," "light, bantering manner," "softness and delicacy," and his "admirable occasional poetry, like pieces of fine goldsmith's work," with their "late archaic prettiness." On his part, Kirkwood calls Anacreon an "ironist" and "satirist"; his "sophisticated intellectual verse" lacks "passion and earnestness." What characterizes "the sophisticated playfulness of his poetry of love and wine" is its "limpid and graceful phraseology," and "graceful self-mockery." Kirkwood notes especially the "theme of moderation" and "strong feeling for civilized behavior" in Anacreon's poetry.

37. In Sparta, where all activity was singlemindedly channeled towards the interests of the state, there were severe restrictions on social differentiation among the citizens, who proudly called themselves "equals" *(homoioi)*. All Spartiates, including their "kings," ate the same food in common messes; luxury was forbidden, softness despised. Unwieldy iron spits were used in place of coinage to

discourage economic disparity. That the vaunted Spartan equality soon ceased to be true in fact means simply that the urge for social differentiation and superior prestige was ultimately stronger.

38. Fränkel, *EGPPh,* 283. On the channeling "into public contexts" of choral songs, displays and distribution of wealth, funeral and marriage processions, sacrifices, religious festivals, see S.C. Humphreys, *Anthropology and the Greeks* (London, Henley, Boston 1978) 219.

39. Fragments of Alcaeus are quoted from E. Lobel and D. Page (edd.) *Poetarum Lesbiorum Fragmenta* (Oxford 1955). I have adapted the translations of D. Page, *Sappho and Alcaeus* (Oxford 1955).

40. See Page, *Sappho and Alcaeus,* 176. For a capsule description of the political strife in Lesbos see Andrewes, *Tyrants,* 92-99.

41. Page, *Sappho and Alcaeus,* 177. See also W. Donlan, "Changes and Shifts in the Meaning of Demos in the Literature of the Archaic Period," *PP* 135 (1970) 391-392, 394.

42. *Sappho and Alcaeus,* 211. Cf. the comments by A.J. Podlecki, "The Language of Heroism from Homer to Pindar" in *Classics and the Classical Tradition* (University Park, Pa. 1973) 159.

43. Interestingly, it is about this time that the custom of burying arms with the corpses of warriors ceased to be prevalent. M. I. Finley, *Early Greece. The Bronze and Archaic Ages* (New York 1970) 102, comments, "it is tempting to link the disappearance of arms from the graves with the development of the hoplite phalanx since arms no longer signified exclusive social status." If this is so, then Alcaeus may be seen as attempting to memorialize the past glory of the individual warrior. His statement, "For it is noble *(kalon)* to die in Ares" (fr. 400 L-P), appears more a romantic glorification of the warrior's role (un-Homeric as the sentiment is) than a reflection of similar Tyrtaean expressions.

44. *GLP,* 139. The fragments of Alcaeus' poetry contain numerous references to mythological events and heroic legends, expressed in Homeric language. Cf. Kirkwood, *Monody,* who notes Alcaeus' "affinity for the Homeric tradition" (pp. 85ff.); see also 71-72.

45. *Kakopatridēs* (literally, "son of a *kakos* father") is found three other times in Alcaeus. In frgs. 75.12 and 106.4 L-P there is not enough context to establish who is meant. In 67.4-5 L-P the word is in the plural, a clear indication that Alcaeus lumped his enemies together as a group of "low-born" men.

46. See Page, *Sappho and Alcaeus,* 169-75; Andrewes, *Tyrants,* 94-95; Bowra, *GLP,* 151. Two facts alone — that Pittacus had been a sworn companion of Alcaeus' circle and had married into the noblest family of Lesbos, the Penthilidae (fr. 70 L-P) — make a "plebeian" Pittacus difficult to imagine.

47. Fr. 429 L-P; cf. frgs. 129.21, 70, 72. On Alcaeus' descriptions of Pittacus see H. Martin, Jr., *Alcaeus* (New York 1972) 30-31.

48. Frgs. 129, 167, 306(9) L-P.

49. For the meaning of *aisymnētēs* and the character of Pittacus' ten-year office see Andrewes, *Tyrants,* 96-99; Martin, *Alcaeus,* 29-31; Bowra, *GLP,* 136 (with notes). Pittacus instituted sumptuary legislation which limited the amount that could be spent on funerals and imposed double fines on crimes committed in drunkenness.

50. Andrewes, *Tyrants,* 55, 118. G. Busolt, *Griechische Staatskunde,* 3rd ed.,

vol. 1 (Munich 1920) 211, gives the ancient sources for the names. These are not the same as subjected native populations who tilled the soil as kinds of serfs; e.g. *helots* in Sparta, *klarōtai* in Crete, *penestai* in Thessaly, although there may be some identification or overlapping.

51. On Alcaeus' rather fierce dedication to wine and his erotic poetry see Page, *Sappho and Alcaeus,* ch. 13, "Women and Wine" (pp. 291-301) and Bowra, *GLP,* 157-63. Page, for some reason, wishes not to believe that Alcaeus wrote of homosexual attachments, but the later tradition, which had all the poetry available to it (e.g. Quintilian 10.1.2; Cicero *Tusc.* 4.33.71, *De nat. deorum* 1.28.79; Horace *Odes* 1.32.6ff.) is unequivocal. For a discussion of these ancient references see Martin, *Alcaeus,* 114-15.

52. *Alcaeus,* 52. Sappho, the great female poet of Lesbos, and a contemporary of Alcaeus, was herself obsessed with love (homosexual), beauty and style. "I love luxury . . ." she once said (fr. 58.25 L-P); another time she castigates her rival Andromeda for being enamored of some "countrified" woman in a "countrified" gown, who "does not even know how to draw her dress about her ankles" (fr. 57 L-P). Fränkel, *EGPPh,* 187, speaks of the concern of Sappho and her circle with "sense, consistency, order and propriety, over dullness, disorder, accident, and coarseness."

53. Cf. fr. 37D and Bowra, *GLP,* 276; also frgs. 412, 416 Page, and Fränkel, *EGPPh,* 299-300: Anacreon's "party poems" preach "moderation and propriety."

54. See Bowra, *GLP,* 297-300. Artemon is called *ponēros* ("worthless," "low," line 5). This is the first recorded instance of class usage of a word which later became part of the arsenal of aristocratic social vocabulary. Before this time *ponēros* meant simply "oppressed by toil."

55. In fr. 353 Page he says that "rebels" or "talkers" *(mythiētai)* rule Samos as *stasiōtai* – and these are identified by a scholiast as seamen or fishermen.

56. Cf. also frgs. 16, 17, 24b, 25, 39, 42D.

57. Jaeger, *Paideia,* I, 121, makes the point that "the rise of the lampoon in the early city-state is a symptom of the increased importance of the demos, the common people." Hipponax follows the tradition of Archilochus and Semonides (a seventh-century Ionian, who wrote a scathing indictment of womankind in a popular vein: fr. 7D). In all respects Semonides' is a peasant's view of women – their defects are qualities contrary to a common man's ideal of the practical and useful: neglect of household duties, intellectual pretensions, lack of common sense, instability, gluttony, promiscuity, love of luxury. The portrait he draws of one type (the "mare's daughter") is especially interesting: she shuns menial work, will not grind, sift, or carry out the filth, refuses to sit before the oven because of the soot, bathes two or three times a day, keeps herself perfumed, combed and wreathed with flowers – a *kakon* to her mate unless he is a *tyrannos* or king *(skēptouchos),* "the kind that takes delight in things like that" (57-70). Cf. a similar poem by Phocylides (fr. 2D).

58. Fr. 3D. See above, pp. 53-54.

59. See Fränkel, *EGPPh,* 228-30; C.M. Bowra, *Early Greek Elegists* (Cambridge, Mass. 1938) 126-27 (cited hereafter as *EGE*). In other respects Xenophanes broke with tradition, especially in his search for a universal conception of the divine as opposed to the anthropomorphic and anthropocentric vision of the gods inherited from Homer and Hesiod.

60. The line is also found in the aristocratically oriented corpus of poems which has come down to us under the name of Theognis (see below, Ch. 3, pp. 93-94), the next line of which goes: "and every man is *agathos* if he is *dikaios*" (lines 147-48). Adkins, who discusses this as Theognis' sentiment, calls it "amazing" and "startling" (*M&R*, 78). But in the light of Phocylides' other pronouncements, and in the context of the anti-aristocratic tradition, it is not at all startling that those to whom the upper-class notions of *aretē* were not significant would see man's highest accomplishment as justice.

61. This is evident both from the fragments and from the somewhat schematic description of Solon's accomplishments by Aristotle (who had all of the poems available to him) in the *Constitution of the Athenians* (Chs. 2-13). Some scholars persist in viewing Solon as an unregenerate aristocrat; others see him as a spokesman for a newly rich middle class. A.W. Gomme, "Interpretation of Some Poems of Alkaios and Sappho," *JHS* 77 (1957) 257, somewhat overstates the democratic position: "There was undoubtedly a democratic movement, that is, one of the many, the poor, against the few rich, in Athens; and Solon led it and guided it." Andrewes' assessment that "In the crisis which called him to power there is no doubt that he stands on the side of the poor," and that Solon "came forward primarily as the champion of the poor against their oppressors" (*Tyrants*, 84-85) is more balanced.

62. A commonplace of Greek ethical thought (cf. Hesiod, *Works and Days* 320ff., Theognis 197ff., Pindar, *Nem.* 8.17), but more strongly expressed here.

63. At least in frgs. 23.21 and 24.18D. It is important to note that otherwise, when Solon speaks of the dominant group, he uses terms which connote possession of power and wealth (frgs. 3.7; 5.3, 7; 10.3; 25.4; 27; cf. 1.72; 4.6). The majority of the population is described in terms denoting poverty or oppression (frgs. 3.23; 24.8-15). He also uses *dēmos* in the narrow class sense (frgs. 5.1, 7; 24.22; 25.1,6). Solon never employs birth words to indicate either group, and, in general, we may conclude that with the exception of class usage of *agathos/esthlos, kakos* and *dēmos*, his terminology is factually descriptive rather than qualitatively judgmental.

64. Cf. fr. 14D, in which the simple pleasures of life are favored over the possession of wealth and luxury.

65. Plutarch, *Solon* 21.5, 23.3; cf. Diog. Laert. 1.55; Diodorus 9.2.5. Tradition records other legislation by Solon, the apparent purpose of which was to strengthen the economic position of the poorer or the landless element; e.g. laws stating that every father had to teach his son a trade and encouraging the export of olive oil and prohibiting the export of other agricultural products. See Starr, *Economic and Social Growth*, 184-86, with notes.

66. For Fränkel, *EGPPh*, 232, this fragment "implies considerable enlightenment that in Solon's opinion goodness has nothing to do with wealth and that it attaches to its bearer permanently." This "emerging view" was a harbinger of the later distinction between "'inward' and 'outward' goods."

67. Starr, *Economic and Social Growth*, 190.

68. *Livelihood of Man*, 168.

◊

CHAPTER THREE

1. Controversy over the authorship of the collection, specifically which lines are by Theognis himself, and their dates of composition, seems never to be finally resolved. For the sake of simplification the author will be referred to as Theognis. Citations are from D. Young (ed.), *Theognis* (Leipzig 1961). The translations are mine, with frequent reliance on the Loeb translation of J.M. Edmonds.

2. *Agathos* is found 76 times in the *Theognidea;* in the *Iliad,* which is ten times longer, the word occurs 87 times. There are 41 instances of *agathos* used of persons, 20 of *esthlos,* 53 of *kakos,* 21 of *deilos* in Theognis.

3. G. Cerri, "La terminologia sociopolitica di Teognide: I," *Quaderni Urbinati* 6 (1968) 7-32, attempts to reconcile the apparent contradictions between Theognis' social and ethical usage of these terms. Cerri correctly sees that *agathos/ esthlos, kakos/deilos* combine both spheres of meaning in Theognis; the unifying element is the complex of aristocratic "presuppositions" (birth, wealth, etc.) and aristocratic "qualities" (loyalty, justice, etc.) which are produced only by a particular kind of upbringing. See P.A.L. Greenhalgh, "Aristocracy and Its Advocates in Archaic Greece," *G&R* 19 (1972).

4. This is not a universal change in fashion, of course. *Agathos* and *deilos* in Solon (fr. 1.39) mean "brave," "coward," and the words are so used frequently by fifth-century authors.

5. To these we may add fr. 100D (of uncertain ascription); also frgs. 382, 391, 419 Page (see above, Ch. 2, note 35). The inward-turning quality of Anacreon's poetry is described by Lesky, *Hist. of Greek Lit.,* 176-77. The fragments of Stesichorus (a Sicilian poet, who died in the 550's) contain similar sentiments. One begins: "O Muse, thrusting away wars and celebrating with me the marriages of gods, the feasts of men and the festivities of the blessed . . ." (fr. 210 Page). The *Theognidea* is firmly in this tradition, as we can see in some tamperings with the martial poetry of the Spartan Tyrtaeus. After quoting the rousing quatrain which urges martial valor (fr. 9.13-16D), Theognis adds a hedonistic postscript, which essentially subverts the Tyrtaean lines (1003-12). For this and other changes see D. Young, "Borrowings and self-adaptations in Theognis," *Miscellanea Critica* I (Leipzig 1965) 309-11.

6. Cf. lines 535-38, 1109-14.

7. M.I. Finley, *The Ancient Economy* (Berkeley and Los Angeles 1973) 41. The destitute man, "altogether without resources," was called *ptōchos,* "beggar." Starr, *Economic and Social Growth,* 123, has estimated that the largest landholdings in Attica were about 30 hectares of farmland, while the smallest plots, minimally sufficient to support a family, might range from two to four hectares (about five to ten acres). Starr further estimates that the Solonian class of *zeugitai* at Athens (those who served as hoplites) possessed an average of 12 hectares per family (pp. 154-55).

8. Starr, *Economic and Social Growth,* 123 ff., coins the term, "semi-aristocrats," to identify a "much larger group, not so well-to-do, probably not so well-born," who, "together with men of ancient lineage . . . helped to form the upper classes of historical Greece" (p. 124). These are the *kakoi* of Theognis and Solon. The "semi-aristocrats" were not a commercial and industrial urban middle class (although some traders and artisans might be included, p. 125); rather, they were

the "middling farmers," landowners of some substance, also identified by Starr as the "hoplite class." They "shared the cultural patterns of men of ancient blood and wealth rather than upholding a distinct social code" (p. 128). Starr's invention of a specific group of this kind strikes me as an attempt to layer Greek society too precisely. And there is an inherent difficulty in Starr's distinction. If, as he maintains, this group "sought to imitate the aristocrats socially," but were regarded by them as *kakoi,* that is, were completely disdained by the élite for their "social assertiveness" (p. 128), where could they have stood in ideological relationship to the aristocrats, so jealous of their own position − except in an adversarial posture? There *was* a middle group (composed of medium farmers and a lesser number of trader/artisans), but it had more the character of a "middle mass" in a society which, by all the evidence we have, recognized only two social strata − aristocrats and the rest − or, in economic terms, "the rich" and "the poor." However much (or little) social and economic gradation there may have been among non-aristocrats, the Greeks themselves never conceptualized it beyond vague references to "the middle." It is true that at the upper level of the middle group distinctions will have blurred somewhat (thus Theognis' complaints about intermarriage), and that the decline of the aristocracy's political power was met by a greater degree of civic participation on the part of non-nobles, resulting (by the fifth century) in a broadening of the power base, and consequently some identification of interest. Nevertheless, despite a certain convergence, the consciousness, on both sides, of the distinction between aristocrats and non-aristocrats remained a fundamental fact of life through the period studied in this book. From this it follows that the value systems of the two groups not only remained distinct (aside from the sharing of a collective body of cultural assumptions), but as the political and economic gap between them narrowed, the socio-psychological differences increased.

9. More traditional statements are 561-62, where he hopes that he may have some of his enemies' wealth and much to give to his friends. He prays that Peace and Wealth may possess the city (885), that he may warm his heart with youth and riches (1122), that he may live "rich, apart from evil cares" (1153).

10. E.g. Tyrtaeus fr. 6.7.8D; Archilochus fr. 58.5D; Mimnermus fr. 2.12D.

11. See also lines 321-22, 523-24, 751-52, 865-66, 1061-62.

12. See 465-66, where the embracing of *aretē* and *dikaia* is contrasted to being overcome by gain, "which is *aischron.*"

13. E.g. 42-52, 1147-50. Greed is also a universal vice, of course; e.g. 83-86, 401-406.

14. J. Ferguson, *Moral Values in the Ancient World* (London 1958) 20: "Theognis, presented with the spectacle of impoverished aristocrats, cannot equate *arete* with wealth."

15. B. Snell, *The Discovery of the Mind* (Cambridge, Mass. 1953) 171: "For Theognis material gain has, in contrast with earlier views, become an enemy of virtue." E.L. Highbarger, "Literary Imitation in the *Theognidea,*" *AJP* 50 (1929) 350-51, notes that Theognis has changed the meaning of *aretē* from that which is purely physical to the sphere of the moral and intellectual. Jaeger, citing lines 149-50: even the *pankakos* man can have wealth, but only the few have *aretē* (see above, p. 83), says, "Theognis holds that arete is the quality which characterizes the true nobleman when the presence or absence of wealth is left out of account:

namely the very rare quality of spiritual nobility" (*Paideia* I, 203).

16. Simonides: Aristotle, in Stobaeus, *Anth.* 86.25; Aristotle: *Pol.* 1293b 10; cf. 1272b 36; 1273a 23, 26; *Ath. Pol.* 1.1; 3.2; Euripides: *Phoen.* 439-42. Arnheim, *Aristocracy in Greek Society*, 170, calls primacy of birth the "bedrock of aristocracy," and of the aristocracy's assertion of its pre-eminence; but, "with the growth of trade new opportunities opened up to the non-noble, and the resultant social mobility made the old equation of birth and worth seem less self-evident than before."

17. Lines 39-52 (cf. 1081-82b) imply power in the hands of aristocratic leaders *(hēgemones)* who have "turned to plunge into great evil-doing." These nobles (to whom Theognis applies the epithet *kakoi*), by aiming at tyranny will ruin the polis. Like all Greek aristocrats what Theognis feared and hated even more than the gradual usurpation of political power by the lower class was the sudden seizure of absolute power by one man. This was the basis of Alcaeus' hatred of Pittacus, and Solon's most pressing concern. The *dēmos*, of course, is despised for being easy prey (they are *philodespotos*, 849). Thus it is never a crime to lay low a "tyrant who devours the *dēmos* " (1181-82); he will not mourn a *tyrannos anēr* any more than a tyrant would grieve at his death (1203-06; cf. 891-94, a reference to Euboea and the Cypselid dynasty). Since the would-be tyrant is usually a fellow aristocrat there is something of an ethical dilemma:

> Neither raise up a man to be a *tyrannos* in hopes, yielding to gain; nor kill him if you have sworn an oath to him by the gods
>
> (823-24).

18. Above, p. 83.

19. The neglect of patriotism is consonant with the few references to war and martial zeal in Theognis and other sixth-century aristocratic poets. Lines 541-42, 603-04, 667-82, 757-68, 825-30, 855-56, 865-68, 947-48, 1003-06, 1043-44 (some of which have been discussed above) are all the references to patriotism or to concern for the polis. Cf. 549-54, 887-90, a war going on. As Fränkel notes, in addition to a lack of "patriotic feeling" in the *Theognidea*, there is "little indication of a feeling of responsibility for others or of service to a cause. Family relationships are very seldom mentioned and there is no mention of the duties of office" (*EGPPh*, 413, and notes 27, 28, 29).

20. See also 35-38, 563-66, 792, 1165-66: associate with the good; 59-60, 65-72, 613-14, 1025-26, 1167-68: the counsel of the *agathoi* is superior, that of the *kakoi* is inferior and untrustworthy.

21. In 979-82 a true friend is one who acts as well as says, and who proves himself *agathos* in deed. Cf. 83-86, 115-28, 1049-54, 1087-90.

22. Other statements that an *agathos* is a good friend, the *kakos* a bad one: 105-14, 853-54, 955-56, 1083-84, 1151-52, 1377-80.

23. E.g. 295-98, 309-12, 323-30, 399-400, 409-14, 467-98, 509-10, 627-28, 841-44, etc. See Bowra, *EGE*, 161-62, for further examples.

24. Cf. lines 355, 395-98, 445-46, 555-56 (=1178 a-b), 591-92, 1029-30, 1162 a-d.

25. According to Fränkel, *EGPPh*, 421, what Theognis means by *tolmān* is "a strong and composed attitude of mind; a spirit of resistance which sets the oppressed on his feet again; a kind of active patience which strengthens those who

have been weakened . . . based upon a peculiar elasticity which is produced by simultaneously recognizing and disregarding the ugly truths . . . for in the behavior of the self-controlled man the dark depths of sorrow are concealed behind calmness."

26. H. North, *Sophrosyne* (Ithaca, N.Y. 1966) 17. Cf. lines 39-42, 377-80, 753-54, 1081-1082 (*sōphrosynē* opposed to *hybris*).

27. See North, *Sophrosyne*, 18-19 on this passage. North also points out that *sōphrosynē* in Theognis 699-718 has a specific intellectual connotation, another new direction.

28. Phocylides' fr. 12D, in which he expresses a wish to be *mesos* in the polis, relates to the ordinary man's lack of pretension (see above, Ch. 2, p. 68. Solon's keen interest in the mean has no "class" significance (North, *Sophrosyne*, 15). It is at this time that the doctrine of "nothing in excess" *(mēden agan)* becomes associated with the aristocratically oriented shrine of Apollo at Delphi.

29. Lines 233, 847. Other lines on intellectual capacity and their moral implications are 59-60, 279-82, 369-70, 453-56, 625-26, 631-32, 1037, 1167-68. See Bowra, *GLP*, 334 (citing lines 279-82): "The nobles arrogated the name of wise to themselves, and thought their democratic adversaries fools."

30. Cf. lines 29-30, 53-60, 289-90, 393-98, 547-48, 749-52. In 39-52 the (aristocratic) leaders are *kakoi* and *adikoi;* see above, note 17.

31. *Paideia* I, 203. Cerri (above, note 3) 14, note 13, gives a summary of the controversy. Adkins, in his discussion of this "amazing" couplet (*M&R*, 78-79) says that this notion "smashes the whole framework of Homeric values," but that it did not become generally accepted and only reemerges as a result of the interior moral speculation of the late fifth and fourth centuries. Arnheim, *Aristocracy in Greek Society*, 164-67, attacks Adkin's position. On Phocylides' maxim, see above, Ch. 2, note 60.

32. In these examples *aretē* still retains its essential sense of "ability," "achievement," "success." Other instances of *aretē* in the collection have this meaning: 129, 317, 402, 624, 654, 904, 971, 1062, 1074. Cerri (above, note 3) 31, note 36, asserts that in the frequent opposition between "few" and "many," these words signify *agathoi* and *kakoi* for Theognis.

33. Fränkel, *EGPPh*, 401; see Fränkel's summary, pp. 422-25, in which he contrasts Theognis' attitude ("aristocratic" in a social sense, but intellectually and spiritually "bourgeois") with Pindar's loftier aristocratic vision.

34. The poems of Pindar are cited from the Teubner text of B. Snell, *Pindarus*, 2 vols. (Leipzig 1964, 1971). The chronology of the odes is that of C.M. Bowra, *Pindar* (Oxford 1964). The translations are my own, with frequent reliance on those of J.E. Sandys in the Loeb edition of Pindar, and R. Lattimore, *The Odes of Pindar* (Chicago 1947). The games were held at regular intervals at Olympia, Delphi, Nemea and the Isthmus of Corinth. The traditional date of the founding of the most prestigious festival, the Olympian, is 776 B.C.; the others were regularized in the early 500's, coinciding with the heyday of aristocratic ostentation.

35. The usage of *agathos* in Pindar reflects this: the *agathoi* are a group set apart from the rest of the citizenry (*Pyth.* 2.81, 96; 3.71, 83; 4.285; 10.71); the *agathoi* are fittest to rule (*Pyth.* 10.71); they are wise (*Ol.* 7.91; *Pyth.* 3.83). Pindar's usage of *eslos* is similar, but somewhat more general.

36. *Cheirōn* occurs twice; in *Isth.* 4.34 it means "inferior" in a physical sense and in *Nem.* 8.22 it is opposed to *esloi* in a generalized ethical sense.

37. Cf. *Pyth.* 1.84; *Nem.* 3.40-41; *Parth.* 1.8-10. The same idea is found in Theognis 797-98: "One man blames, another praises the *agathoi*, but of the *kakoi* there is no mention at all."

38. *Ol.* 2.10-11; 10.20; 11.19-20; 13.13; *Pyth.* 5.17-19, 76; 8.44-45; 10.12; *Nem.* 1.27-28; 5.40-41; 6.8, 15-16; 11.12, 33-38; *Isth.* 1.39-40; 3.13-14. Pindar's insistence on "the genealogical principle" is well demonstrated by P. W. Rose, "The Myth of Pindar's First Nemean," *HSCP* 78 (1974) 151-55.

39. A. Andrewes, *The Greeks* (New York 1967) 201. The numerous local festivals, on the other hand (like the Panathenaea at Athens, a pet project of the tyrant Pisistratus), were more consciously civic and patriotic and gave greater scope to the religious, athletic and cultural expressions of the populace.

40. See above, Ch. 2, p. 65.

41. D. Kagan, *The Great Dialogue. A History of Greek Political Thought From Homer to Polybius* (New York 1965) 54. Greenhalgh (above note 3) 204-207, shows that while the concept of the aristocracy's "hereditary capacity" and their "hereditary fitness to rule" is stated with little reservation in Pindar, the *Theognidea* recognizes the "problem of noble failure" (e.g. lines 305-308), a significant difference in outlook.

42. V. Ehrenberg, *From Solon to Socrates* (London 1967) 175ff.; cf. also p. 123.

43. Other Pindaric statements on wealth are consistent: wealth must not be hoarded but enjoyed and distributed (*Nem.* 1.31-32; *Isth.* 1.67-68); greed is dangerous, but is regarded as a universal vice and not connected with the *kakoi* (*Pyth.* 3.54; 4.139-40; *Nem.* 11.47-48; cf. *Pyth.* 1.92; 8.13; *Nem.* 7.18; 9.33).

44. E.g. *Ol.* 9.70ff.; *Nem.* 3.36-37; 10.73ff.; *Isth.* 6.35ff. See Bowra, *Pindar*, 386-88.

45. *Ol.* 2.86; 7.91; 9.100; 11.10; *Pyth.* 1.42.

46. In *Pyth.* 5.107-15 the "understanding" *(synetoi)* praise the victor, who is wise, courageous, strong and skilled in poetry and athletics; and in *Nem.* 8.41 the *sophoi* are linked with the just *(dikaioi)*. Cf. *Isth.* 5.11; *Nem.* 6.4-5.

47. In *Ol.* 2.83-86 Pindar says that his shafts are aimed at the "understanding" *(synetoi)* but the crowd *(to pan)* needs interpreters; and in *Ol.* 5.16 those who are successful and prosperous "seem *sophoi* even to the citizens *(politai).*"

48. Cf. *Ol.* 13.11-12, where the poet speaks of his unerring boldness *(tolmā eutheia)*. In *Nem.* 7.59 the victor's father has "a daring spirit for noble deeds" *(tolmā kalōn)*, and in *Nem.* 10.30 *tolmā* is opposed to a "toil-avoiding heart." See also *Pyth.* 5.117.

49. North, *Sophrosyne*, 24-26.

50. See W. Donlan, "The Origin of *Kaloskagathos*," *AJP* 94 (1973) 365-74.

51. J.D. Beazley, *The Development of Attic Black Figure* (Berkeley and Los Angeles 1951) 64; D.M. Robinson and E.J. Fluck, *A Study of the Greek Love-Names* (Baltimore 1937) 66-69.

52. The lines which follow this couplet (935-38) provide a good example of the change in values. They are obviously adapted from Tyrtaeus (fr. 9.37-42D), but Tyrtaeus is referring to honor won only in battle, while for Theognis it is the combining of (now generalized) *aretē* and *kallos*. Other erotic references in the

Theognidea to beauty are 994, 1017-19, 1259-62, 1279-82, 1319-22, 1327-28, 1335-36, 1341-44, 1345-50, 1365-66, 1369-70, 1377-78. At the beginning of the *Theognidea* the Muses and Graces are made to say, "whatever is beautiful *(kalon)* is dear *(philon)*, and what is not *kalon* is not *philon*" (17). Here beauty, as Fränkel says, is "at once physical and moral beauty" (*EGPPh,* 402; cf. 418).

53. In *Nem.* 11.11-14 Pindar praises the victor's father, the victor's beauty ana his "inborn fearlessness," and ties together wealth, good looks, and might in the games. See also *Ol.* 10.99-105; *Isth.* 2.3-5. Homosexual love and the pleasures of conviviality are occasional themes in Pindar's poetry (e.g. frgs. 123; 124 a.b).

54. Fränkel, *EGPPh,* 490-91, and note 8.

55. He could, then, praise democratic Athens and write odes honoring tyrants while condemning tyranny at home. Even here, as Ehrenberg points out, "Pindar stresses the old family descent of the tyrants; thus he can see their states as examples of *eunomia,* as though they were aristocracies" (*From Solon to Socrates,* 177, note 122).

56. A.G. Woodhead, *Thucydides on the Nature of Power* (Cambridge, Mass. 1970) 68; a fault also shared by the democratic factions in the fifth century, as Woodhead points out.

57. Fränkel, *EGPPh,* 337, 487-96.

58. B.R. English, *The Problem of Freedom in Greece From Homer to Pindar* (Toronto 1938) 100. Pindar attempted to recreate the easy and natural aristocratic panhellenism of the Homeric epics, but achieved it only by ignoring the realities of quarreling city-states and narrow class interest.

59. Fränkel, *EGPPh,* 426. Cf. pp. 428, 432, 460.

Ω

CHAPTER FOUR

1. Citations of Simonides are from E. Diehl, *Anthologia Lyrica Graeca;* the translations are my own. For a perceptive analysis of the Scopas fragment see Fränkel, *EGPPh*, 307-12; the poem corrects "the system of norms and values then in force," and initiates ideas that are "entirely new and revolutionary," namely the abandonment of the archaic way of thinking in antitheses and the substitution of a "relative mode of thinking." Another poem, preserved in a papyrus fragment first published in 1959 and believed to be by Simonides, contains similar ethical thought. See W. Donlan, "Simonides, Fr. 4D and *P. Oxy.* 2432," *TAPA* 100 (1969) 71-95.

2. In his article on Theognis' language (see above, Ch. 3, note 3), G. Cerri contrasts the outlooks of Simonides, Theognis and Pindar and concludes that in the two Simonidean poems there is a conscious repudiation of "the aristocratic ethic" (pp. 31-32).

3. *From Solon to Socrates*, 173; cf. fr. 106D.

4. See Pindar fr. 110 Snell; Ehrenberg, *From Solon to Socrates*, 173-77; Bowra, *Pindar*, 110-117; P. Green, *Ancient Greece, An Illustrated History* (New York 1979) 102-03.

5. *Kakos* here has not a social but a moral meaning. Other statements of Simonides reflect a shifting of focus away from conventional aristocratic ideas; e.g. fr. 55D: "Appearance *(to dokein)* forces even the truth"; fr. 37D on *aretē*, reminiscent of Hesiod, *W&D* 289-92, but more speculative; fr. 8D: "For all things come to one horrible Charybdis, both great achievements *(aretai)* and wealth *(ploutos)*." See also frgs. 6, 9, 10.3-4, 11, 26, 48D. The message is that life is difficult, mortal achievement is illusory, all is in the hands of the gods. Other sentiments are more traditional (e.g. 57D, on pleasure), but in general Simonides' poetry is grounded in realism and in common-sense morality — hard work, piety, cooperation — which, translated into the political realm, means that "the new democratic man is fully responsible for his actions" (T.B.L. Webster, *Political Interpretations in Greek Literature* [Manchester 1948] 24).

6. The "modernity" of Simonides sometimes makes us forget that he was an almost exact contemporary of Xenophanes (*ca.* 570-475). Fränkel, *EGPPh*, 325, calls both of them relativists, apostles of enlightenment, fighting for "a rational ordering of values and for a practical code of ethics." Simonides is "the clever and lucid advocate of a rational revision of prevalent modes of thought and behavior . . . . the arrogance of self-conscious nobility must be replaced by bourgeois propriety" (p. 400).

7. Citations of Bacchylides are from *Bacchylidis carmina cum fragmentis*, ed. H. Maehler post B. Snell (Leipzig 1970). The translations are my own.

8. Bacchylides' emphasis on virtues which are both civic and pious is also seen in Ode IV.3, where Hiero, the tyrant of Syracuse, is called "just ruler of the city" *(astythemis)*, and in Ode III. 83-84, where Hiero is advised to "make glad his heart by doing pious deeds *(hosia)*, for this is the highest of gains."

9. Bacchylides was not opposed to wealth, of course, and he displays none of the bitterness on the subject often seen in Theognis; his general attitude is conventional: wealth is a good thing (fr. 4.61-62; V.53; III.81-82); greed is bad, moderation is good (XV.57ff.; fr. 1; I.165-68).

10. It should be noted that for Bacchylides *esthlos* and *chrēstos* were probably synonymous terms – the *esthlos* is the man "useful" in the community. Aristocrats and non-aristocrats in the fifth century both claimed title to the words.

11. Lesky, *Hist. of Greek Lit.*, 203; W.C. Greene, *Moira. Fate, Good and Evil in Greek Thought* (Cambridge, Mass. 1944) 81.

12. P.W. Rose, "The Myth of Pindar's First Nemean," *HSCP* 78 (1974) 152-53; see above, pp. 97-98.

13. Bowra, *GLP*, 373ff., discusses the background and the historical problems of the various *scolia*. The Attic *scolia* are cited from Page, *PMG*. The translations are my own.

14. See also frgs. 892, 903 Page.

15. Four fragments (893-896 Page) which, taken together, are called the "Harmodius Song," celebrate the slaying of the Athenian tyrant Hipparchus, son of Pisistratus, by two aristocratic lovers, Harmodius and Aristogeiton. There are many problems of dating and interpretation of these poems, in which the word *isonomos* ("with equal laws") first occurs, a word later to be a democratic catchword. See Bowra, *GLP*, 391-96 and M. Ostwald, *Nomos and the Beginnings of the Athenian Democracy* (Oxford 1969) *passim*. But, aside from these historical questions, the central fact is that they commemorate a tyrannicide by two aristocratic lovers. The poems thus indicate aristocratic hatred of one-man rule, pederastic friendship, and, very significantly, early employment of propaganda to enhance the aristocratic image.

16. Similar are frgs. 901, 904, 905 Page.

17. Thuc. 2.40.2. The translation is adapted from Rex Warner, *Thucydides. History of the Peloponnesian War* (Baltimore 1972).

18. G.E.M. de Ste. Croix, *The Origins of the Peloponnesian War* (Ithaca 1972) 349.

19. *Ibid.* 35.

20. *M&R*, 207.

21. The practice of "liturgies" was established in Athens in the fifth century; individual wealthy citizens were required to fit out a warship (trireme) or to bear the expense of a public chorus, as well as other, less costly, functions. This form of taxation was an excellent way for the author to manifest his dedication to the community, and most men of wealth with political ambitions made the most of the opportunity.

22. E.g. *gennadas* (noble), *agenēs* (of no birth), *dysgenēs* (of low birth) are found (apparently) first in the fifth century. For a fuller analysis, with contextual citations, see W. Donlan, "Social Vocabulary and its Relationship to Political Propaganda in Fifth-Century Athens," *Quaderni Urbinati* 27 (1977) 95-111.

23. Other valuative designators which appear either for the first time or with frequency include *sōphrōn* (prudent, moderate), *dexios* (clever), *ponēros* (wicked), *mochthēros* (wretched, knavish), *phaulos* (insignificant). One of the most interesting of the aristocratic words is *chrēstos* (useful, worthy), an old word, used during the archaic period with political force but in the context of civic usefulness, opposed, often, to aristocratic luxury. But in the fifth century it was appropriated by oligarchs who proclaimed *themselves* the useful members of the polis.

24. See R.A. Neil, *The Knights of Aristophanes* (Cambridge, Eng. 1909), App. II, "Political Use of Moral Terms."

25. See W. Donlan, "Changes and Shifts in the Meaning of *Demos* in the Literature of the Archaic Period," *PP* 135 (1970) 381-95; "The Origin of *Kaloskagathos*," *AJP* 94 (1973) 365-74. Also de Ste.Croix (above, note 18) 871-76. *Dēmos* and its derivatives had negative connotations only in aristocratic usage, of course. Similarly, *kaloskagathos*, by the early fourth century, had been taken over by non-aristocrats and we find the orators using it proponents of the radical democracy. Subsequently it, and most of the other social terms, lose their social bite and become general designations of ethical behavior without regard to social status.

26. See Neil (above, note 24) 209, who translates *hoi pacheis* as "the bloated." Neil notes that in Attic the word is found mainly in Herodotus and Aristophanes.

27. *EGPPh*, 321. The following description of the political attitudes of the sophists is drawn from E.A. Havelock, *The Liberal Temper in Greek Politics* (New Haven and London 1957). See also W.K.C. Guthrie, *The Sophists* (Cambridge, Eng. 1971).

28. Havelock, *Liberal Temper*, 342-43.

29. See Guthrie, *The Sophists*, 153. The translations are from K. Freeman, *Ancilla to the Pre-Socratic Philosophers* (Cambridge, Mass. 1966).

30. It is of no matter really whether or not the author himself held these sentiments to be true; the point is that they represented to the reading or listening audience the kinds of statements that proponents of particular views would be likely to make. The translations of the Athenian dramatists are my own.

31. The fifth-century Athenian dramatists often state vehemently the democratic doctrine that the *people* decide the destiny of the state, not a single ruler. See, e.g. Aeschylus, *Suppliants* 356-75, 517-18, 600-24, 698-703, 942-49; *Persians* 234-42; *Agamemnon* 1348-65; Sophocles, *O.C.* 75-80, 907-30, 1032-33; *Antigone* 726-39; Euripides, *Heraclidae* 422-24; *Suppliants* 399-454. Very explicit are Euripides, *Suppliants* 352-53 and *Phoenissae* 535-45, on equality.

32. Compare Euripides, *Helen* 1678-79: "For the gods do not hate *hoi eugeneis*, but their sufferings are greater than the mob's *(hoi anarithmētoi).*"

33. The paradox of the "noble slave" was a favorite of Euripides, e.g. *Ion* 854-56: "For one thing brings shame *(aischynē)* to slaves — the name. In every other way a slave is no more inferior *(kakiōn)* than the free, as long as he is *esthlos.*" Cf. *Helen* 1640-41; frgs. 511, 831 (Nauck). For other statements by Euripides on slaves see Guthrie, *The Sophists*, 156-58.

34. Impoverished nobles: Euripides, *H.F.* 588-92 and V. Ehrenberg, *The People of Aristophanes* (New York 1962) 110, and note 8. The upper class was naturally ill-disposed to men of no family who had become wealthy; cf. Aristophanes, *Wasps* 1309-10, Euripides, *Suppliants* 741-44. See also W.R. Connor, *The New Politicians of Fifth-Century Athens* (Princeton 1971) 155-56. The term *neoploutos* (newly-rich), found first in Aristophanes, seems to have been a pejorative (cf. Cratinus, fr. 208, *neoploutoponēroi*).

35. See Ehrenberg, *People*, 247-48, with notes. Ehrenberg's ch. 9, "Money and Property," is a measured exposition of the complex of attitudes towards wealth in the fifth and fourth centuries B.C. at Athens.

36. The date, authorship and purpose of this political pamphlet is much disputed. It may have been written as early as the 440's or as late as the 420's. See G. Bowersock, "Pseudo-Xenophon," *HSCP* 71 (1966) 33-55; also H. Frisch, *The*

Constitution of the Athenians (Copenhagen 1942). For a discussion of the socioeconomic terms in this work see G.E.M. de Ste. Croix, "The Character of the Athenian Empire," *Historia* 3 (1954) 24-25. The author groups *ponēroi, penētes, dēmos* in opposition to *gennaioi, plousioi* and *chrēstoi* (1.2). In 1.4 *ponēroi, penētes, dēmotikoi, dēmotai, cheirous* are opposed to *chrēstoi,* while in 1.9 *dexiōtatoi* and *chrēstoi* stand in contrast to *mainomenoi* (the mad) and *ponēroi,* and in 2.18 *dēmos, plēthos, penētes, dēmotikoi* are ranged against *plousios, gennaios, dynamenos.* See also 1.13, 2.14 (*dēmos* opposed to *plousioi*), 2.19 (*dēmos* equivalent to *penētes*), 2.10 *(dēmos, ochlos* opposed to *plousioi, oligoi, eudaimones).*

37. Cf. Euripides, *Electra* 37-38, frgs. 22, 95, 247, 249, 326 Nauck. At the same time, the opposite point of view can be maintained: e.g. Eur. fr. 232;cf. 235. This represents a kind of "fall back" position, and demonstrates the confused welter of opinion regarding the relative weight of birth and wealth in the fifth-century's treatment of a volatile social issue.

38. Nor, as a matter of fact, does he refute the claim to superiority based on the wisdom of the upper class – the many are implicitly contrasted with the wise counsellors, their role is merely to listen and to vote.

Although Pericles in the Funeral Oration naturally minimizes class distinctions, when he does allude to the subject he implies differences of wealth and poverty (Thuc. 2.37, 40, 42, 43). Ehrenberg, *People,* 250-51, comments on *Suppliants* 238ff. that this is a "purely theoretical" exposition, and that there "never existed any distinct social groups or classes to correspond to those three types." Ehrenberg is doubtless correct, but the point is that increasingly in the latter half of the fifth century the upper class pressed hard its natural advantage in this area and succeeded in keeping democratic apologists on the defensive, even forcing them to employ rhetorical categories which favored the wealthy few.

39. Cf. de Ste. Croix, *Origins of the Peloponnesian War,* 35, 90.

40. Which is precisely the point made by the Old Oligarch: the democracy is conducted for the benefit of the useless poor against the *chrēstoi* wealthy; the contributions of the rich in the form of liturgies are a ploy by the poor to impoverish the rich.

41. The arguments *for* democracy were also couched in the rhetoric of moral right. Theseus' defense of democracy in the *Suppliants* was that under written laws *(gegrammenoi nomoi)* "the weak and the rich have equal *dikē,"* and it is possible for the weaker to speak up against the fortunate when attacked: "Armed with *dikaia* the lesser *(meiōn)* may overcome the mighty *(megas)."* Anyone at all may bring forward some "useful counsel" *(chrēston bouleuma)* and thereby gain fame (433-41; cf. *Phoenissae* 531ff.). Otanes' plea for democracy against monarchy in Herodotus 3.80 is also based on moral arguments. He speaks of the *hybris* of the monarch, the lack of self-restraint caused by unrestricted power, the envy, jealousy, injustice and savagery that necessarily follows from one-man rule. But the rule of the *plēthos* "has the fairest name of all, equality before the law *(isonomia)."* So too, in *Suppliants* 238-45, while the divisions are economic the judgments are moral; the rich are useless and greedy, the poor are envious, beguiled by *ponēroi* politicians; those "in the middle" guard the *kosmos* of the polis.

42. Cf. *Electra* 253, where Electra calls the peasant "a poor man *(penēs)* but *gennaios* and reverent *(eusebēs)* to me." Also, fr. 53 Nauck.

43. See also 473-75, 489-98, 502-504, 627-30, 750-73, 779-81, 860-70.

44. Compare 510-16: Poverty is the reason why men perform necessary and useful work; 593: all good things *(agatha)* come from Poverty; Euripides fr. 327: a poor man is often more pious than a rich man.

45. In tone Cleon's remarks are similar to those of the Sicilian Athenagoras (above, p. 142). The chorus in Euripides' *Ion* (834-35) prefers a friend who is "an ordinary man but upright" *(phaulos chrēstos)* to one who is "wiser but evil" *(kakos sophōteros)*.

46. Thucydides is a prime example. It is not correct to term him a doctrinaire anti-democratic (like the Old Oligarch), but for him, as for the aristocratic authors of the sixth century, qualities like *sōphrosynē* and *gnōmē* were pre-eminently characteristics of the upper class. He consistently applied these to statesmen whom he admired, like Themistocles and Pericles, and denied them to men like Cleon and other leaders of the "extreme democracy." See Woodhead, *Thucydides on the Nature of Power*, 44-46; North, *Sophrosyne*, 102; P. Huart, *Gnomē chez Thucydide et ses contemporains* (Paris 1973).

47. Examples of this kind of "self-consoling" argument are frequent in Euripides; e.g. the powerless lower class is really better off than the upper class with all its troubles: *I.A.* 16-19, 446-50; birth, wealth, and power are not what determine loyalty, friendship, honest character: *Orestes* 1155-57; *Andr.* 639-41; *H.F.* 633-36; *Heraclidae* 1-5, 743-47; *Ion* 621-47; *Phoenissae* 531-67; the noble slave whose body is in bondage but whose soul is free: *Helen* 726-33; *Ion* 854-56. Cf. *Andr.* 695-705; *Ion* 834-41.

48. *Aristocracy in Greek Society*, 170-72. For lines 367-72 see above p. 213. Adkins discusses these passages at some length *M&R*, 177-78, 195-96; *MV & PB*, 115-117). Orestes, he says, "has been shocked into questioning traditional assumptions." He continues, ". . . nowhere else in the extant complete plays of Euripides is any male character commended as *agathos* for self-control or for any cooperative excellence" (*MV&PB*, 116). This is an oversimplification (see e.g. *Orestes* 902-31, *Hecuba* 592-602, and above pp. 136-37). Adkins preserves his thesis that only the success standard counted, even in the fifth century, by interpreting lines 386ff. to mean "self-control renders a man *agathos*, because men who are self-controlled are good at administering both their cities and their households." That is, if *sōphrosynē* is effective in terms of the success standard, it will be valued (*MV&PB*, 117). Adkins errs in insisting that the upper class (and hence Greek society as a whole) simply did not value highly the "cooperative" virtues. We have seen, to the contrary, that the upper class did, in fact, and by claiming them as specifically their own, aristocrats maintained their edge of superiority. The non-noble argument presented here by Euripides is an attempt at counter-claim and is not some new impulse.

49. Electra's peasant husband displays the same kind of common-sense wisdom in *Electra* 404-30 (his final appearance in the play) where he cleverly parries with her on the subject of wealth and poverty. Cf. Euripides, frgs. 168, 377 on bastards.

50. *Sophrosyne*, 75. Cf. Sophocles, *Philoctetes* 874.

51. In a variation of the *physis/nomos* dichotomy Euripides presses for equality by contrasting good qualities that are available to all men "by nature" with the appearance of such. For example, in the Electra passage "appearance"

(dokēsis), "empty opinions" *(kena doxasmata,* repeated in the *Melanippe* fragment), "hulks of flesh, empty *(kenai)* of mind, statues," are opposed to *physis.* Euripides implies that the mere appearance of excellence is what the upper class uses to intimidate and deceive the lower class. This is given more explicit utterance by an old slave in the *Electra,* who muses to himself on seeing Orestes and Pylades (550-51):

> *Eugeneis* it seems, but this may prove false, for many who are *eugeneis* are *kakoi,*

and by Andromache, who says to Menelaus:

> Oh, reputation, reputation *(doxa),* you have raised to mighty honors countless mortals who were nothing. I call blessed those who have good fame *(eukleia)* based on truth *(alētheia);* but to those whose fame is from lies *(pseudē)* I grant only the chance appearance of wisdom *(tychēi phronein dokein).*
>
> *(Andromache* 319-23)

Cf. *Electra* 394-95; *Phoenissae* 531-58. It is clear that Euripides has not worked out the problem completely; the formula *ouden ōn* (being nothing) is applied both in the aristocratic sense, applicable to the lower class, and in the moral sense of nobles who are, in reality, nothing. The focus on appearance vs. reality must be connected with the upper-class emphasis on style of life, calculated to impress the lower class.

Ω

CHAPTER FIVE

1. See above pp. 140-41 and Frisch (Ch. 4, note 36) 211-14. The Old Oligarch also says that the *dēmos* are exploiting the rich, who pay for choral performances, athletic contests and the equipping of triremes; the poor have the enjoyment of these things, for which the rich expend their money, the purpose being the impoverishment of the rich. On Greek education in general see Marrou, *A History of Education in Antiquity*.

2. Ehrenberg, *People*, 99; for a full discussion of the social effects of education, with citations from Old Comedy and other fifth-century sources, see *People*, Chs. 10 and 13.

3. See J.H. Oliver, *Demokratia, the Gods and the Free World* (Baltimore 1960) 134.

4. See C.R. Beye, *Ancient Greek Literature and Society* (Garden City 1975) 168-69. On the "cult of masculinity," see Starr, *Economic and Social Growth*, 130-33. The red-figured vases of the period after the Persian Wars, like those of the archaic period, continue to concentrate on the leisured pursuits of the upper class: athletics, hunting, drinking parties, pederasty. In his short treatise *On Hunting (Kynēgetikos)* Xenophon extols the virtues of this manly art; it makes the body healthy, improves sight and hearing, retards old age, and is the best training for war. "For men who are sound in body and mind *(psychai)* are always at the edge of success" (12.5). Again, "A good education *(paideusis kalē* = physical training) teaches a man to observe the laws and to talk and listen about *ta dikaia*" (12.14).

5. Guthrie, *The Sophists*, 50.

6. In 1450ff. the chorus congratulates Philokleon on his adaptation to a life which is "dainty and soft."

7. E.g. of a cavalry officer in *Lysistrata* 561 and of a homosexual aristocrat in *Clouds* 100; cf. *Knights* 1121. See *Knights* 1331-32, *Clouds* 984 on the (by then) old-fashioned custom of wearing the *tettix* or "cicada" in the hair-knot.

8. Compare *Clouds* 545; *Ploutos* 170-71, 571-74; *Birds* 1280-83.

9. The word is *Komētamynia*. Amynias was an aristocrat, general in 423/2, suspected of Spartan sympathies, notorious for his long hair, effeminacy and foppishness. K.J. Dover, *Greek Homosexuality* (Cambridge, Mass. 1978) 142, notes that "long hair was regarded as characteristic of wealthy and leisured young men," and that the slighting references to long hair were expressions of "class antagonism." The verb *komaō* "is used in comedy in the sense 'give oneself airs,' 'think oneself a cut above other people'" (p. 78).

10. The proposal that the latter be given precedence in mating with Athenian women is seen as "a democratical notion" *(dēmotikē gnōmē)* and a "mocking" of the former.

11. Compare *Clouds* 872ff., 985ff., 1002ff., 1045ff.; Pherecrates frgs. 2, 29; Plato Comicus fr. 208; Cephisodorus fr. 3; Phrynicus fr. 3; Cratinus frgs. 98, 100; *Adespota* 56; Lysias 4.7-8, 16.11. See Ehrenberg, *People*, 104-105, 243.

12. Cf. 74, 243. Hunting was another of the aristocratic pursuits that made distinctions of class so visible. See *Knights* 1382-83 and *Wasps* 1202-04.

13. *Wasps* 1025-28; *Peace* 762-63.

14. *Knights* 732-40, 867-77; *Clouds* 973-83, 1022-23, 1088-1100; *Acharnians*

716; *Wasps* 686-91; *Ecc.* 102ff.; Lysias 3 *(passim);* 14.26. See Ehrenberg, *People,* 100-102.

15. See W.K. Lacey, *The Family in Classical Greece* (Ithaca 1968) 157-58. Cf. Aristophanes fr. 338 (from *Thesmophoriazusae* II) where *lakōnizein,* "to play the Spartan," is glossed by ancient commentators as "to be a pederast."

16. Dover, *Greek Homosexuality,* 151; see pp. 194-96.

17. Dover, *Greek Homosexuality,* 198.

18. Dover, *Greek Homosexuality,* 151. Dover states that the central characters (and bulk of the audience) of comedy were more heterosexually oriented. Prerequisites for homosexual courtship were "impressive gifts" and "leisure," not available to the non-wealthy (p. 150).

19. Dover, *Greek Homosexuality,* 201-02. Cf. P. Slater, *The Glory of Hera* (Boston 1968) 59. Beye (above, note 4) 157, identifies upper-class homosexuality with imitation of Sparta and the desire for an aristocratic exclusiveness which had overtones of kinship affiliation. A.W. Gouldner's discussion (*The Hellenic World,* 60-64) is enlightening in this regard. He concludes that "pederasty must be most common among the males most deeply involved in the contest system, and thus most common among the upper class or aristocracy. This, in fact, appears to be the case. In particular, the section of the aristocracy that affects the Spartan manner, the *Lakōnizontes* (or Spartan sympathizers), view pederasty as a Spartan and hence noble tradition."

20. Certainly it is not the teaching of Socrates that is parodied in the *Clouds,* nor does Aristophanes give an accurate portrayal of the instruction furnished by the sophists to the wealthy young men of Athens. Aristophanes, as artist and moralist, is constrained to fix concrete blame for what he and others saw as dangerous departures from older and more socially productive ideals. By concentrating on Socrates and the distorted popular image of the sophists (few in his audience had ever heard one teach) the poet confounds, perhaps purposely, cause and effect. Aside from the moral and philosophic "messages" put in the mouths of the two Arguments (Wrong Argument disclaiming, for example, the existence of justice, utilizing "sophistic" methods), the picture of upper-class manners and lifestyle that emerges conforms exactly to our other information on the subject. See K.J. Dover's Introduction to his edition of the *Clouds* (Oxford 1968).

21. Brasidas was the most prominent Spartan general of the time; the clothing and beard-style described here are Spartan.

22. E.g. Thuc. 8.48.3; 854.4; 8.81.2; cf. Aristophanes, *Lysistrata* 577.

23. *Knights* 257. For other citations see Ehrenberg, *People,* 98, note 9 and 109-10. In Old Comedy partisans of the democracy seem positively paranoid about the possible subverters of the constitution. For a recent, brief discussion of the political clubs see Connor, *New Politicians,* 25-29.

24. To the modern mind Alcibiades' defection, which actually included plotting the military destruction of his own country, is unspeakable treason (every American school child remembers the awful lesson of Benedict Arnold); yet Alcibiades' behavior is but another illustration of the precedence of the claims of class over all other appeals. Alcibiades gives an *apologia* in the same speech (6.92.2-4) saying that he was an exile because of the *ponēria* of those who drove him out, he was a lover of his country *(philopolis)* when he held his citizen's rights, but not when he was wronged; he is, in fact, a true *philopolis,* because he is striving to

recover a country he has lost. Alcibiades' sophistic argument perfectly represents the aristocratic tendency to separate themselves from the rest of the community. We are not surprised to learn that Alcibiades had previously re-established himself as *proxenos* (public representative) to the Spartans and that he was an hereditary guest-friend *(patrikos xenos)* to a Spartan ephor. The name Alkibiades was, in fact, as Thucydides tells us (8.6.3), a Spartan name.

25. Examples abound; see Ehrenberg, *People (passim)*, and for a recent discussion see de Ste. Croix, *The Origins of the Peloponnesian War*, App. 29, "The Political Outlook of Aristophanes." De Ste. Croix notes that Aristophanes treats two very prominent politicians of the day, Alcibiades and Nicias, quite gently, and that the rich (except for "demagogues" who are accused of getting rich from politics) are seldom satirized (pp. 360-62). The negative portrayal of democratic politicians acting in a democratic manner has often beguiled modern observers. Thus Jaeger can say of Cleon: "Athenians who were accustomed to the magnificent manners and intellectual nobility of Pericles turned with disgust from the common tanner whose vulgarity brought discredit on the whole nation" (*Paideia* I, 366).

26. Connor, *New Politicians*, 171ff., offers an explanation for Old Comedy's prejudice against Cleon and other demagogues: they were attacked precisely because they consciously repudiated the old values and the old style: "He offended not because he was contemptible, but because he showed contempt for a system that others had accepted" (p. 174).

27. The Greek attitude towards banausic occupations brings up the subject of slavery, which, along with attitudes towards race, has hardly been mentioned, despite their importance to a full understanding of social ideology. Equality of individuals for the Greeks was restricted to those who shared real or fictive kinship; and, despite sporadically expressed feeling that slaves and barbarians ought to be regarded as equal, this attitude persisted throughout antiquity. Because of a number of complex factors — among which was technological stagnation, which necessitated slave labor as the only means of increasing production — slavery was an apparent economic necessity for the Greeks. Since chattel slaves (in contrast to the various forms of helotage) were totally outside the framework of civic rights and obligations, they did not constitute a "social class," and hence do not figure at all in discussions of social problems.

28. Austin and Vidal-Naquet, *Economic and Social History*, 131-41; S. C. Humphreys, "Economy and society in classical Athens," in *Anthropology and the Greeks*, 136-58. De Ste. Croix, *Origins of the Peloponnesian War*, sees the war itself as a struggle between oligarchy and democracy, extended to the dependent states of each power (pp. 34-49).

29. *New Politicians*, 196-97. See the whole discussion on pp. 175-98. Alcibiades represents a third alternative, by appealing alternately to the *dēmos* and to the oligarchs; but his *style* was never anything but purely aristocratic. See also P. MacKendrick, *The Athenian Aristocracy: 399 to 31 B.C.* (Cambridge, Mass. 1969) 3-27, who details the careers of aristocrats and *nouveaux riches* in the "unaristocratic fourth century."

30. *Sophrosyne*, 137. One of the charges against the younger Alcibiades was that he had fraudulently served in the (less dangerous) cavalry instead of the infantry. In his defense of Mantitheus (see above, p. 161) Lycias is at pains to

show that Mantitheus, although enrolled as a knight, preferred hoplite service (16. 13), and that his private and public life were free from the vices of drinking, dicing, etc., that he was a true democrat and aided the polis as much as his means would allow.

31. Adkins, *M&R*, 210-13. See Humphreys, *Anthropology and the Greeks*, 233: "Attic society was becoming more complex and more mobile; the old aristocratic conception of *aretē*, in which class attributes, status obligations, and more abstract moral qualities were inextricably mingled, was no longer adequate. Virtue had to be democratic, the same for all men; at the same time it had to be rational, adaptable to all circumstances."

32. North, *Sophrosyne*, 174. This same kind of argument can be found in fourth-century orators who were unfriendly to the democracy. See North, *Sophrosyne*, 146, on Isocrates' *Niocles* (46), where the *sōphrosynē* and *metriōtēs* which are present by means of reasoning and good judgment are superior to the same qualities which come through nature and chance. Otherwise the old fifth-century arguments on the primacy of birth, wealth, life-style, muted to some extent, and given a bourgeois flavor, are duly produced by Isocrates and other *laudatores temporis acti*.

33. Arnheim's conclusion, *Aristocracy in Greek Society*, 159, is typical: ". . . the dominant ideology amongst the ancient Greeks was an aristocratic one." Cf. Austin and Vidal-Naquet, *Economic and Social History*, 16: ". . . aristocratic values were by and large not seriously challenged."

34. *Economic and Social Growth*, 130.

35. Terms like "social revolution," "class struggle," "class warfare," are much too extreme to describe the internal strife *(stasis)* of Greek *poleis*. The actual extent of bloody class war was limited in Greece until well into the fifth century, when economic differentiation became sufficiently severe to produce a true polarization of interests. A case in point is the restraint of the restored democracy in Athens in 403. After the crude excesses of the oligarchical "Thirty" in 404, which included executions and banishments on a large scale, the democratic regime did not retaliate in kind but reacted with remarkable mildness and moderation. Cf. Aristotle *Ath. Pol.* 50.3.

36. Andrewes, *The Greeks*, 192-194.

Ω

INDEX

- Abdera, 131.
- Achaeans, 8.
- *achreios,* 32, 117, 122.
- *achrēstos,* 170.
- *adikia,* 145.
- *adikos,* 71, 91, 93, 199.
- Aeschines, 176.
- Aeschylus, 204.
- Aesop, 49.
- Africa, 104.
- *agathos,* 4, 15, 16, 32ff., 41, 72ff., 77ff., 86, 87, 89ff., 104f., 107, 109, 110, 113, 114, 116, 119, 120, 126, 127, 131, 144, 148, 163, 176, 177, 184, 187, 189ff., 190, 195, 196, 206.
- *agenēs,* 203.
- *agnōmosynē,* 92.
- agriculture, 22, 26, 33, 36, 70, 74.
- *aidōs,* 47, 92, 93.
- *aischros,* 54, 79, 94, 114, 135, 137, 140, 145, 192, 197.
- *aischynē,* 204.
- *aisymnētēs,* 62, 193.
- *akolasia,* 171.
- Alcaeus, 59-63, 65, 81, 104, 120, 198.
- Alcemeonids, 119, 123, 164.
- Alcibiades, 168ff., 173, 175, 209, 210.
- Alcibiades, son of Alcibiades, 174f.
- *amathēs,* 146, 148, 157, 160.
- *amathia,* 145, 148ff.
- Anacreon, 55ff., 63ff., 67, 79f., 92, 120, 196.
- Ananius, 67.
- *andreia,* 120.
- *andreios,* 151, 152, 159.
- *anepistēmosynē,* 172.

- *anoia*, 170, 171.
- Antiphon, 131.
- *aphneios*, 184.
- *aphrōn*, 80, 90, 93.
- *aphrosynē*, 117.
- *apistos*, 172.
- *aporoi*, 128.
- *apragmōn*, 122.
- *apragmosynē*, 122.
- Archaic period, 35ff., 57f., 63, 67, 81, 86, 95, 109, 119, 155.
- Archilochus, 44-49, 53ff., 61, 65, 81, 90, 100, 194, 197.
- *archōn*, 66, 69, 132.
- *aretē*, 6, 7, 18, 23, 33, 34, 41ff., 66ff., 74, 81, 83, 84, 91ff., 100, 102, 103, 105, 106, 107, 109ff., 114, 116, 117, 118, 125, 145, 157, 176, 177, 197, 199, 200, 202, 211.
- Argives, 10.
- Aristophanes, 133, 145-59, 157, 159, 161, 163, 164, 166, 167, 173, 204, 209, 210.
- *aristos*, 19, 23, 32, 127, 135, 143, 144, 150, 151, 156, 187.
- Aristotle, 39, 48, 85, 179, 195, 197.
- Ascra, 46.
- Asia, 2, 104.
- Asius, 54.
- Athenagoras, 142, 206.
- Athens, 68ff., 106, 113, 123ff., 131, 136, 140, 156, 158, 166, 168ff., 196, 200, 201, 209, 211.
- Attica, 69, 119.
- *autarkeia*, 172.

- Bacchylides, 116ff., 202, 203.
- *basileus*, 2, 6, 16, 20, 22, 24, 25, 27ff., 31, 34, 50, 69, 122, 187.
- *beltiōn*, 127, 142, 145, 148, 170, 175.
- *bdelyros*, 157.
- birth, see lineage.
- Boeotia, 26.
- *boulē*, 6, 124, 156.
- Brasicas, 209.

- Callinus, 42, 44, 50, 65, 114.
- Ceos, 113, 116.
- *charis*, 56, 91, 125.
- *cheirōn*, 16, 128, 200, 205.

INDEX

- chief, 17ff., 25, 26ff., 38, 69; see *basileus*.
- chiefdom, 2, 9, 13, 17ff., 25, 31, 33, 69.
- *chrēstos*, 66, 117, 136, 137, 138, 145ff., 148, 152, 157, 176, 203, 205, 206.
- Cicero, 57, 194.
- class, social, 9, 18ff., 23, 32ff., 36f., 38, 39f., 44, 47, 48, 49ff., 57, 59, 62, 64, 65, 69, 71f., 75, 78, 81, 84, 86, 88, 89, 90, 94ff., 107, 109, 115, 117ff., 122, 126ff., 136, 142, 144f., 148f., 152, 156ff., 161ff., 177f., 190, 205ff., 210, 211.
- Classical period, 7, 35, 95, 113ff., 155ff.
- Cleisthenes, 123, 124.
- Cleon, 133, 148ff., 168, 172, 172, 206, 210.
- colonization, 33, 37.
- Crete, 119.
- Critias, 47, 158.
- Cylon, 70, 161.
- Cyrene, 105.

- Dark Age, 1ff., 20, 25, 58, 177, 178, 183.
- *deilos*, 50, 77, 78, 89, 90, 93, 95, 96, 107, 118, 120, 128, 191, 196.
- *dēmagōgia*, 146, 157, 210.
- democracy, 48, 108f., 115, 122ff., 130, 131, 133f., 140ff., 156, 158, 168, 174, 176, 205, 209ff.
- Democritus, 131.
- *dēmokratia*, 123, 124, 129, 142, 171, 172.
- *dēmokratikos*, 129.
- *dēmos*, 8, 12, 18, 24, 29, 41, 42, 47, 59f., 71, 73, 75, 84, 86, 87, 93, 122, 123, 124, 126, 129, 141ff., 148, 149, 153, 156ff., 168, 170ff., 174, 176, 179, 186, 187, 189, 195, 198, 205, 208, 210.
- *dēmotēs*, 132, 205.
- *dēmotikos*, 129, 170, 176, 177, 205, 208.
- *dexios*, 156, 159, 203.
- *dikaios*, 10, 32, 90, 93, 94, 146, 147, 148, 152, 157, 167, 195, 197, 200, 208.
- *dikaiosynē*, 68, 93.
- *dikē*, 10, 11, 27ff., 48, 50, 71, 93, 116, 205; see justice.
- *dokēsis*, 207.
- *doxa*, 43, 87, 90, 92, 207.
- Draco, 70.
- *dynamis*, 85, 86, 105.
- *dynatos*, 128, 170.
- *dysgeneia*, 135, 140, 147, 203.
- *dysgenēs*, 138, 140, 147, 203.

- economy, 4, 22, 26, 33f., 25ff., 51f., 66, 68f., 70, 74, 81ff., 142, 172ff.
- education, 145, 156ff., 166f., 176.
- Egypt, 11.
- *eidos*, 6, 7.
- Ephesus, 42, 64.
- Ephialtes, 125.
- *epieikeis*, 127.
- epinicians, 95.
- *epiphanēs*, 175.
- *epistēmē*, 177.
- *esthlos*, 4, 32, 50, 61, 72, 77ff., 81, 83, 87, 89, 90, 92, 93, 96, 113, 117, 118, 120, 127, 134, 137, 147, 184, 191, 195, 196, 199, 200, 203, 204.
- *ethos*, 83, 138, 150.
- *euandria*, 138, 150.
- *eudaimōn*, 205.
- *eugeneia*, 133, 134, 136ff., 141, 147, 152.
- *eugenēs*, 68, 80, 85, 97, 127, 132, 134, 135, 140, 141, 146, 147, 150, 152, 157, 207.
- *eugnomosynē*, 176.
- *eukleēs*, 114.
- *eukleia*, 118, 207.
- *eunomia*, 11, 65, 72, 100, 105, 116, 145, 201.
- *eupatridai*, 62, 70, 71, 119.
- Eupolis, 140.
- *euporoi*, 128.
- Euripides, 85, 135-39, 144, 147, 150ff., 158, 198, 204ff.
- *eusebēs*, 205.
- *exochoi*, 25.

- *gennadas*, 163, 203.
- *gennaios*, 49, 127, 136, 138, 144, 150ff., 205.
- *genos*, 38, 68, 137, 140, 141, 175.
- *gēomoroi*, 62.
- *geras*, 4, 19.
- *gnōmē*, 92, 93, 138, 148.
- *gnōrimoi*, 127.
- Gyges, 48.
- *gymnastika*, 156.

- Heraclitus, 143.
- Hermippus, 163.

INDEX 217

- Herodotus, 124, 132, 144, 161, 171, 204.
- Heroic Age, 1ff.
- heroic ideal, 2ff., 40ff., 44ff., 54, 57, 59ff., 134, 190.
- Hesiod, 14, 26-34, 36, 39, 44, 46, 48ff., 53, 68, 83, 93, 102, 106, 165, 191, 194, 195.
- *hetairia,* 168.
- *hetairos,* 23, 88.
- Hiero, 102, 202.
- *hippeis,* 62, 162.
- *hippobotai,* 62.
- Hipponax, 64f., 67, 82.
- Homer, 1-8, 14, 18-29, 32f., 42ff., 49, 52ff., 60f., 80, 92, 100, 106, 108f., 161, 165, 191, 194, 201.
- *homoioi,* 192.
- *homonoia,* 179.
- homosexuality, 53, 63, 89, 120, 129, 164ff., 175, 194, 200, 203, 209.
- hoplite, 39f., 44, 60, 70, 74, 116, 160, 196, 197.
- Horace, 194.
- hospitality, 10ff.
- Hybrias, 121.
- *hybris,* 11, 28, 48, 50, 71, 72, 84, 93, 117, 186, 189.
- Hyperbolus, 172,

- Ibycus, 57, 65, 92.
- *Iliad,* 1f., 6ff., 12ff., 20ff., 27ff., 39, 48, 50, 55, 196.
- Isagoras, 124.
- *isēgoria,* 159.
- Isocrates, 211.
- *isonomia,* 205.
- *isonomos,* 203.
- Ithaca, 9, 13, 17.

- justice, 12f., 27ff., 48ff., 68, 78, 94; see *dikē.*

- *kakopatris (idēs),* 61, 62, 80, 82, 193.
- *kakos,* 4, 11, 16, 27, 28, 32, 54, 72ff., 77ff., 93ff., 107, 113, 117, 128, 132, 134, 136ff., 144f., 147, 176, 184, 187, 188, 193ff., 198ff., 202, 204, 207.
- *kakotēs,* 93.
- *kallos,* 94, 106, 200.
- *kalos,* 106, 107, 121, 129, 134, 137, 147, 156, 175, 193, 201.
- *kaloskagathos,* 129, 133, 134, 146, 157, 160, 173, 204.

- kinship, 8f., 13, 31f., 38, 70, 124, 191; see lineage.
- *klarotai*, 194.
- *kleos*, 92, 114.
- *komaō*, 161.
- *komētēs*, 161, 164.
- *kompsos*, 161.
- *koros*, 84, 103.
- *kosmios*, 175, 177.
- *kouphologia*, 172.
- *kydos*, 4, 23, 58, 108, 117.

- *laos*, 8, 18, 25, 28, 41, 42, 186.
- law, 70, 73, 130.
- Leonidas, 114.
- Lesbos, 81.
- life-style, 22f., 52ff., 56ff., 62f., 65f., 73, 75, 89, 91, 100, 106, 126, 143f., 146, 155ff., 207, 208, 209, 211.
- lineage, 2, 9, 12, 15f., 38, 49, 61f., 68, 69f., 75, 78, 80, 81, 85, 93, 97ff., 119, 127f., 131f., 133ff., 143, 144ff., 140f., 155, 158, 159, 168, 178f., 183, 196, 206, 211.
- liturgies, 126, 203.
- lyric poets, 35ff., *passim*.
- Lysias, 161, 175, 210.

- Macedon, 115.
- *malakia*, 172.
- *maniōdēs*, 172.
- manufacture, 33, 36f., 189.
- Marathon, 116.
- Megacles, 164.
- Megara, 77.
- *megas*, 50, 150, 205.
- mental qualities, 90, 92f., 95, 104f., 126ff., 139, 143ff., 170f., 178, 199, 205.
- *mesos*, 72.
- metic, 156.
- *metrios*, 171, 176, 211.
- Miletus, 66.
- Mimnermus, 54f., 57, 63, 65, 67, 72, 77.
- *misthioi*, 128.
- *misthophorioi*, 128.
- *mochthēros*, 128, 172, 203.
- *moira*, 94.

INDEX 219

— *monarchos*, 179.
— moral qualities, 78, 83ff., 87ff., 95, 103ff., 113f., 118ff., 126ff., 136, 139, 143ff., 170f., 175, 178.
— *mousikos*, 157.
— Myrsilus, 61.
— Mytilene, 60, 61, 148.

— Nebuchadrezzar, 60.
— Nicias, 169, 210.
— *nomos*, 130, 138, 158, 206.

— *ochlos*, 127, 136, 141, 144, 171, 205.
— *Odyssey*, 1f., 6ff., 10ff., 17ff., 23f., 26, 28f., 49, 50, 87, 90.
— *oikos*, 2, 4, 9, 13, 14, 23, 38, 183, 186.
— *olbios*, 94, 128, 141.
— *olbos*, 102.
— "Old Oligarch," 141, 144f., 156, 171, 174, 205, 206, 208.
— *oligarchia*, 123, 170.
— *oligarchikos*, 176.
— oligarchy, 123f., 142, 144, 158, 168, 176, 210.
— *oligoi*, 94, 125, 127, 205.
— Olympic games, 169, 199.

— *paideia*, 166, 167.
— *paideusis*, 167, 208.
— *panaristos*, 32.
— Paros, 44, 46.
— *parrhēsia*, 159.
— *pauroi*, 94.
— peasant, 26, 36, 51, 66, 121, 162, 188.
— *penēs*, 82, 85, 128, 140, 141, 147, 152, 205.
— *penestai*, 194.
— Penia, 148, 149.
— *penichros*, 81.
— Pericles, 122, 125, 140, 148, 171ff., 205, 206, 210.
— Persia, 155.
— phalanx, 39f., 74, 79, 190.
— *phaulos*, 148, 203, 206.
— *philodespotos*, 198.
— *philopolis*, 209.
— *philotēs*, 9, 185.
— Phocylides, 66f., 93, 94, 194, 199.
— *phyā*, 97, 98.

— *physis*, 130, 135, 137, 138, 150, 152, 153, 158, 176, 177, 206, 207.
— Pindar, 58, 77, 95-111, 113-19, 131, 199ff., 202.
— Pisistratids, 119, 203.
— Pisistratus, 70, 123, 200, 203.
— Pittacus, 59ff., 73, 75, 198.
— Plataea, 115f.
— Plato, 47, 158, 165, 177, 179.
— *pleistos*, 108.
— *plēthos*, 85, 127, 205.
— *plousios*, 81, 85, 128, 142, 147, 162, 205.
— *ploutos*, 102, 103, 140, 202.
— *poinē*, 12.
— polis, 3, 8, 9, 37ff., 42, 43, 44, 51, 52, 57, 59, 60, 65, 69, 70, 71, 74, 75, 87, 100, 108, 109, 116, 121, 122ff., 129, 131, 132, 134, 141, 142, 145, 156, 157, 171, 173, 174, 176, 178, 179, 186, 190, 205, 211.
— *politeia*, 125.
— *politēs*, 8, 38, 51, 52, 67, 123, 170, 200.
— *polloi*, 127, 142ff., 150, 169.
— *polymathēs*, 159.
— Polycrates, 56, 57, 132.
— *polypragmosynē*, 122.
— *ponēria*, 145, 170, 209.
— *ponēros*, 128, 137, 141, 144, 145, 147, 148, 156, 171, 176, 194, 203, 205.
— population, 32, 33, 37, 156.
— poverty, 64, 81ff., 140, 147, 156, 173f., 197, 205, 206, 208; see *penia*.
— *prostatēs*, 141, 142.
— *ptōchos*, 196.
— *prōtoi*, 118, 140, 170.
— Pythermus, 66.

— Quintilian, 194.

— religion, 20ff., 29, 38, 68, 69, 99f., 123.
— Rhegium, 57.
— *rhētōr*, 158.

— Samos, 50, 132.
— Sappho, 194.

INDEX

- *scolion*, 119ff., 160, 203.
- Scopas, 114, 116.
- *semnos*, 162, 164.
- Semonides, 194, 198, 202.
- Sicily, 104, 169.
- Simonides, 85, 113-16, 118f., 202.
- slavery, 204, 210.
- Socrates, 161, 166, 209.
- Solon, 68-75, 77, 81, 84, 87, 100f., 123, 165, 196, 198, 199.
- *sophia*, 92, 95, 108, 145.
- sophists, 130f., 138, 158f., 166, 204, 209.
- Sophocles, 131, 133ff., 204.
- *sophos*, 104ff., 108, 117, 148, 153, 159, 200.
- *sōphrōn*, 80, 90, 93, 105, 138, 145ff., 150, 157, 172, 175, 176, 203.
- *sōphrosynē*, 90, 91, 93, 95, 105, 138, 148, 149, 152, 167, 171, 206, 211.
- Sparta, 36, 41, 149, 157, 168, 171, 190, 209.
- *stasis*, 38, 66, 70, 73, 211.
- Stesichorus, 196.
- *synoikismos*, 69.
- *synomotai*, 168.
- Syracuse, 96, 202.

- technology, 35f.
- Thasos, 46.
- Thebes, 30, 105, 115.
- *themis*, 116, 186.
- Themistocles, 206.
- *Theognidea*, 77-80, 82-97, 106ff., 109ff., 113f., 117ff., 131, 196ff., 202.
- Theognis, 77-80, 82-97, 106ff., 109ff., 113f., 117ff., 131, 196ff., 202.
- *Theogony*, 26, 28f.
- Thessaly, 115.
- Thrace, 131.
- Thucydides, 53, 106, 122, 125, 140, 142, 148ff., 158, 169ff., 206.
- *timē*, 4, 13, 23, 54, 58, 78, 87, 90, 102, 117, 118, 120, 186, 190.
- *timios*, 55, 81.
- *tlēmsoynē*, 90.
- *tolmā*, 105, 198, 200.
- trade, 33, 36f., 51, 74, 140, 196.
- tribal culture, 2ff., 9. 13, 18ff., 29f., 38, 42, 75, 124, 178.
- Trojan War, 1, 14.

- Troy, 9, 17, 30.
- *tyrannos*, 39, 62, 70, 123, 179, 194, 198.
- tyranny, 39, 51, 53, 56, 61f., 70, 75, 115, 123, 132, 149, 179, 189, 198, 201; see *tyrannos*.
- Tyrtaeus, 40-44, 47, 54, 59, 65, 77, 84f., 92, 100, 114, 190, 196, 197, 200.

- vase painting, 52f., 66, 107, 208.

- *wanax*, 2.
- wealth, 4f., 19, 23, 26, 32ff., 38, 51ff., 58, 64, 66, 71ff., 78, 79, 80ff., 94f., 101f., 109, 117, 118, 127f., 139ff., 143, 146ff., 150ff., 155, 158, 159, 168, 173f., 178f., 196, 197, 200, 202, 204ff., 208, 211.
- *Works and Days*, 26-32, 49f.

- *xenios*, 186.
- Xenophanes, 53, 65f., 100, 202.
- Xenophon, 140, 208.
- *xynesis*, 148, 150.
- *xynetos*, 142, 148, 151, 200.

Selected Papers

CHANGES AND SHIFTS IN THE MEANING OF DEMOS IN THE LITERATURE OF THE ARCHAIC PERIOD

The word δημοκρατία first occurs, so far as we can tell, in the fifth century B.C. Its coinage, like that of similar abstract political terms such as ὀλιγαρχία and ἀριστοκρατία, illustrates a growing awareness of political theory in that century.[1] The usage of the word δημοκρατία also shows how political terms, even new ones of a technical nature, change semantically. Whether δημοκρατία was originally coined by those who favored or opposed popular government is not known, but its later connotations were decidedly different, depending on the user.[2] Employed by someone who was well disposed towards democracy δημοκρατία signified rule by the whole of the citizen population, while anti-democrats invariably implied that it meant control by the poorer, less stable segment of the citizenry.[3] The injection of bias into the usage of descriptive political terms is not a surprising phenomenon to the viewer of the historical scene, ancient or modern. Few words which occur in a socio-political ambience escape becoming "catch-words" used by opposing groups in dissimilar ways. Nevertheless, in the case of δημοκρατία the ambiguous usage is in large part traceable to the various shadings of meaning acquired through generations by the root word δῆμος.

By the middle of the fifth century δῆμος had generally come to denote the greater mass of free citizens, large in number but of lower economic and social standing than the relatively few of substantial wealth and good birth, very often with a pejorative connotation. Thus δῆμος is equated with terms like πολλοί, πλῆθος, πένητες, πονηροί, ὄχλος, δειλοί, and so on.[4] In earlier literary usage δῆμος was not used pejoratively and did not denote a social class. At some point, then, this word, originally "neutral," gained socio-political connotations. I shall attempt to trace the process of development from a neutral to a socially charged term.

Etymologically δῆμος seems to be related to an I.E. verb which connotes cutting or dividing (cf. δαίομαι; Old Irish *dam* = "band of men," "Gefolgschaft").[5] In the Mycenaean tablets *da-mo* signifies both the land belonging to a community and the people which inhabits, possesses and farms the communal land. It is the "village" in both the geographical and human sense, with an identity and will of its own.[6]

An examination of the usage of δῆμος in the Homeric epics confirms in general outline what we know of the Myceneaen *damo*. In Homer δῆμος signifies either an area of (probably cultivated) land or its inhabitants, who make up the aggregate of the dwellers in a community. The two meanings, "land" and "people" sometimes merge, and there are instances where the context does not reveal which is meant.[7] This confusion demonstrates the close connection between the two concepts: land and people are one.

An analysis of the Homeric usage of δῆμος referring to people, reveals that it usually denotes all the free inhabitants of a community, excluding the immediate leadership. This exclusion is not always immediately apparent, for there are instances in Homer where δῆμος appears to indicate the total community of people. Thus in *Il.* 20.166 πᾶς δῆμος is described as gathering for a lion hunt, and in *Il.* 11.328 the two sons of Merops are called the "best men of the δῆμος."[8] A wealthy companion of Hector, Podes, was honored by him μάλιστα...δήμου (*Il.* 17.576–77). These passages seem to suggest that even men from the noble warrior group are included in δῆμος. In *Od.* 21.17 we are told that Odysseus had gone to Messene to collect a debt "which πᾶς δῆμος owed him." The passage makes it clear that the debtors are the whole of the Messenian state, not a portion thereof. On the other hand, there is often a clear distinction made between the δῆμος and someone set above or outside it. Neleus, in *Il.* 11.704, kept much booty and "gave the rest to δῆμος to divide." In *Il.* 18.490–508 δῆμος (= λαός) is apparently differentiated from the γέροντες. The δῆμος gives a γέρας to the "leaders and counsellors" of the Phaeacians in *Od* 7.150;[9] in 8.157 Odysseus makes his plea "to the king and the whole δῆμος" and in 7.11 the poet says that the δῆμος listened to Alcinous as if to a god.[10] Similar is *Od.* 16.425, where Antinous' father had fled to Odysseus' house as an exile "fearing the δῆμος," who were finally restrained by Odysseus.[11]

The clearest indications in Homer that δῆμος excludes the leadership are *Il.* 12.213 where Polydamas, a man of high standing in the community, refers to himself as δῆμον ἐόντα as opposed to Hector, and in *Il.* 2.198, where Odysseus treats a "man of the δῆμος" differently from a βασιλεύς or an ἔξοχος ἀνήρ (one who "stands out," line 188). Further evidence for the meaning of δῆμος in Homer is found in the adjectives δήμιος, δημοβόρος and the substantives δημογέρων and δημιοεργοί.[12]

From this brief review it may be concluded that δῆμος in the epics denotes the whole population but usually excludes the immediate leadership, specifically the chieftain (βασιλεύς) or, occaasionally, others of high standing,

Changes and Shifts in the Meaning of Demos 227

in a capacity of leadership. Thus men of stature like the sons of Merops, Podes and Polydamas may be included in the term δῆμος because they are not in command. With the exception of *Il.* 2.198–206 δῆμος is never spoken of in disparaging terms, nor is it regarded either as a social class or as a political unit. It is, simply, the people.

The scant evidence provided by the Homeric Hymns supports these conclusions. Thus in *h. Dem.* 151 the six βασιλεῖς of Eleusis are said to have great power and δήμου τε προὔχουσιν; in the same hymn Demeter orders πᾶς δῆμος to build her a temple (line 271).

We are warranted, I believe, in seeing a slight, but significant, shift of emphasis in Hesiod's usage of δῆμος in *Op.* 256–62, where the poet says that δῆμος "pays" for the wickedness of the βασιλεῖς. Here, as usual, δῆμος means the whole people exclusive of its leaders, but for the first time we have an intimation of oppression by the βασιλεῖς and an awareness of opposition on the part of the δῆμος —a tension not observed in the Homeric poems.[13] The distinction, in any case, between δῆμος and leaders seems more emphatic, and we must consider whether this shift of emphasis becomes more pronounced in the lyric poets of the seventh and sixth centuries.

In his *Eunomia* Tyrtaeus employs the terms δημότας ἄνδρας (frg. 3a. 5D) and δήμου πλήθει. In each case the terms refer to the whole of the free male population, but carefully distinguished from the national leadership, the βασιλεῖς and the γέροντες. The separation of the elements which make up the community appears more precise than in the earlier Homeric usage. The δημόται ἄνδρες and the δῆμος are regarded as distinct constitutional entities, with defined functions, rights and responsibilities. The Tyrtaean evidence, as well as that of the "Great Rhetra" which he paraphrases here, shows the word δῆμος in a much more precisely delimited sense. It still means, as in Homer and Hesiod, the citizen body; but now it has, as it were, a constitutional "life," being regarded as an organ within the *polis*, able to be distinguished from other organs.[14]

At the same time, however, δῆμος is used in a more inclusive sense in another fragment of Tyrtaeus (9.15D) where bravery in the ranks is called ξυνὸν δ' ἐσθλὸν... πόληί τε παντί τε δήμωι. Here a close connection between the political entity (πόλις) and its human constituency (δῆμος) is emphasized, and no distinction is made between people and leadership.[15] This all-inclusive meaning is found in Callinus (frg. 1. 16–17D), who says that a man who has not fought bravely is "not dear to the δῆμος nor missed" while the brave defender is mourned by the ὀλίγος and the μέγας. Here δῆμος (= λαὸς σύμπας, line 18) embraces the total community of men, high and low.[16] This "undifferentiated" meaning of δῆμος, equivalent to πόλις, retains its vitality in the succeeding centuries side by side with the more limiting, "political" meaning of the term.

A noteworthy instance of δῆμος is found in Alcman frg. 17.7 (Page), in which the poet states that he does not eat food elegantly prepared (ἠΰ τετυγμένον) but yearns for τὰ κοινά like the δᾶμος. Alcman appears to be making a distinction between the common mess of the δᾶμος and the more elaborate food consumed by others. We must be careful not to think that δᾶμος here means anything like the "common people"; rather that Alcman distinguishes between the whole adult Spartan population and some (unknown) individuals or group here regarded as somehow outside it.[17]

Thus far, down through the seventh century, δῆμος appears not to have acquired any social implications. In the instances examined it signifies sometimes the whole population (the "people" as the human element of the state), or the "people" regarded as an entity separate from the leadership. The evidence, scanty as it is, shows clearly that in the latter usage the sense of separateness is understood on the constitutional level, but not really on the social or class level. Even in Hesiod, δῆμος means no more than the whole people face to face with its traditional leaders.[18]

That the undifferentiated meaning for δῆμος holds through the sixth century is evidenced by a dedication from Anacreon, in which occurs the phrase εὐθυδίκων Εὐωνυμέων ἐνὶ δήμωι (frg. 105.3D; the geographical sense is preserved along with the human), and Xenophanes 2.8–9D, where a victor in the Olympian games would have food δημοσίων κτεάνων ἐκ πόλιος. The public treasury embraces the concept of the whole πόλις, with no sense of distinction. Similarly, when Hipponax prays that his enemy be condemned to die by a "vote" in the βουλὴ δημοσίη (frg. 77.4D) he probably is referring to public stoning. In this case βουλὴ δημοσίη is used in a humorous way to mean the whole community.[19]

Turning now to the evidence of Solon's usage of δῆμος we see a definite shift in focus. The undifferentiated concept of δῆμος still holds to a limited degree but in most of the occurrences the cleavage between δῆμος and leaders is pronounced. Moreover, we note a semantic shift toward the later dichotomy between δῆμος (conceived of as the common people, the masses) and a social group which is elevated above it. In truth, Solon did not make the kind of sharp, judgmental distinction seen in the late fifth and fourth centuries, but a careful examination of the text shows that Solon was approaching a social meaning for δῆμος.

In frg. 3 D, "Eunomia," Solon directs his indignation at the ruling group of birth and power who are exploiting their economic advantage in Attica. In line 7 of this poem he says that "the mind of the leaders of the δῆμος is unjust." We cannot say with precise certainty who these ἡγεμόνες were, but the simplest and most obvious identification is with a small group of wealthy, powerful citizens, the upper class "nobles."[20] Δῆμος, then, will be the people, all the free citizens exclusive of the dominant group. The context of the poem shows that δῆμος is not equivalent to πόλις but is considered by Solon as part of the πόλις (cf. lines 1–6: "our polis" will not be destroyed by the will of the gods, but the townsmen themselves [ἀστοί] want to ruin it, yielding to gain). On the other hand δῆμος is not regarded as a class or party, but as the people, differentiated from the group which has emerged from it as a separate entity. This is evident from lines 23–24:

ταῦτα μὲν ἐν δήμωι στρέφεται κακά· τῶν δὲ πενιχρῶν
ἱκνοῦνται πολλοὶ γαῖαν ἐς ἀλλοδαπήν.

The κακά are the wrongful activities of the "leaders" and the attendant civic evils, στάσις ἔμφυλος and πόλεμος, which lead to eventual destruction of the total community, the πόλις (9–22). The μέν and δέ show that δῆμος and πενιχροί are not equivalents. The δῆμος is the whole people minus the group which is exploiting it; the "poor" form a portion of the δῆμος.[21]

Further evidence of the cleavage between the δῆμος and the group in control is provided in frg. 5.1D where Solon says that he gave to the δῆμος as much γέρας as was sufficient, neither taking away nor adding to their τιμή, while those "who had power and who were admired for their wealth" did not suffer. The contrast between δήμωι μέν and οἳ δ' εἶχον δύναμιν κτλ. makes it clear that Solon sees these as two separate elements of the πόλις. This is underscored by his use of the terms ἀμφότεροι and οὐδέτεροι in the same fragment (lines 5–6). There are, in other words, two contesting groups in Athens: those who are both powerful and wealthy, and everyone else. The δῆμος is again, in this instance, the "people," not a faction or the masses of the poor. Aristotle thought that Solon meant the masses (τὸ πλῆθος), as he says in *Ath. Pol* 12, quoting further from Solon: "The *dêmos* would thus best follow the *hêgemones*, by being neither too much in check nor pressing hard..." (frg. 5.7–8). But here, too, Solon is simply contrasting the people with the leaders.[22] The ἡγεμόνες of this fragment may be considered in a more strictly constitutional sense than the leaders mentioned in frg. 3, and this perhaps explains why the sense of separation is less compelling here. At any rate, the combination of δῆμος and ἡγεμόνες equals the concept of πόλις.[23] The fragment quoted by Diodorus as Solon's warning about the approaching tyranny (10D) is also instructive for the Solonian usage of δῆμος. He says, first, that a πόλις is destroyed because of powerful men (μεγάλοι ἄνδρες, line 3).

This is a general statement: the *totality* of the political order is brought to utter ruin by strong men. Then comes a specific charge: because of its ignorance (ἀϊδρείη) the δῆμος enslaves itself by choosing a μόναρχος. The warning is directed to a segment of the πόλις, the δῆμος, which, of its own accord, will opt for a tyrant, thereby destroying the whole state.

The meaning of δῆμος in the opening lines of frg. 24 is not immediately clear. By saying that he "gathered the δῆμος together," Solon may mean the "whole people" in the undifferentiated sense, or that he gave the "people" (i.e., the citizens exclusive of the wealthy ruling group) a feeling of group identity. If the opening lines are understood thus:

> In what respect did I cease before I accomplished
> the things for which I had gathered the *dêmos* together?[24]

i.e., that he did, in fact, accomplish his objectives, then the latter meaning makes more sense. Indeed, in lines 15–17 (cf. frg. 23.18) Solon boasts that he had done what he promised, specifically, that he removed the boundary stones, brought back both those who had been sold into slavery abroad and those who had gone into exile because of poverty, and freed those who were slaves in Attica. Whatever the precise details of the σεισάχθεια were, it is plain that the beneficiaries of his reforms were citizens in economic distress, and that they were victims of *varying* degrees of social and economic hardship. The identification of these people with δῆμος in line 2 is compelling. And the identification seems certain when, in lines 20–22, he says:

> Had any other man than I taken the goad...
> he would not have restrained the *dêmos*.

Δῆμος in lines 2 and 22 refers to that portion of the population which benefitted from the reforms, namely the broad mass of citizens, who, in one degree or another were experiencing the evils of economic pressure from above. The appeal which Solon makes in this poem is clear. For the δῆμος he accomplished the economic "disburdenment" which he had promised; and, in addition, he wrote "ordinances" which provided equal justice for *all* citizens (τῶι κακῶι τε κἀγαθῶι, lines 18–20). Another would have yielded to further demands from the δῆμος but to try to please both sides would have meant civil strife, and the whole corporate body (πόλις) would have been deprived of many men (20–25). The closing figure of a wolf at bay (26–27) underscores in a poetic manner the embattled αἰσυμνήτης; resisting pressure from opposing groups. Precisely the same dichotomy is noted in frg. 25.1–5, where δῆμος is opposed to ὅσοι δὲ μείζους καὶ βίαν ἀμείνονες. In lines 6–9 he again speaks of restraining the δῆμος and employs the simile of an arbitrator who stands midway between contesting groups.

The clear and definite impression of Solon's usage of the term δῆμος is that for him it signified neither the total community (πόλις) nor "the commons" or "the masses," as the term was used later, but the citizenry exclusive of the minority which was in a position of power and control. Δῆμος in Solon has no undercurrent of contempt or sense of innate inferiority and it includes more than the poorest citizens. It is regarded as having a corporate will and power (at least potentially) equal to its rival group. Nevertheless, by giving a clear-cut identification to the two groups in the state Solon shows that δῆμος was emerging as a distinct socio-political concept in Athens. The "party" or "factional" meaning of δῆμος and its identification with the mass of poor citizens, which is its predominant sense later on, is adumbrated in the Solonian usage.

There are two instances of δῆμος in the fragments of Alcaeus, who, like Solon, was writing within a political context at approximately the same time. But, unlike Solon, Alcaeus does not treat δῆμος as a separate element. In frg. 70 L-P he deplores the "soul-devouring discord and the intestine fighting…which brings *dâmos* into destruction and gives Pittacus his desired glory" (lines 10–13). Δᾶμος is set off against the immediate leader, Pittacus, who is now in power in Mytilene, but it does not suggest any social division of the state. Δᾶμος here appears to be equivalent to πόλις; in line 7. The same phrase, "devours the *polis*," occurs in frg. 129 L-P in reference to Pittacus, who had apparently joined forces with Myrsilus, and had broken oaths sworn by the faction of Alcaeus and Pittacus. The oath, paraphrased by Alcaeus, was either to die at the hands of the men who were then (in power?)[25] or to kill them "and deliver *demos* from its woes" (17–20). In this fragment, as in the one previously cited, δᾶμος appears as the "people" exclusive of the immediate leadership, but with no indication that it is a separate group within the πόλις; it is, rather, the human element of the δῆμος. Why Alcaeus, an aristocrat, gives no hint of a party sense for δῆμος is a question to which we shall return.

Theognis' usage of δῆμος shows evidence of the same growing social gulf observed in the poems of Solon. In 43–52 he expresses his concern for the πόλις; saying that ἀγαθοί never destroyed a πόλις, but κακοί, who for money and power "both corrupt the *dêmos* and give judgments to the *adikoi*." When this happens the πόλις will not stay long in peace. In these lines Theognis considers the πόλις as the total corporate entity, while δῆμος is a part, susceptible to the machinations of its unjust leaders, the κακοί. Messina (op.

cit., 237), maintains that δῆμον φθείρουσι (45) is strictly equivalent to πόλιν ὤλεσαν (43), and, therefore, that πόλις and δῆμος are synonymous. But the progression of ideas is: ἀγαθοί destroy no πόλις; κακοί spoil or corrupt δῆμος and give judgment to the unjust. These things lead to civil disorder (στάσιες, ἔμφυλοι φόνοι) and, ultimately, to μούναρχοι.[26]

In lines reminiscent of these, but offering a positive prescription for rule, the separate elements appear more clearly defined:

πατρίδα κοσμήσω, λιπαρὴν πόλιν, οὔτ' ἐπὶ δήμωι
τρέψας οὔτ' ἀδίκοισ' ἀνδράσι πειθόμενος (947–48).

Here we have the whole political body, the πόλις, set off against the δῆμος and those whom he terms ἄδικοι ἄνδρες.[27] This note of separateness comes through even more clearly in 233–34, where the ἐσθλὸς ἀνήρ is termed "a citadel and a tower to the empty-minded *dêmos.*" Theognis assumes here an aristocratic group which is set off against a stratum of society which is inferior to it. The social tension is also implicit in these lines; the man whose *natural* place is at the head and set above receives little honor (τιμή) from the δῆμος. The separation is not simply that of people and leaders but of opposing groups in active discord. Κενεόφρων is the first disparaging epithet applied to δῆμος in our sources. The notions that δῆμος is inferior, deserves to be treated harshly, and desires to be led come through forcefully in 847–50:

Λὰξ ἐπίβα δήμωι κενεόφρονι, τύπτε δὲ κέντρωι
ὀξέϊ καὶ ζεύγλην δύσλοφον ἀμφιτίθει·
οὐ γὰρ ἔθ' εὑρήσεις δῆμον φιλοδέσποτον ὧδε
ἀνθρώπων, ὁπόσους ἠέλιος καθορᾶι.

Theognis, like Solon and Alcaeus, perceived that the greatest danger to the πόλις was the emergence of a single ruler, a τύραννος, μόναρχος, whose appeal was to the δῆμος, the people at large. The emergence of the strong man in the several Greek states meant that the old dichotomy of δῆμος and leaders was widened as the new leader, the tyrant, threatened the hegemony of the traditional leader-class. One result was a heightened sense of differentiation on both sides.

The political rhetoric could also be conciliatory as well as disparaging. Thus Theognis can say, even while recognizing the awful impiety of the statement, that it is no sin to kill a δημοφάγον τύραννον (1181–82). In the same vein he says that the κακοί "corrupt the *dêmos*" (45). Generally, however, Theognis' political invective tended to portray the δῆμος as weak and malleable, as κενεόφρων (233, 847) or φιλοδέσποτος (849).[28]

This attitude perhaps explains why Alcaeus employs δῆμος in the undifferentiated sense. In Mytilene the political turmoil was not, in the view of most historians, a class struggle, but was a contest among various aristocratic factions for hegemony.[29] So Alcaeus would not be ranged against the δῆμος as was Theognis, who had seen the "traditional" social system overturned, nor in the middle, like Solon, arbitrating between two opposing groups, but actively vying for their support. It was to his advantage to make πόλις and people virtually identical.[30]

We may summarize briefly the usage of δῆμος to the end of the archaic period:[31] On the Mycenaean tablets and in the Homeric poems δῆμος denotes either the land of the community or the free population which lived on the land. The "geographical" meaning for δῆμος survives only rarely in literature after Homer, and, except for passages which are epic in manner, δῆμος indicates people, not an area. In the epics, but very rarely, δῆμος may signify the total community; usually it indicates the whole of the free people, exclusive of the immediate leadership, especially the local chief, the βασιλεύς. After Homer the semantic differentiation in the usage of δῆμος tends in general to be more pronounced, but in degree rather than in kind. There are indications that δῆμος comes to be regarded as a separate "constitutional" element in the state, while the concept of the leadership is widened to the extent that it appears as a group with its own separate aims. There is a note of social tension between δῆμος and βασιλεῖς in the usage of Hesiod, while in Tyrtaeus δᾶμος appears as a constitutionally defined division of the state, apart from the kings and elders. Alcman also hints at the consciousness of a growing social gulf. At the beginning of the sixth century in Athens Solon's usage demonstrates an awareness of δῆμος as a politically and socially self-conscious entity ranged in opposition to a group characterized as men who were wealthy and powerful. Theognis also treats δῆμος as a separate element of the πόλις; but, additionally, in the *Theognidea* the δῆμος is regarded as inferior in a judgmental sense to those who are its rightful leaders, the ἐσθλοί. It is in the lines of Theognis that δῆμος is first coupled with pejorative epithets which show a definite upper class bias against the people as a whole.

Nevertheless, there is not a simple progression of differentiation in the archaic usage of δῆμος since it is also used throughout the period in an undifferentiated sense, with no obvious emphasis on the separation between people and leadership. It is certain, then, that the term δῆμος underwent no *technical* change in meaning; throughout this period it signified the free people exclusive of the immediate leadership. But, in contexts which emphasized political or social problems, the word acquired specialized shades of meanings —with the expanding sense of political awareness came new dimensions in the signification of δῆμος.[32]

NOTES

[1] For the appearance of δημοκρατία see J. A. O. Larsen, *Cleisthenes and the Development of the Theory of Democracy at Athens*, in *Essays in Political Theory presented to George W. Sabine* (Ithaca, N.Y., 1948), 1–16, and V. Ehrenberg, "Origins of Democracy," *Historia* I, 1, 1950, 515–48. Ehrenberg cites A. Debrunner, "Δημοκρατία" in *Festschrift für E. Tièche* (Bern, 1947), 11–24, who argues that the terms μοναρχία and ὀλιγαρχία provide the pattern for δημοκρατία; Ehrenberg feels that ὀλιγαρχία and δημοκρατία appeared at the same time (p. 534). Ἀριστοκρατία is not seen earlier than Thucydides (3.82).

[2] See Larsen, op. cit., 13–14.

[3] E.g. Thuc. 6.89; Xen. *Mem.* IV 2.36–37; Aristote *Pol.* 1280A. For other examples and a general discussion of the dual concept of δημοκρατία see G. E. M. de St. Croix, "The Character of the Athenian Empire," *Historia*, 3, 1954, 22–25. Cf. also R. Sealey, "Ephialtes," *CP*, 59, 1964, 20–21, for overtones of disapproval in the early usage of δημοκρατία.

[4] See O. Reverdin, "Remarques sur la vie politique d'Athènes au Ve siècle," *Mus. Helv.*, 2, 1945, 201–12. Cf. Pseudo-Xen. *Ath. Pol.* 3.10 where τὸ βέλτιστον is opposed to δῆμος which is made equivalent to τὸ κάκιστον.

[5] H. Frisk, *Griechisches etymologisches Wörterbuch* (Heidelberg, 1954)

[6] See L. R. Palmer, *The Interpretation of Mycenaean Greek Texts* (Oxford, 1963), 85 ff., 188. For an attempt to explain the Mycenaean *damo* as a "class" of agricultural "producers" as opposed to a warrior class (λαός) and a priestly class see A. Yoshida, "Survivances de la tripartition fonctionelle en Grèce," *Rev. Hist. Rel.*, 166, 1964, 21–38, and M. Lejeune, "Le δᾶμος, dans la société mycénienne," *REG*, 78, 1965, 1–22. In the epics and in later literature there is little difference discernible between δῆμος and λαός (cf. *Il.* 15.738, 24.776–77).

[7] E.g., *Od.* 4.666, 6.34, 6.274, 8.36, 8.390, 13.14, 17.558, 19.73, 21.331.

[8] Von Schoeffer, "Demos," in *R.E.*, Band V, 153–61, asserts, erroneously, that δῆμος in *Il.* 11.328 and 12.447 refers to "gemeines oder niederes Volk," but the sons of Merops in 11.328 were not "commoners"; see Adolf Fanta, *Der Staat in der Ilias und Odyssee* (Innsbruck, 1882), 13, note 2. In 12.447 Hector lifts a stone which "two men, the best of the *dêmos*" could scarcely lift. This means simply that Hector's strength was greater than that of any two men in the whole community.

[9] Cf. *Od.* 13.186.

[10] Cf. the expression "honored like a god by *dêmos*": *Il.* 5.78, 10.33, 11.58, 13.218, 16.605; *Od.* 14.205. Of the men thus honored, Agamemnon, Aeneas and Thoas were leaders in the direct sense; Dolopion and Onetor were priests and Castor was the fictitious father of the "Cretan" Odysseus. As warrior kings or priests the characters from the *Iliad* stand separate from the community. It is not unreasonable to suppose that the rich Castor was a village chieftain.

[11] Cf. also *Od.* 14.239, 16.75 (= 19.527), where the "voice of the *dêmos*" i.e., public opinion, expressed in assembly (cf. *Od.* 15.468) acts as a compelling force on someone in a position of leadership. In *Od.* 2.239 Mentor contrasts the suitors to ἄλλῳ δήμῳ which implies that in this situation the suitors are part of the δῆμος, as opposed to the single chieftain, Odysseus; but in *Od.* 16.113–25 πᾶς δῆμος is treated as separate from Telemachus and the suitors, who are chiefs in their own districts. Other instances which treat δῆμος as the body of citizens, but as an entity apart from the leadership are *Il.* 18.295–96, 24.776. In a few passages in Homer a distinction is made between πόλις and δῆμος (*Il.* 3.50, 24.706; *Od.* 6.3, 11.14), between γῆ, δῆμος and πόλις (*Od.* 8.555), between γῆ, δῆμος and ἀνέρες (*Od.* 13.233). It is difficult to know the precise distinction, but I suspect that the emphasis is geographical rather than human: city (proper) and "district." Cf. T. A. Sinclair, *A History of Greek Political Thought* (London, 1951), 15, who suggests "city" and "country."

[12] Δήμιος: *Od.* 2.32, 2.44, 3.82, 4.314, 8.259, 20.264, simply makes a distinction between "public" (belonging to or relating to the community) and private; but in *Il.* 17.248–51 the

war-leaders "drink δήμια" i.e., provided by the δῆμος (cf. δημόθεν *Od.* 19.197). In *Il.* 1.231 Achilles calls Agamemnon δημοβόρος βασιλεύς i.e., a leader who misuses and misapplies the substance which belongs to the whole community (cf. καταδημοβορῆσαι *Il.* 18.301, "for public consumption"). Δημογέροντες (*Il.* 3.149, 11.372) "elders of the *dêmos*," almost by definition, exist apart from the main community in a position of leadership or authority; in fact, Ilus in *Il.* 11.372 was a king. The δημιοεργοί (*Od.* 17.383, 19.135), are those whose special skills are at the services of the whole community.

[13]G. Ferrara, "Solone ed i capi del popolo," *Par. Pass.*," 9, 1954, 336, sees a greater significance in this usage of Hesiod; δῆμος is the mass of the citizens exhibiting its political impotence which stems from its social inferiority. In reality, Hesiod is merely describing the evil effects of bad leadership on the people as a whole. The other instances of δῆμος in Hesiod are geographical (*Op.* 527; *Theog.* 477, 971).

[14]W. G. Forrest, *A History of Sparta: 950–192 B.C.* (London, 1968) and others have correctly stressed the new awareness by the Spartan δᾶμος of its potency and identity. Ferrara, op. cit., 335–36, and A. F. Messina, Δῆμος in *alcuni lirici*, in 'Ἀντίδωρον *U. E. Paoli oblatum* (Genova, 1956) 229–30, properly note that δῆμος and δημόται in Tyrtaeus indicate all the citizens with full constitutional rights (the ὅμοιοι), but they fail to stress that a clear and precise distinction is being made between δῆμος and leaders.

[15]Messina, op. cit., 230.

[16]Ferrara, op. cit., 335; Messina, op. cit., 230. Δῆμος occurs twice in fragments of Archilochus (9.1, 85.1 D) in the undifferentiated sense of "people."

[17]Cf. V. Ehrenberg, "Der Damos im archaischen Sparta," *Hermes*, 68, 1933, 288–305, who stresses the sense of importance and self consciousness of the Spartan δᾶμος at this time. The phrase ὁ δᾶμος ἅπας is found in frg. 119, and in 3.74, a girl, Astymeloisa, is termed μέλημα δάμωι. The contexts are too fragmentary for analysis but δᾶμος in both instances seems to be used in the undifferentiated sense.

[18]The ambiguity inherent in the word δῆμος has been recognized by scholars. Thus D. L. Page, *Sappho and Alcaeus* (Oxford, 1955), 177, says: "Alcaeus, like Homer, Hesiod and Alcman, uses the word *damos* to signify the whole citizen-body of the state excepting its overlords." A. Andrewes, *The Greek Tyrants* (New York, 1956), 35, notes: "*Demos*, the people can mean the whole community, including everyone within it... It can also mean, not everyone, but the mass of the people in contrast to a privileged class...." The problem is to determine at what point and for what reasons *dêmos* acquired new senses of meaning.

[19]See O. Masson, *Les Fragments du poète Hipponax* (Paris, 1962), 168–70. Whether the βουλὴ δημοσίη in the famous inscription from Chios (Tod, 1) presupposes the existence of another (aristocratic) βουλή or not, is a disputed point; nevertheless, it is important to note that even the undifferentiated usages of δῆμος during the period 700 to 600 and beyond display a distinct awareness of δῆμος as a real and vital element of the community. We have seen that from Mycenaean times down through the Homeric period δῆμος was not employed as the term for the total community, but referred to the citizen body exclusive of the leadership. If, in the undifferentiated usages we have been examining, δῆμος appears equivalent to πόλις then it is not unreasonable to suspect that this may reflect an "egalitarian movement" in certain states, which attempted to equate the concept of the total community with the free population, disregarding the existence of a group or class set above or outside it. This may possibly explain why on earlier Athenian inscriptions (e.g., Tod 11, late sixth century) the prescript reads ἔδοξεν τῷ δήμῳ instead of τῇ βουλῇ καὶ τῷ δήμῳ. Cf. V. Ehrenberg, "An Early Source of Polis-Constitution," *CQ*, 37, 1943, 14–18, whose attempt to answer the question is unsatisfactory. Significantly, Ehrenberg cites an early (ca. 600 B.C.) inscription from Dreros in Crete which mentions only πόλις in the prescript, while later Cretan inscriptions regularly couple κόσμοι with πόλις.

[20] So I. M. Linforth, *Solon the Athenian* (Berkeley, 1919), 198 and Ferrara, op. cit., 340. Linforth, who discusses the problems of identification of δῆμος, ἡγεμόνες and ἀστοί is correct in identifying ἀστοί with all the citizens (p. 197). Cf. A. Masaracchia, *Solone* (Firenze, 1958), 254.

[21] Masaracchia, op. cit., 265, interprets ἐν δήμωι as "nel paese." Messina, op. cit., 232 sees *dêmos* here as the whole community, "lo Stato," with also a trace of the old concept of "the land," but it appears to me much simpler to see δῆμος here and in line 7 as meaning the people as opposed to the leaders. The adjective δημόσιον occurs twice in frg. 3 (lines 12, 26) with the undifferentiated meaning of "public."

[22] Messina, op. cit., 233–34, rightly observes Aristotle's anachronistic interpretation. She is also correct in seeing that the contrast is between "tutto il popolo" and the leaders, but she appears not to see that in Solon's usage δῆμος is emerging as a distinct and clearly separate concept.

[23] See Ferrara, op. cit., 341–44, for an interesting interpretation of the differences between the "leaders" of frg. 3 and frg. 5. But, in any case, Solon has firmly in mind the idea of a collective entity, δῆμος, which is regarded as distinct and separate from a group which is set above it.

[24] So, Masaracchia, op. cit., 346–47, 354. Linforth, op. cit., 184, reaches essentially the same conclusion. I do not believe that Solon is referring to the establishment of a "popular party"; that would be anachronistic.

[25] C. M. Bowra, *Greek Lyric Poetry* (Oxford, 1961), 143 and D. Page, op. cit., 163.

[26] Κακοί cannot here be "plebe" as Messina holds (op. cit., 237), because they are motivated by the same desires for wealth and power as the "leaders of the *dêmos*" in Solon frg. 3 (cf. Ferrara op. cit., 339). The phrase δημόσιον κακόν (50) is used in the undifferentiated sense of "public."

[27] If these lines belong to the previous couplet (945–46), then the "program" sounds very Solonian; the just and sober leader walks the middle path between opposing factions.

[28] So also in frg. 10 Solon says that the δῆμος succumbs to the slavery of a μόναρχος because of its "foolishness." Cf. frg. 5.10 D where he implies that the mind of the δῆμος is not ἄρτιος, and 23.1–7, where, as Plutarch says, Solon puts in the mouths of οἱ πολλοὶ καὶ φαῦλοι a speech censuring him for not seizing a tyranny which, from the point of view of this sort of man, was something desirable.

[29] Santo Mazzarino, "Per la storia di Lesbo nel VI secolo. a.C.," *Athenaeum*, 20, 1943, 38–78.

[30] Page, op. cit., 177, believes that for Alcaeus δᾶμος, meant "the entire populace including the noble families, contrasted with the ruling power, whether king or tyrant or oligarchy." I believe, however, that Alcaeus uses δᾶμος in the undifferentiated sense deliberately, although it is possible that, in the absence of any true class tension in Lesbos, the older significance still held true.

[31] The usage of δῆμος in the fragments of Simonides and Pindar is conventional: the whole population or the people exclusive of the leadership.

[32] I am indebted to my colleague, Mr. A. Allen, for his lucid comments and suggestions on the nature of δῆμος.

THE TRADITION OF ANTI-ARISTOCRATIC THOUGHT IN EARLY GREEK POETRY

One of the more stubbornly held historical assumptions concerning the period from the eighth through the sixth centuries B.C. in Greece is that it was, preeminently, an aristocratic age: in the nascent Greek city-states small groups of hereditary nobles dominated political, social and economic life, while the common people had little say in their governance, were often exploited economically and were regarded as socially inferior. As the many, the *demos,* they counted for little, suffered much, enduring their lot, for the most part, in passive silence. The major political changes that took place during this period are usually seen as the result of class struggle in which the masses, protesting against the excesses of their noble lords, fought to obtain basic legal rights, economic relief and political equality. In general, modern historians emphasize the revolutionary aspect of the archaic age—the attempts by a depressed populace to wrest concessions from an entrenched and obdurate oligarchy.[1]

But to concentrate thus on notions of protest, struggle, reaction, incurs the risk of presenting a one-sided picture of social conditions. For example, the aristocratic ideal, elaborately and splendidly spelled out in the Homeric epics, is usually viewed as the normative system of values for the whole culture,[2] and the few voices acknowledged as being in disagreement (e.g., Hesiod, Archilochus) are regarded as unique and idiosyncratic.[3] This point of view assumes an aristocratic hegemony in the ideological as well as the political sphere, leaving no room for an alternative possibility—that during the archaic period in Greece there existed a deep-rooted and self-conscious literary expression of anti-aristocratic opinion.

Scholars have, to be sure, been long aware of certain anti-aristocratic biases in statements by lyric-age poets, critical of the noble or heroic ideal; but there has been little systematic analysis of the extent and exact nature of such utterances or of the precise basis for their rejection of the aristocratic system of values. Collected below, in summary form, are the well-known passages from the lyric poets which may be considered as counter to the aristocratic view. These have been divided into three groups: criticism of traditional values that are associated with the epic or heroic ideal, criticism of the aristocratic way of life or of qualities associated with aristocrats, statements that reflect a nonaristocratic or lower class outlook. There is, of course, some overlapping in this schematization, but in general the categories indicate adequately the particular aspects of the anti-aristocratic bias.

1. Criticism of epic-heroic values.

> Archilochus 6D:
> Rhipsaspis: the heroic code of valor is rejected in favor of personal safety.
> Archilochus 13D:
> Heroic ideal of friendship reduced to usefulness.
> Archilochus 60D:
> Epic stress on external appearance as an index of worth rejected in favor of the real and the useful.
> Archilochus 61D:
> Glory of combat reduced to grim reality.
> Archilochus 64D:
> Epic idea of posthumous fame rejected in favor of reward now (Cf. Stesich. 245 Page).
> Tyrtaeus 9. 1–12D:
> Epic and aristocratic *aretai* rejected in favor of ability to stand firm in ranks.
> Tyrtaeus 9. 13.–22D:
> *Aretê* restated in terms of what is useful to the whole community (*xunon esthlon*); the epic qualities of *anêr agathos* are reduced to steadfastness in ranks. (Cf. 6. 7.1–2).
> Tyrtaeus 9. 23–44D; Callinus 1. 6–21D:
> Individual fame and glory seen in terms of approbation by the whole community for service to the community.[4]
> Xenophanes 2D:
> Rejection of traditional physical *aretai* and success which comes from these in favor of his own *sophia*. The basis for rejection is that these skills are not useful to the polis.
> Phocylides 10D:
> Identification of *aretê* with justice.
> Phocylides 11D:
> Criticism of the mere appearance of soundness based on outward appearance.

The Tradition of Anti-Aristocratic Thought 239

2. Criticism of aristocratic values and of aristocrats.

> Archilochus 22; 70D:
> Common man's suspicion and mockery of the success-standard of wealth, power and influence.
> Archilochus 94D:
> Appeal to Zeus as the overseer of right and wrong, and as judge of *hybris* and *dikê*. (Cf. Solon 1. 16–25; 3. 15–16).
> Archilochus 97D:
> Ironic reference to noble birth.
> Solon 1. 11–13D:
> Rejection of wealth gained through violence and injustice.
> Solon 1. 71–73D:
> Criticism of the greed of the wealthy.
> Solon 3. 5–13D:
> Criticism of those in power, whose greed, injustice and violence lead to antisocial acts.
> Solon 3. 14–26D:
> Criticism of the powerful: they do not heed justice; their actions are harmful to the whole polis, internally and externally; aristocratic clubs bring ruin to the community. The powerful are equated with the unjust throughout.
> Solon 4. 4–8D:
> Warns the wealthy to restrain their arrogance and greed, and to be moderate in their desires.
> Solon 4. 9–12D:
> Criticism of the wealthy in the strongest terms; he identifies himself with the *agathoi* poor against the *kakoi* rich, and opposes *ploutos* to *aretê*.
> Xenophanes 1. 21–24D:
> Rejection of ancient and modern themes of violent *stasis* as fit subjects for feasts, on the grounds that these are not *chrêsta*.
> Xenophanes 3D:
> Criticism of the useless display, luxury and arrogance of the Samian aristocrats. The implication is that these led to Lydian tyranny.[5]
> Phocylides 3D:
> Criticism of noble birth as inferior to skills helpful to the community.

3. Non-aristocratic values.

> Semonides 7D:
> Presents a peasant view of womankind—the defects of women are qualities contrary to the peasant values of usefulness and practicality:

neglect of household duties (2–6, 57–62); intellectual pretension and curiosity (7–9, 12–20); lack of common sense (21–26); instability (10–11, 27–42), gluttony (24, 46–47, 56); promiscuity (48–49); love of luxury (63–70).[6]

Semonides 7D:
> The good wife exhibits qualities which conform to the peasant value of usefulness: increase of livelihood (85); sobriety (90–91).

Alcman 17. 6–8 Page:
> Preference for food that the *damos* eats over food luxuriously prepared.

Alcman 123 Page:
> Praise of cooperation (μέγα γείτονι γείτων).

Solon 14D:
> Praise of the simplest material goods as equal to the highest wealth.[7]

Anacreon 361 Page:
> Rejection of wealth and power (in favor of simpler things?).[8]

Phocylides 2. 6–8D:
> The good wife is industrious.

Phocylides 4D:
> A small polis, well-ordered, is preferred over luxurious Ninevah.

Phocylides 7D:
> Wealth consists of a piece of good farmland.

Phocylides 9D:
> Gaining a livelihood takes precedence over *aretê*.

Phocylides 12D:
> To be *mesos* in the polis is best.

Ananius 2D:
> Simple food is preferable to gold.

Hipponax 16, 17, 24A, 24B, 25, 29, 39, 42D:
> Total preoccupation with food and the simple necessities of life; mocks his own poverty.[9]

Taken together these passages reveal a remarkable consistency of outlook. It is evident, first of all, that some "virtues" which are important in the epic-aristocratic system (e.g., courage, skill, fame) are seldom criticized for themselves, but the focal point for these is now the community not the individual.[10] On the other hand, certain manifestations of the aristocratic ethos are criticized: arrogance, acquisitiveness at the expense of others, luxury, outward display, mere appearance. More important to note is that explicitly and implicitly the basis for approval or disapproval of values is usefulness. The aristocratic-heroic ideal, in short, is subjected to a test of *utile*, and where it fails it is rejected. This concept of usefulness is often stated in terms of the commonalty, and there the criticism is essentially that the aristocratic values are antisocial. Additional social themes, consistently stated throughout the period, are a strong dislike of the improper exercise of authority, a distaste for violence and civil strife, the primacy of justice and fair-dealing, and the idea that social injustice is punishable by divine retribution. Also notable are attempts to restate the idea of *aretê* in a communal rather than an individual context.

Seldom, however, do these statements appear in the form of outright protest; there is little obvious sense either of serious discontent or of oppression. We note, rather, the well-defined expression of a point of view that has its foundation in a solid sense of worth. This sense of worth is seen in the positive aspect of the tradition which reveals a set of counter values as solidly established as the aristocratic values. These also focus primarily on usefulness and practicality, often stated in terms of the larger community. In this aspect of the tradition what may be called "peasant" virtues are commended: hard work, thrift, simplicity, cooperation, common sense, utility.

It is reasonable to conclude that such consistency of attitude over a lengthy period is expressive of a literary convention that was critical of upper class values and that professed the merits of the peasant class. If the lyric poets of the seventh and sixth centuries were writing within the context of such a tradition these same themes should be reflected in the literature of an earlier period. Certainly the *Works and Days* and *Theogony* display these attitudes in abundance, and it is hardly necessary to dwell at length on the Hesiodic bias against aristocratic values in favor of a peasant system of values. In fact, the close similarity in content and tone between the statements of the lyric poets and Hesiod demonstrates that there was a frame of conventional attitudes which goes back at least to the beginning of the seventh century.[11]

The obvious question at this point is whether the tradition originated with the Hesiodic school or whether Hesiod was himself a continuator of a tradition of anti-aristocratic, pro-peasant expression. It can be shown, I believe, that the tradition was operative earlier than Hesiod; despite their dedication to the value-system of the warrior-nobility, the Homeric epics reveal significant traces of an egalitarian tradition.

The Thersites incident in *Iliad* 2 is the first recorded instance of anti-aristocratic, anti-heroic sentiment. Despite much controversy concerning the role and position of Thersites in the book, certain facts pertinent to this discussion are clear. As he is presented in this episode, Thersites was no novice at public speaking or at expressing his discontent. He is called ἀμετροεπής and had a vast fund of disorderly insults, which he used, with apparent regularity, in his role as a crowd-pleaser, against the *basileis*, especially against Achilles and Odysseus (lines 212–221). Even Odysseus calls him λιγὺς ἀγορητής (246). Thersites' speech is short, eighteen lines, but in it are clearly expressed some of the themes familiar in the tradition: the king's greed and selfishness, his violent disregard of fair-dealing. Another theme, also observed in the later expression of the tradition, is that the leader (*archos*, line 234) has a responsibility to the larger community on whom he ultimately depends. For unmistakable in Thersites' speech is the implication that the rank and file are the basis of the king's power and wealth.[12]

Not only is Thersites presented as a frequent critic of the leadership, he also expresses in a pungent and effective style a point of view antithetical to the heroic ideal. Implicit in his description of the Trojan campaign, which for him was nothing more than an expedition to win booty and ransom, is a denial of the heroic code that motivated the aristocratic warriors. In Books 1 (121 ff.) and 9 (307 ff.) Achilles also reviles Agamemnon, but his speeches are full of the heroic ethic wholly lacking in Thersites' broadside. Thersites' realistic, pragmatic, common soldier's view of warfare is in all essentials the same as Archilochus'.[13]

There is one other trace in the *Iliad* of a major theme of the tradition. Only once, but most emphatically and dramatically, does the *Iliad* link the idea of justice to an avenging deity. This is the famous simile of the flood that an angry Zeus sends down on men (16. 387–88):

οἳ βίῃ εἰν ἀγορῇ σκολιὰς κρίνωσι θέμιστας,
ἐκ δὲ δίκην ἐλάσωσι, θεῶν ὄπιν οὐκ ἀλέγοντες.

The giving of "crooked decrees" violently and without regard to the gods, is, as Lesky points out, "entirely in the manner of Hesiod."[14] But, more importantly, this commentary on ethical-political right and wrong, later observed not only in Hesiod but in other statements of the anti-aristocratic tradition, is here presented in complete form, all the elements worked out. Already in the eighth century it has the feel of a traditional concept. Further, if public business during the Homeric period was entirely in the hands of the aristocrats, as some historians maintain, then these lines constitute no less a statement than that Zeus himself punishes nobles who are guilty of political injustice!

A similar concern with this kind of social justice is even more evident in the *Odyssey*. Thus in 18. 138–142 Odysseus obliquely warns the suitors against violence and lawlessness, hinting that these will bring punishment from the gods. And, in lines which recall a fragment of Archilochus (94 D), the gods are said to wander in disguise (17. 487):

ἀνθρώπων ὕβριν τε καὶ εὐνομίην ἐφορῶντες.[15]

In another arresting simile, Odysseus likens Penelope to a "blameless king" who, because he is god-fearing, just and a good leader, prospers along with his people (19. 109-14). This combination of social virtues which produce prosperity for the whole community is also important in Hesiod and in the lyric poets.[16]

Of even greater significance than these manifestations of the tradition are the incidents in the *Odyssey* that concern Odysseus, in his disguise as a beggar, the swineherd Eumaeus, and the cowherd Philoetius. A very large portion of Books 1-22 is devoted to the curious friendship that develops between the returning king and his loyal slaves. Eumaeus especially personifies the virtues of the peasant ethic: cooperation, thrift, hard work, piety, common sense. He, above all, is scandalized by the behavior of the suitors, and the qualities of character he exhibits are set off against the violence, greed, arrogance and impiety of the aristocratic suitors.[17] Their actions are not only in contrast to Eumaeus' *peasant* soundness but also do violence to the heroic code, which they, as the "best men of the community," the *aristoi*, are supposed to embody.[18]

Eumaeus is much more than a good servant—Homer explicitly states that he was a trusted friend to Penelope, Telemachus and Laertes.[19] He becomes a close friend of the beggar Odysseus, and when Telemachus arrives at the swineherd's hut Eumaeus functions as the courteous host, observing all the rules of heroic etiquette (16. 46 ff.). A further, important, implication of these episodes is that men in lowly positions, by their own good qualities, can excel in an aristocratic society. This is done pointedly in Book 22, where Odysseus, Telemachus, the swineherd and the cowherd fight shoulder to shoulder (all four, incidentally, equally armed as heroic warriors) against a superior force of suitors. Twice Eumaeus and Philoetius get their man with accurate spear casts; Eumaeus, like Telemachus, receives an honorable wound, and Philoetius is allowed an heroic vaunt over a fallen suitor.[20] By emphasizing the bonds of comradeship between men of royal blood and slaves, and by showing men of no rank in heroic postures the poet appears to have made a clear statement that excellence and achievement result not from birth and breeding only but from intrinsic worth. It is most tempting, indeed, to see social commentary in the fact that the real heroes of the second half of the *Odyssey* are men of the lower class and not aristocrats.[21]

One noteworthy aspect of the episodes of Book 22 is the assumption by Odysseus that Eumaeus and Philoetius would acquit themselves well in the battle with the suitors, despite a total lack of soldierly training. This may well reflect a folk motif—because they were good peasants they would be good warriors.[22] A further implication that these scenes fall within the context of a tradition favorable to the lower classes is Odysseus' promise that their loyalty and courage will be materially rewarded. In 21. 213–216 he promises that if the suitors are defeated he will give the slaves wives and possessions and houses near his own; he promises further that they will be *hetairoi* and *kasignêtoi* of Telemachus—a startling upgrading of their material and social positions.

A somewhat analogous situation is found in the story told by Odysseus, the "Cretan" (14. 199–359). The fictional Odysseus began at a disadvantage, as the son of a wealthy Cretan and a slave woman; at his father's death he was given only a tiny allotment by his brothers (line 210). But, because of his prowess (εἵνεκ' ἐμῆς ἀρετῆς, line 212) he was able to marry well, and to become eminent among the Cretans, even attaining international prominence as a hero in the Trojan war. Both Odysseus' fictional account and the narrative of Eumaeus and Philoetius show that even in a "closed society," commonly assumed as the normal situation in the epics, socio-economic advancement on the basis of personal merit alone was a literary motif.

While none of the examples cited constitutes by itself definite proof that the epics were influenced by a tradition of anti-elitist sentiment, taken together they form a clear and coherent pattern of awareness of such attitudes. Certainly their existence in the *Iliad* and *Odyssey* demonstrates that during the eighth century the chief themes of anti-aristocratic expression had already been formulated and were sufficiently powerful to intrude even the aristocratic epics.[23]

In conclusion, the fact that there was an early, sustained, and well-articulated anti-aristocratic tradition, coupled with a conscious emphasis on the values of the common man, is significant to any historical assessment of the so-called "social revolution" of the archaic period. The existence of this dual tradition implies that the basis for social change was deeply rooted in a firm sense of identity and self-esteem of the peasant class, and, further, that a feeling for justice, equality and common dignity formed a stratum of democratic orientation which found constant public expression during the seventh and sixth centuries. The social historian may well caution himself against emphasizing the weakness and discontent of the "masses" during the archaic period, and should stress more the positive forces which produced so much important social, economic and political change.[24]

NOTES

[1] E.g.: G. Busolt, *Gr. Gesch.*, 1[2] (Gotha 1893) 627–628; *id.* 2[2], 254; J. Beloch, *Gr. Gesch.*, 1, 1[2] (Strasbourg 1912) 214, 306–308, 347–378; Glotz–Cohen, *Hist. Grecque*, 1 (Paris 1925) 218–222, 237–238, 410–411; E. Meyer, *Gesch. des Altertums*, 3[3] (Stuttgart 1936) 280–283,

321–323, 510–512; G. de Sanctis, *Storia dei Greci.* 1⁸ (Firenze 1967) 282–284; U. Wilcken, *Gr. Gesch.*⁹ (Munich 1962) 97; J. B. Bury, *Hist. of Greece*³ (London 1955) 118.

²N. G. L. Hammond, *A History of Greece* (Oxford 1959), can say, "Different as the poets of the Greek states were in temperament and outlook, they had one point in common. They were all aristocrats" (p. 173). Cf. F. Schachermeyer, *Gr. Gesch.*² (Stuttgart 1969) 84–85: "So formte die Adelskultur nicht nur den Ritter, an ihr formte sich auch der kleine Mann. Sie wurde dadurch zur gemeinhellenischen Gesittung." This is a dominant theme of W. Jaeger's *Paideia,* which is even stated as a universal truth: "Culture is simply the aristocratic ideal of a nation, increasingly intellectualized" (Vol. I, 2nd Eng. ed., tr. by G. Highet [New York 1965] 4).

³Thus W. G. Forrest, *The Emergence of Greek Democracy* (New York and Toronto 1956), speaking of Hesiod, says that the *demos* "in whatever sense the word had from time to time, failed to produce a voice that has survived, with this one exception" (p. 58). Some, e.g. Jaeger (above, note 2) 69 ff., emphasize the originality of Hesiod in formulating the peasant ideal: "the prophet of a new age." Others, like A. A. Trever, "The Age of Hesiod: A Study in Economic History," *CP* 19 (1924) 157–168, make him an early spokesman of class conflict. Cf. the common view which regards Archilochus' antiheroic stance as the result of his personal condition, so A. Lesky, *A History of Greek Literature,* tr. by J. Willis and C de Heer (London 1966) 110: "…the explanation lies in his origins. Archilochus was a bastard."

⁴Cf. Simonides' "encomium" on those who fell at Thermopylae (531 Page), where the *andres agathoi* win the "glory of Greece" as the reward for their service. Here the community is expanded, but the sentiment is the same.

⁵See C. M. Bowra, "Xenophanes, Fragment 3," *CQ* 35 (1941)119–126. Douris of Samos cites some lines of the poet Asius as proof of the ostentatious luxury of the Samians in this period (*FGrHist* 76 F60).

⁶The picture of the mare's daughter is especially revealing (lines 57–70): she shuns menial work (δούλι' ἔργα), will not grind, sift or carry out the filth; she refuses to sit in front of the oven because of the soot, washes herself two or three times a day, annoints herself with perfume, keeps her hair combed and wreathed with flowers. In short, the wife of an aristocrat, not of a peasant. The peasant distinction between outward appearance and usefulness is seen most clearly in 67–70: she is καλὸν θέημα to others, but a κακόν to her mate, unless he is a τύραννος or σκηπτοῦχος, "the kind that takes delight in things like that."

⁷Fr. 13, on the other hand, expresses just the opposite, aristocratic, idea.

⁸See B. Snell, *The Discovery of the Mind,* tr. by T. G. Rosenmeyer (Cambridge, Mass. 1953) 48 and 312, n. 5, who equates the tone of this fragment with Archil. 22.

⁹The significance of Hipponax must not be understated. The savage realism, the street slang, and the humorous personal references to his own life place him firmly in the tradition. More important is that, when a poet reproduces vividly detailed scenes from daily low life, we must presume both an audience used to such themes and a literary tradition accustomed to handling topics that had lower class appeal.

¹⁰The new communal ideal expressed by Tyrtaeus and Callinus is treated by Jaeger (above, note 2) 87–97. See also Snell (above, note 8) 171–174.

¹¹E.g., *Works and Days.* Zeus as protector of the weak and humbler of the proud: 5–8; distaste for violence and strife: 12–16, 161–166, 182–194, 213–216, 320–322; violence, greed and injustice of those in power: 38–39, 202–212; divine retribution for injustice: 217–224, 238–273, 333–334. primacy of justice: 225–235; appreciation of simple things: 40–41; common sense: 293–297; industriousness: 298–309, 381–382, 398–413, 493–503; social cooperation: 342–351; thrift: 361–371; peasant view of women: 60–105, 373–375, 695–705.

¹²Booty is gotten by "us", "me" (lines 228, 231); "we" help him (238). In addition, there is the strongly expressed assertion of the potential of the common soldiery for taking independent collective action (lines 235–238).

[13]The fact that Thersites is described in odious terms by the poet, and is ignominiously silenced by Odysseus does not lessen the impact of his outburst. On the contrary, the savage caricature, the beating with the sceptre, and the acquiescence of the rank and file to his silencing serve to underscore the seriousness of the conservative reaction to that kind of anti-aristocratic display. The fact remains that for the poet and his audience it was possible for a man to step out of ranks and berate his betters. To argue that what Thersites did was highly unusual is not sufficient—if what he did was unthinkable, then neither poet nor audience could have contemplated it. In a provocative book, *Hesiods Erga in ihrem Verhältnis zur Ilias* (Frankfurt 1959), H. Munding maintains that *Il.* 2 is a post-Hesiodic addition, composed as a travesty of the peaceful, unwarlike peasant ethic of Hesiod. In this "Hesiodreaktion" Thersites is an epic caricature of Hesiod himself (pp. 110–150). Munding's views seem to have found little acceptance, but his companion thesis that *Works and Days* self-consciously opposes a peasant morality to Homer's aristocratic ethic (pp. 12–96) is in the right direction. Munding wants to believe that the legendary contest between Homer and Hesiod may actually have occurred; it is simpler, as I have tried to show, to believe that Hesiod expressed themes that were in a conscious tradition of anti-aristocratic thought, and that this tradition was not wholly lacking in the epic poems.

[14]Above, note 3, 69.

[15]Cf. 14. 83–84.

[16]*Theogony* 80–92; *Works and Days* 225–237. In 238–247 (Cf. 260–262) where the "whole polis" suffers for the violence and injustice of its leaders the point is made strongly that such behavior is antisocial—a prominent theme in Solon (fr. 3. 14 ff.).

[17]E.g., his industriousness, skill and success as a peasant: 14. 3. ff., 524 ff.; his piety: 14. 388 ff.; his indignation with the suitors: 14. 80 ff.

[18]See Jaeger (above, note 2) 20–21. Jaeger is forced by his assumptions to maintain that although "the shameless behaviour of the suitors is constantly stigmatized as a disgrace to them and to their class" the poet's admiration for the nobility is not diminished.

[9]*Od.* 15. 353–379; 16. 11–29, 135–145; 17. 505–552, 589–597.

[20]Lines 108–115, 265–268, 277–291. Homer's favorable depiction of Eumaeus has often been explained by the fact that he was of royal blood, and, therefore, "noble" by birth. But the qualities most in evidence are those of a good servant, not of a high-souled aristocrat. In any case, Philoetius, whose character is the same as Eumaeus', and who also proves capable of competing as a warrior, has no claim to gentle birth.

[21]In addition, Eurycleia is presented as a paragon of common sense and loyalty. Penelope exemplifies in all respects the peasant view of a good wife. It is also worthy of note that Laertes is essentially a small farmer, not a royal person (1.189–193; 24. 226 ff.). Is it entirely coincidence that two *demiourgoi*, Phemius and Medon, alone of the group in the hall, are considered guiltless and spared (22. 330–377)? The children of Dolius, Melanthius the goatherd, and Melantho, Penelope's serving girl, are wicked, and suffer grim deaths (22. 465–477). Both are closely allied to the suitors. Eumaeus rebukes Melanthius for his violence (ὑβρίζων), pride and wastefulness (17. 244–246); Melantho is the type of the "bad" peasant woman: insolent, faithless, promiscuous (18. 321 ff.). Dolius, on the other hand, is a faithful servant to Penelope (4. 735), and retainer to Laertes (24. 222). Originally, perhaps, there were two—one, the father of the bad servants (who lived up to his name) was superseded by Dolius of the (probably later) final book, who, with his six sons displayed the same courage and loyalty as the good servants Eumaeus and Philoetius. The rag-tag "army" of Odysseus, Telemachus, Eumaeus, Philoetius, Laertes, Dolius and his sons, which confronts the relatives of the suitors fits very neatly into a propeasant tradition (24. 496 ff.).

[22]Cf. 18. 351–386, the exchange between Odysseus and Eurymachus. The suitor taunts Odysseus with being a beggar and not wanting honest work; Odysseus retorts that he is a good farmer and a good warrior as well.

The Tradition of Anti-Aristocratic Thought

[23] It has been well-established that peasant views and attitudes permeate both epics. See H. Strasburger, "Der soziologische Aspekt der homerischen Epen," *Gymnasium* 60 (1953) 97–114, who gives many examples. For further examples see also H. Levy, "Odyssean Suitors," *TAPA* 94 (1963) 145–153 and P. Walcot, *Greek Peasants, Ancient and Modern* (Manchester, Eng. 1970) 16–20. These agree generally that the economic and social background of the Homeric epics and of the Hesiodic poems is essentially the same, but the evidence they give shows mainly that the economic-cultural milieu of the poems is simple and rural, and that the upper layer of society had many values in common with the peasants.

[24] Contrast the view of Forrest (above, note 3) 65–66, for whom the task of the archaic period was "to create, virtually *ab initio*, the idea of a state composed of citizens who by virtue of their citizenship alone had certain unquestionable rights… In a word, to invent the notion of an autonomous human being and to apply it rigorously throughout all levels of society."

THE STRUCTURE OF AUTHORITY IN THE *ILIAD*

In *Iliad* 15.294–300, Thoas, one of the younger Achaean warriors, addresses a group of his companions in a moment of fierce fighting against Hector:

> But come, as I say, let us all *peithesthai*. Let us order the *plêthus* to return to the ships; but we ourselves, who declare we are *aristoi* in the army, let us stand and see if facing him first we will check him, lifting our spears against him; and I think that even though he is eager he will fear in his heart to enter the throng of the Danaans. So he spoke, and they listened to him well and they *peithesthai* him.

This scene is typical of hundreds of similar passages in the *Iliad*, in which someone issues an order or makes a request to others. Some are long and elaborate, others are short, but all of them can be reduced to a small number of categories which illustrate the mechanics of commanding and leading in the epic.

The purpose of this paper is to attempt a methodology that will furnish a structural model of authority in a society in which the workings of the authority-system were neither precisely defined nor clearly stated. Thus the analysis of Homeric leadership—how men induced other men to act—is schematic rather than literary. Such an approach is open to the criticism that pertinent considerations such as subjective human motivations for action, ironic or tragic intent on the poet's part, the pragmatic or plot-demands of a given situation, and so on, are ignored. The easiest response to this correct criticism is that the method of enquiry essayed here simply offers another perspective of the text; consequently both literary and linguistic analysis are largely excluded in favor of abstract structural descriptions of leadership situations in the *Iliad*. It is hoped that this approach will provide a conceptual frame which will illuminate one aspect of the cultural foundations of an archaic society.

The question of "historical reality" cannot be addressed directly here. Whether the "political system" observed in the *Iliad* reflects an actual system which can be located spatially and temporally, or whether it is entirely a poetic fiction, or an amalgam of the real and the imagined, are problems which can never be solved definitively. The system of leadership and authority in the *Iliad* may properly be analyzed in respect to its own inner logic. On the other hand, it is a reasonable hypothesis that the socio-psychological conditions underlying the processes of commanding and leading in the poem ought to correspond in some meaningful way to an eighth-century audience's perception of the observed reality, and, to a significant degree, would be experientially familiar.[1]

The procedure followed in this investigation was to isolate every instance in the *Iliad* in which someone attempts to exercise "Leadership Authority" (LA), which is defined as:

> The subject's (the person willing a mode of activity) ability, recognized, claimed or assumed, to make decisions, issue orders, or suggest specific courses of action with the expectation that the decisions/orders/suggestions will be persuasive or compelling to others.

The initiation of LA will, or will not, result in *others acting in accordance with the expressed wish of the subject*. Situations in which LA succeeds are given the broad category, "Type A." When LA fails it is a "Type B" situation. As has been noted, these scenes vary from very simple to rather complex multiple-response situations; accordingly, neat and precise categorization in every case was not possible. Nevertheless, despite ambiguity in a few instances, the resultant count is essentially accurate: of approximately 320 LA situations in the *Iliad* 280 are Type A, 40 are Type B.[2] Since Type A situations are preponderant we may assume that this type forms the usual or statistically "normal" pattern of initiative/response within the society of the warrior-group. That is, whenever a subject attempts LA his chances of success in "persuading" the addressee(s) are 87%.

The most frequently successful LA subjects are the major figures in the poem whose power or whose ability as warriors and counsellors are recognized and celebrated in other situations: Hector, Achilles, Agamemnon, Nestor, Ajax, Odysseus, Priam, Diomedes, Menelaus, Idomeneus, Patroclus, Sarpedon.[3] From this we may reasonably conclude that what enables a character to induce others to do his bidding is related to that character's power or ability. We can state this more formally: the capacity to initiate a course of action depends on possession of either *established social position* or *standing based on ability*.

A digression is necessary at this point to define these terms as they are used here.[4] "Established social position" (henceforth "position") states the

The Structure of Authority in the *Iliad* 251

universally agreed-upon relationship between the holder of position and social groups, which affirms that the holder is privileged, by virtue of his position, to exert control or predominance within the group. Thus Ajax, son of Oïleus, has position among the Locrians, which means that the Locrians acknowledge Ajax as their leader, heed him and follow him. Among the Achaeans Agamemnon has position, which means that the mass of the Achaeans and all others with position agree that Agamemnon is predominant. Both the bases of position and the nature of the predominance elude precise classification. For example, the basis of Agamemnon's (and others') position is a complex of inheritance, remote divine sanction, age, personal wealth and numbers of followers. There are, in addition, less "concrete" bases for position, namely the vaguely expressed notion that the leader holds his position by consent of the communal group itself, and the (related) notion that position is dependent on ability. The nature of the control exercised is not clearly delimited and ranges from persuasion, to coercion. Furthermore, position exists on an almost totally undifferentiated continuum, in that all who hold position are *basileis* and share, more or less equally, the descriptive nomenclature of position. "Standing based on ability" (henceforth "standing") is the recognition accorded by others of a figure's ability and achievement. The bases of standing are visibly apparent—a nexus of physical and mental skills—and need little elucidation.

It is imperative to emphasize at the outset that position and standing are essentially inseparable elements of a unitary nexus, which can be differentiated only by the sort of structural analysis employed here; the Homeric *basileus* is both leader and warrior/counsellor. At the point of social development depicted in the *Iliad* position without standing is an almost impossible conception (hence the necessity for Agamemnon to be perceived also as pure warrior— e.g. in his *aristeia*, 11.91–247). It must also be noted that within the cognitive frame of the poem position is a much more intricate element than standing. Because the bases of standing are clearly defined in the society, and because their effects are visibly obvious, both a typology of skills and a rough gradation of standing may be constructed: Achilles is the best warrior by far; Ajax is next; Odysseus excels in speaking, Nestor in counsel, and so on. Position, on the other hand, is more problematical. Because its bases are complex and not precisely defined, because all figures with position are perceived to some extent as *pares*, and, especially, because ability (which is *the* basis of standing) is a prerequisite of position, a description of a "hierarchy" of position is impossible.[5] There is one apparent exception. Although in general it is not possible to establish an absolute ordering within position, there is universal agreement in the poem that Agamemnon and Hector have highest position within the whole of their societies. If it were so that in all LA situations in which they were participants Agamemnon and Hector initiated action, or, having attempted LA, they were always successful, the structural model of authority in the *Iliad* would be relatively simple: at the top of either group one figure with supreme authority, whose will was always translated into action, and directly below him a lesser stratum of authority whose relative position and standing were more or less undifferentiated. Such is not the case; initiative is often assumed by other participants in LA situations, and in a number of cases Agamemnon and Hector are unsuccessful in initiating LA. They occupy, in other words, the position not of *supremus* but of *primus inter pares.*

Thus, although it is *statistically evident* that some position or standing is a necessary precondition for LA and that figures with the greatest position and standing initiate action most frequently, there is an inherent uncertainty concerning the relative influence of position or standing as determinants of LA in any given situation. Or, to state this in schematic terms, LA situations do not exhibit a pattern analogous to a formal chain-of-command or to a conical system of authority. Often (as in the example which introduced this paper) LA is assumed situationally by an individual in response to the exigencies of the particular moment and easily relinquished when the moment has passed. There is frequent interchange of authority-roles without reference to a hierarchy of position or standing, so that in many Type A situations the LA subject is of lesser standing than the addressee; in addition there is a significant (though much smaller) number of instances in which the successful LA subject is inferior in position to the addressee (Type A^2). Most notably there occur several situations in which the LA subject, although superior in position, is unsuccessful (Type B^1; see note 2).

A description of the structure of authority in the *Iliad* must therefore account not only for the question of the primacy of position or standing in general but also for the special circumstance of the acknowledged "supreme" leader who, by virtue of his highest position, will usually initiate action successfully, but not always. Clearly there is potential for social disharmony arising from uncertainty about the relative weight of the factors of position and standing as determinants of action. And in the case of the figure with the highest position, the *primus,* any conflict poses a serious threat to the smooth functioning of the authority system.

As a matter of fact oppositional tension is situationally minimal; almost 90% of LA situations are Type A. A third constituent factor is therefore hypothesized to explain the structure of Leadership Authority: a principle of "collective authority" or "collectivity." These somewhat awkward terms are meant to express the complex phenomenon of the *authority of the group* which, unlike position and standing, is perceptible not only at the highest echelon but throughout the whole of the society. At the upper level collective authority denotes the operation of a sense of "collegial cooperation," which serves to "defuse" potential discord among those figures with position and standing. On the level of the society as a whole collective authority reflects a wider group-authority which, although vaguely expressed in the poem, is nevertheless clearly manifested, and, as will be seen, is the basic condition from which all other forms of authority derive.

At the leader-level of society collective authority works as follows. Whenever a figure attempts LA, once attempted it is usually successful, regardless of the relative position/standing of those involved in the situation, provided that the subject has sufficient "stature" in the community. Functionally, this cooperative give-and-take guarantees that competition in the sensitive area of initiating action will be minimal. It can hardly be overemphasized that initiation, *archê*, is a major point of potential tension among strong-willed individuals. In a culture like that of the *Iliad*, in which the competitive spirit is a primary value, a moderating social mechanism is necessary to enable the high degree of cooperation essential for a common effort. Collective authority insures that in a group composed essentially of *pares* the question of who are *primi*, that is, who will exercise authority in a given situation, need not continually be put to the test.[6]

When it works properly, the collegial exchange of authority-roles permits socially "correct" reactions in LA situations. In 12.342–72, Menestheus, leader of the Athenians, hard-pressed in the battle before the Achaean wall, orders his herald Thootes to summon the Aiantes to help. Thootes delivers Menestheus' request verbatim: the two Aiantes or at least Telamonian Ajax and Teucer are to come. Ajax responds by ordering Ajax son of Oïleus to remain in place with Lycomedes, and goes to Menestheus' aid along with Teucer and Pandion.

A more extended example of collective authority is found in 17.651–723, in the battle for the corpse of Patroclus. Ajax orders Menelaus to find Antilochus and to tell him to inform Achilles of Patroclus' death. Menelaus obeys, but, before leaving, enjoins the Aiantes and Meriones to stand fast. Having found Antilochus Menelaus orders him to go to Achilles, and Antilochus obeys. Menelaus sends Thrasymedes to the Pylians to replace the loss of Antilochus. Returning to the battle around Patroclus, Menelaus tells the Aiantes that together they should devise some plan. Telamonian Ajax orders Menelaus and Meriones to lift up the corpse and bear it away, while he and the other Ajax fight a delaying action.

These and similar episodes are made up of a series of Type A situations in which the LA subjects and addressees assume and relinquish authority-roles easily and without friction.[7] The patterns of initiation and response which are observed, although fluid, are not formless. Within Leadership Authority the structural elements of authority based on position, authority based on standing (ability) and collective authority are in balance. Logically, the socially effective working of the authority-system depends on the harmonious interrelationship of these factors. As we have seen, position appears functionally to be the more dominant element (figures with highest position will most frequently initiate action), but because of the intrinsic ambiguity between position and standing an express ratio of value cannot be stated without raising serious questions about the primacy of the one or the other as the basis for initiating action, i.e. without establishing an oppositional polarity. The factor of collective authority is the overarching element which serves to obviate potential conflicting claims. It must be stressed that collective authority, *qua* structural element, normally operates on the preconscious level, i.e. as an inherent social condition. It can be defined as a culturally deep-rooted sociopsychological mechanism, the underlying origin of which is the (again preconscious) presumption of an essential oneness of the group. Like position and standing it achieves the level of conscious articulation only when severe imbalance threatens to disrupt social stability.

Since, by definition, the LA process works properly in Type A situations, evidence of strain in the process will be found in the anomalous Type B situations. Detailed contextual analysis of those portions of the *Iliad* which are characterized by Type B or other "unusual" situations reveals even more clearly the structure of command and leadership. The main series of episodes are, of course, related to the Quarrel between Agamemnon and Achilles.[8]

The first occurs at the beginning of Book 1. The priest Chryses prays to "all the Achaeans and especially to the two sons of Atreus" for his daughter's ransom; the Achaeans shout assent, but Agamemnon refuses (1.15–25). Although Chryses is outside the social system of the Greeks, he makes his claim to LA as a priest of Apollo; he holds his badge of standing, the fillets on a golden staff, and founds his appeal on Apollo's authority (*hazesthai*, 21). The Achaean host recognizes the legitimacy of the claim (*aideisthai*, 23). The king's negative response (26–32) both rejects the expressed will of the army and explicitly denies the authority implied by the priest's standing (28). Implicit in this double Type B^2 situation (see note 2) is Agamemnon's reliance on his (as yet unstated) claim to superiority of position to override a competing claim of standing and the principle of group-authority.[9]

LA initiative is seized by Achilles in summoning the *agora* (1.54), in his suggestion to Agamemnon that a seer be consulted (62–64), and in his promise of protection to Calchas (85–91). It is in these exchanges that the polarization

The Structure of Authority in the *Iliad*

of position and standing is first evident. Calchas requests Achilles' protection "in words and hands" against Agamemnon, "who *krateein* mightily over all the Achaeans and whom the Achaeans *peithesthai*, for a *basileus* is *kreissôn* when he is angry at a *cherês* man (Type A², 1.77–80). Achilles' reply, that no one, "not even...Agamemnon, who declares himself to be by far *aristos* of the Achaeans," will harm the seer (88–91), approaches being a clear statement of opposition between Achilles' standing-authority and the king's position-authority. Agamemnon's belated and grudging Type A response (he will give the girl back, 116), because it is coupled with the demand for a compensatory *geras* on the grounds that "it is not seemly" he should be *agerastos* (119), in fact increases the tension. Similarly, Achilles' repetition of the request to surrender Chryseis, together with his offer of increased compensation (127–29), ought to constitute the "usual" cooperative compromise, but it contains a Type B² element in that Agamemnon demanded a *geras* "immediately" (118), while Achilles promises compensation when Troy is sacked. The situation is further complicated by Achilles' insult (*philokteanôtate*, 122) and his indirect appeal to a wider group-authority, when he says that the common (*xynêïa*) booty has been apportioned and it "is not seemly for the *laous* to gather together these things again" (126).

As the Quarrel of Book 1 continues, the stated oppositions of position and standing are more pronounced. First, Agamemnon, appealing to his position-authority, threatens to take a *geras* from Achilles, Ajax or Odysseus (131–39). He closes this portion of the Quarrel with an explicit affirmation of his claim to LA based on position. He will, himself, take Achilles' prize, Briseis, "so that you may know well how much I am *pherteros* than you, and that another may fear to call himself *îsos* to me and liken himself to me to my face" (184–87). Achilles, on his part, contradicts Agamemnon's position-authority ("how may someone of the Achaeans *peithesthai* your words of his own free will?"), accuses the king of abusing his position and its privileges, exalts his own standing as a warrior, and, complaining about the diminution of his *timê*, threatens to sever himself from the jurisdiction of Agamemnon's position (149–71).

The climax of the confrontation opens with insults by Achilles of Agamemnon's own standing as a warrior (225–28) and of his position (cf. *dêmoboros basileus*, 231). He directly attacks Agamemnon's claim to primacy based on position by implying that Leadership Authority is actually grounded in the group—"and now the sons of the Achaeans who give judgments (*dikaspoloi*) bear it [*skêptron*] in their hands, and they guard *themistai* from Zeus" (237–38)—and insists that *his* standing has greater social value than the king's position (240–44). At this point Nestor intervenes in an attempt to restore the principle of collegial cooperation. His speech (254–84) demonstrates a conscious-level awareness of the structural elements of LA and the socially destructive effects of imbalance. Because of the Quarrel a "*mega penthos* is come upon the Achaean land" and the strife would make the Trojans rejoice (254–58). The legitimate prerogatives of the elements of position and standing and their socially allowable limits within the sphere of collectivity must be reintroduced (1.275–84).

> Neither do you, even though you are *agathos*, take away the girl, but let her be, since the sons of the Achaeans gave her as a *geras* to him first. Nor you, son of Peleus, wish to strive against a *basileus* in might, since never does a *skêptouchos basileus* have an equal share of *timê*, to whom Zeus has given *kydos*. But if you are *karteros* and a goddess mother bore you, he is *pherteros*, since he *anassein* over more people. And you, son of Atreus, cease your *menos*; but I beseech you to give up your anger against Achilles, who is a mighty bulwark of evil war for all the Achaeans.

The final speeches of Agamemnon and Achilles show both antagonists having arrived at something approaching an abstracted understanding of their social roles. The king complains: "But this man wishes to be above everyone else, he wishes to *krateein* everyone, to *anassein* everyone, and to *sêmainein* everyone; there is someone, I think, who will not *peithesthai*" (287–89). Achilles says: "I would be called *deilos* and *outidanos* if I yield to you in everything that you say; give these orders to others, do not *sêmainein* me; for no longer do I think I will *peithesthai* you" (293–96).

The lengthy episode of the Quarrel, which opens the *Iliad*, verifies the hypothesis that the structural elements of leadership authority are position, standing and collectivity, that the socially "correct" exercise of authority requires an harmonious configuration of these elements, with position as the normally dominant factor and collectivity as the necessary mediating factor. It is to be noted that despite the severe imbalance the structure remains precariously intact and does not collapse, because the dominance of position is maintained, and because collegial compromise is not entirely absent. Agamemnon does restore Chryseis, Achilles does not go home as he had threatened; neither does he physically attack the king nor resist the taking of Briseis; in addition, both antagonists make sporadic conciliatory gestures. The exchanges also exhibit a conscious perception of the social dangers which attend deterioration of the integrity of the structure.[10]

The ground situation is one of unanimity in which all the members of the group, at every level, share a common set of attitudes concerning the

The Structure of Authority in the *Iliad*

initiation of action. Consequently, we may assume that the overriding concern is to restore collective authority and to repair the imbalance. Imbalance is centrifugal, leads to social dysfunction, which brings material consequences which are harmful to the whole; accordingly, a major thematic line of the poem is the progress from centrifugal to centripetal. Examples abound.

Agamemnon's puzzling decision to "test" the army and to involve the second-echelon leaders in the restraining of the anticipated rush (2.72–75) may be interpreted on the structural level as an attempt by the king both to reestablish his own diminished position-authority and to oblige the *hêgêtores* to a public commitment of loyalty to the figure with highest position. Almost certainly Nestor's announcement to the *boulê* that had anyone but the king reported the dream it would be considered false, represents a deliberate affirmation by the lower leadership of the precedence of position-authority. Beyond a doubt Odysseus' lectures to the leaders and the *dêmos*, both of which emphasize divine legitimation of kingly authority (directed to the "office" and not the person), have this purpose (2.203–6; cf. 196–97):

> In no way will all we Achaeans *basileuein* here; *polykoiraniê* is not *agathon*; let there be one *koiranos*, one *basileus*, to whom the son of crooked-counselling Kronos has given *skêptron* and *themistai* so that he may *bouleuein* for them.

The speech of Thersites (2.225–42), a Type B^2 situation, is directed against Agamemnon's abuse of his position (although not against position-authority itself). From Thersites' low-level perspective Agamemnon is the bad leader whose sense of the group is defective: "It is not seemly for one who is *archos* to lead the sons of the Achaeans into evil" (233–34). Odysseus' rebuttal (2.246–64) is a social object lesson; he repeats the phrase Nestor had used to Achilles in 1.277 (paraphrased by the host in 2.277), not to strive against kings, and strikes Thersites with the sceptre, symbol of position-authority. Odysseus' address to king and *agora* is directed towards unanimity and is approved with acclaim (2.284–335). Nestor takes up this and related themes: strife is divisive and counter-productive (2.337–43); he urges Agamemnon to resume his old role as leader (344–45); he curses those who would be dissidents (346–59); he tells Agamemnon to counsel well and to heed another's advice (360–63). In turn, the king welcomes Nestor's advice, publicly regrets the Quarrel, assumes some blame, and himself restates the principle of collectivity: "If ever we shall counsel a single counsel (*es ge mian bouleusomen*), then no longer will there be a putting off of evil for the Trojans, not even for an instant" (379–80). Agamemnon then issues tactical commands like a correct leader, and the Argives applaud enthusiastically (2.381–97). In schematic terms, the Type B episode of Thersites is followed by a series of nine Type A situations involving the leadership and the army, which restores the balance between position-authority and collective authority (2.225–446).

Subsequently, whenever an LA situation threatens social stability immediate steps are taken to restore correct proportion among the elements of position, standing and collectivity. In the Type B[1] situation in 9.17–49, in which Diomedes rejects Agamemnon's second proposal to return home, the warrior assails the king on the grounds that his superior position is insufficient to initiate action: "The son of crooked-counselling Kronos has endowed you by halves; with the *skêptron* he has given you to be honored above all, but *alkê* he has not given you, which is the greatest *kratos*" (9.37–39). The Greeks approve; Nestor commends Diomedes' standing as a warrior/counsellor, invoking his own standing as a more experienced counsellor as a warrant for his LA (9.61–75):

> Nor will anyone *atimein* my word, not even *kreiôn* Agamemnon. *Aphrêtôr, athemistos, anestios* is that man who loves chilling war among the people (*polemos epidêmios*).... But then, son of Atreus, you *archein*, for you are *basileutatos*...and when many are assembled you *peithesthai* the one who devises the best *boulê*.

In the *boulê* that follows Nestor drives these points home (9.97–102):[11]

> With you I leave off and with you I begin because you are *anax* of many *laoi* and Zeus has endowed you with *skêptron* and *themistai* that you may *bouleuesthai* for them. Therefore it is right for you especially to speak and also to listen, and to accomplish this for another, whenever his spirit urge him to speak for good. For on you hinges whatever he may initiate (*archein*).

Agamemnon moves towards the desired center by following the prescription for correct social conduct, admitting his mistake and offering recompense. By so doing he formally endeavors to repair the imbalance between position-authority and standing-authority ("worth many *laoi* is the man whom Zeus loves in his heart," 116–17), while yet affirming the precedence of position as the dominant factor of LA: "And let him yield place to me, inasmuch as I am *basileuteros* and declare myself elder in birth" (9.160). The attempts of the Embassy to effect collegial cooperation are rebuffed by Achilles, who continues to insist that his standing supersedes the other factors. He refuses to

The Structure of Authority in the *Iliad*

recognize the priority of position-authority: "And the daughter of Agamemnon, son of Atreus, I will not marry.... Let him pick another of the Achaeans, someone who is fitting for him and who is *basileuteros*" (9.388–92). He is, nevertheless, not immune to the centripetal force of the claim of the group on him, and in changing his mind from imminent departure to a half-promise of cooperation, Achilles also moves towards the center.

The tensions generated by competing claims of position and standing are intense; when the two elements are strongly represented the possibility of social discord is great. In the case of the Quarrel the stark juxtaposition of the opposing claims and the failure of collectivity produce a disharmony which affects the whole community. Such situations can be avoided only when oppositional polarity is muted in favor of collegial cooperation. An illustration is the potentially discordant confrontation between Glaucus and Hector in 17.140ff., in which Glaucus accuses Hector of cowardice and bad leadership for having abandoned the corpse of Sarpedon (see 16.656–65) and for not facing Ajax in the battle for the corpse of Patroclus. He threatens to abandon the war and return to Lycia with his troops. Hector's reply, although an angry rebuttal of the charge of cowardice, constitutes a cooperative gesture to Glaucus and ends with a positive assertion of Hector's leadership of the combined forces (17.170–87).[12]

The restoration of the element of collective authority means also a restoration of correct proportion of the factors of position and standing in initiating action. The exchanges between Agamemnon and Achilles in Book 19 are a public affirmation that a balance has been effected. There is no need to analyze these exchanges in detail, except to point out that all the sore points of the Quarrel are smoothed over. Achilles rather casually asserts that Briseis was not worth quarreling over (a contradiction of his previous sentiments), accepts partial blame for the Quarrel, implies that his insistence on his standing-authority was socially harmful and yields LA to Agamemnon (19. 56–75). Agamemnon's response (19.78–144) is addressed to Achilles, but, significantly, includes the whole of the *agora* in the reconciliation. By "blaming" Zeus, Moira, Erinys and Ate the king gives the Quarrel a cosmic dimension—the epic's way of saying that discontinuity in collective authority is so enormous a breach of social normality that its cause must be viewed as the workings of an external *force majeure*. His speech ends in a totally conciliatory manner with his offer of alternatives to Achilles, who, in turn, graciously yields authority back.[13] The king is given another reminder of the necessity to subordinate the claims of position to collectivity by Odysseus: "Son of Atreus, henceforth will you be *dikaioteros* towards another; for in no way is it blameful for a *basileus* to appease a man when he is first to be angry" (19.181–83).[14]

As has often been remarked, the Funeral Games of Book 23 show the group sharing in complete harmony. In terms of the factors of LA the contest scenes represent the final balancing. In every case Achilles' behavior is marked by deference to the position of Agamemnon, as in 156–57: "Son of Atreus, for to your words especially will the *laos* of the Achaeans *peithesthai*...." Achilles becomes the embodiment of collegial cooperation: in the incipient quarrel between Ajax son of Oïleus and Idomeneus (492–94), in the question of the second prize for Eumelus (536–39), in the wrestling contest between Odysseus and Ajax (735–37). The resolution of the potentially ugly Type B situation involving Menelaus and Antilochus in 23.426–30 is a model of collegial cooperation (587–611). The spirit of group harmony reaches its symbolic climax at the end of the games, in the poem's final exchange between Agamemnon and Achilles, where Achilles honors both Agamemnon's standing as a warrior and his position as chief (23.890–95):

> Son of Atreus, for we know how much you are ahead of everyone, and by how much you are *aristos* in *dynamis* and javelin-throwing; go to the hollow ships with this prize, but let us give the spear to hero Meriones, if you wish it in your heart, for so I urge. So he spoke, and *anax* of men Agamemnon did not *apeithein*.

If the foregoing descriptive analysis of the structure of LA in the *Iliad* is correct, certain summary conclusions may be stated. Chief among these is the notion that the principle of collective authority is a primary cultural given which operates reflexively to insure communal harmony. When the structural elements of LA are in proper balance the system of command and leadership permits an apparently effortless interchange of authority-roles, limiting friction between "juniors" and "seniors" or between these whose place and importance in the society are based on potentially conflicting claims (position or standing) concerning the initiation of decisions which affect the whole group. The successful operation of this centripetal collectivity has been demonstrated in the statistically preponderant Type A situations which give the surface impression of a fluid, almost formless, system of Leadership Authority.

A final example shows the structure imbedded in the elaborate modes of address which typically include all addressees, both "primary" and "secondary," and which take into account participants' position and standing. In a *boulê* (9.697–711) Diomedes as LA subject addresses "Most glorious son of Atreus, *anax* of men, Agamemnon," then enlarges the range of addressees to include all those present: "But come, as I say, let us all *peithesthai*," issuing his commands to the entire group. The scene ends: "So he spoke, and all the

The Structure of Authority in the *Iliad*

basilêes assented, admiring the word of Diomedes, tamer of horses."[15] The "formulas" of *boulê* and *agora*, in which LA is authorized by universal assent, evidence the structural deep-rootedness of group-authority, which, as we have seen, emerges as a consciously expressed element only when it is contradicted. Position-authority and standing-authority are more "visible" as structural elements in Leadership Authority, though neither is given formal ideation nor attains complete differentiation. Despite serious ambiguities in definition and some questioning of its validity it is evident from the text that position-authority is universally recognized as the necessarily weightier element in initiation of action.[16]

And here we approach the heart of the structure of command and authority among the early Greeks. Group-authority is the primal element, the matrix, as it were, of normal social interaction. It is not an unreasonable hypothesis that its historical foundation is prior, hearkening back to a distant time when leadership initiative was a matter of situational impulse in a society where all action was essentially collective, and "leaders" emerged according to the situational demands and fell back into the "ranks." In such cases leadership is equivalent to initiative. Its basis, then, would be a higher degree of psychological authority, predicated on possession of superior physical strength and skills. Obviously, individual "natural" leaders will have asserted themselves frequently, and collectively will have constituted a leadership "class" among the group; some, no doubt, will have served as quasi-permanent leaders until circumstances forced their "retirement," thus providing a social model for the type of the permanent leader. In the course of social evolution the leadership principle emerges in response to the increasing complexity of communal organization. At this stage of development social stability demands not leaders but the idea of leader, the position of leader as the transcendent symbol of the authority of the group, imbedded in the matrix of collectivity and issuing from it.

The authority of the leader is dependent on the collective authority from which it derives and must be in constant touch with that principle. In such a scheme any imbalance or deficiency is socially harmful. But if a primary danger to the structure is an undue distancing between the individual with position and the collective whole, another source of danger, no less destructive, is the challenge to authority based on position posed by the competing principle of authority based on ability. For inherent in the idea of position-authority is the condition that the individual who holds the position of leader may be inferior in those skills and attributes which the society values, and which, in fact, are necessary to the continuing prosperity of the group. The possibility of such a challenge is implicit in the very nature of the structure we have been describing, since the position of leader demands possession of those qualities to a great degree, and is, in fact, organically derived from those qualities.

The crisis of the leadership-structure in the *Iliad* may reflect this schematic model at the point at which the factors of position-authority and standing-authority are no longer mutually compatible but have begun to compete in a socially disruptive manner, and are inadequately responsive to group-authority. The solution of the *Iliad is* to preserve the structural balance—restore collective authority, reassert the principle of position-authority and reduce the friction between the claims of position and standing. This solution proves to be a tenuous one because of the inherently ambiguous and conflictual nature of the relationship between position and standing. Since it is the primal social impulse collectivity emerges as the dominant factor and subsumes the other elements in the interests of social stability. Shortly thereafter most groups in Greece organize themselves according to the principle of collective hegemony by which the position of the leader becomes typically several "offices" which share authority to initiate and which rationalize (and "tame") the various leadership roles by institutionalizing them. The polis, which comes into being at this time, both mirrors and fosters the process of collectivization of authority.[17]

NOTES

[1] For a recent succinct statement of the question see P. W. Rose, "Class Ambivalence in the Odyssey," *Historia* 24 (1975) 131–32. Rose's conclusion, that the epics form "a picture of social, political, and economic relationships familiar to the poet and his audience," seems to me the correct view. At the least we may accept the opinion of A. W. H. Adkins, *Moral Values and Political Behaviour in Ancient Greece* (New York 1972) 10: "It seems difficult not to conclude that the values and society depicted [in the Homeric poems] are related to some actually existing society, whose identity it is unnecessary to discuss here." That the socio-political background of the epics is "Mycenaean" or post-700 B.C. seems highly unlikely. Whether Homer's "world" is to be located in the tenth or ninth centuries (M. I. Finley, *The World of Odysseus* [New York 1954] 43) or in the eighth does not affect the argument of this paper. The basic assumption of my point of departure is expressed by J. M. Redfield, *Nature and Culture in the Iliad* (Chicago and London 1975) 20: "In the *Iliad*...individuals are not seen as free, self-defining creatures confronting a society whose structure and values they are free to accept or reject. Rather, the Homeric actors are seen as embedded in a social fabric; they are persons whose acts and consciousness are the enactment of social forces which play upon them." (See also pp. 23, 71, 75, 78–79, 99, 251, note 16).

[2] The categories were further broken down into Types A^1 and B^1, in which the LA subject is superior or equal in position to the addressee(s), and Types A^2 and B^2, in which the subject is of lesser position. The resultant statistics are: Type $A^1 = 237$; $A^2 = 42$; $B^1 = 26$; $B^2 = 14$. The total numbers of LA situations (319) and the totals of Type A (279) and Type B (40) may be subject to slight correction. Tabulation and category-analysis were done independently by me and two assistants, with only slight variation in totals.

The Structure of Authority in the *Iliad* 263

Only human to human exchanges were counted, except in cases where gods were disguised as mortals. Analysis of LA situations among the gods should provide an interesting counterpart to mortal LA situations, but to have included them here would require a lengthy digression and might pose problems of interpretation. All human to human LA exchanges, except the most trivial (e.g. orders to servants) were counted.

³Arranged in order of frequency of successful LA, from Hector (42) to Sarpedon (5). In addition to these, some twenty-five or so individuals or groups exercise LA successfully one or more times.

⁴To my knowledge no satisfactory terminology of social stratification or social differentiation in ancient Greek society has been developed. Terms like "class," "rank," "status," are often employed by students of archaic Greece inappropriately. A. W. Gouldner (*The Hellenic World: A Sociological Analysis* [New York 1969] 14) uses the term "established social rank," referring specifically to Agamemnon. However "rank" conveys the idea of a rigid hierarchical relationship which does not adequately describe the situation of the leader *vis-à-vis* the group. "Standing based on ability" is my own expression to identify "those who seek honor through competitive military achievement in conformance with the warrior code." (*ibid.*).

⁵How, for example, is Menelaus to be located on a relative scale of position within the group of Achaean *basileis*? He is Agamemnon's brother, the expedition to Troy is in his cause, and he leads a contingent of sixty ships, but it could not be said for certain that his position among the Achaeans is higher than (say) Odysseus' who leads twelve ships. In any case, even if it could be established that Menelaus has higher position than Odysseus, this does not guarantee precedence in initiating action. See 10.234–40, where Menelaus is both *cheirôn* (in ability) and *basileuteros* (in position).

Standing is not totally unambiguous either; it would not be possible to make an agreed-upon ordering of *all* Iliadic figures in terms of ability. It would be equally difficult to construct a hierarchy of skills or to determine the ideal admixture of skills. Although socially harmful conflict between figures who claim superiority of standing is quite possible (we think immediately of the quarrel between Ajax and Odysseus over the arms of Achilles), the poem has chosen not to make this a visible issue.

⁶In the Catalogue of Ships (2.487–759) the words which are used to describe the "rulers" of the various contingents all convey the basic notions of "leading" and "initiating"; *hêgemôn, archos, archein, hêgemoneuein, hêgeisthai, agein, kosmeein*; cf. *anarchos, hepesthai*. The exception is *koiranos* (487, 760), a "ruling" word, but it really occurs outside the catalogue proper. In a warrior society, like that of the *Iliad*, the idea of leading seems prior to the idea of ruling; leading implies the possibility of competition, or, at the least, a continuing effort to stay ahead.

An analysis of all socially diagnostic words (many of which appear untranslated in the quotations) would be a desirable adjunct. The ambiguity (interconnectedness?) of the relationship of position, standing, collectivity is often mirrored in the terminology—e.g. *archô* (begin/rule), *peithô* (persuade/obey), *basileus -teros -tatos*.

⁷Cf. 5.171–240; 6.77–105; 7.47–66; 7.109–200; 7.279–305; 9.96–173, 10.204–53; 13.726–87; 14.62–134; 17.238–59; 17.469–515. Even when there is some friction collegial cooperation operates to smooth it over. In 19.68–276 there is a minor controversy (with Type B exchanges) about whether to begin battle immediately or to have breakfast; by the time the ring is closed the question has been resolved to everyone's satisfaction. See below, note 14.

⁸Obviously, not all Type B situations are evidence of social strain; almost a half are inconsequential negative responses: e.g. 5.174; 5.221; 5.249; 6.258; 6.354; 19.68; 19.148; 19.206; 19.303; 20.463; 21.74; 23.39; 24.208. The characteristic of "significant" Type B situations is the disagreement of LA subject and addressee as to what constitutes the proper course of action (almost always in reference to the group). Conversely, in Type A situations the perceptions of subject and addressee concerning the correctness of the intended act are mutually agreeable.

[9]Redfield (note 1, above) 94 correctly assesses the importance of this scene. Although Chryses "stands somewhat outside the status order" he has "special powers," and by refusing him and the host "Agamemnon is undercutting his own position; his kingship (while inherited) is an accountable position, an instrument of public and collective authority. When Agamemnon ignores the folk, he is cutting himself off from the source of his own power and abandoning his claim to moral authority."

[10]It is interesting that in line 299 Achilles switches from second singular to second plural (*epei m' aphelesthe ge dontes*),an indication that Agamemnon's position-authority is perceived as ultimately derived from the authority of the group (which presumably might have interceded for Achilles). Achilles, no less than Agamemnon, separates himself from the collective whole, which, put in the untenable position of having to "choose" between the two potent claims of position and standing, opts (as often) for passivity; in effect, this means "victory" for position-authority.

[11]Cf. 14.83–102, where Odysseus rejects the king's third proposal to abandon the expedition. As in the other episodes in which the weakness of the ranking figure is detailed, Agamemnon's position-authority is not questioned but is actually affirmed: *sêmainein, anassein* (85) and lines 92–94. It is his ability to exercise LA that is doubted. Again, the situation is set straight by recourse to collectivity as Agamemnon easily assents to Odysseus' refusal and to Diomedes' seizure of LA (14.104–34). Once the principle of collective authority has been restated Agamemnon's position-authority is allowed to reassert itself (2.381–99; 9.68–69; 14.133–34). It is clear that while the primacy of position-authority is maintained, its functional efficiency is intimately connected with collectivity and standing-authority.

[12]Agamemnon is involved in a similar situation. In Book 4 he is the "correct" *archos*, alternately encouraging and chiding (4.232ff.). In 338–48 he remonstrates with Menestheus and Odysseus for hanging back; Odysseus replies hotly and the king backs down gracefully (4.350–63). Shortly thereafter a similar scene with Diomedes and Sthenelus takes place (4.370ff.); Diomedes accepts the criticism silently and angrily stops Sthenelus when he talks back to the king (4.401–18). Both scenes represent collegial resolution of tension, the first reinforcing standing-authority, the second position-authority (cf. esp. lines 402, 415–17).

Significant examples of the social dangers caused by imbalance in the elements of LA are Type B situations involving Hector and Poulydamas. In 12.211ff. Poulydamas prefaces his advice not to attack the Greek ships with an acknowledgment of the opposition between his standing-authority and Hector's position-authority (211–15). Hector's negative response widens the imbalance by contrasting his superior position to Poulydamas' inferior standing as a counsellor and warrior, thus eliminating the possibility of cooperative mutuality (231–50). In another Type B situation Poulydamas urges the Trojans in *agora* to retreat to the city and to avoid the aroused Achilles (18.254–83). Hector again denies Poulydamas' LA, "pulling rank" and denigrating his comrade's standing (18.293–97). This disastrous breech of the collective principle inspires one of Homer's few comments on the actions of his heroes: "For Hector they praised when he devised *kaka*, but Poulydamas no one praised, who counselled *esthlê boulê*" (18.312–13). Hector later regrets: "But I did not *peithesthai*; surely that had been much better" (22.103). These episodes contrast with the Type A[2] situation in 13.726–53 between Hector and Poulydamas in which Hector accepts the tactical advice offered. Interestingly, Hector is at least as equally reluctant as Agamemnon to yield his position-authority to collegial cooperation. See Poulydamas' statement of this in 13.726–29.

[13]Purely literary interpretations can sometimes miss important movements in the poem. For example, C. H. Whitman (*Homer and the Heroic Tradition* [Cambridge, Mass. 1958]) fails to see the social significance of this scene: "Nor is there any real reconciliation with Agamemnon; the gracious formalities are a bore" (179); "...his reconciliation with him is a mere formality, perfunctorily observed by Achilles with complete boredom, while the king makes long self-excusing speeches" (193).

The Structure of Authority in the *Iliad*

[14]The complex of exchanges in 19.56–275 is a paradigm of collectivity. Set within an extraordinary "augmented" *agora* (40–46), they begin and end with Achilles as LA subject (56–73; 270–75) and embrace a minor, almost comic, disagreement which is resolved by collegial cooperation. In 68–69 Achilles urges immediate resumption of battle; Agamemnon offers him a choice of fighting or waiting to inspect the gifts (139–44) Achilles insists on immediate action (148–50); Odysseus suggests breakfast, a review of the gifts, an oath concerning Briseis, and a feast (171–80); Agamemnon agrees to these and further suggests a sacrifice (187–97); Achilles again urges immediate action (206–208); Odysseus vehemently defends his plan (216–33). The upshot is that the Greeks take time out for the gift-giving, sacrifice and prayer (242–68), and Achilles, after his own short prayer, tells the Greeks to go to eat (270–75).

[15]See also 2.284–335; 7.325–44; 9.31–51; 9.52–79; 9.162–73; 17.333–43; 23.48–54; 23.235–49; 23.272–87. Special note is to be taken of 7.399–411, in which Diomedes answers for the Greeks to the Trojans, the Achaeans express their approval, Agamemnon relays this as the will of the Achaeans and of himself, and issues his final orders. Cf. 14.109–34. An example of "unconscious" collectivity is found in the Type B^2 situation in 7.345–97. Antenor addresses the *agora* of the Trojans and their allies, suggesting the return of Helen and the treasure; Paris refuses, saying he will give back the *ktêmata* but not Helen; Priam accepts Paris' decision and orders Idaeus the herald to report this to the Greeks. Idaeus does so, but adds that it was the Trojans' bidding (*keleuesthai*) that Paris restore Helen. Antenor's suggestion is thus projected as the will of the whole group. *Boulê* and *agora* are the formal societal institutions for the expression of collective and group-authority; thus the formulas which end them invariably convey the oneness of the group.

[16]Cf. Redfield (note 1, above) 92; "A community has need of such a dominant figure; the existence of a single paramount authority limits conflict, guarantees solidarity, and enables the community to function."

[17]I wish to express warmest thanks to Professors P. B. Harvey, Jr., R. A. Prier, P. W. Rose, and W. F. Wyatt, Jr., who read an earlier draft of this paper and provided many helpful criticisms. I am especially grateful to Professor Prier, whose suggestions (and disagreements) proved particularly valuable.

THE UNEQUAL EXCHANGE BETWEEN GLAUCUS AND DIOMEDES IN LIGHT OF THE HOMERIC GIFT-ECONOMY

The exchange of gifts is the climax of a long episode, the meeting of two foes on the field of battle, who discover that they were ξεῖνοι πατρώϊοι by virtue of a ξεῖνος-bond established by their grandfathers. Diomedes proposes an exchange of military gear (τεύχεα) as a witness to onlookers of their guest-friend relationship. Leaping from their chariots, they grasp hands and pledge their trust.

ἔνθ' αὖτε Γλαύκῳ Κρονίδης φρένας ἐξέλετο Ζεύς,
ὃς πρὸς Τυδεΐδην Διομήδεα τεύχε' ἄμειβε
χρύσεα χαλκείων, ἑκατόμβοι' ἐννεαβοίων.

(*Il.* 6.234–236)

[And then Zeus, son of Cronus, took away Glaucus' wits;
he exchanged armor with Diomedes, son of Tydeus,
gold for bronze, a hundred cattle worth for nine cattle worth.]

This ending has always struck critics as odd; many have thought it intentionally humorous.[1] Conventionally, epic heroes are crafty and cunning, no more so than when they are protecting their wealth and their honor. Glaucus especially, as a direct descendant of Sisyphus, would be expected to have his wits about him in any transaction involving these.[2] Therefore, the idea that the Lycian chief would so miscalculate his giving is inherently incongruous. But, if that is all the point, that Zeus deluded Glaucus into outgiving outrageously when he should have given only equal value, then the poet is charged with putting a clumsy and inappropriate ending to one of the great moments of the *Iliad*. Since antiquity, scholars have puzzled over these three lines in an effort to supply a credible motivation for Glaucus' act. In his recent article, Calder (34) proposes a sociological explanation: Glaucus outgave Diomedes on purpose, and by so doing he displayed his superiority over the other.

Calder's explanation stems from the recognition that the epics describe an exchange system whose purpose was not the maximization of material profit but the establishment and maintenance of personal relations. In such "gift economies," the highest premium is placed on generosity and display; superiority in gift-giving equates to superiority in social prestige. "Power, authority and status are achieved by giving rather than receiving."[3] However, this exchange of gifts is not an example of competitive display on Glaucus' part.

As members of a gift society, the poet and his listeners knew the complicated rules and social purposes of gift-giving, including, of course, the strategy of competitive giving. There are two prominent examples of this in the *Iliad*, the lavish donation offered by Agamemnon to Achilles (9.121) and the equally costly outlays by Achilles in the funeral and games for Patroclus (23.29,166, 237). These are linked together. Agamemnon's δῶρα were meant not merely to compensate for outrage, but also, by their extraordinary abundance, to elevate his own prestige and to put Achilles under severe obligation. The offer, if accepted, would have made Agamemnon the "winner" in τιμή and would have given him power over Achilles.[4] Achilles' counterstroke, long delayed, was to out-display his rival with a splendid funeral and feast in honor of Patroclus, followed by an openhanded distribution of treasure as prizes in the games. The unparalleled holocaust of sheep, cattle, dogs, horses, and captured Trojans makes this a true potlatch, in which all the valuables were destroyed or given away.[5] If the exchange between Glaucus and Diomedes had been a similar example of the "potlatch principle," the poet would not have presented it as an incident of divinely inspired stupidity.[6]

Nevertheless, Calder has rightly identified the social role of gift-giving as the key to this "perennial puzzle in Homer." In following his lead, I shall try to show that Glaucus did overgive intentionally, but that the poetic point of the episode's "nearly burlesque ending" (Leaf) is that Diomedes, not he, was the superior in status.

I

Since incidents of gift-giving abound in the epics, we are well informed about the sociology of the gift in Homeric society. Gift-giving encompasses a broad array of gift-situations and relationships: traders' dues, ransom, peace compacts, rewards for services, tribute to chiefs, donations from chiefs, recompense for insult, marriage transactions, and guest friendship. Of these, only the last two formally prescribe an exchange of gifts; the rest are one-way transactions.[7] Within this diversity, all gift transactions share basic features.

The Unequal Exchange

Gifts are given either as compensation for specific acts, positive or negative, or in expectation of some future service or favor. The gifts themselves are always things of high value, sometimes animals, but much more frequently treasure goods (κειμήλια). There is always a social element present in the transaction, though the degree of sociability varies according to the type of relationship. There is one other common feature. Ceremonies of giving, especially at the elite level, convey important information about rank and prestige.

As it happens, in the majority of gift-giving situations the distinctions of rank among the participants are previously known and recognized. Status and rank are defined by the relationship and are so stated by the transactions themselves. In traders' dues and ransom, for example, the recipient of the gift is the obvious superior, whereas in rewards for services rendered the gift-giver is manifestly the social superior.[8] This is also the case in gifts to and from chiefs. The upward spiral of goods, personal services, special awards, and perquisites given to a leader by his people is a manifestation of his superiority over them. Conversely, the obligatory downward flow of largesse from the chief also expresses his superiority over the gift-receivers.[9]

On the other hand, in marriage transactions, compensation for insult, and in guest-host relationships the status differential is often not clearly defined beforehand. In these cases the gift transaction itself serves to make explicit or to establish the relative social standing of the participants.

This is very clear in respect to the marital transactions of the Homeric elite, among whom marriages, both within and outside the *demos*, were political alliances, carrying with them long term obligations of reciprocal service. According to Homer, marriage arrangements among the ἀγαθοί were highly flexible, exhibiting several residential and gift-giving schemes. This variety in marriage patterns has been seen as a problem. Snodgrass used the coexistence of presumably opposing categories of giving ("bridewealth" vs. "dowry") to argue that Homeric society is a conflation of different historical stages. On the contrary, optionality in post-nuptial residence and gift arrangements is quite consistent with the fluid power relations within the epics. The giving and exchanging of marriage gifts served to calibrate relative prestige and authority among the loosely ranked top families.[10] The bidding of bridegifts (ἕδνα) by suitors is a pure example of establishing primacy by competitive giving. The suitor who promises the most δῶρα wins the bride and the social connection he and his family want. By outgiving his rivals, he establishes his superiority over them, and so elevates his worth to the bride's family. The principle is exactly the same when a man recruits a desirable son-in-law into his *oikos*, without the requirement of wooing gifts (ἀνάεδνον) and, often, with promises of gifts to the groom. Acceptance of the offer is a clear statement by the groom that he recognizes the authority of the bride's father over him. The new husband is in the place of a son; his loyalty and services belong to his wife's father and brothers; his children belong to his wife's family.[11]

Status ambiguity is a potential problem in insult situations, where the participants would be men of equivalent rank. Such encounters are particularly sensitive because they touch the tenderest nerve of personal honor. In the interests of social harmony the breach must be healed, *and* the proper honor and dignity of both men must be preserved. The gift transaction is a definitive public statement of their relative status.

The cases of Euryalus and Odysseus in *Odyssey* 8.133, and of Antilochus and Menelaus in *Iliad* 23.566, show the socially correct form. Insult provokes angry indignation, leading to an apology and offer of a δῶρον; the offer is accepted graciously by the victim, who adds a conciliating speech of his own. Although the situation bristles with tension, the parties move towards amity *via* a series of delicate manoeuvers designed for maximum face-saving on both sides. In the incident at Scheria the gift itself complements the apology in a perfectly fitting way. Euryalus' gift of a fancy sword and sheath symbolically calls back the insult that Odysseus looked like a merchant and not an athlete, and confers on the still anonymous stranger his proper status as a warrior.[12]

Status is a central consideration in the cheating incident of *Iliad* 23. Accused by Menelaus of "shaming my *arete*," Antilochus readily apologizes to the older and higher-ranking man, and offers him the prize mare and "some other better thing from my house." Though he is the aggrieved party, Menelaus ends up giving his prize to Antilochus, "in order that these men here may know that my spirit is never arrogant and unbending" (570–611). So Menelaus appears magnanimous and generous, as befits his superior status; the gift-*receiving* Antilochus is even more firmly indebted to the Atreidai.[13]

The insult situation between Agamemnon and Achilles is a negative image of these properly managed situations; the negotiations, which take up large portions of Books 9 and 19, are a caricature of the normal routine. Agamemnon's offer of δῶρα is belated and unaccompanied by a public apology. Odysseus' diplomatic suppression of Agamemnon's claim to superior rank (9.160–161) in his otherwise *verbatim* repetition of the gift offer (262–299) shows how crucial the question of their relative status was in the incident. Achilles' refusal, though inevitable under the circumstances, is also a breach of the convention. Their public reconciliation (19.56–275) likewise bristles with competitive tension. Agamemnon responds to Achilles' renunciation of his χόλος with an apology that is not quite an apology, and restates his offer of the gifts. Achilles offhandedly dismisses the gifts and manoeuvers to prevent a public display. When, at Odysseus' insistence, the gifts are produced for all to see, Achilles' response is short and ungracious; he does not acknowledge the gifts.

In presenting a perverse variation of the insult situation, the poet meant, and the audience understood, that both men were using gift-giving as a weapon in their ongoing *agon* over honor and status. The poetic message is that Achilles emerged the ultimate winner, because he took the gifts of Agamemnon on his own terms (unlike Meleager in Phoenix's story) and then outdazzled his rival with a brilliant display of generosity. Nor should we fail to note Achilles' final stroke. In the last contest of the games, Achilles awards first prize for spear-throwing to Agamemnon without a competition (23.884). It is a gracious compliment, and a fitting climax to their painful progress towards a semblance of amity. Yet the audience will also have noticed that the ἄεθλον was thereby transformed into a free δῶρον. Agamemnon departs from the narrative under obligation to Achilles.[14]

It is clear from the preceding discussion that every occasion of gift-giving in Homeric society was also a public declaration of the relative status of the participants. When political superiors give, their gifts are recognized as instruments of control; the obligations they create are the obligations of service. And when a man of lesser renown gives to one of higher renown, the obligation created is the favor and good will of the superior. Competitive giving can occur only when relative status is uncertain or in contention. In these cases, as we have seen, the gift itself is a statement about the status relationship between giver and receiver, and establishes, at least temporarily, a superior-subordinate condition.

II

We come, at length, to ξενίη, where the puzzle of Glaucus and Diomedes resides. "Guest friendship," as Finley says (above, note 3, 99) "was a very serious institution." It was also quite different from other personal relationships, both in its formal structure and in the symbolic role of the gifts that accompanied it. Guest friendship extended rights and duties proper to kinship and close comradeship beyond the *demos* to foreigners. The bonds of φιλότης were inherited by succeeding generations. The obligations, however, though sacred, operated only intermittently; repayment of the favors became due only on a return visit, which might be years later. The favors themselves were considerable and valuable. The guest-ξεῖνος received protection, food and lodging, certain "diplomatic" services, and parting gifts of treasure (κειμήλια).[15]

The relationship was also a formal exchange partnership. This feature, unique to ξενίη, was highly functional in Dark Age Greece, where treasure items were scarce. For next to raiding, guest friendship was the chief means of circulating highly prized prestige objects beyond the local area. We should also note that the obligation to return gifts of at least equal value was a self-selecting mechanism, insuring that only men of approximately equal wealth became exchange partners. Networks of ξεῖνοι were thus indispensable to the ambitions of the pre-state βασιλεῖς, as indeed they continued to be to aristocrats in the archaic and classical πόλεις, even though such personal alliances often conflicted with state interests.[16]

It is important at this point to distinguish between simple hospitality (τὰ ξείνια) to a stranger, and the formal bond of guest friendship. Custom, reinforced by divine sanction, demanded that any stranger (ξεῖνος) who appeared at the door be given protection and sustenance. The giving of obligatory or altruistic hospitality does not automatically establish a continuing ξεῖνος-relationship. For that to occur, it is necessary that both men agree to a relationship, declare it formally, and symbolically cement it by an exchange of gifts on the spot.[17] One scarcely needs to add that a commitment to a transgenerational political alliance *cum* exchange partnership was not entered into casually, but only after the most careful weighing, by both parties, of the potential advantages and disadvantages. In one sense, ξενίη is perfectly symmetrical. Both parties expect the benefits to balance; otherwise they would not have entered into the contract. Nevertheless, there is a structural imbalance in guest friendship which is peculiar to it. Within the cycle of visit and return visit, the guest-ξεῖνος is the clear beneficiary. For, while it is true that ξενίη is ultimately balanced, the intermittent nature of the relationship gives the guest-ξεῖνος an important material advantage by providing him with a temporary fund of treasure goods. These, displayed and given away, are the necessary coinage of prestige and power among the elite.[18]

Just how important this surplus was to the βασιλεῖς is shown by their preoccupation with amassing delayed gift-debts. The theme is woven into the plot of the *Odyssey*. Odysseus emerges into the real world of Ithaca *via* the magical Phaeacians, who put all to rights economically for Odysseus by giving him more guest gifts than all the Trojan plunder he had lost at sea (*Od.* 13.135). This is the fantasy motif of the guest who receives and never has to repay. The same motif occurs in the lie of Odysseus/Eperitus, who tells Laertes how five years before he had given "Odysseus" an extremely generous array of δῶρα ξεινήϊα (*Od.* 24.273). "Stranger," replies Laertes, "You bestowed these gifts in vain, in your countless giving; for if you had found him alive in the land of Ithaca, then he would have sent you off having reciprocated well with gifts and good hospitality; for that is *themis* for the initiator" (24.283–286; cf. 1.316–318). Here we see both the fantasy of unrequited getting and its reverse, the dread of the host-ξεῖνος of giving with no hope of a return.[19] A more everyday example is the suggestion of Menelaus that he and Telemachus make a tour of the surrounding regions. "Nor will anyone send us away as we are, but will give one thing at least, either a good bronze tripod, or a cauldron, or two mules, or a gold cup" (*Od.* 15.82–85).[20]

This is not meant to imply that all the benefit is to the receiver. A reputation for being a generous host increases one's τιμή.[21] The host "owns" the debt. His generous hospitality and abundant gifts impose a heavy obligation on the guest-ξεῖνος, insuring that when the ξεινοδόκος is in other men's lands he will get as good as he gave. But, as Herman points out, there is no way for ξεῖνοι to enforce the obligation.[22] That is the severe limit of a relationship that purports to turn strangers into friends. The obligations of guest-friend φιλία mimic those of ἑταῖροι and kin without the social constraints that attend these "within" relationships. So, while the giver is under great pressure to be generous—perception of stinginess in ξείνια would jeopardize a return—the debt is a deferred benefit, cancelled if the partner dies or chooses to be unjust.[23]

This brings us to the question of relative status. Differences or ambiguities in status between ξεῖνοι have nothing to do with rivalry or competition, since foreign ξεῖνοι do not oppose one another for τιμή within the same *demos*. However, the higher the status of a ξεῖνος in his own community, the more valuable he is as a guest friend. Therefore, superior-subordinate in ξενίη is a function of one partner perceiving the relationship as of greater utility, or as the source of greater prestige, to himself than to the other. In his study of ξενίη, Herman found that formal status or official position within one's own community was of relatively little importance in forming a ξένος-relationship.

> What mattered most was the possession of a quality which the other needed, and that is why, in fact, a bond of ritualized friendship did not necessarily involve exact social equals.[24]

Herman suggests that outgiving is an expression of this inequality of need. The promise of large gifts may signal that the giver "is willing to recognise the power of the recipient over him. The gift thus becomes a mark of submission...."[25] There is, in fact, some evidence of submissive/subordinate giving by Homeric ξεῖνοι. When news reached Cyprus that the Achaeans were were sailing to Troy, Cinyras sent Agamemnon an elaborate θώραξ as a ξεινήϊον (*Il.* 11.19). The unsolicited gift was plainly intended to flatter Agamemnon and win his favor (cf.

χαριζόμενος βασιλῆϊ, 23), with the purpose, we may suspect, of excusing Cinyras from the expedition (cf. *Il.* 23.296). Maro, the priest of Apollo in Ismarus, gave Odysseus ἀγλαὰ δῶρα of gold, silver, and wine (*Od.* 9.196). The form of giving is ξεινήϊα, but the purpose was clearly to buy protection (199) for Maro and his family during Odysseus' raid against the Cicones (9.39).

Let us summarize the "rules" of giving in Homeric ξενίη. Giving is never meant to overawe or to display superiority. ξενίη partakes of the φιλία of kinship and comradeship; hence, giving can only be a mark of respect and affection. Within the continuing relationship, the status of ξεῖνος-receiver is the more advantageous status. These rules are, of course, known and understood by everyone. We would expect, therefore, a more or less uniform reaction to stories about asymmetrical giving between ξεῖνοι. My opinion, based on what has been said, is that the listeners' imaginations would supply a narrow spectrum of appropriate motives for being more generous. The outgiver wants or needs the φιλία of the other; the relationship is of greater prestige to him; he holds the other in higher esteem or respect; the other is acknowledged the better man, or the more valuable friend.

III

Let us test these deductions. There are four incidents of direct gift-exchange in Homer. Three accompany the initiation or reinitiation of a ξεῖνος-relationship, the fourth is the temporary pact of φιλότης made by Hector and Ajax, ending their duel.

In only one of these situations is there an exchange of equal value, the initiation of ξενίη between Odysseus and Iphitus (*Od.* 21.11). Odysseus and Iphitus of Oechalia met by chance in Messenia. Iphitus gave Odysseus the bow of his famous archer father Eurytus (thus honoring Odysseus as the bowman); Odysseus reciprocated with a sword and spear. Odysseus was a stripling (παιδνός, 21), just beginning his public career (16–21). Their chance meeting was in a neutral place, the house of a mutual ξεῖνος, Ortilochus. Homer calls the ritual exchange the "beginning of a loving guest friendship" (ἀρχὴν ξεινοσύνης προσκηδέος, 35). The *hapax* προσκηδής emphasizes the kinlike quality of the bond. The conditions of their meeting show that the relationship was intended to be one of disinterested equality. The exchange of armor of equivalent material and significant value is the poetic expression of their equality of status.

In the other three examples of direct exchange, all from the *Iliad*, Hector, Bellerophon, and Glaucus give more than Ajax, Oeneus, and Diomedes. The

The Unequal Exchange

situation of Ajax and Hector (7.283) is a very clear demonstration of how status differences are expressed by means of unequal exchange. As the loser in the duel, Hector is situationally the subordinate. He initiates (cf. 286) the compact of φιλότης, and gives a silver-studded sword, with sheath and baldric. Ajax counters with a ζωστῆρα φοίνικι φαεινόν (305).

The Homeric ζωστήρ is a rather shadowy piece of military equipment. It appears to have been a broad belt worn around the waist as protection for belly and groin, made either of bronze, bronze plates sewn over leather, or simply of leather. Here there seems no doubt that a leather belt is meant.[26] Ajax's answering gift is unmistakably of lesser worth than Hector's. The audience will have understood this unequal exchange as a sign of his superiority and of Hector's submissive status. The symbolic content is heightened by the fact that the unglamorous ζωστήρ is a purely defensive item, while the sword is the instrument of attack at close range.[27]

The initiation of ξενίη between Oeneus and Bellerophon is related by Diomedes (6.215). Oeneus, he says, had once hosted (ξείνισ') Bellerophon for twenty days.

οἱ δὲ καὶ ἀλλήλοισι πόρον ξεινήϊα καλά·
Οἰνεὺς μὲν ζωστῆρα δίδου φοίνικι φαεινόν,
Βελλεροφόντης δὲ χρύσεον δέπας ἀμφικύπελλον.
(6.218–220)

[And they handed each other fine gifts of guest-friendship.
Oeneus gave a belt, bright with crimson dye,
and Bellerophon a two-handled cup made of gold.]

The modern presumption has been that the exchange was equal; but the giving of gold for leather in the same story as the giving of gold for bronze ought to give us pause. It is significant that the same "formula" (it occurs only these two times) is used for Oeneus' gift and for Ajax's lesser gift (7.305). Only in these two places is a ζωστήρ a gift item. Otherwise, military gear as gift objects consists of swords, breastplates, spears, or bows.[28]

The δέπας (= ἄλεισον) is a common object, small and not of very great value. A δέπας ἀμφικύπελλον is the loser's prize in the boxing match, where first prize is a mule (*Il.* 23.654). Still, a gold cup is an eminently fitting guest gift. A "very fine" ἄλεισον χρύσεον is a special personal gift from Alcinous to Odysseus (*Od.* 8.430). Menelaus offers Telemachus three horses and a δίφρος, plus a καλὸν ἄλεισον.[29] We recall that a χρύσεον ἄλεισον is included among the potential guest-gifts one might collect on a "tour" (*Od.* 15.85). One of the items of ransom for Hector's corpse was a δέπας περικαλλές, a gift from the Thracians, called a "great possession" (μέγα κτέρας).[30]

On balance, the evidence warrants the conclusion that Bellerophon's gift of a gold cup outmatched Oeneus' leather belt. Ancient critics thought so.[31] Just as important as the objective value of the gift, however, is its symbolic meaning. The δέπας is the instrument of drinking and libation, hence of conviviality, hospitality, and of cementing trust and loyalty. "I will give you," Menelaus promises Telemachus, "a καλὸν ἄλεισον, that you may make libations to the immortal gods reminful of me all your days" (*Od.* 4.591–592).[32] The message conveyed by Bellerophon's countergift is that he warmly welcomed the pact of φιλότης and was eager to see it flourish. Symbolically the imperishable cup promised that when Oeneus should visit Bellerophon in Lycia his reception would be even more friendly, his gifts more splendid.

If we have correctly decoded the message of the gift in this scene, Bellerophon, by outgiving Oeneus, admits a subordinate status in the relationship. Why Bellerophon should have been so eager for a ξεῖνος-relationship with Oeneus—or, more exactly, why the poem has Diomedes signify this to Glaucus—constitutes a parallel problem to the Diomedes-Glaucus exchange.

We turn, finally, to the exchange of ξεινήϊα between Diomedes and Glaucus. The total circumstance is highly unusual; for it is not a normal guest-host situation, but is also a meeting of enemies on the field of battle. Inevitably, therefore, the encounter—whether an invention of our poet or a story he inherited—contains overt elements of a battlefield truce. In either situation, the poetic message conveyed by the unequal exchange is clear: Glaucus affirms, before the two armies, that he is the subordinate.

This is quite apparent when we consider the episode in its broader aspect, the meeting between enemies. Diomedes is the unmistakable superior; he confronts Glaucus at the height of his martial glory. The episode is the final exploit of his extraordinary ἀριστεία. He begins, as Craig notes, with an invitation to Glaucus to fight and be killed.[33] Even after he recognizes their ξεῖνος-bond, Diomedes continues to dominate. His words, though "gentle" (214) are a clear vaunt of superiority (227–229).

πολλοὶ μὲν γὰρ ἐμοὶ Τρῶες κλειτοί τ' ἐπίκουροι
κτείνειν ὅν κε θεός γε πόρῃ καὶ ποσσὶ κιχείω
πολλοὶ δ' αὖ σοὶ 'Αχαιοὶ ἐναιρέμεν ὅν κε δύνηαι.[34]

[For there are many Trojans and their famous allies for me
to kill, whichever one the god gives me to catch,
and for you, too, many Achaeans to kill, whichever one you can.]

The entire episode, insofar as it is a temporary truce, has obvious parallels to the truce between Ajax and Hector in Book 7. The larger gift, therefore, is quite easily interpreted as a gift of submission. There can be no doubt that the listeners were supposed to have the idea that during the entire episode Glaucus "was conscious of his inferiority in the presence of the overbearing Diomede."[35]

Yet, at line 215 the poet abruptly changes the psychosocial context. Glaucus goes from nameless ἐχθρός to ancestral φίλος; their gifts are the expression of a ξεῖνος-bond, forgotten and now happily reestablished. But this is the context in which Glaucus lost his wits and made a shameful exchange. It would be difficult to deny that the bard's intent was to show Diomedes the superior in the ξεῖνος-situation as well. The favored explanation of the early commentators, opposed to the notion of Glaucus as victim, was that the Lycian, inspired by his father's injunction, μηδὲ γένος πατέρων αἰσχυνέμεν (211), gave gold for bronze so that he would not appear to be less generous than his grandfather. This charitable explanation has the merit of pointing up the fact that Bellerophon's gift of gold was on Glaucus' mind when he exchanged gifts with Diomedes. The obvious corollary to this idea, however, is that Diomedes "set up" Glaucus. Most seriously, it does not explain why Homer would show Glaucus displaying noble generosity and in the same breath "find fault" with him for it.[36]

Here is my explanation of lines 234–236. It is apparent from the beginning of their encounter that Diomedes was playing cat and mouse with Glaucus. His opening speech is ironic. Who are you? If you are a god, I will not fight you, but if you are a mortal I will kill you (6.123–143). This from a man who had been given the ability to recognize gods (5.127) and who had just fought and wounded Aphrodite (5.336) and Ares (5.855) and defied the mighty Apollo (5.434). In his second speech (6.215–233) Diomedes orchestrates the rituals of ξενίη. He recognizes the ξεῖνος-relationship and chooses to reinitiate it. He assumes the controlling role of the ξεινοδόκος, thus taking the part of his grandfather Oeneus and putting Glaucus in the role of Bellerophon. Significantly, Diomedes' account of the original ξενίη focuses almost exclusively on the gift and the more valuable countergift. The listeners had abundant signals of Diomedes' total control of the situation and of his dominance over Glaucus. Attuned to the subtle etiquette of the gift and its poetic function, they were prepared to see Glaucus assume the position of the subordinate ξεῖνος, attempting by means of a more generous initiatory gift to bind them closer in φιλία.

It seems, then, that the point of lines 234–36 is not that Glaucus outgave, for that was conventionally expected, but that he was so bewildered he gave at the humiliating ratio of 11 to 1. That is the real bite of the poet's joke, and is to be explained by Diomedes' cunning manipulation of his psychological advantage. Glaucus, prepared for a duel to the death, is taken unawares by the sudden and unexpected shift from enmity to φιλία. Diomedes' offer of an exchange on the spot forces him to make a crucial immediate calculation. Unprepared, affected by Diomedes' aura of invincibility, conditioned by Diomedes' statement that Bellerophon had given gold to Oeneus, anxious to please his new ξεῖνος, Glaucus reacts in confusion to Diomedes' gift of bronze (φρένας ἐξέλετο Ζεύς) and makes a face-losing exchange. I am suggesting, then, that the entire ξεῖνος-scene was tailored to create a poetic expectation that Glaucus would display submissive giving. The audience was fully cognizant that an intimidated Glaucus was being gulled by a superconfident Diomedes; and in the climactic exchange of ξεινήϊα was expecting some such surprise "punch line" as they heard.[37]

Two questions remain. First, why would the poet want to show the illustrious Glaucus as a submissive giver? In the *Iliad* there are numerous instances of supplication and ransom. All such examples of overt submissive behavior on the field of battle are by Trojans (or allies) to Achaeans.[38] The gifts that are offered are patently gifts of submission, statements by the givers that the receivers are superior in *arete* and τιμή. Such incidents are part of the general Iliadic plan of Hellenic superiority. We may now add to the list the poetically more subtle examples of battlefield submission by Hector to Ajax and Glaucus to Diomedes.

These are more subtle because they take place within the context of φιλία. Nevertheless, as we have repeatedly emphasized, the audience was given plenty of stylistic clues that φιλία was only a mask. The inherent contradiction (which in the case of Diomedes and Glaucus is almost surrealistic) of battlefield foes exchanging gifts of friendship was itself a sufficient signal that the episodes were symbolic occasions. That, plus the clear indications that the two Achaeans were more potent in valor, and, especially, the gifts themselves, will have told contemporary hearers that Hector and Glaucus were performing public acts of submission.

This brings us to the final question of poetic motivation. We have already remarked at length on the elaborate staging of the episode. Let us look at the format one more time. The encounter starts off, conventionally, as the preliminaries to battle, with vaunt and return vaunt. Typically, there would follow the duel to the death and the despoliation of arms by the victor. Naturally, Diomedes would be the odds-on favorite. As it turns out, Diomedes is the victor and he symbolically despoils Glaucus. Homer intricately transposed Diomedes' expected duel with a major opponent (which would have been a conventionally fitting climax to his ἀριστεία) into a duel of another sort, a contest of wit and will. The listeners will have readily caught on to this strange new twist, and will have become instantly aware that the *agon* they were witnessing had been shifted to the level of μῆτις, "wily intelligence." Detienne and Vernant have shown that for Homeric men μῆτις is more than a quality of mind; it is

> itself a power of cunning and deceit. It operates through disguise. In order to dupe its victim it assumes a form which masks, instead of revealing, its true being. In *metis* appearance and reality no longer correspond to one another but stand in contrast, producing an effect of illusion, *apate*, which beguiles the adversary into error and leaves him as bemused by his defeat as by the spells of a magician.[39]

Diomedes in this scene reveals himself as a master of μῆτις.

The poet's "joke" itself stands as a complex and artfully elaborated (ποικίλος) example of the lesson it illustrates: that the Achaeans were superior to the Trojans and their allies in μῆτις as well as in βίη. Or, rather, we should say with Detienne and Vernant that cunning intelligence is the essential part of Hellenic κράτος—"in a sense, the absolute weapon" (13).

The supreme epic example of Achaean μῆτις (and of Trojan ἀπορία in its presence) is the Wooden Horse, a perfect combining of Hellenic cunning and might. The μῆτις behind the δόλος (*Od.* 8.494) of the wooden horse and the μῆτις of Diomedes' κέρδος display equally "the most prized cunning of all: the 'duplicity' of the trap which always presents itself as what it is not and which conceals its true lethal nature beneath a reassuring exterior."[40]

NOTES

[1]For a summary of ancient and modern explanations, see W. M. Calder III, "Gold for Bronze: *Iliad* 6.232-36," in *Studies Presented to Sterling Dow, GRBS Monograph* 10 (Durham, NC 1984) 31–35 (hereafter cited as Calder).
[2]Glaucus bore the name of his paternal great grandfather, Glaucus, son of Sisyphus.
[3]C. A. Gregory, *Gifts and Commodities* (New York and London 1982) 55. These ideas, based on the pioneering work of Malinowski, Mauss, and Polanyi, were first systematically applied to Homeric society by M. I. Finley in *The World of Odysseus* (revised edition New York 1978 [original edition 1954]). For an analysis of the Homeric exchange economy, see W. Donlan, "Reciprocities in Homer," *CW* 75 (1981–82) 137–175.
[4]The appropriate recompense would have been the return of Briseis and "something else" besides. See pp. 46–47.
[5]The commonest examples of competitive giving in Homer are marriage gifts (see below) and feast-giving (to win followers and a reputation for liberality). See Donlan (above, n. 3) 163–164. B. Qviller, "The Dynamics of the Homeric Society," *SO* 56 (1981) 109–155, at 125 calls gift-giving "the economic corollary to martial contests and fighting." See S. C. Humphreys, *Anthropology and the Greeks* (London 1978) 151. On the archaeological (burial) evidence for "competitive destruction of wealth as a means of ranking households," see I. Morris, "Gift and Commodity in Archaic Greece," *Man* 21 (1986) 7–13.

⁶Calder's explanation is that the story was a Mycenaean inheritance, and that "the Geometric poet no longer understood the custom" (34). This is contradicted by the textual evidence as well as some archaeological evidence of competitive display. It is, indeed, quite likely that Bronze Age chiefs practiced competitive giving among themselves, since it is a nearly universal custom. If so, there is no reason to think that such practices, typically associated with pre-market societies, would have disappeared in the much more basic economy and society of the Dark Age. All indications are that gift-giving as a means of social integration and social control played a more prominent role in the Iron Age than earlier.

⁷This does not mean that in gift-giving (as opposed to gift-exchanging) there is no expectation of reciprocity; some sort of return, sometime, is always expected. Merely that in some marriage transactions and in ξενίη an equivalent (treasure) return is demanded. Certain forms of compensatory giving, such as "blood price," fines (θωή), and μοιχάγρια are highly particularized and have quasi-legal status. Traders' dues and ransom, though technically δῶρον-transactions, have minimal social purpose; like payment of χρέα, they are "doing business." Giving to beggars and other wandering unfortunates is part of obligatory ξείνια. See Donlan (above, n. 3).

⁸Of course, the receiver of a reward gets τιμή; but the greater honor goes to the giver, whose ability to reward demonstrates his social potency, his wealth, and his generosity. The gift sustains and strengthens the relationship, leaving the way open for further services and rewards.

⁹The continuous flow of mutual exchanges forms a *system* of reciprocities. This system is the economics of the highly personal leader-people relationship. A reputation for generosity was an essential element of the political control of a βασιλεύς. See Donlan (above, n. 3) 159–163, 169.

¹⁰This is an endless argument. For an exposition of the entire question, see I. Morris, "The Use and Abuse of Homer," *CA* 5 (1986) 81–129. On marriage and status, see 106–113.

¹¹See Morris (above, n. 10) 107; Donlan (above, n. 3) 145–147. Hence, Agamemnon's offer of his choice of daughters ἀνάεδνον was not attractive to Achilles, as he makes clear (9.388–400). It is the wealthy, powerful houses, like Priam's and Nestor's that attract sons-in-laws (*Il.* 6.242; *Od.* 3.386). These are often men who for one reason or another had left their home communities (e.g., *Il.* 6.192; 14.121; *Od.* 7.311). A good example of the service-groom is Othryoneus of Cabesus, who had no ἔδνα to marry Cassandra, and promised instead service in the war (*Il.* 13.363). Idomeneus makes an insulting joke about this to his corpse (13.374). There is debate whether the ἔδνα at *Od.* 1.276–278 (referring to Penelope and the suitors) means "bridegifts" or "dowry"; see Morris 109. In support of the former interpretation, we might note the fact that the same lines are repeated (2.196–198) by the suitor Eurymachus, who later brought Penelope a gold chain as a wooing gift (18.295).

¹²*Od.* 8.401. It is significant that this is the only military item among all the Phaeacian gifts of clothing, gold, tripods, and cauldrons (8.392, 403, 430; 13.13).

¹³In *Od.* 22.54, each of the suitors promises τιμή worth twenty cattle, in bronze and gold, to Odysseus. Here, of course, the apology and gifts could not be accepted. For another potential insult/gift situation, see *Od.* 2.132; Morris (above, n. 10) 109.

¹⁴One presumes that the cauldron was the first prize, though the spear is mentioned first (884). I think it is meaningful that the *spear* goes to Meriones (893).

¹⁵Finley (above, n. 3) 66, 99–103; E. Benveniste, *Indo-European Language and Society*, Eng. tr. by E. Palmer (London and Coral Gables 1973) 83, 293–294; Donlan (above, n. 3) 148–151. For delay of return visit, see *Od.* 1.209; 19.221; 24.115, 309.

¹⁶G. Herman, *Ritualised Friendship and the Greek City* (Cambridge, Eng. 1987).

¹⁷Herman (above, n. 16) 41–69. There is no such thing as non-reciprocal ξείνια, of course. Ideally, every man is a potential guest or host, according to circumstance. That sacred general obligation is surely the origin of formal ξενίη. However, a declared ξεῖνος-relationship is of a different order entirely.

¹⁸W. Donlan, "Scale, Value, and Function in the Homeric Economy," *AJAH* 6 (1981) 101–117.

The Unequal Exchange 281

[19]Next to the collective guest gifts of the Phaeacian βασιλεῖς, the ξεινήϊα of Eperitus are the most generous in the epics, almost as numerous as the ransom gifts for Hector's body (lines 276–277 = Il. 24.230–231). This adds to the fantasy effect. Most κειμήλια transactions consist of one to three items, reflecting the reality of treasure (metal) scarcity in the Dark Age. See Donlan (above, n. 18) 102–103.

[20]Eagerness to collect ξεινήϊα is a character trait of Odysseus. He tells Alcinous that he would stay a year longer in Scheria if it meant getting more gifts (Od. 11.355). Though this gets him into trouble (9.224; 10.34), Odysseus has few peers in the art of gift-acquiring (19.282–286; cf. 19.239, 272; 14.285, 321; 15.159; 24.283. A suitor mockingly says that no one is κακοξεινώτερος than Telemachus, because he keeps a beggar-guest (Odysseus) who eats much but gives back nothing in return (20.376). Stanford (at Od. 15.54) is moved to remark that "the etiquette of Homeric hospitality was coming very near to being exploited as a 'racket'."

[21]E.g., Od. 3.346–355; 4.612–619 (cf. 15.113); 11.338–341; 14.402; 18.223; 19.334. The house of Odysseus was known for its good hospitality; e.g., Od. 1.176; 19.314, 379, etc.

[22]Herman (above, n. 16) 30–31. See Od. 19.313–316. ξεινοδόκοι might also be perfidious; e.g., Il. 6.178; 11.138 (cf. 3.205); Od. 21.25.

[23]Good hospitality and fitting guest gifts, then, are strong reminders of the other partner's moral responsibility. "For a ξεῖνος remembers all his days a ξεινοδόκος who shows φιλότης" (Od. 15.54–55). Cf. Od. 1.309–318; 4.591–592, 613–614; 8.430–432; 15.78, 113.

[24]Herman (above, n. 16) 37. A good example is Agamemnon's ξενίη with the Ithacan Melaneus, whose house Agamemnon used as a base to recruit the paramount βασιλεύς Odysseus (Od. 24.115). See Finley (above, n. 3) 103.

[25]Herman (above, n. 16) 89. The nomenclature, of course, is strictly equal. Regardless of their relative status, partners are simply ξεῖνοι or φίλοι ξεῖνοι.

[26]See in general, H. Brandenburg, *Archaeologia Homerica*, Band I, Kap. E, Teil 1 (Göttingen 1977) 119–143. H. Lorimer, *Homer and the Monuments* (London 1950) 246–247, thinks leather is meant; so Leaf (at 6.219) and Ameis-Hentze (at 7.305). This seems certain from Od. 23.201, ἱμάντα βοὸς φοίνικι φαεινόν (of Odysseus' bed).

[27]In all other mentions of ζωστήρ (except 6.220), the belt is pierced by a weapon, resulting in a serious wound (Il. 4.132) or death (Il. 5.539; 17.519; 20.414).

[28]Once, a boar's tusk helmet is given as a ξεινήϊον, a valuable heirloom with a long pedigree (Il. 10.266).

[29]Od. 4.591 (= δέπας ἀμφικύπελλον, 15.102, 120). The cup is midway in value between Menelaus' main gift, a splendid silver and gold *krater*, and a woman's *peplos*.

[30]Il. 24.234; this is the καλὸν ἄλεισον which Priam offers to Hermes as a gift for guiding him safely to Achilles (429).

[31]Porphyry 1.96.11–20 (Schrader); Eustathius 638.44–45 (van der Valk).

[32]Od. 4.591–592. See Od. 8.430, where again the purpose of the special gift-cup is to remind the receiver of the giver. Cf. Od. 3.40–64; 15.147–159; Il. 16.225.

[33]J. D. Craig, "ΧΡΥΣΕΑ ΧΑΛΚΕΙΩΝ," *CR* n.s. 18 (1967) 243–245, at 243.

[34]Eustathius says that in line 228 Diomedes ἐσέμνυνεν ἑαυτόν...τὸν μέντοι Γλαῦκον οὐ πάνυ σεμνύνει τὸ "ὃν ἂν δύνηαι"(638.37–38). The scholia on lines 227–229, however, say that Diomedes is not overbearing (Erbse II. 171.76–81). Cf. at 214 (169.33–34).

[35]Craig (above, n. 33) 244. The idea of a cowed Glaucus is at least as old as Horace *Serm.* 1.7.17. It should be noted that the duel between Ajax and Hector is the next major martial episode, separated by the domestic scene of Hector and Andromache. All three episodes portend the eventual Achaean victory.

[36]See Σ 234 (171.92–95, 1–2); Porph. 1.96.11–17, 33–97.6; Eust. 638.44–53. Diomedes is explicitly excused from the charge of craftiness: Σ 230 (171.88–89); Eust. 638.62–64. Line 234 is tortuously explained as ἀντὶ τοῦ ὑπερηύξησε τῇ φιλοτιμίᾳ, ὡς τὸ "γέρας ἔξελον" Σ

6.234; Porph. 1.96.33; 1.97.16; Eust. 638.52). Alexander Pope accepted this as having "the nobler Air," even though it "dishonours" Diomedes for proposing the exchange. See Calder 31. Cf. C. M. Bowra, *Homer* (New York 1972) 68, "... but the laugh is to the credit of Glaucus, who is carried away by generosity."

[37]According to M. Maftei, *Antike Diskussionen über die Episode von Glaukos und Diomedes im VI. Buch der Ilias* (Meisenheim am Glan 1976), behind the face-saving version preserved to us is another level of criticism which said that Diomedes was lying from the outset, and that his call to renew the ξενίη "war nur ein übler Trick, mit dem Diomedes den Glaukos aus schmutziger Gewinnsucht übertölpelte" (52; see 2, 13, 14–18). See above, nn. 34 and 36.

[38]See V. Pedrick, "Supplication in the *Iliad* and the *Odyssey*," *TAPA* 112 (1987) 125–140, at 127; J. Gould, "*Hiketeia*," *JHS* 93 (1973) 74–103, at 80, n. 38.

[39]M. Detienne and J.-P. Vernant, *Cunning Intelligence in Greek Culture and Society*, Eng. tr. by J. Lloyd (Hassocks, Sussex 1978) 21. They take as their Homeric example of μῆτις another complex ruse, the trickery of Antilochus in *Iliad* 23 (11–26). The youthful Diomedes is an ideal balance of might and cunning intelligence (cf. *Il.* 9.53–54). Four times he gives the leaders precisely the right advice (7.399; 9.31; 9.696; 14.109). He initiates the spy-raid on the Trojan camp (*Il.* 10.220).

[40]Detienne and Vernant (above, n. 39) 27. I should like to express my appreciation to the Director and staff of the *Thesaurus Linguae Graecae*, at Universtiy of California, Irvine for access to the facilities of the TLG data bank.

THE PRE-STATE COMMUNITY IN GREECE*

> The city-state was embryonically present in the chiefdoms of the ninth century B.C.; most importantly, the concept of a *koinonia* as a comprehensive unity with known boundaries, a central place, and a "national" identity, had emerged by then. Integration of the polis-community out of separate settlements was connected to the rise of paramount chiefs. Crystallization of the community, therefore, was a "political" process; the eighth-century transition to the true state took place within an already evolved structural frame.

There is general agreement that the *polis*-state had appeared in Greece by about 700 B.C. On the other hand, little is understood about its formative stages, which occurred during the obscure Dark Age (roughly 1150–750 B.C.). We are especially uninformed about the underlying structure of early Greek society; and yet a firm understanding of how "community" evolved is a necessary condition for analysis of the final transition from the pre-state to the state. The purpose of this paper, therefore, is to reconstruct the antecedent forms of the state. The plan is, first, to describe the pre-state community in its eighth-century form, and then to trace its origins back to the beginning of the Dark Age. I hope in this way to show that the transition to the city-state was a predictable and uniform political process. My conclusion is that both the structure of the Classical city-state and its inner dynamics were highly evolved by the ninth century.

We will concentrate on the fundamental concepts, "household," "land," and "people," which throughout history constituted what might be called the "exostructure" of the Greek community. By tracing the development of *oikos*, *demos*, *laos*, and other institutions—for which there is diachronic evidence extending back beyond 1200 B.C.—we can expect to understand better the social transformations that determined the establishment of the *polis* in the eighth century.

Before the seventh century, the evidence for the primary elements is scattered and uneven. There is some information about the Mycenaean community in the Linear B tablets; then there is a break in literary evidence until the Homeric epics and Hesiod. After 700, datable writings begin to provide an historically objective picture of these concepts, which is extremely helpful for analysis of their earlier evolution. A continuous, though sparse, archaeological record, covering the entire period, supplies important information about changing demographic, subsistence, and habitation patterns.[1] Since they are incontrovertibly "real," the physical remains also serve as the control by which to evaluate findings based on non-physical data. And, since the material evidence is roughly datable, it provides a fairly secure time-frame for such findings. Finally, linguistic analysis of the words *oikos, demos,* and *laos* yields some information about the historical changes undergone by these entities.

The most abundant early evidence for the cardinal elements of household, people, and territory is found in the Homeric epics and Hesiod. With Hesiod we are on firm historical ground, since we know he was a real person, and that his poems were written down in his lifetime, around 700 B.C. For these reasons, we agree that when Hesiod sang (for example) of those who give "straight *dikai*"

> to *xeinoi* and *endemoi*...their *polis* prospers and the *laoi* flourish in it; and peace, the nurse of youth, comes over the *ge*

he was using these words in their contemporary sense.[2]

With Homer there is not the same certainty; and some scholars seriously question the validity of the poems as social-historical documents.[3] For our present purposes, however, we need consider only whether the Homeric usage of the words *oikos, demos, laos,* etc., may be trusted as historical evidence. There are sound reasons for thinking so. These verbal artifacts, which were in continuous use throughout the Dark Age, represented not only the basic social elements within the fictional epics, but also the corresponding real-life institutions. In any body of hearers, at any given time, they would have aroused universally shared images; for it is difficult to conceive how, even in the deliberately archaizing epics, a singer's evocation of these concepts would not have approximated his audience's experience of them.[4] Even more convincing is that these elements, as described in the epics, are clearly recognizable as antecedent forms of the historically known institutions. The *oikos* of Homer, for example, is obviously the same social unit as the *oikos* of Hesiod and the later Greeks, while it also betrays certain transitional features, as we shall see. Therefore, accepting the conventional dates for the epics (ca. 750–700

B.C.), we may conclude that the *Iliad* and *Odyssey* provide an authentic description of these primary institutions, at a time no later than the second half of the eighth century.

I

1. *Oikos*. The primal element of community was the household. *Oikos*, which meant both the family and the family's house and land, was the basic unit of society throughout Greek history. The Greeks tended always to idealize it as self-sufficient and autonomous. In the mature city-state this ideal of autarky was inevitably limited by the actualities of highly evolved economic, social, and legal systems, which greatly channeled its activities.[5]

By contrast, it appears that in pre-polis Greece *oikos* had a much greater degree of actual autonomy. The material evidence shows a simple farming and pastoral economy, with little craft specialization or division of labor, and minimal commerce. Until the eighth century, population was very low, settlements were small and isolated, and land was plentiful. Under such conditions, every household would have been economically self-sustaining in almost every respect.[6]

That the pre-state *oikos* enjoyed considerable political independence also seems clear. Our earliest literary sources reveal only the rudiments of the administrative and judicial apparatus which formed the government of the later polis. Nor is there any evidence that superordinate social groups like clans, phratries, and tribes regulated the activities of the early *oikos*.[7] Finley makes the important point that in the critical area of marriage there is no suggestion of involvement beyond "the groom, his father and brothers, and the girl, her father and brothers."[8] Consistently in Homer and Hesiod, a person's primary point of reference is his or her parents, spouse, siblings, children, and property. There is no identification with any broader kin group; in fact, *oikos* is the only formal kinship unit named in Homer and Hesiod.

The "supremacy of the *oikos* over all other groups and ties," is thus the crucial feature of the early Greek community.[9] It fortunately happens that most of our information is about the highest ranking houses, those that dominated the "ordinary" households (which were structurally the same, of course, but with less wealth and manpower). The eminent *oikos*, as Finley noted, consisted of three distinct elements: the family, the labor force, and retainers.[10]

The core of the *oikos* was the family; a man, his wife, and their children, living together in the same house. It is presented as a usual practice in Homer for sons to remain in the *oikos* after they married, thus forming a household of several brothers and their families, under the rule of the father, the undisputed head. Normally, daughters left the *oikos* upon marriage, but in a number of

Homeric cases sons-in-law were induced to join their wives' fathers' households. Priam's is an extreme example of such a large extended family; wife, several concubines, sons (fifty; nineteen by Hecabe) and daughters (twelve), wives and husbands of Priam's sons and daughters, young grandchildren, all of whom inhabit a large complex of buildings.[11] Less exotic, but identical in form, is the well-described *oikos* of Nestor in *Odyssey* 3. The old man is its head; other members are Nestor's wife, his six sons, and their wives, his married daughters, and their husbands.[12]

The clear purpose of these marriage and residence customs was to maximize the number of fighting men, the principal source of the *oikos*' strength. "You once said," Sarpedon scolds Hector, "that you could defend the *polis* alone, without the folk (*laoi*) and allies (*epikouroi*), with your sisters' husbands (*gambroi*) and your brothers (*kasignetoi*)."[13] Conversely, a family without brothers is dangerously short of manpower. The disguised Odysseus asks Telemachus if his troubles with the suitors were caused by inadequate support from his *kasignetoi*, "in whose fighting a man puts his trust, even if a great feud (*neikos*) arises" (*Od.* 16.97–98). Telemachus explains that he is defenseless precisely because he has no brothers; Zeus had made the family line run to single sons.[14] Achilles, an only son, is concerned about his *oikos*' survival for the same reason (*Od.* 11.492–503; cf. *Il.* 19.328–37). The death of aged Phaenops' only two sons in war meant the extinction of his *oikos*; "relatives (*cherostai*) divided up his possessions" (*Il.* 5.152–58).

The second element of the *oikos* consisted of unfree workers (*dmoes, dmoai, oikees*). They, and to a lesser extent the *thetes* (free hired hands, loosely or seasonally attached to the household), shared in the life of the *oikos*, but only as inferiors, assigned to the hard labor and drudgery. Since domestics and hirelings served under constraint, their loyalty and reliability may have been questionable. Nevertheless, when necessary, these low-status "members" could provide manpower for the *oikos*. Antinous inquires whether Telemachus' shipmates on his voyage to Pylos were "chosen youths of Ithaca or his own *thetes* and *dmoes*" (*Od.* 4.641–44). Odysseus and his son killed the suitors, and later faced down their kinsmen with the help of a small band of faithful workers.[15]

The third element of the high-ranking household, the "retainers," were free men, non-kin (or distant kin) in willing service to the *oikos*-head. The regular word for them in Homer is *therapon* (attendant), a broad term, covering a range of standing, from simple attendant to esteemed warrior-companion.[16] We are told the backgrounds of a few retainers. Lycophron, a *therapon* of Ajax, had fled his land after killing a man (*Il.* 15.430–32). Patroclus was brought to Peleus' house as a boy by his father, having killed another youth over dice. He was reared there and "named" *therapon* of Achilles (*Il.* 23.83–90). Phoenix ran away from home because of a quarrel with his father over a concubine, and was treated like an "only son" by Peleus (*Il.* 9.447–84). Hermes, in the guise of a *therapon* of Achilles, said that he was one of seven sons, chosen by lot to follow Achilles (*Il.* 24.396–400).[17] In whatever way they came to be attached to an *oikos*, retainers were bound to it by the strongest ties of obligation and personal loyalty, and were, in turn, welcomed as highly valued additions to the *oikos'* manpower.[18]

The large Homeric family of brothers, brothers-in-law, and close retainers (adopted brothers, in effect) was not a feature of the polis, which knew only the nuclear family. The words *daer* (husband's brother), *galoos* (husband's sister), *einater* (husband's brother's wife), important identifiers in this type of household, do not occur in literature after Homer.[19] This "tendency towards narrowing the circle," as Finley puts it, is already evident in the epics. Although the well-manned compound family (Priam, Nestor) is portrayed as the desirable norm, the actuality is as frequently the isolated—and vulnerable—single family (Odysseus, Achilles, Agamemnon). An extraordinary account of what awaits an only child whose father has died is given by Andromache in *Iliad* 22.477–507. The orphaned Astyanax, she laments, will be in dire want, and will be completely cut off from companionship—a situation impossible to imagine in the huge family of Priam, but a possible scenario in a society of isolated families. As Nestor's son says,

> A son whose father has gone away has many woes in his halls,
> when he has no other helpers, as now Telemachus' father is gone,
> nor are there others in the *demos* who might ward off evil.[20]

We will explore later the possibility that the Homeric *oikos* represents a transitional stage from a multi-family unit to a single-family unit. For now, it is sufficient to recognize that *oikoi* in Homer and Hesiod, whether large or small, stood alone. This fact of isolation is the key to the political dynamic observed in the epics. Poor or weak families needed the help and protection of powerful friends; wealthy families, with high ambitions, needed additional adherents.[21]

A great warrior in Homer had numerous followers—"companions" (*hetairoi*) or "friends" (*philoi*)—attached to him and his house. Like other status terms in Homer, *philoi/hetairoi* were broad, describing both the intimate associates, tightly bound to the *oikos*, and others less closely connected—distant relatives or non-relatives—who could be called on to augment the *oikos'* manpower. Ambition demanded followers; a man's authority depended on, and was measured by, the number of men he could persuade to follow him. What bound all *hetairoi* to their leader was personal loyalty; but beyond the tight circle of boon companions, loyalty was alloyed with self-interest. In return for their aid, followers expected to be rewarded with feasts, booty, gifts; otherwise they, and their families, might choose to support someone else. Homer bitingly portrays the calculated loyalty of the Trojan Antimachus,

> who beyond all others had taken the gold of Alexander, glorious gifts, and did not allow Helen to be given back to fairhaired Menelaus (*Il*. 11.123–42).

When Halitherses publicly foretells the imminent return of Odysseus, Eurymachus the suitor angrily accuses him of "looking for a *doron* for your *oikos*, which [Telemachus] might give you."[22]

There were, of course, other kinds of bonds besides the tie of personal loyalty to a powerful man. Households were also linked by marriage and by neighborhood. The webs of amity, obligation, and dependence connecting kinsman to kinsman, villager to villager, produced strong local solidarity groups. These networks of relatives and neighbors were fundamental structures. In the pre-state period (and, indeed, beyond) most of the activities of ordinary life took place within the overlapping "communities" of kindred and village. The superordinate bond, nevertheless, seems to have been personal allegiance to a leader. And the operational political groupings appear as informal, flexible coalitions of lesser households orbiting around a grand house.[23]

2. *Demos*. The arena in which the able and ambitious leaders (*basileis*) competed with one another for honor and prestige, and for the followers who were both the means and the sign of their eminence, was the *demos*. As in later times, *demos* in Homer and Hesiod names the largest conceivable unity: the "land" and the "people." The limiting genitives of *demos*-"land" are always a named people or the named territory they inhabit, as ἐν δήμῳ 'Ιθάκης; (*Il*. 3.201; κατὰ δῆμον πάντων Φαιήκων (*Od*. 6.34).[24]

In action, *demos*-"people" is always portrayed as the populace at large, expressing a common will or experience. *Pas demos* gathers together for a collective project (*Il*. 20.166); owes a debt in common (*Od*. 21.17); divides spoils (*Il*. 11.704); gives *geras* to the leaders (*Od*. 7.150); builds a temple (*h. Dem*. 271); pays for the wickedness of its rulers (*Op*. 261). Leaders are honored by *demos* (*Il*. 5.78, etc.); *demos* hearkens to the leader (*Od*. 7.11); the opinion (*phemis*) of *demos* constrains individuals (*Od*. 14.239; 16.75 = 19.527); one beseeches or fears *demos* (*Od*. 8.157; 16.425); *pas demos* is angry (*Od.* 16.114).[25] *Demos* represents the outermost limit of belonging; outside his *demos* a man is in the "*demos* of others," in an alien land, cut off from home, family, and friends.[26]

Ge (earth, land) and *patre* (ancestral land) are also used synonymously with *demos* to express the exostructure of land/people and household. Nothing is sweeter, Odysseus says,

> than one's *patris* and parents (*tokees*), even though a man lives far away in a rich *oikos* in an alien *gaia* apart from his *tokees* (*Od.* 9.34–36).

Hector exhorts the Trojans,

> It is not unseemly for a man to die fighting in defense of his *patre*; but his wife and his children after him and his *oikos* and his lot of land (*kleros*) are safe, if only the Achaeans go away with their ships into their *patris gaia*.[27]

Sometimes *demos* is linked closely with *polis* in variations of the formula δῆμός τε πόλις τε. Paris is a great woe (as Hector is a great joy) to his "father and *polis* and *pas demos*" (*Il.* 3.50). The close connection between these concepts is also seen in parallel expressions such as Τρώων πόλιν (*Od.* 3.85); Τρώων ἐνὶ δήμῳ (*Od.* 1.237); Φαιήκων ἀνδρῶν δῆμόν τε πόλιν τε (*Od.* 6.3); Φαιήκων ἀνδρῶν ἐν πίονι δήμῳ (*Od.* 13.322); Φαίηκες μὲν τήνδε πόλιν καὶ γαῖαν ἔχουσιν (*Od.* 6.195).[28] Quite clearly, the epic poet and his listeners identified the word-concepts "land/people" with a central place, the principal settlement of the land. When they catch sight of Odysseus returning from Circe's house, his *hetairoi* weep with joy, "as if they had come to *patris* and *polis* itself of rugged Ithaca, where they were raised and born."[29]

3. *Laos*. *Laos* in Homer is usually equivalent in meaning to *demos*-"people." To the question, "Do the *laoi* hate you *ana demon*?" Telemachus replies, "*pas demos* does not hate me, nor is angry with me."[30] Antinous fears that Telemachus will call the *laoi* to the assembly, and that "they will do us evil and will drive us from our *gaia*, and we would come to the *demos* of others."[31]

Traditionally, Homeric scholars have taken *laos* to mean the "soldiery," the men under arms; or, in peace, the (common) "people." The word, however, exhibits certain peculiarities of usage which show that it was not simply an interchangeable synonym of *demos*. Thus, while *demos* persists as the regular word for the "people" in Greek, the employment of *laos* after 700 becomes almost exclusively "poetic."[32] Unlike *demos,* it occurs in both the singular and plural forms (more frequently in the plural, though with no apparent distinction in meaning). In the *Iliad, laos* refers to the combined Achaean or Trojan forces, as well as to single contingents.[33] And, in a number of instances, *laos* seems to denote a group of warriors attached personally to a particular hero.[34]

Consideration of these peculiarities led Jeanmaire in 1939 to theorize that Homeric *laos* meant the assembled "warriors" of a particular land, liable to summons by the "king"; and that little by little, the word came to designate (in the later *Odyssey*) the "body of the citizens in a given state." In its "primitive sense," however (recoverable from the earlier *Iliad*), *laos* had meant a group of warriors who owed personal allegiance to a chief—his "companions" (*hetairoi*).[35] According to this widely accepted theory, then, *laos/laoi* had originally denoted discrete segments of the populace, and had come, in Homer, to mean the "people" as a single unit. This notion of *laos/laoi* as the whole "people," the "folk," is well developed in Hesiod.[36]

Analysis of the concepts "household," "land," and "people," has shown that the framework of the classical Greek community was solidly established by at least the middle of the eighth century. By then, the comprehensive *demos* possessed a highly refined sense of its collective character as the land and the people, including a sentimental, "patriotic" recognition of itself as the "earth," the "fatherland." There is also a positive identification of this whole with the major settlement, the *polis* (or *astu*), the "central place" of the land and people.[37]

As historians are careful to point out, however, this social system is not yet the true state. Thus, while the essential political-legal institutions of assembly, council, and law court are firmly in place, they are still informal and undeveloped. There are no magistracies and boards: impersonal offices which exist permanently and independently of the men who fill them. There are only vague indications of the formal administrative and military divisions which provided the internal organization of the later city-states.[38]

Nowhere is the elementary state of constitutional development more apparent than in the behavior of the *demos/laos* in the *agore*. A well-known example is the assembly of the Ithacans in *Odyssey* 2. As his initial step into manhood, Telemachus calls the people together, for their first assembly in twenty years.[39] Aegyptius, an elder, rising first, asks who the summoner is; and whether he has news of the army's return or speaks to them of "some other *demos*-matter" (τι δήμιον ἄλλο). Telemachus announces that it is not a *demion*, but "my own *chreios*," the threat to his *oikos*. At this point the *laos* assumes "its normal position of neutrality."[40]

Even though Odysseus was their paramount chief, and despite emotional appeals by Telemachus and Mentor to shame them into decisive action against the suitors, the people do not interfere. They elect to regard the matter as a private dispute between the house of Odysseus and his *hetairoi* (Halitherses, Mentor) and the combined suitors. For all its awareness of itself as a coherent entity, the Homeric *demos* still acts as a collection of separate loyalties, wherein men follow and obey particular leaders. It is not yet a body of citizens, loyal to an abstract "state," bound by laws enforced by a central authority. In brief, the narrow divide separating the personal chiefdom from the impersonal state had not yet been crossed—though clearly it was about to be.[41]

Which brings us to a final observation. The imminent progress to the "true" Greek state was a process of transformation *within* an existing frame. Important political, economic, and social events occurred in Greece between about 800 and 675 B.C. All of them—the spread of epichoric alphabets, the founding of the Olympian festival, overseas colonization, the first interstate war, urbanization—happened within the context of highly defined communities. Among these events, and coming last in time, was the establishment of the formal machinery of organization, regulation, and coercion—features that technically define the state form. The political developments that produced the state originated and matured inside an exostructure that had already achieved its "classic" form.[42]

II

Having described the pre-state community, we turn now to its origins. There is more or less general agreement with Lejeune's definition of Mycenaean *damo* as a "local administrative entity, devoted to agriculture," one of several "districts" into which the Mycenaean state was divided. It is also believed that Linear B *damo* signified the free inhabitants of the district, and that the *damo* had its own internal political structure. There is abundant evidence that in classical times δῆμοι were districts (villages and their lands) within the confines of both Ionic and Dorian states.[43]

Scholars have therefore proclaimed a direct evolutionary link between the Late Bronze Age structures and those of the archaic state. According to Maddoli, for example, each *damo* had an "administrative center," a particular village, which was the seat of the district's governing body. After the collapse of the centralized ruling structure, certain of these villages became "centripetal nuclei" in respect to smaller or weaker villages. These centers Maddoli identifies as the many Homeric *poleis*—villages that had been strong defense-points during the turmoil of the early Dark Age.[44] Andreev discerns a similar pattern.

In the aftermath of Mycenaean decline (eleventh–tenth centuries), the Greek landscape came to be dotted by numerous small, independent communities, composed of groups of families. The focal point of these "pygmy states" was the fortified settlement, the *polis,* ruled over by the founder and "tribal leader" (*Stammesführer*), the *basileus.*[45]

These and similar theories, which stress continuity of political forms, suggest a plausible model for the evolution of community in Dark Age Greece. By the time the last vestiges of centralized authority had disappeared (by 1150–1100), the fairly extensive Bronze Age kingdoms were already disintegrating into smaller parts. These would have been natural units, villages and hamlets, along with their farms and close-in pastures. The word for the territory (and its people) was *damos;* the word for its main settlement was *polis.* We must suppose that the social, economic, political system of the small *damos*—now totally disconnected from any central administration—was simple. It would have consisted of a small group of families, engaged in subsistence farming and herding, who followed the lead of their ablest man. The local leader, a "big man" type, was called *basileus,* formerly the title of a lesser Mycenaean official with local jurisdiction, the *qa-si-re-u.*[46]

This simple type of polity (together with its Bronze Age, "Achaean," nomenclature) survived the shocks of the early Dark Age: the final waves of destruction, incursions of new ethnic groups, massive depopulation. To judge by the evidence, this system, with all its elements, was exported to Asia Minor, beginning around 1050 B.C. According to the traditions, the Ionian emigrants set out in small groups, collected and led by *basileis,* who founded numerous settlements (*poleis*). The archaeological record confirms that these small settlements were of diverse origins, apparently independent at first, consolidating into larger units only much later.[47]

The remarkable fact is that on both sides of the Aegean, and on the islands, such communities eventually, and more or less simultaneously, evolved into city-states. This pattern of development, which occurred independently in diverse regions of Greek habitation, is a compelling indication that the embryo of the *polis*-state existed by about 1050 B.C. in the form of the small, self-contained community (*damos*), made up of separate households (*oikoi*) concentrated in a village (*polis*), and "governed" by an emerging protonobility (*basileis*).[48]

In retrospect, the subsequent evolution of community appears as a process of crystallization, based on the primary pattern. In time, separate communities (*damoi/demoi*) came to regard themselves as the *demos,* a single "land-people." One settlement (for whatever various reasons) emerged as the main population center and as the center of political, economic, and religious activity in the *demos.* Crystallization ended either at some natural boundary or by collision with another *demos'* frontiers. This is the picture of the eighth-century community given to us in the Homeric epics.

What we are most unsure about is how the separate small communities found in the early Dark Age coalesced into the incipient city-states described in Homer. New methods of settlement-pattern analysis, initiated by geographers, are a promising approach to the questions of how one locus of habitation gains a superior importance over others, and how individual units unite to form a larger unit. Application of such techniques and models to Dark Age Greece has just begun, however, and the data produced so far are too few to draw definite conclusions.[49]

One thing these studies have made clear is that the development of central places is tied to the development of central persons. Indeed, amidst the multiple factors involved in the formation of the various pre-states, one is identified as having been common to all Greek societies; namely the universal tendency of local chiefs to seek precedence over other local chiefs, thereby forming wider political hierarchies. Although such "pyramids" were quite unstable, they provided a pattern of political leadership which looked beyond purely local (village, deme) boundaries to more integrated forms of political association. It will be useful, therefore, to focus more closely on the obscure subject of Dark Age politics and its role in the development of the community.

In the post-Mycenaean *damoi*, as we saw, there was very little social or economic differentiation; "political" groups would have consisted simply of an eminent man at the head of a band of local kinsmen and neighbors. It is quite probable that the closely knit kin/villagers/followers were known to one another as *philoi* ("friends"), *hetairoi* ("companions"), *etai* ("kinsmen")— ancient words, which in the epics express similar kinds of relationships.[50] There is also good reason to believe that in their function as a military group these men were called *laos,* a word of obscure origin. In the Mycenaean tablets *laos* appears only in proper names and as a component of the title *lawagetas,* who seems to have been a high personage, subordinate to the *wanax* alone. Despite much uncertainty about the nature and functions of Late Bronze Age *laos* and *lawagetas,* the latter is commonly identified as "war-leader," and *laos* the "army," either as a special class of warriors or as the "people" in their capacity as the warriors.[51] We have seen that before the decipherment of Linear B, Jeanmaire and others had already concluded that the "primitive" *laos* was a group of warriors loyal to a chief, his "companions." It is a reasonable inference, therefore, that within the small communities of the Submycenaean period, *laos* continued in use as the word for the "warriors," that is, the men of fighting age who followed their local *basileus,* himself an outstanding warrior. At that level, of course, the personal "followers" of a *basileus* and the "people" of the community would have been the same, the *laos*.[52]

The essential feature of the follower system was the independent household. It is important, therefore, to know when the *oikos* achieved the form familiar to us from Homer and Hesiod on. Though slight, the indications are that the single-family *oikos* was an early development from a larger kinship unit. Linguists derive *oikos* from an Indo-European root **wik-*, which yields Sanskrit *viš*, 'settlement, house, clan'; Iranian *vîs*, 'settlement, village'; Latin *vicus*, 'town, quarter', etc. This has led to the conclusion that Proto-Indo-European **wik-* denoted a settlement composed of several interrelated extended families, whose separate dwellings, clustered together, formed a "clan village."[53] It has been tentatively suggested, on the basis of the Linear B evidence, that the Mycenaean *oikos* was an extended kinship group, a "clan."[54] And it is quite possible, though we have no evidence aside from the mysterious *phulai,* that the pre-migration Dorians were organized by clans. The *Iliad* and *Odyssey* preserve no sense of such a structure, but they are aware of a stage when the extended family was the normal social unit.

It may be, then, that the Greeks once had a compound family "oikos," a large living unit, which devolved into the single extended family, and, eventually, into the nuclear-family *oikos,* already standard in Homer. An explanation for such a change may be sought in the disturbances of the late thirteenth through the eleventh centuries, which were severe enough to cause larger units to segment. Destruction or abandonment of traditional settlements, wide-scale movements and migrations, and, of course, a huge drop in the number of people, all could have contributed to a rapid splintering into smaller primary units. If in fact such a process did occur, it would thus seem to have been completed before 1000 B.C., by which time a measure of stability had returned to Greece. An early date for the appearance of the small, autonomous household is also indicated by the fact that the legendary traditions retain no memory of possible earlier clan-like structures, but revolve around single chiefs and their houses. This conclusion is also consistent with the indications that the overseas settlements of the late eleventh century were founded by small follower groups, and that the evolution of the *oikos*-alliance system there paralleled the course of political development on the mainland.

It was on this basis of small associations of households that a more complex system of ranking arose. As habitation became more settled, ambitious *basileis* enlarged their spheres of influence by recruiting non-local supporters—other small bands of households loyal to their own "big man"—thus building up regional pyramids. The bonds in either case were similar, in that all followership was based on personal loyalty. But the relationship between a *basileus* and followers outside his local base lacked the mechanical solidarity of kindred and neighborhood; by their nature, these extra-local ties were more truly "political." This development would account for the anomalies observed in the epic usage of *laos*. The word that had earlier designated the "men folk" of a local community became the collective name for the "men folk" of the integrated community, while simultaneously losing currency as the following of a particular chief; a meaning it retained only vestigially in the epics. And *hetairos*, "companion"—a referent of strictly personal allegiance, with no built-in connotations of kinship or locality—was extended in application to cover all degrees of political/military followers.[55]

The result of this political dynamic was that after some generations one *basileus* achieved an uneasy dominance over the other *basileis* within a particular territory and people, and was recognized by all as the paramount chief. This was the type of political arrangement familiar to the epic audiences. In Homer, the ranking *basileus* was a man of outstanding ability, whose *oikos* was wealthy enough to support several retainers and numerous followers. His position as paramount, coveted by many, entitled him to special honors and rewards, conferred by the *demos*, including the "right" to pass the chiefly office on to his son. His most important responsibility was to lead the warriors on raids or in defense of the territory. The chief was also the acknowledged head of the council of "elders," and played the major role in communal rituals and in the arbitration of justice.

Despite the great authority attained by strong Dark Age chiefs, the position of ranking *basileus* remained an achieved status. Political power continued to be based on shifting pyramids of personal followers—the fatal defect of chiefdoms. Stable, centralized kingship eluded the grasp of even the most successful *basileus*. The informal nature of the alliance system and the essential equality among the *basileis* thus kept the paramount's rule tenuous. Around 700 B.C., in most Greek communities, the unstable chiefdom ended when the *basileis* instituted a formal system of power sharing through short-tenured offices and collegial boards. But by then, as I have argued, the structure of the city-state had been firmly established.

The emergence of the pre-state and the expanding political role of the elites occurred together. We may suspect, therefore, a reciprocal relationship between the rise of chiefdoms and the establishment of "national" boundaries and political centers. Local traditions ascribed political and territorial union to a single powerful *basileus*; modern historians have tended to see synoecism as a lengthy process rather than as a single event. Although the process of boundary formation is still too dim to be reconstructed with any certainty, it is at least reasonable to suggest that the efforts of successive strong leaders to achieve regional control effected a significant, and lasting, measure of cohesion among traditionally separate segments.[56]

Certainly, in his various "centralized" roles, the Homeric *basileus* represents a unifying figure within the *demos*. This is especially true of his role as leader in defense, but the *basileus* is also a focus of communal solidarity in peace. This is the thrust of Odysseus' praise of the "blameless *basileus*" whose benevolent and wise leadership ensures the well-being of the community: "The *laoi* prosper (*aretao*) under him" (*Od.* 19.109–14). Hesiod's Muse-favored *basileus* is also such a centripetal figure: "And all the people (*laoi pantes*) look to him as he decides the laws with straight judgments..." (*Theog.* 83–92).

III

To assign an absolute chronology to these developments is difficult. It was argued above that the small, autonomous household, nucleated settlement, deme, and simple ranking were all present by about the mid-eleventh century; and that the integrated community, central place, elaborated ranking, and an incipient central organization had been achieved by at least the mid-eighth.

Archaeology provides our best information for more precise dating within these brackets. A general survey of the evidence shows that throughout the Submycenaean and Protogeometric periods there were only loose scatters of small settlements, presumably self-sufficient and independent. The few buildings and goods recovered are unimpressive; there are no indications of economic or social differentiation. By Early Geometric the picture changes to reveal stable, settled life throughout most of the Greek areas, with clear signs of increasing intra- and inter-regional communication. Around that time (900 B.C.) there begin to appear relatively substantial population centers, often in the form of clusters of small villages, which are the recognizable precursors of the capital towns of the archaic period. Ninth-century burials contain a greater frequency and a higher standard of luxury goods, signalling an economic surplus controlled by an elite stratum of consumers.[57] The early ninth century, then, is the earliest time for which there is material evidence consistent with the crystallization process described above, and the rise of a preeminent class.

At the beginning of the next century, new circumstances appear evident to archaeologists. Chief among these was a widespread rise in population, accompanied by the bringing of hitherto uncultivated pastures and marginal land under the plow.[58] Even if the demographic upcurve should prove not to have been as steep or as sudden as Snodgrass and others believe, there is no denying that early eighth-century Greece experienced a marked growth in population and quickly felt its economic and political consequences. Bintliff, following a line popular among processual archaeologists, suggests that the surge in population, and the exploitation by the wealthy of the outlying land, triggered the transformation of the "achieved, chief/'big man' structures...into an ascribed hereditary squirearchy, dominating the peasantry and the possession of the land itself."[59] According to this model, which is highly plausible, the politico-economic transition from the pre-state to the city-state is thus to be dated from the early decades of the eighth century.

Altogether, the indications are positive enough to conclude that the final formative stage of the pre-state polity occurred during the ninth century. This period, from about 900 to shortly after 800, was the florescence of the low-level chiefdom portrayed in the *Iliad* and the *Odyssey*.

*

I have not dealt directly with the final transition to the *polis* form, since that involves detailed discussion of the eighth-century political/economic transformations within specific states. My more modest purpose here has been to make those transformations more intelligible by establishing the prior history of the community.

We saw that the structural form of the city-state originated in the simple polity that emerged after the disintegration of the Bronze Age kingdoms, and that the growth of pre-states was a concurrent phenomenon over a wide zone of the Greek world, in response to similar sets of conditions. It has also been shown that the political system of the Early and Middle Geometric Periods was a prime agent of centralization. The horizontal and vertical networks generated by the evolution from a big-man society to the basilarchy had a centripetal effect, uniting local interests into territorial unities, creating regional power and cult centers, and promoting the growth of central institutions.

Most important for our understanding of the city-state is the knowledge that the Greek *koinonia* was "political" from the start. The ties that bound households together hierarchically were, in the main, ties of deferential friendship. Throughout the Dark Age, single households were nearly autonomous units that stood in reciprocal, nearly equal, relationships with their leader-houses.

This pretty well describes the political character of the developed states, in which a citizenry of free householders engaged in a continuous tensioned dialectic with its aristocratic rulers, who were themselves embroiled in stasiotic contests for pre-eminence—aided by personal supporters from among the citizenry.

What all this amounts to is this: the *polis* form merely enveloped, without radically changing, the political style of the pre-state community. We should keep this principle in mind when we turn to the formation of individual *poleis*. Each *polis* had its own particular historical development, but their basic configuration, inherited from the Dark Age, was the same. The archaic Greek states were born as nations of farmer-warriors, upon whose good will the success of their leaders ultimately depended. The special genius of the Greeks was that they developed a complex civilization while retaining the communal form and political spirit of the low-level chiefdom. It was precisely this that made the *polis* unique among the states of the ancient Mediterranean.

NOTES

* Research for this article was greatly facilitated by the use of the *Thesaurus Linguae Graecae* at the University of California, Irvine. The author wishes to express his thanks to the Director and staff of the project.
[1] J. Haas, *The Evolution of the Prehistoric State*, New York 1982, is a detailed analysis of what archaeology by itself can and cannot tell about prehistoric social change. For Greece, see P. Cartledge, *Sparta and Lakonia. A Regional History, 1300-362 B.C.*, London, Boston and Henley 1979, 8ff.
[2] *Op.* 225–28.
[3] E.g., A. M. Snodgrass, "An historical Homeric Society?," *JHS* 94, 1974, 114–25; A. G. Geddes, "Who's Who in 'Homeric' Society?," *CQ* 34, 1984, 17–36.
[4] J. M. Redfield, *Nature and Culture in the Iliad. The Tragedy of Hector*, Chicago 1975, 78–79.
[5] W. K. Lacey, *The Family in Classical Greece*, Ithaca 1978.
[6] M. I. Finley, *The World of Odysseus*, rev. ed., New York 1978, 60–61.
[7] F. Bourriot, *Recherches sur la nature du genos. Étude d'histoire sociale Athénienne—périodes archaïque et classique*, Paris 1976; D. Roussel, *Tribu et Cité. Études sur les groupes sociaux dans les cités grecques aux époques archaïque et classique*, Paris 1976; W. Donlan, "The Social Groups of Dark Age Greece," *CPh* 80, 1985, 293–308.
[8] M. I. Finley, *Economy and Society in Ancient Greece*, New York 1981, 243.
[9] *Ibid.* p. 244.
[10] Finley (above n. 6), 104.
[11] *Il.* 6.242; 24.160, 248, 495. Epic descriptions of the dwellings of the elites are garbled reminiscences of Late Bronze Age "palaces." Throughout the Dark Age, archaeology reveals, houses were modest one or two room affairs, suitable for a single small family. On the other hand, excavators have recently uncovered large buildings, dating from the eleventh century in the case of the so-called "heroon" at Lefkandi and from the tenth century in Nichoria (the so-called "chieftain's house"). See M. Popham, E. Touloupa and L. H. Sackett, "The hero of Lefkandi," *Antiquity* 56, 1982, 169–74; W. A. McDonald, W. D. E. Coulson and S. Rosser, *Excavations at Nichoria in Southwest Greece*, vol. 3, Minneapolis 1983, 19–58.
[12] *Od.* 3.386–469. Only Peisistratus, the youngest son, unmarried, and his unmarried sister, Polycaste, live in the central portion of the house with their parents. The others have their own rooms, *thalamoi*, set off from the main dwelling. All seven brothers of Andromache had lived *en megarois* (*Il.* 6.421). In Scheria, Alcinous' five sons (two married, three bachelors) also live at home (*Od.* 6.62). Alcinous wants Odysseus to marry Nausicaa and be part of his *oikos* (*Od* 7.311). Menelaus' son's new wife comes to live in the paternal *oikos*; his daughter leaves to marry Achilles' son (*Od* 4.5–12). The mythical Aeolus married off his six sons to his six daughters (*Od* 10.5).

[13] The obvious advantage of uxorilocality (see also *Il.* 6.192; 14.121; *Od.* 7.312) to an *oikos* is immediate increase in manpower. The next generation of children will also belong to the mother's paternal house. Prestige is also a factor; dominant houses keep their females and gain males. Bastard sons are also warriors: e.g., *Il.* 5.69; 6.21; 8.281; 11.102. For further discussion of marital alliance, see W. Donlan, "Reciprocities in Homer," *CW* 75, 1982, 145–47.

[14] *Od.* 16.115–20; cf. 11.174–76. Homeric *kasignetos* probably also refers to first cousins; see H. P. Gates, *The Kinship Terminology of Homeric Greek*, Baltimore 1971, 14–16.

[15] On faithful and unfaithful slaves, see Donlan (above n. 13), 157. The natural resentment of this class, leading to treachery, is illustrated in *Od.* 15.417–70. Slaves in Hesiod: *Op.* 405, 469, 502, 559, 597. Thetes: *Il.* 21.441; *Od.* 11.489; 18.357.

[16] C. G. Thomas, "From Wanax to Basileus: Kingship in the Greek Dark Age," *Hispania Antiqua* 6, 1978, 202–04.

[17] Cf. the simile of *A.* 24.480–82, a man kills a man in his *patre*, and "comes to the *demos* of others, to a rich man's house." For other examples of adopted suppliants, see C. A. Trypanis, "Brothers Fighting Together in the *Iliad*," *RhM* 106, 1963, 289–97. For the possible economic function of such "strays," see B. Qviller, "The Dynamics of the Homeric Society," *SO* 56, 1981, 139.

[18] G. Nagy, *The Best of the Achaeans*, Baltimore and London 1979, 292, says that *therapon* originally designated one's *alter ego*. This is especially true of Patroclus. Lycophron is also *pistos hetairos* (*Il.* 15.437). Automedon and Alcimus perform as personal attendants of Achilles, and are at the same time his close *hetairoi* and outstanding warriors. We have a detailed picture of the character and activities of Meriones, *therapon* of Idomeneus, in *Il.* 13.246–329, 23.112–24, 859–88.

[19] Finley (above n. 6), 77–78; Gates (above n. 14), 23–26, 34, 42–43.

[20] *Od.* 4.164–67; cf. 2.58–59. *Od.* 6.180–185 is evidence that the nuclear family was the "normal" family unit for the poet and audience. Hesiod talks only of the isolated nuclear family; see Roussel (above n. 7), 35–37. Several times Hesiod expresses concern about the fragility of this small unit (*Op.* 244, 325, 376).

[21] W. G. Forrest, *The Emergence of Greek Democracy, 800–4000 B.C.*, New York and Toronto 1966, 49.

[22] *Od.* 2.186. Cf. *Od.* 4.525; *Il.* 17.225. For an extended discussion, see Donlan (above n. 13), 163–69, and "The Politics of Generosity in Homer," *Helios* 9, 1982, 1–15. Cf. O. Murray, "The Symposion as Social Organization," in R. Hägg (ed.). *The Greek Renaissance of the Eighth-Century B.C.: Tradition and Innovation*, Stockholm 1983, 196–97. A chief's authority and prestige were measured by the number of his followers. See H. Jeanmaire, *Couroi et Courètes*, Lille 1939, 56–57.

[23] Donlan (above n. 7), 301–05.

[24] Cf. *Il.* 16.437; *Od.* 1.237. The only exceptions are metaphorical usages at *Od.* 24.12 and *op.* 527; and at *Il.* 2.547, where Athens = *ptoliethron* = "*demos* of Erechtheus."

[25] See also *Il.* 3.56; 6.442; 18.295, 500; *Od.* 2.101, 239, 8.259, 15.468. *Demos* in Homer and Hesiod does not have its later connotation of "lower class." See W. Donlan, "Changes and Shifts in the Meaning of *Demos* in the Literature of the Archaic Period," *PP* 135, 1970, 382–85; Geddes (above n. 3), 19–27.

[26] Hence the importance of the *xeinos*-relationship in epic society. Exile from the *demos*: *Il.* 6.158; 9.634; 19.324; 24.481; *Od.* 2.366; 8.211, 15.228, 238; 16.381; 23.118.

[27] *Il.* 15.496–99; cf. 12.243. The formula, "to see (his) *philoi* and to reach (his) well-built *oikos* and (his) *patris gaia*," occurs eight times in the *Odyssey*. Ithaca is called *patris gaia* in *Od.* 10.420, 462; 19.461. Cf. *Il.* 24.480; *Od.* 13.325; 15.228, 272, 382; 23.120.

[28] Cf. *Il.* 15.737; 24.706; *Od.* 6.191; 8.555; 11.14; 14.43; *Op.* 527.

[29] *Od.* 10.416–17. See J. V. Luce, "The *Polis* in Homer and Hesiod," *PRIA* 78, 1978, 9: "The name of the *polis* is also the name of the entire territory"; J. V. Andreev, "Könige und

Königsherrschaft in den Epen Homers," *Klio* 61, 1979, 368–69: "Die Begriffe Gemeinde und Stadt selbst sind bei ihrer Verwendung im Epos eng miteinander verbunden."

[30]*Od.* 16.95–96 (= 3.214–15), 114.

[31]*Od.* 16.375–82. See *Il.* 18.490–508; 22.408; 24.776, 789; *Od.* 2.41–81; 3.304; 6.194; 8.472; *Th.* 84–90; *Op.* 222, 225–27.

[32]H. van Effenterre, "Laos, laoi et lawagetas," *Kadmos* 16, 1977, 38–41.

[33]E.g., *Il.* 1.54; 2.120, 280, 438; 6.80; 13.492, etc.; *Od.* 3.140.

[34]E.g., *Il.* 2.664; 4.377, 407; *Od.* 6.164; 9.263; 14.248. Cf. *Il.* 2.577, 580, 675; 3.186; 4.91, 202; 13.710; 16.551; 17.390; 20.383; *Od.* 24.428. See Jeanmaire (above n. 22), 56–58.

[35]Jeanmaire (above n. 22) 55–59, 97–99. So also E. Benveniste, *Indo-European Language and Society*, trans. E. Palmer, London and Coral Gables 1973 371–72: *Laos* "expresses the personal relationship of a group of men to a chief...the retinue of a chief." Cf. Nagy (above n. 18), 83. Benveniste also points out (following Jeanmaire) that the political titles *poimen, orchamos, koiranos, kosmetor* are construed exclusively with *laos*, never with *demos*. (*Anax, agos,* and sometimes *orchamos,* take *andrôn*.)

[36]*Th.* 84–90, 430; *Op.* 227, 243, 763, 768; *Sc.* 472. The apparent change in the meaning of *laos*, dimly discernible in the epics, is an important clue to the political development of the community. See below, Section II.

[37]Luce (above n. 29), 15. See C. G. Thomas, "Homer and the *Polis*," *PP* 106, 1966, 5, 13; R. J. Hopper, *The Early Greeks*, New York 1976, 115; Andreev (above n. 29), 368–69.

[38]R. A. Posner, "The Homeric Version of the Minimal State," *Ethics* 90, 1979, 27–46; Homeric society is a "cohesive community," with rudimentary institutions, but is "prepolitical." W. G. Runciman, "Origins of States: The Case of Archaic Greece," *Comp. St. in Society and History* 24, 1982, 351–77; Homeric society describes the "semistate" (a polity which has no potential for statehood) in transition to the "protostate" (a stage which inevitably culminates in statehood). This transition took place during the eighth century, according to Runciman. I prefer the term "pre-state" to describe the chiefdom society of the ninth and eighth centuries.

[39]*Od.* 2.6–259. The extraordinary length of time without a gathering of the people is, I think, an exaggeration of reality, meant to coincide with the proportionately long absence of the paramount. That assemblies in the pre-state were irregular, however, rings true sociologically.

[40]*Od.* 2.15–49. Thomas (above n. 37), 11. It must be emphasized, nevertheless, that the will of the assembled *demos*, in its capacity to say yes or no, was ultimately supreme; the *basileis* had very limited means of coercion. For a dramatic example of an aroused *demos*' power, see *Od.* 16.424–30.

[41]One index of this is the assumption that an embassy turning up in a foreign land may have come on a *prexis demios* (*Od.* 3.82; 4.314).

[42]See C. Renfrew and M. Wagstaff, *An Island Polity. The Archaeology of Exploitation in Melos*, Cambridge, Eng. 1982. Renfrew argues that small-scale societies (with small populations, small territory, with no spatial hierarchy) are capable of developing into states. The transition "from chiefdom to state...need not involve any increase in territorial scale..." He concludes that "The essential transformation in Melos was not one of territorial aggrandisement, but of internal organization accompanied by population increase" (p. 283).

[43]M. Lejeune, "Le δᾶμος dans la société Mycénienne," *REG* 78, 1965, 6; G. Maddoli "Δᾶμος e βασιλῆες: contributo allo studio delle origini della *polis*," *SMEA* 12, 1970, 27–36; C. G. Thomas, "The Dorians and the Polis," *Minos* 16, 1977, 216–18.

[44]Maddoli (above n. 43), 36–40.

[45]Andreev (above n. 29), 378–79. This fits the pattern observed by archaeologists for the late Bronze Age and early Dark Age. Large regional centers, with a network of subordinate settlements, are replaced by tiny villages and hamlets, scattered in smaller districts. See J. Bintliff, "Settlement patterns, land tenure and social structure: a diachronic model," in C. Renfrew and S.

Shannon (edd.), *Ranking, Resource and Exchange: Aspects of the Archaeology of Early European Society*, Cambridge, Eng. 1982, 107.

[46]B. C. Dietrich, "Prolegomena to the Study of Greek Cult Continuity," *Acta Classica* 11, 1968, 166–67, gives a similar scheme, based on interpretation of the Pylos tablets. The early post-Mycenaean *damos* "was a social unit with apparently a particular topographic location." For summaries of the evidence on the *qasireu*, see C. G. Thomas, "The Nature of Mycenaean Kingship" *SMEA* 17, 1976, 106–07, and "Wanax to Basileus" (above n. 16), 190–91.

[47]See Hopper (above n. 37), 68–82, esp. 76, 81. Hopper concludes that the migrants to the Asian coasts were a "mixed lot" of successive groups. "[T]he initial settlements were small, and therefore the first settlers were in small bands...joined by others later... [T]here were many of these small settlements." According to Hopper, the absorption, subordination, or elimination of the smaller communities by the larger ones was completed before 700 B.C.

[48]C. Roebuck, "The Early Ionian League," *CPh* 50, 1955, 35–36. The Ionian migrants "came with the organization of a weak post-Mycenaean kingship such as probably existed at the time of their departure. This was reproduced in the Ionian towns." So also C. G. Thomas, "The Roots of Homeric Kingship," *Historia* 15, 1966, 404. On the survival of Mycenaean political vocabulary in all Greek regions, see Thomas (above n. 43), 211–17.

[49]The underlying factor that is the most important, and at the same time the most difficult to pin down, is the *prior* sense among groups of people that they somehow belonged together and were to be distinguished from others who spoke the same dialect and shared the same cultural traits. Geography and topography were no doubt implicated in this, but are not sufficient explanations. Scholars are necessarily vague about the mysterious phenomenon of cultural communities in early Greece. See, e.g., C. Roebuck, "Some Aspects of Urbanization in Corinth," *Hesperia* 41, 1972, 106; Cartledge (above n. 1), 4; A. Snodgrass, *Archaic Greece. The Age of Experiment*, Berkeley and Los Angeles 1979, 26–28; R. J. Buck, *A History of Boeotia*, Edmonton 1979, 88. The Ionian experience suggests that "ethnicity" and "tribalism" were highly flexible concepts; one was an "Ionian" or a "Milesian" by virtue of being accepted as a resident in the area. On the ease of transfer from one *demos* to another, see *Od.* 15.238–42; *Op.* 635–40.

[50]On the semantic connections between *philos, etes,* and *hetairos,* see Donlan (above n. 7), 300–01, with notes.

[51]Thomas, "Nature" (above n. 46), 99, 100, 105, with bibliography; van Effenterre (above n. 32), 43.

[52]For the theory that the small local groups were also called *phula,* see Donlan (above n. 7), 297, 303–04. It is significant than in the fifth century *etes* could mean the "citizen" of a polis, as opposed to a magistrate; see A. Andrewes, "Phratries in Homer," *Hermes* 89, 1961, 134.

[53]Benveniste (above n. 35), 165, 167, 176, 251; O. Szemérenyi, *Studies in the Kinship Terminology of the Indo-European Languages.* Acta Iranica 16, Teheran-Liege 1977, 24, 33–34, 100, 151, 191, 205; P. Friedrich, "Proto-Indo-European Kinship," *Ethnology* 5, 1966, 16, 29. G. Thomson, *Studies in Ancient Greek Society. The Prehistoric Aegean*, New York 1965, maintained that *demos* and "clan" were identical (pp. 113, 326–27, 351).

[54]Dietrich (above n. 46), 169. There is serious doubt, however, that "clans" in the strict anthropological sense (a corporate, named group, which holds property in common and acts as a collective unit) existed among the proto-Greeks. See now, S. C. Humphreys, "Fustel de Coulanges and the Greek 'genos'," *Sociologia del diritto* 8, 1983, 35–44; cf. Donlan (above n. 7), 301–02. On the devolution of the extended family, see Humphreys, "Kinship in Greek society, c. 800–300 B.C.," *ASNP* 4, 1974, 357–58

[55]Followers are recruited *ana* or *kata demon* (e.g., *Od.* 2.291; 4.530, 652, 666; cf. 4.167). Mycenaean *eqeta* (= *hepetes*) has been equated with Homeric *hetairos;* cf. *Od.* 4.536; 15.262 (*hetairoi*) *hoi heponto.* Dietrich (above n. 46), 168, suggests that the Bronze Age *hepetes* was a "nobleman," possibly a military commander of a localized *damos.* Such a meaning could correspond

to the Homeric usage of *hetairos* as "close companion," the loyal subordinate of a *basileus*—a usage which was then broadened in the wider community to identify any "follower." On the "pyramids," see Forrest (above n. 21), 48–50, 55.

[56]Thomas (above n. 16), 196–200; the *basileis* were the agents of political reunification in Attica, and of federation in Ionia. Compare Runciman (above n. 38), who argues that it is the accumulation of political power that produces states. There is evidence to suggest that the "phratry" developed during the ninth century as the communal reflection of the political/military pyramids (Donlan, above n. 7, 305–08).

[57]A. Snodgrass, *The Dark Age of Greece*, Edinburgh 1971, 378–80, 402–16; J. N. Coldstream, *Geometric Greece*, New York 1977, 50–106, 303–14; CAH^2 III.I (1982) 666–72 (Snodgrass); 703–13 (Hammond); R. Hägg, "Burial Customs and Social Differentiation in 8th-Century Argos," in Hägg (above n. 22), 27–30.

[58]A. Snodgrass, "Archaeology and the Rise of the Greek State," *Inaugural Lecture*, Cambridge and London, 1977, 10–15; *idem* (above n. 49), 22–25, 35–36; Coldstream (above n. 57), 20–109, 152, 221, 306, 367; T. W. Gallant, "Agricultural Systems, Land Tenure, and the Reforms of Solon," *ABSA* 77, 1982, 115–16, 122.

[59]Bintliff (above n. 45), 110, n. 5.

HOMERIC τέμενος AND THE LAND ECONOMY OF THE DARK AGE

Great uncertainty surrounds the interpretation of Homeric τέμενος, even though the descriptions of it are clear and consistent within both epics. Τέμενος has historical significance because the descriptions of τεμένη in Homer provide our only details about land-tenure in pre-polis society. All discussions of τέμενος, therefore, revolve around the land-tenure system. Yet the Homeric τέμενος does not fit at all neatly into conventional models of early Greek landholding.[1] The stumbling block has been the automatic assumption that the land from which new τεμένη were taken was land already under cultivation. This paper is an attempt to place τέμενος in its proper position within the land economy of the Dark Age.

I

Τέμενος occurs thirteen times in Homer. Four of the mentions refer to τεμένη of divinities, and appear to have substantially the same meaning as in classical Greek—an area of land assigned to the god, in which was located an altar for sacrifice.[2] The other nine references are to τεμένη held by living men, an institution that is not generally found in the archaic and classical periods.[3]

In Homer, τέμενος is a piece of arable land "cut out" (τέμνειν; cf. τάμον, *Il.* 6.194; 20.184; ταμέσθαι, *Il.* 9.580). In all the examples, the τέμενος is held by or promised to a man of high status. In three passages the cutters-out are specifically named: οἱ Λύκιοι (for Bellerophon, *Il.* 6.194), γέροντες Αἰτωλῶν (for Meleager, *Il.* 9.574), Τρῶες (for Aeneas, *Il.* 20.184). In the other six passages, the τέμενος is already in possession, and there is no information about the transaction.[4]

Since all the holders (or potential holders) are identified as βασιλεῖς or sons of βασιλεῖς, it has been generally assumed, with reason, that a τέμενος was granted only to men of chiefly status. It is also apparent that the grantors (those who "cut out") were a collective—the δῆμος as a whole. In addition,

- 303 -

the texts show unambiguously that once granted by the community a τέμενος remained in permanent possession and was inheritable by later generations. This is certain not only from Iphition's τέμενος πατρώϊον (*Il.* 20.391), but also from Anticleia's statement to Odysseus that "no one yet has your καλὸν γέρας, but Telemachus unhindered τεμένεα νέμεται...." (*Od.* 11.184).[5]

In addition to the foregoing information, the poems give some details about the kind of land that made up a τέμενος. First of all, the τέμενος is substantial. Those belonging to Sarpedon and Glaucus and to Odysseus are called μέγα (*Il.* 12.313; *Od.* 17.299); the piece of land promised to Meleager is πεντηκοντόγυον, "of 50 γύαι" (*Il.* 9.579).[6] Qualitatively, the τέμενος is consistently very fertile, well-watered agricultural land. In four instances, it is said to be half orchard/vineyard and half plowland.[7] The τέμενος βασιλήϊον on Achilles' shield is shown as being harvested by workers, reaping the wheat (or barley) and binding the sheaves (*Il.* 18.550). Odysseus' τέμενος is clearly agricultural land, since the heaps of straw and mule and cattle dung lying in his front yard are used to manure it (*Od.* 17.297).

The fertility and moisture of the soil are emphasized. Meleager's μέγα δῶρον was to be cut from the "richest plain of lovely Calydon ... an exceedingly fine one (περικαλλές)" (*Il.* 9.578). Iphition's ancestral τέμενος is located by the marshy Lake Gugaie at the confluence of the Hullos and Hermos rivers (*Il.* 20.391); that of Sarpedon and Glaucus by the banks of the Xanthus (*Il.* 12.313). Alcinous' τέμενος and "blooming orchard/vineyard" (ἀλωή)—which we must suppose was part of his τέμενος —were situated in a meadow (λειμών) that surrounded a grove of poplars sacred to Athena and a spring (*Od.* 6.291).[8]

Only in this last description are we given detailed information about the location of a τέμενος. From the sea shore, where Odysseus had been washed up, the road to the πόλις/ἄστυ goes first past the out-fields and farmplots (ἀγροί, ἔργα, 6.259), then past the meadow, poplar grove, and spring, "near the road" (6.291). After this, the road crosses a narrow isthmus to the high wall around the πόλις, and thence to the ἀγορή and twin harbors. Alcinous' τέμενος, therefore, lies outside the isthmus wall, at the near edge of where the farmland begins, "as far from the πτόλις as a man's shout will carry" (6.294).[9] Like the other τεμένη, it is very desirable land: fertile, well watered, close to town, and by a road.

The texts are also informative as to *why* a community granted a τέμενος. The giving of a gift as compensation for service is a common feature of Homeric social relations, which are consistently expressed in terms of obligation and counter-obligation. This type of reciprocity is explicit in the cases of Meleager, promised a μέγα δῶρον by the Aetolian γέροντες in return for "coming out and defending" Calydon (*Il.* 9.576), and of Aeneas, whose suppositious award of a τέμενος by the Trojans would have been for killing Achilles (*Il.* 20.176).

These examples of awards for a specific service to the community are, of course, quite compatible with the notion that a τέμενος was granted to a popular chief as compensation for his ongoing obligations as a leader of the people. The high honors given to Sarpedon and Glaucus (τετιμήμεσθα μάλιστα) in Lycia, among which was the holding of a τέμενος, require them, as Sarpedon says, to fight in the forefront of the Lycians (*Il.* 12.310). In Bellerophon's case, the awarding of a τέμενος was linked to his elevation to chiefly rank, after he had demonstrated his worth as a warrior by passing several hero-tests of benefit to the people (*Il.* 6.179).[10]

Though no formal connection between the granting of a τέμενος and high performance as leader is indicated for the other τέμενος-holders, it is significant that all of them are distinguished in the texts as effective, popular chiefs. Thus, the young Iphition was πολέων ἡγήτορα λαῶν and his father Otrynteus (whose τέμενος Iphition inherited) was πτολίπορθος (*Il.* 20.383). Odysseus and Alcinous were both paramount βασιλεῖς, greatly respected by the people for their wise leadership.[11] Τεμένη may have been cut out expressly for them, or, just as likely, been inherited from their fathers, who had also been powerful, revered chiefs. Nausithous, the founder of Scheria, had made the original division of the plowlands (*Od.* 6.10), and it is quite likely that a τέμενος was reserved for him as a γέρας.[12] Finally, it is instructive that Anticleia in Hades describes Telemachus as in firm possession of his father's "splendid honor" (καλὸν γέρας), though in strict chronological terms he would have been only about fourteen at the time. Telemachus, she says, "administers τεμένεα and partakes of equal feasts, to share which is fitting for a man with authority to judge (δικασπόλον ἄνδρ᾽), for all men invite him" (*Od.* 11.185). For our purposes, what is significant about Anticleia's statement is that she portrays her grandson as enjoying the rewards and performing the duties of a respected chief.

To this point analysis of the texts has presented few problems of interpretation. Not only are the references to τέμενος clear and consistent within both epics, they also display a neat symmetry with other elements of the Homeric distributive system. Community members are alloted a parcel of arable land, κλῆρος, for their subsistence and, as members of raiding parties, are guaranteed an equal portion of the spoils. The chiefly τέμενος is to the κλῆρος as the γέρας (the extra portion of the booty reserved to the raid-leader) is to the equal δασμός.[13] Τέμενος and γέρας—things "cut out" or "chosen out"—thus belong to the category of "chiefly-due," the material recognition of the high position and communal responsibilities of the βασιλεύς.[14]

Difficulties arise, however, when we ask out of *whose* land a τέμενος was cut. The nineteenth-century thinking about land-tenure, heavily influenced by contemporary sociological theory, was that land was held and farmed under an ancient "open-field" or "common-field" system. In that scheme, the τέμενος was a grant of land, a "royal domain," given to the king by the people out of the communally tilled land. Since the land was periodically redistributed among the members of the community, no one lost his share of the common land. Though the royal τέμενος was the only type of private land found in Homeric times, it was the opening wedge of a new system of private land ownership.[15] "The *témenos* is the germ of private property emerging within the tribal system."[16]

In 1957, M. I. Finley decisively challenged this tenacious theory, rejecting the existence both of conditional tenures and of cultivated *ager publicus*.[17] Most scholars today agree with his conclusion that all cultivated land was held privately and permanently, without condition, and could be handed down or otherwise transferred by the owner.[18] The argument for a regime of private family holdings, as opposed to communal landholding, is in fact totally convincing. The Homeric household, both as a social and as a subsistence unit, was conceptually inseparable from the land (οἶκος is simultaneously house, family, work force, and property). Moreover, the social standing, pride, and religious-symbolic existence of οἶκοι were bound to the unbroken occupation of ancestral plots. It is highly unlikely that there was ever a "stage" of collective land-holding in Greece. For the Dark Age, we should accept the principle that once a piece of land was put into cultivation, the labor invested in it conferred permanent title.

There is a great difficulty here, however. If there was no *ager publicus*, then new τεμένη would have to have been taken from private land, since, according to all interpretations of the relevant texts, the τέμενος land was land already in cultivation. Finley proposed that the recipient of a τέμενος was invited "to choose from the best of the privately held lands." D. Hennig, in a recent study, agrees that this is the only possible solution to a difficult problem.[19] But this sidesteps the crucial question of the social mechanisms by which the owners of these choice farmlands were induced to give up their private holdings. Finley is not much help. He is both vague and contradictory about where the authority to give τεμένη resided (either in "royal power" or "community power") and suggests merely that there existed "techniques for obtaining compensation," citing *Odyssey* 13.13–15, where the Phaeacian chiefs are advised to recoup the expense of gifts to Odysseus by "gathering among the δῆμος.[20]

But this is not a matter of households giving up agricultural surplus or animals but of surrendering the land they worked. That were a gift indeed.

The Dark Age polity, insofar as we can deduce it from Homer and the archaeological remains, was loosely structured. Political organs like the law court and assembly were still largely informal; custom set and supervised the rules of social behavior. Can we imagine a Dark Age δῆμος able, as an entity, to decide whose farmland was to make up the new property of a βασιλεύς, and then to see to its redistribution? Few today would suggest that "royal power" possessed the means—or would be allowed—to coerce so drastic a gift, an act amounting to internal piracy.[21] Again, what "compensation" could possibly have been given in exchange for good cultivated land? On the other hand, the clear statement of the epics is that the giver of τεμένη was the δῆμος. This must mean that in some formal sense the land was its to give.

If we accept a system of private property in the Dark Age, there is only one possibility. New τεμένη were cut out of uncultivated (i.e., unowned) arable land and not, as traditionally assumed, from land already being farmed. This surplus arable was *ager publicus* and its distribution resided in "community power." This can be demonstrated.

II

From the early twelfth century to the second quarter of the eighth, all Greece was severely underpopulated. Modern estimates—based on graves, number and size of settlements, and field surveys—show a drop in population to between one-half and one-quarter of the high levels of the thirteenth century. For example, between LH III B and III C the number of known occupied sites in Laconia fell from 39 to 7, and in Messenia from 67 to 13. The population of Messenia in the eleventh century was 10 per cent of what it had been in the thirteenth century. Laconia appears to have been actually uninhabited between ca. 1050 and 950. Only four occupied sites are known in the southern Argolid between 1200 and 900; and in Boeotia only three of 55 Bronze Age sites were inhabited in the early Iron Age. All this "adds up to a picture of depopulation on an almost unimaginable scale."[22] Although the downward spiral leveled off around 1000, and population likely began to rise gradually during the ninth century, the whole of the Dark Age may be fairly characterized as a period of abundant land and very few people.

Land use and land tenure during the Dark Age reflected the demography. The tiny villages were situated near fertile plowland. The level or gently sloping farmland, within convenient walking distance of the settlement, shaded off to higher slopes, and thence to the steeper and wooded mountain lands that formed the territorial boundaries of the community.[23]

The coastal and alluvial plains supported plow and hoe cultivation of cereals, fruit trees, grape vines, and vegetable gardens. The moist lowland meadows and the fallow plowlands were used for grazing. As always in the Mediterranean regions, the upland slopes and mountains served as summer pasture for flocks. Lower hillslopes with thinner, rockier soil or the remote mountain valleys, under cultivation in more populous times, were left untilled. During the depopulated Dark Age there would have been little incentive to plant these marginal lands, whose lesser return was not worth the extra labor and travel time.

The land tenure-system in these small societies could not have been very complicated. Homeric δῆμος meant both the "land" and the "people." As the "land," δῆμος is a well defined territorial unit; δῆμος as "people" embraces all those who live there. This identification, which was ancient in Homer's time, shows that then, as later, the ultimate "owner" of the δῆμος was the δῆμος.[24] All notions of rights in land derive from this fundamental, unreflective, principle. A second principle, also obvious, is that land put into cultivation became the "private property" of the member-cultivator and his family, by virtue of the labor invested in it. A man's land allotment, κλῆρος, was as fully and permanently his property as his house, animals, and personal belongings. As long as he remained an accepted member of the community, neither the community nor any individual was entitled to take the source of his livelihood from him.

It must be emphasized, again, that what gave land value was labor, and only worked land was private property. Land that could not be cultivated (like wooded mountain slopes) or did not seem worth cultivating (like marginal land and areas of marshy meadows) was "no-man's-land" (or rather every man's land), available without restriction to any community member for grazing, gathering, and foresting.[25] At that time, the δῆμος will have had no corporate interest in grazing and foresting rights. Such land, in abundance, was simply there, to be used by all. The primary use of this free land was for pasturing the many flocks and herds that appear in Homer as the criterion of wealth. De facto, the few men "rich in flocks," that is, the βασιλεῖς and other important men, dominated use of these pasture lands. This was especially true of the grassy meadows (λειμῶνες) found in the plains and valley bottoms, the only suitable land for pasturing large numbers of cattle and horses, the most highly prized animals, emblematic of elite-status.

We may say with complete assurance that corporate interest was confined to the good cultivable land, that is, the deep-soiled plainlands and low slopes adjoining the πόλις. All cultivation took place within this portion of the δῆμος, called the "plain" (πεδίον) or the "field(s)" (ἀγρός/οί) by Homer.[26] Although much of it was given over to grazing, the πεδίον/ἀγρός was above all the life-sustaining grainland, the primary source of subsistence for "men who eat bread."[27] The good land embraced by the terms πεδίον and ἀγρός was the reason for settlement in the first place, and formed an indissoluble unit with the village. Κλῆροι and τεμένη came from it. The question of permanent rights in this heartland—that is, the right to work it—will have been of vital concern to every man and woman in the community. Even if we did not have the evidence of Homer, we would have to conclude that its allocation lay with the community as a whole.[28]

Beyond lay the uncultivated "margin" (ἐσχατιή), whose border with the arable land (ἀγροῦ ἐσχατιή) marked the boundary of communal concern with land rights.[29] We can assume that if any member of the community was so minded, he could automatically claim permanent rights by cultivating it. There is a probable mention of this in *Odyssey* 18.357. The suitor Eurymachus offers the beggar Odysseus a job as a hired hand (θητευέμεν), "gathering stones for fences and planting tall trees," in land he was cultivating ἀγροῦ ἐπ' ἐσχατιῆς. This scene is significant in showing that those in the best position to improve the "free" land were men of chiefly status, like Eurymachus, with their greater resources in manpower and equipment.[30] We will come back to this point later, but now let us return to τέμενος.

Consideration of the evidence for population, land use, and land tenure in the Dark Age has led to the conclusions (1) that there was surplus arable in the πεδίον/ἀγρός, which was used for grazing, and therefore was common land; and (2) that the community as a whole controlled its conversion to farmland. It is logical to suppose that τεμένη (and new κλῆροι as well) were taken from this uncultivated *ager publicus*. Against this is the traditional interpretation of the texts, which is that τέμενος land was already under cultivation at the time of its transferral.

Let us consider first the three passages in which nearly identical formulas are used to describe τέμενος land.

Il. 6.194–95 (to Bellerophon)
καὶ μέν οἱ Λύκιοι τέμενος τάμον ἔξοχον ἄλλων
καλὸν φυταλιῆς καὶ ἀρούρης, ὄφρα νέμοιτο.

Il. 12.313–14 (to Sarpedon and Glaucus)
καὶ τέμενος νεμόμεσθα μέγα Ξάνθοιο παρ' ὄχθας
καλὸν φυταλιῆς καὶ ἀρούρης πυροφόροιο.

Il. 20.184–86 (to Aeneas)
ἦ νύ τί τοι Τρῶες τέμενος τάμον ἔξοχον ἄλλων
καλὸν φυταλιῆς καὶ ἀρούρης, ὄφρα νέμηαι....

We note that in the first and third passages, possession (νέμομαι) is potential; in the second it is actual. And only in the case of the already held τέμενος is ἄρουρα indicated to be under cultivation (πυροφόροιο). By itself, ἄρουρα means simply arable or cultivable land. In most occurrences in Homer it has a very general sense of "land" or "earth," with no specific connotation of its character as plowland.[31] The actual condition or use of a particular ἄρουρα is identifiable only by its qualifiers or by the context.[32] Thus, while ἄρουρα most often (and naturally) signifies land already in use, it may also refer to arable land that has not yet been prepared or planted, as in *Odyssey* 6.10 where Nausithous, the founder of Scheria, ἐδάσσατ' ἀρούρας, and in *Odyssey* 9 (108–111, 357–358) where grain and vines grow uncultivated in the ζείδωρος ἄρουρα of the non-farming Cyclopes. Ἄρουρα in *Iliad* 6.195 and 20.185 clearly falls into that general category of tillable land.[33] In his employment of the formula the poet appears to have carefully distinguished between the plowlands promised to Bellerophon and Aeneas, not yet planted, and the ἄρουρα of Glaucus and his brother, already in possession and planted in wheat.[34]

In the one other instance of a τέμενος promised but not possessed there are definite indications that uncultivated land is meant. Meleager's τέμενος (*Il.* 9.579) is to be τὸ μὲν ἥμισυ οἰνοπέδοιο,/ ἥμισυ δὲ ψιλὴν ἄροσιν πεδίοιο. The adjective οἰνόπεδος (ground or soil fit for wine)[35] occurs just three times in Homer: here, as a neuter substantive, and twice as a modifier in the phrase ἀνὰ (κατὰ) γουνὸν ἀλωῆς οἰνοπέδοιο (*Od.* 1.193; 11.193; cf. *Hy. Merc.* 207). Regularly in Homer a producing vineyard or orchard is called ἀλωή or ὄρχατος;[36] the appearance of the noun οἰνόπεδον is unparalleled; it cannot mean a planted vineyard here, but rather land suitable for grapevines.[37]

The noun ἄροσις occurs only here and at *Odyssey* 9.134, in a description of an uninhabited island opposite the land of the Cyclopes. It contains both meadows (λειμῶνες) and ἄροσις λείη, level land suitable for plowing, but obviously uncultivated. So too, the ψιλὴν ἄροσιν of Meleager's promised τέμενος is best taken as ground good for plowing, bare of trees and brush, but not yet worked.[38]

The μέγα δῶρον promised to Meleager by the Aetolians was not the best of the cultivated land, but rather the right to cultivate unworked land in the πεδίον. Such a procedure did not deprive households of their farmplots, and therefore required no compensation and imposed no economic hardship on the people. In fact, as we shall presently see, the τέμενος played a functional role in the Dark Age land economy.

III

There are indications that τεμένη were allocated from land that required improvement, most prominently poorly drained bottomlands. Frequently in Homer the πεδίον is described as cut by a river, in whose floodplain were marshy, thickly vegetated meadows.[39] As was said above, these uncultivated meadowlands (λειμών, also ἕλος, "marsh") were used for grazing horses and cattle;[40] but the texts make it clear that they were also considered good for vines and fruit trees. The deserted island off the coast of the Cyclopes' land, lush and wooded, would have made a "fine settlement," as Odysseus notes with a farmer's eye (*Od.* 9.131–135):

"For it is in no way bad, and would bear all things in season. For on it are λειμῶνες by the shores of the gray sea, watered and soft (ὑδρηλοὶ μαλακοί); the vines would be imperishable. And on it is ἄροσις λείη; always, season after season, they would reap a very deep grain crop, since the subsoil is very rich."

This land is exactly like the well watered land of the Cyclopes opposite, which spontaneously yielded wheat, barley, and vines but was used solely for pasturing sheep and goats (cf. 108, 167). Trees and grapevines, watered by four springs, grow in wild abundance around Calypso's cave, surrounded by moist, flowery λειμῶνες (*Od.* 5.63).

The lushness of the meadows, which made them attractive for gardens, was offset by their susceptibility to overwatering. In a flood simile, a river, swollen by winter rains, "scatters" the dikes (γέφυραι) built to restrain it (*Il.* 5.87–92; cf. 16.384):

"Neither do the bulwarks (ἕρκεα) of the blooming ἀλωαί hold it back as it comes on suddenly, when Zeus' rain lays heavy, and many fine ἔργα of industrious men are ruined by it."

To prepare the wetlands for cultivation, which might involve extensive drainage and irrigation works, and then to maintain them, required a large workforce. In addition, vines are especially labor intensive. In the Homeric world only the few top houses had the labor (and the metal tools) needed to work this kind of land on a sizeable scale.

As we saw earlier, the τεμένη in Homer are composed both of orchard/vineyard and plowland, and are regularly situated by a water source. Alcinous' τέμενος is explicitly said to be located in a λειμών.[41] Though the evidence is by no means conclusive, the language of the poems suggests a standard procedure for the cutting out of a τέμενος. The garden portion (φυταλιή, ἀλωή) would be taken from moist meadowland; the arable (ἄρουρα, ἄροσις), assuming that it lay adjacent, would no doubt be better drained, but still requiring works to convert it into grain-producing fields.[42]

Τεμένη might also be cut out of other land besides moist bottomland, though the principle remains the same. There were no λειμῶνες on Ithaca or the other islands, as Telemachus pointedly informs Menelaus (*Od.* 4.602). Though it is "rugged" and lacks the level meadows that are necessary for horsebreeding, Ithaca is nevertheless very good for grain (σῖτος) and produces wine and a variety of timber; it has good pasture for goats and cattle. There is constant rainfall and dew, and abundant water sources (ἀρδμοί).[43]

In this land of steep wooded hills and narrow, sloping sea plains, Odysseus held a τέμενος μέγα (*Od.* 17.299; cf. 11.185). We are told only that it was manured, but that is sufficient to show that it was a garden (orchard/vineyard) rather than a grainfield.[44] Just such a piece of land is Laertes' ἀγρός, located ἐπ᾽ ἀγροῦ, far from town, to which Laertes had exiled himself out of grief for Odysseus.[45] He had "acquired" it (κτεάτισσεν) many years before—it was flourishing when Odysseus was a boy (παιδνός). Now Laertes lived there permanently with the δμῶες: an old Sicilian woman, who took care of him, old Dolius, and their six sons, who worked the ἀγρός along with the retired chief. It is vineyard, orchard, and garden; Homer refers to it variously as ἀλωή (6), ὄρχατος (4), κῆπος (2).[46] It is a large operation, with a permanent house and shedding, growing many vines and many fruit trees: fig, olive, pear, and apple.

Not surprisingly, considering the topography of Ithaca, Laertes' garden was located on hilly ground. No doubt Laertes' men had to clear the land of thick vegetation and construct terraces and channels to hold the soil and protect it from the frequent heavy rains. Many years later, it still required a large permanent staff. When Odysseus visits it, Dolius and his six sons are out gathering stones and other material to be ἀλωῆς ἕρκος (24.224). Laertes himself spends his declining years in constant, backbreaking toil on it.[47]

Was Laertes' orchard/vineyard a τέμενος, or was it "free" land reclaimed by Laertes, like Eurymachus' land ἀγροῦ ἐπ᾽ ἐσχατιῆς (*Od.* 18.357)? Scholars are divided, and the Greek (24.205–206) can support either meaning.[48] I incline towards the former interpretation because Laertes' garden is consistently said to be in the ἀγρός, not on the margin. It is highly likely, in fact, that Laertes' ἀγρός was the garden τέμενος of Odysseus, mentioned in 17.299. The identification is supported by one important piece of evidence. In 4.735, Penelope requests someone to tell Δολίον...γέροντα, δμῶ᾽ ἐμόν...[ὅς] μοι κῆπον ἔχει πολυδένδρον to inform Laertes about Telemachus' journey from home. Plainly, she is referring to the κῆπος of Laertes, which here, as Laertes' son's wife, Penelope calls her own.

To summarize, τεμένη taken from moist meadowlands in the πεδίον and τεμένη cut out of steeper land in the ἀγρός share common characteristics. Both

Homeric τέμενος and the Land Economy

are potentially rich farmlands that require improvement to make them initially productive, and a great deal of attention to keep them up.

All this leads to the conclusion that as a social and economic transaction the δῶρον of a τέμενος was more balanced and more integrative than has been generally perceived. Let us quickly review the social relations. The advantages to the recipient are obvious. First and foremost, the award was a γέρας, a mark of signal honor from the δῆμος. Second, the possession of additional arable in the πεδίον/ἀγρός was a material benefit. Chiefs had large households to feed, and their position obliged them to set an abundant table. In addition, a surplus over consumption helped to support a growing (since 900) activity in the manufacture and trade of luxury goods.[49] Yet it is significant that half of τέμενος land was devoted to orchard and vineyard, that is to the abundant production of fruit and wine. The garden portion of a τέμενος was thus something of a luxury, a showplace that proclaimed the owner's high standing in the community. That is clearly the nature of Alcinous' ὄρχατος τετράγυος adjacent to his house—a true wonder of fruit trees, vines, and vegetables, all ripening at different times of the year, irrigated by two springs.[50] Every family will have had a vegetable plot, and most will have had some trees and vines; but only the richest would have extensive orchards and vineyards, since these are so labor intensive. To possess an unending abundance of fruit and wine, things that enhance the quality of life, was a very visible proof of preeminence. Thus, though we should not minimize the practical aspects of the δῶρον, it is clear that its essential value was that of a status symbol.[51]

The δῆμος benefited as well. The other side of chiefly privilege is *noblesse oblige*. The gift of arable land to βασιλεῖς imposed a counter obligation to be generous with its fruits. This entailed liberality on a day-to-day basis, as well as a special type of generosity; for there were times when the chief's surplus of grain was needed to lighten the effects of drought, flood, blight, or enemy raid.[52] Such big and little acts of public generosity confirmed the chief's authority as leader and bound him and people closer together. A further symmetry is evident in the circumstances of the transaction. The creation of new arable may be seen as a kind of public works, in that it produced an extra source of grain, close to the population center, on which the community had some moral claim in times of shortfall. This was accomplished entirely at the expense of the recipients, who were the members of the society best equipped to do it. Furthermore, the reclaimed land was from "common" pasture, i.e. land that was already heavily utilized, if not monopolized, by the elite for grazing their large herds and flocks.

The mostly symbolic value of the τέμενος is explained by the fact that wealth and prestige were not measured in land but in animals. Large-scale slaughtering of animals for feasts was the principal mode of chiefly largesse. Generous feasting of associates and followers was the standard way to win esteem and gain new supporters. Since good grainland was plentiful, and only a few unfortunates lacked the means to grow their own bread, chiefly distribution of grain would be an extraordinary measure, reserved for emergencies. And in the highly localized, subsistence-based economies of the Dark Age, there was scant possibility of bulk transport of grain as an exchange commodity. Thus, even for the βασιλῆες there was little incentive to expand grainfields. Jameson puts the matter succinctly. The Dark Age "king can do little with large estates of arable land and their surplus (and so does not possess them) whereas cattle are conspicuous for status and useful for ritual and social functions."[53]

In other words, landownership was not a means of social control in the Dark Age. The fundamental fact of the chiefdom economy is that the surplus production of the politically ambitious (consisting primarily of animals) had to be continually and lavishly *expended* in exchange for authority.

IV

We have succeeded in assigning τέμενος its proper role and importance in the social economy. Though τέμενος was a single, and rather minor, element of the economy, it was completely harmonious with all the other elements of the internal exchange system. The gift and acceptance of a τέμενος functioned as a mechanism of integration, conferring benefits on giver and receiver and strengthening the ties between them. As an economic transaction the τέμενος exemplified the ideals of fairness and balance. As a social transaction it reiterated the ethics and values of the contemporary political system: honor and prestige, competitive display, gift and obligation. Its chief significance for us lies in its strong affirmation of the personal and reciprocal nature of the ruler-people relationship during the Dark Age.

At some point, probably by the early seventh century, the custom of giving τεμένη to living men was essentially discontinued. The reason why is clear. A sharp rise in population during the early eighth century put pressure on the land. For the first time in 400 years farmland became scarce. A major consequence of land shortage was the decline of large-scale herding, inefficient in terms of land use, in favor of cereal production. Henceforth wealth and status were measured by land ownership and not by the size of flocks and herds.[54]

Thus the process began whereby a few families came to own a disproportionate share of the land. Exactly how this was managed we are not told, but it is easy to guess. Since the basis of livelihood was now scarce, control of it meant automatic social control—without the constant expense of feasting. Given this incentive, the important men would have marshalled all their power and resources to acquire more fields. The free land outside the ἀγρός, formerly little exploited, but now worth the effort of cultivating it, could be easily appropriated by men with the manpower and the "capital." The *ager publicus*, from which the τεμένη were cut, was just as easily taken over. When proprietary rights to land near the settlement became a high priority, the elite could base their claim on customary use, since their cattle and horses had pastured in the λειμῶνες and their sheep and goat flocks had dominated the hillier grazing grounds for generations. Against any other claim to these lands, the βασιλεῖς could assert, "this is our land."[55] Indeed, as the texts make clear, they already possessed squatters' rights to the theoretically "common" pastures. Odysseus has a full-time staff of herders in the ἀγρός, living there amidst a complex of pens, folds, and other "works." And, as we have repeatedly emphasized, only the elite had the ready means to convert moist pasturelands to plowlands.

However it was accomplished, in the competition for land the chiefly class was the clear winner; and in a comparatively short time (three or four generations) this group was transformed from relatively small-scale farmers to a profit-motivated landed gentry, whose status as aristocrats depended on the production of large saleable surpluses of agricultural goods.[56] This was the fundamental premise of the polis economy; for the rest of Greek history the need to turn a profit from the land intimately affected every layer of society and every aspect of social life.

The τέμενος is part of the history of that momentous change, and though minor in itself has been a valuable aid in describing the evolution of the process. Τέμενος has also served as a dynamic symbol of the change. Its awarding commemorates the traditional system, in which the relationship between leaders and δῆμος was one of fairness, mutual obligation and generosity. Its passing marks the emergence of a different system, in which the leader-people relationship was characterized by injustice, exploitation, and greed.[57] In its surviving form—a δῶρον by the δῆμος to a tutelary deity or benefactor hero—there is a reminder of the old ways.

NOTES

*This article was substantially aided by the use of the Thesaurus Linguae Graecae at the University of California, Irvine. I wish to thank the Project Director and staff for access to the facilities of the TLG and for their unfailing kindness.

[1]For a review of the problems, with bibliography, see I. Hahn, "Temenos and service land in the Homeric epic," *A Ant Hung* 25 (1977). Τέμενος is the only land-holding term common to Linear B and Homer. A tablet from Pylos reveals a *wanaktero temeno* and a *rawakesijo temeno*, both followed by the grain sign, L. Palmer, *Mycenaeans and Minoans*[2] (London 1965) 99. The holding of agricultural τεμένη by the highest ranking individuals thus survived into the Dark Age. The social relations of the Mycenaean *temeno* are unknown; however, the apparently important role of the Mycenaean *damo* and the distinction between *kitimena* and *kekemena* land support in principle the view espoused here, that from earliest times the community controlled the allocation of uncultivated land.

[2]*Il.* 2.696 (Demeter); 8.48 (Zeus); 23.148 (Spercheius); *Od.* 8.363 (Aphrodite). See K. Latte, Τέμενος, *RE* 5A (1934) 435–37; B. Bergquist, *The archaic Greek temenos* (Lund 1967).

[3]There are some indications that the practice may have lasted after 700 in some places; e.g., the Battiads in Cyrene (Herod. 4.161), the Spartan *basileis* (Xen. *Const. Lac.* 15.3).

[4]*Il.* 12.313; 18.550; 20.391; *Od.* 6.293; 11.185; 17.299.

[5]Possibly, though not necessarily, the τεμένη of Sarpedon and Glaucus (*Il.* 12.313) and of Alcinous (*Od.* 6.293) were inherited by them from Bellerophon and Nausithous respectively. For νέμομαι = to acquire legally by way of apportionment, see. E. Benveniste, *Indo-European language and society* (Coral Gables 1973) 69.

[6]Γύης may have been the amount of land that could be plowed in one day, approximately one acre; but this is uncertain. See W. Ridgeway, "The Homeric land system," *JHS* 6 (1885) 323–325; G. Thomson, *Studies in ancient Greek society. The prehistoric Aegean* (New York 1949) 317–18; W. Richter, *Die Landwirtschaft im homerischen Zeitalter* (Göttingen 1968) 14, 99.

[7]*Il.* 9.579; 6.195; 12.314; 20.185.

[8]See also *Il.* 6.194; 20.184; 23.148; *Od.* 11.184.

[9]Thomson (supra n. 6) 360.

[10]See Richter (supra n. 6) 9.

[11]Alcinous: *Od.* 7.10; 8.387; 11.346, 353, etc. Alcinous initiates every action in Phaeacia during Odysseus' stay. Odysseus: *Od.* 2.230; 4.687; 14.138; 19.108, etc. As paramount, Odysseus had the personal authority to save the life and property of a lesser βασιλεύς from the wrath of the δῆμος (*Od.* 16.418).

[12]See G. M. Calhoun in A. J. B. Wace and F. H. Stubbings, *A companion to Homer* (New York 1962) 436.

[13]Thomson (supra n. 6) 329–31; H. van Effenterre, "Téménos," *REG* 80 (1967) 18.

[14]On chiefly due see W. Donlan, "Reciprocities in Homer," *CW* 75 (1982) 158–160. As paramount, Agamemnon feels a heavy sense of responsibility for the Achaeans: *Il.* 1.117; 2.24; 10.1, 91, etc.

[15]Ridgeway (supra n. 6) 335–339. Cf. Leaf at *Il.* 12.421; Ameis-Hentze at *Il.* 9.580. See Hahn (supra n. 1) 302. A notable early exception was N. Fustel de Coulanges, *The ancient city* (New York 1965 [1864]) 60ff., for whom the "right of property" was a basic premise of Greek and Roman culture.

[16]Thomson, *Prehistoric Aegean* (supra n. 6) 329, 357; cf. *Aeschylus and Athens* (London 1966) 38.

[17]M. I. Finley, "Homer and Mycenae: property and tenure," *Historia* 6 (1957) 133–159. The recent decipherment of the Linear B tablets had stimulated a revival of interest in the communal ownership and cultivation theory.

[18]A. Andrewes, *The Greeks* (New York 1967) 97–98; C. G. Starr, *The economic and social growth of early Greece, 800–500 B.C.* (New York 1977) 150–151.

[19]Finley (supra n. 17) 156, following W. Erdmann, "Homerische Eigentumsformen," *ZRG* 62 (1942) 355–356. D. Hennig, "Grundbesitz bei Homer," *Chiron* 10 (1980) 44. Hahn (supra n. 1) 313–314 concludes that Homeric τέμενος is a garbled memory of the Mycenaean *temeno*, "royal land," managed by the Mycenaean kings for the maintenance of religious sanctuaries. Van

Homeric τέμενος and the Land Economy

Effenterre (supra n. 13) 22–26, offers an even more complicated explanation on linguistic grounds.These are pure conjectures, but point up the grave difficulties presented by the apparent mixing of communal and private ownership of land in Homer.

[20]Finley (supra n. 17) 156. The other passages cited by Finley (*Od.* 2.74; 22.55) are even less relevant.

[21]Richter (supra n. 6) 12. This is not to say that Dark Age strong men were averse to confiscating the cultivated fields of neighboring groups, as in *Od.* 4.174, where Menelaus contemplated resettling Odysseus and his λαοί in an outlying village in Argos after clearing out its inhabitants; cf. *Il.* 9.149. Even within communities defenceless widows and orphans could be deprived of their ἄρουραι (*Il.* 22.489); but the taking of land by force from fellow πολῖται was something else entirely. In *Od.* 16.428 we have a contrary example of the δῆμος threatening to "eat up the plentiful and pleasant living" of a βασιλεύς (see supra n. 11).

[22]A. Snodgrass, *Archaic Greece* (Berkeley/Los Angeles 1980) 20. For Laconia and Messenia, see W. A. McDonald and G. R. Rapp, *The Minnesota Messenia expedition: Reconstructing a Bronze Age regional environment* (Minneapolis 1972) 143; P. Cartledge, *Sparta and Laconia* (London 1979) 68, 70, 92, 118. Argolid: T. H. van Andel and C. Runnels, *Beyond the acropolis. A rural Greek past* (Stanford 1987) 98, 101, 173. Boeotia: A. Snodgrass, *An archaeology of Greece* (Berkekey/Los Angeles 1987) 201. A similar drastic decline is reported for Melos and other islands: C. Renfrew and J. M. Wagstaff (edd.), *An island polity: The archaeology of exploitation in Melos* (Cambridge, Eng. 1982) 140–142. For other areas, see V. R. d'A. Desborough, *The Greek Dark Ages* (London 1972) 19. Why this process occurred, and why it lasted so long, are complete mysteries. Apart from unsubstantiated hypotheses of natural disasters, like disease or famine, or wholesale slaughter by invaders (unlikely) or near total emigration (also unlikely), one can only suggest that depopulation was a symptom of the general economic decline after ca. 1200.

[23]Any general description of the landscape and of land use in Greece is necessarily a composite one, because of considerable regional variation. Nevertheless, the Aegean landscape is sufficiently uniform and the ancient evidence consistent enough to construct a valid composite picture. Still very useful is A. Jardé, *The formation of the Greek people* (New York 1970 [1926]) 1–35. See now van Andel and Runnels (note 22) 13–25, 31.

[24]On δῆμος as the inclusive social unit and what this meant in the Dark Age, see W. Donlan, "The social groups of Dark Age Greece," *CPh* 80 (1985) 298–302; also, "The pre-state community in Greece," *SO* 64 (1989) 13–15. In the loosely structured societies of the Dark Age, any free man allowed to dwell within its boundaries was a member of the δῆμος and had a right to live off the land. But where, and how well, a man lived was determined by a variety of conditions and circumstances. Some free men, for whatever reasons, were clearly marginal, like the ἄκληρος man in *Od.* 11.488, whose land must have been in the ἐσχατιή. Cf. Ridgeway (supra n. 6) 332. Land-poor thetes and landless beggars (like Irus in the *Odyssey*) were even more marginal members of the community, but their lack of access to land was not due to structural impediments, but to individual circumstances, largely, one suspects, to lack of kinsmen.

[25]Richter (supra n. 6) 12–13, 42.

[26]See, in general, Richter (supra n. 6) 92–93. πεδίον is the "plain" proper, the level land immediately adjoining the settlement, access to which is by a main road (ὁδός) from the πόλις/ ἄστυ. Cf. *Il.* 3.263; 6.393; 11.167; 15.681; 24.329; *Od.* 3.421; 15.183. ἀγρός appears to be the cultivable land further away from town. E.g., *Il.* 23.823; *Od.* 1.190; 4.757; 6.259; 11.188; 16.383; 24.212, 308. It has often the meaning of "country" as opposed to town, both geographically and culturally. E.g., *Il.* 11.676; 15.272; *Od.* 6.106; 11.293; 16.3, 27, 150, 218; 21.85. Though ἀγρός is "far from" town, it is still accessible by a road (*Od.* 13.268; 17.204), and travel time to it is not excessively long. Eumaeus travels from the furthermost ἀγροί (pastures) to town in the space of a morning (*Od.* 16.155, 333) and returns before dark (16.452). Telemachus makes the same journey from dawn to early morning (*Od.* 17.26–32). Odysseus and Eumaeus traversed this

distance from late afternoon to supper time (17.190, 260). The distance from town to Laertes' ἀγρός was much shorter (*Od.* 24.205; cf. 6.259; 15.427). Like πεδίον, the ἀγρός is closely connected conceptually to the town as a unit (*Od.* 8.560; 14.263; 17.18; 22.47).

[27]*Il.* 5.341; *Od.* 8.22; 9.89, 191; 10.101. The verb σιτέομαι is used generically to mean "eat" (*Od.* 24.209). Cf. *Il.* 13.322; 21.76; *Od.* 1.349; 6.8; 13.261. See Richter (supra n. 6) 107.

[28]"The community's right to dispose of new land, and to control a part of it permanently thereafter, is as fundamental as the householder's right to his *kleros*, and no more so." A. Burford Cooper, "The family farm in Greece," *CJ* 73 (1978) 175.

[29]*Od.* 4.517; 5.489; 18.358; 24.150. The general notion of ἐσχατ- (noun, adj., verb) is location at the edge or furthest point, beyond which is something else; e.g., *Il.* 2.616; 9.484; *Od.* 1.23. Thus ἀγροῦ ἐπ' ἐσχατιῇ (ἦν) is the furthest edge of the ἀγρός, beyond which was land left uncultivated; see *H. Ven.* 122. So Odysseus has goats grazing ἐσχατιῇ, while his pigs forage ἀγροῦ ἐπ' ἐσχατιῇ (*Od.* 14.104; 24.150), i.e., on land that is marginally cultivable. See Jardé (supra n. 23) 14; Hennig (supra n. 19) 48, n.38. In Classical times, the evidence indicates, the ἐσχατιή was still mainly "publicly owned pasture," which was sometimes rented out by the state. Burford Cooper (supra n. 28) 172–173.

[30]T. W. Gallant, "Agricultural systems, land tenure, and the reforms of Solon, *BSA* 77 (1982) 116–117. Here, at the margin, is also where the poorer citizens would live; e.g., *Od.* 5.488.

[31]*Il.* 3.115; 4.174; 7.421; 10.7; 18.104; *Od.* 19.433; 20.379. Πατρὶς ἄρουρα (*Od.* 1.407; 10.29; 20.193) means simply "native land," like πατρὶς γαῖα; ἄρουρα retains this generalized meaning even when qualified by specific epithets like ζείδωρος. E.g., Odysseus, set down on the sandy beach at Ithaca, kissed ζείδωρον ἄρουραν (*Od.* 13.354; cf. 5.463); so *Il.* 2.548; 8.486; 9.141, 283; 21.232; *Od.* 2.328; 3.3; 7.332; 11.309; 12.386; 19.593; 23.311. In these instances, ἄρουρα means simply the ground where men live, as opposed to the wilds or wasteland. Cf. Richter (supra n. 6) 93ff. For a more detailed analysis of the variant meanings of ἄρουρα, see B. Mader, *LfgrE* 1335–40.

[32]Grainfields: *Il.* 6.142; 11.68, 558; 12.314; 13.707; 14.122; 18.541, 544; 20.226; 21.465; 23.599; probably also *Il.* 12.422; 21.405; 22.489; cf. *Il.* 3.246 (wine); *Od.* 4.229 (φάρμακα).

[33]See Finley (supra n. 17) 136, n. 4; 153, n. 6.

[34]Φυταλιή, which occurs only in these three passages in Homer, is assumed to mean a producing orchard or vineyard. The word has been read on a tablet from Knossos (*pu-ta-ri-ja*), but its meaning there is uncertain. Hennig (supra n. 19) 41, thinks this is an old formula, "mechanically handed down," representing the donation of τεμένη in the ninth or tenth centuries; cf. Richter (supra n. 6) 96. It is possible that φυταλιή was originally an adjectival form meaning "land suitable for plants," as ἄρουρα is "land suited for tilling."

[35]So the lexica; e.g., Cunliffe: "with soil fit for producing wine; vine bearing"; Ebeling: *vinifer, viniferax*.

[36]And sometimes κῆπος (garden). See Richter (supra n. 6) 96. Significantly, perhaps, κῆπος in Cyprus meant "uncultivated land"; H. Frisk, *Gr. Etym. Wörterbuch* I 482. Cyprian ἀλωή is also glossed as κῆποι (Frisk I 82); ἀλωή (etymology unknown) also means "threshing floor" (*Il.* 5.499; 13.588; 20.496; Hes. *Op.* 599, 806). The only obvious connection between ἀλωή "orchard/vineyard" and "threshing floor" is that both are levelled, improved ground. Cf. *LfgrE* s.v. ἀλωή.

[37]Later, of course, as infilling occurred, οἰνόπεδον signifies a producing vineyard; e.g., Theognis 892. Cf. Richter (supra n. 6) 97, n. 698.

[38]So Richter (supra n. 6) 95. Lattimore translates correctly: "The half of it to be vineyard and the half of it unworked ploughland of the plain to be furrowed." Mader, *LfgrE* (1333) takes it as an already tilled piece of common land.

[39]*Il.* 2.461,467; 4.483; 5.597; 6.506 (=15.263); 11.492; 12.283; 16.151; 17.747; 20.221; 21.300, 350; *Od.* 4.602; 14.473. Cf. *Il.* 5.87; 9.151 (= 293); 10.466; 12.283; 23.122; *Od.* 5.72; 11.539, 573; 24.13; Hes. *Theog.* 279.

⁴⁰*Il.* 2.775; 6.506; 11.677; 14.445; 15.630; 16.151; 18.520, 574; 20.221; *Od.* 3.421; 4.601; 21.48; *H. Merc.* 72; *H. Cer.* 174; cf. *Il.* 4.475; 22.309. See Richter (supra n. 6) 41–43.

⁴¹*Od.* 6.296; Cf. *Il.* 2.695; 23.148.

⁴²On protection of arable land by banks and dikes, see Jardé (supra n. 23) 39–42; Stubbings in *Companion to Homer* (supra n. 12) 528. Proximity of pasture and tillage: *Il.* 12.283; *Od.* 4.601; gardens and grainlands: *Il.* 14.122. The description of the ἀλωή in the Shield (*Il.* 18.561) shows that κάπετος and ἕρκος were part of a protective system against overwatering. Cf. Richter (supra n. 6) 106–07. Aristotle says that during Trojan War times Argos was marshy (ἑλώδης) and therefore incapable of supporting more than a few inhabitants, while now it is drier and thus well cultivated (*Meteorologia* 352a).

⁴³The landscape of Ithaca: *Od.* 1.186; 4.601; 9.21; 11.184; 13.233, 344, 407; 14.96; 20.185; 15.503; 24.205, 358.

⁴⁴M. Jameson, *Agriculture and slavery in classical Athens*, *CJ* 73 (1978) 129. Though grainfields were not manured, they will have benefited from the droppings of animals pasturing on the fallow stubble.

⁴⁵*Od.* 1.190; 11.187; 24.205, 336.

⁴⁶For the nuances of these terms, see Richter (supra n. 6) 96–97.

⁴⁷Cf. the epithets τετυγμένος (24.206), ἐϋκτιμένη (24.226, 336). On the importance of terrace walls and drainage ditches, see Jameson (supra n. 44) 128. In the modern Argolid this is "hard, time-consuming work," and terraces often collapse from lack of maintenance. The wealthiest farmers pay for such work to show off their status. Cf. van Andel and Runnels (supra n. 22) 145–147.

⁴⁸κτεατίζω and μογέω can refer to war in Homer, but more often mean simply "acquire" and "toil."

⁴⁹J. N. Coldstream, *Geometric Greece* (New York 1977) 50–71.

⁵⁰*Od.* 7.112. This is not part of Alcinous' τέμενος, which lay outside the town, though its nature is the same.

⁵¹Orchard/vineyards are conspicuous items of chiefly property in the *Iliad* as well. Artemis was angered because Oeneus failed to offer her the first fruits of his ἀλωή and sent a wild boar to tear up the δένδρεα μακρά (*Il.* 9.533). Tydeus had πολλοὶ φυτῶν ὄρχατοι, as well as abundant grainfields and flocks (*Il.* 14.122). The marginal land cultivated by Eurymachus is orchard/vineyard (*Od.* 18.357). Cf. *Il.* 21.36, 77; Richter (n. 6) 141, 145. Though the *Iliad* records some trade in wine (7.467; 9.71), wine and olive oil were mainly for domestic consumption.

⁵²A large 10th–9th century building at Nichoria, identified as a "chief's dwelling," appears also to have had important communal functions, and was possibly a "collection-distribution center for the whole village." W.A. McDonald *et al.*, *Excavations at Nichoria* III (Minneapolis 1983) 53; cf. 58, 324, 358. Similar Dark Age buildings elsewhere, e.g., the so-called "heroon" at Lefkandi, may have had like communal functions; M. R. Popham et al., "The hero of Lefkandi," *Antiquity* 56 (1982) 169–74. Evidence for the distributive functions of chiefs in Homer is limited, aside from the generous distribution of meat to friends and followers. See Donlan (supra n. 14) 163–166. On the other hand, feasts of meat also included bread and wine. More to the point, both Homer and Hesiod say that good rulership promotes the fertility of the soil, animals, and women (*Od.* 19.109; *Op.* 225). I take these as references to good management and generosity rather than to any "magical" qualities inherent in the chieftainship. For a concrete example, see *Od.* 7.131: the πολῖται of Scheria have their local water supply from one of Alcinous' springs.

⁵³Jameson (supra n. 44) 126, n. 21.

⁵⁴Snodgrass (supra n. 22) 19–25, 35–37, 55; Gallant (supra n. 30) 115; O. Murray, *Early Greece* (Stanford 1983) 47, 65–66, 107–108. Despite controversy over the suddenness and extent of the rise (I. Morris, *Burial and ancient society* [Cambridge, Engl. 1987] 156–159), there can be no doubt that most of Greece experienced a significant increase in population during the

eighth century nor that this was an event of the utmost importance. Even the thinly populated, poor-soiled Southern Argolid "experienced a steady expansion of settlement" around 750, leading to infilling of the landscape, including the cultivation of "virgin" marginal land; van Andel and Runnels (supra n. 22) 104–105.

[55] See Snodgrass (supra n. 22) 38–40; Murray (supra n. 54) 177, 184–185. Prudent marriages among the endogamous elite would have been another strategy for consolidating landholdings in the cultivated πεδίον. It must be emphasized that what was at stake was not simply land, but land in the πεδίον/ἀγρός, i.e., the best land, near the population center.

[56] After about 750, the economic options of the landowners became considerably greater. As producers of surplus cereal crops, the elite will have gained an important economic edge over subsistence producers. As time went on, they could exploit the seasonal labor of underemployed farmers, further increasing their profits. The elite could also opt to keep using meadowlands for horses and cattle, considerably reduced in number and therefore of even higher status. Or (after 700) they could cultivate olives and vines on a large scale as cash crops. On this "ascending spiral" of economic superiority, see, in general, Gallant (supra n. 30) 116–117. For the southern Argolid, see van Andel and Runnels (supra n. 22) 105–106, 167–168.

[57] Amply recorded by Hesiod at the beginning of the seventh century and by Solon at the end.

DUELLING WITH GIFTS IN THE *ILIAD*: AS THE AUDIENCE SAW IT

The "wrath" (*mênis*) of Achilles and the "quarrel" (*neikos*) between him and Agamemnon are the controlling themes of the *Iliad*. Probably no other Homeric question has received more attention, yet with less agreement among critics, than the "meaning" of these to the poem. This present attempt to explain the Wrath and Quarrel incorporates a sociocultural reading that puts the original audience in the foreground and tries to imagine the action as they might have imagined it when they heard what we read today. Obviously, if we can know what the audience knew, we will know the poem better. We cannot discover from the poems alone how the audiences received the poems. For that we need a considerable social context; and that requires an excursus into the complicated and controversial historiography of "Dark Age" Greece (roughly 1100–700 B.C.)

1. Knowing What the Audience Knew
An increasing volume of archaeological research centered on the Dark Age during the past decades has significantly broadened our knowledge of that previously blank period, so that we may now claim a pretty good understanding of its culture, especially for the better attested Geometric Period (900–700 B.C.), when epic was developing into its final form. Much of the new data has come from wide-area or "survey archaeology," which concentrates on the rural landscape and its non-elite settlements (as opposed to the traditional emphasis on single major sites). Regional surveys also employ the multidisciplinary methods of the "new archaeology" or "social archaeology," so-called because it attempts to elicit information about the entire system represented by the material finds: settlement patterns, demography, economic strategies, and even social and political organization and belief system.[1]

From their material profiles, the small communities of this period closely fit the models of social and political organization called "ranked society" and "chiefdom" by anthropologists. Morton Fried (1967) describes the "ranked society" as an evolutionary stage between "egalitarian" and "stratified" (or "state") societies, indicated by the differential in access to or control over resources and status positions. In a rank society the elites have a monopoly on the positions of authority but cannot withhold access to the means of subsistence, the step that heralds the arrival of the stratified stage. Fried's rank form broadly corresponds to Elman Service's (1975) "chiefdom" level of sociopolitical integration in his postulated series of a "segmental stage" (the egalitarian band and tribe), the "chiefdom," and "archaic civilization" (i.e., the state). The "chief," who holds an institutionalized "office," is a man of great personal authority and prestige, yet with very limited power to coerce.

These ethnographic parallels come readily to mind when we contemplate the remains of the little farming villages of the time, unassuming clusters of one- and two-room mud-brick houses, with populations of a few dozen to several hundred people, often containing, as the only imposing structure in the settlement, a greatly enlarged version of the basic house, identified by the investigators as the "chief's house."[2] Since the "new archaeology" has its roots in social anthropology, current Mediterranean archaeologists have naturally gravitated to these analytical models to explain the material developments they observe,[3] just as anthropologically oriented historians have found them useful to explain Homeric society.

Of course, the pertinent question is not the objective reality of the society in which the singers and their audiences lived, but how closely, if at all, the fictional world of the poems reflected that material and social reality. This is a controversy that has long boiled among archaeologists and historians; it cannot be avoided here, but I will try to be brief.

The *Iliad* and *Odyssey*, in essentially the form we have them today, were composed between about 750 and 700 B.C. All agree that they were not only the creations of a single, or perhaps two separate, brilliant poet(s), though they certainly were that, but also—and this has been our key to understanding the poetic process—they were composed within an ancient and unbroken oral-poetic tradition reaching back centuries through the long, materially poor Dark Age into the rich Late Bronze Age.[4] The highly advanced "Mycenaean" civilization, which collapsed and vanished shortly after 1200 B.C., was the dimly remembered setting of the poems, the time the Greeks recalled as their Heroic Age.

Herein lies the controversy. Many scholars take the position that since epic poetry was a continuous process of oral performance-composition by generations of illiterate bards, using and changing, subtracting from and adding to, the hoard of formulas and formulaic elements, the "world" described in the *Iliad* and *Odyssey* must therefore be an artificial, eclectic amalgam of material features, social institutions and customs spanning nearly five centuries.[5]

That notion of a crazy-quilt pattern of many cultural layers has been vigorously opposed by a growing body of historical-anthropological analysis of the texts, which has demonstrated that the social milieu created by the poets forms a coherent social system that is consistent within each of the poems and also between them.

The great and early champion of this view, that the epics offer us the "raw materials for the study of a real world of real men, a world of history not of fiction," was M. I. Finley, whose ground-breaking *The World of Odysseus* (published in 1954) introduced classicists to the potential of an anthropological approach to the epics. Although his idea that Homer presents us with an actual historical society has met with considerable resistance, Finley's reply to his critics twenty years later remains irrefutable. Either the oral poets were drawing on a real society or, "by a most remarkable intuition," they had stitched together an interlocking system of institutions and values that anthropologists three thousand years later would discover to be universal social patterns.[6]

The simple fact is that when we peel away the obvious heroizing embellishments and deliberate anachronisms that helped to create the desired "epic distancing," the picture of life that emerges matches the observed material and economic conditions of the Dark Age villages. Moreover—and this would seem to clinch the argument—Homeric society conforms both in general and in detail to the anthropological model of the semi-egalitarian ranked society. These congruences give us faith that we see reflected in the epics the image, though admittedly an indirect and distorted one, of a living social order.[7]

This position gets support from what appears to be a universal rule of storytelling: a basic plausibility and verisimilitude. The circumstances and settings may be utterly unreal, yet still the story is rooted in the social and psychological experiences of the listeners.[8] We can easily illustrate this from Homer. Although ninth- and eighth-century weapons were made of iron, Homeric warriors fight only with bronze weapons, like the Mycenaeans. The major heroes drive up to the battle lines in two-horse chariots, dismounting to fight on foot; this is generally considered to be a garbled memory of Mycenean chariot warfare. These anachronistic details we recognize as standardized conventions that transport the hearers to that imaginary "time when." On the other hand, we know for a fact that wars and raids were a constant and major element of contemporary life, and so we do not doubt that what the poems say about the qualities and attributes that made up a good warrior, or about the drive for honor and the fear of public shame that pushed men into mortal combat, or the joy and terror of battle, or the sufferings of innocent victims, corresponded to the listeners' opinions about these things. Were it otherwise, the dissonance would be insupportable.

Homeric chiefs and their guests consume enormous numbers of cattle, sheep, goats and pigs in huge feasting-halls decorated in bronze, silver and gold, drinking endless quantities of wine out of gold and silver cups, waited on by a throng of attendants. These hyperboles are spice for the imagination; yet underlying the exaggerations and Mycenaean evocations is a core of reality. Like their counterparts in ethnographically attested advanced big-man and -chief societies, Dark Age chiefs (*basileis*) did in fact give lavish meat-feasts, in order to display their wealth and win followers and gain renown; and, of great importance for our reading of such scenes, the listening audiences understood the instrumental purposes behind these displays of largesse.

This brings us to the heart of the question. Greek epic poetry is highly sociological in content; in both the *Iliad* and the *Odyssey* the elements of plot, theme, character and motivation revolve around status- and power-relationships. A coherent sociology of Homer is absolutely necessary, therefore; without it, we could not make any sense of such matters. The question is, should we derive the "mentalities" from an artificial, totally self-contained poetical universe, as indicated by the "many layers" theory, or from the empirically verifiable institutions and behaviors of the living society? Remarkably, with some notable exceptions, Homeric literary critics have preferred to do the former.[9]

Still, even an imaginary construct needs a coherent social and social-psychological frame. The unfortunate model of choice, since the beginning of modern Homeric scholarship, has been feudal-age Europe. Archaeology and anthropology have had some effect in toning down the more blatant identities, and so we are spared from the "liege lords," and "vassals" and "feudal tenures" that peppered the commentaries of the last century and the first half of this one. The essential model remains ingrained in Homeric scholarship, nevertheless; current translations, commentaries and literary studies continue to speak of kings and queens, princes and aristocrats, serfs and peasants, palaces and royal estates; "knights" still follow a code of chivalry elevated above the "simple concerns of the commons."

So great a distortion of the underlying sociological reality is bound to distort our understanding of the poetry. We come closer to its spirit when we connect poets and their audiences together in their shared experience of the world about them. In the following pages I set forth what I believe to be a reasonable description of that sharing process. Unlike written poetry, which is strictly a private act, oral poetry, which is produced in performance, is more a collaboration between the "singer" (*aoidos*) and his immediate audience. Surely, the *Iliad* and *Odyssey* (and all other surviving specimens of oral epic) are the polished products of many such composition-performances. In that setting, poet and audience cooperate within the shared knowledge, not just of the traditional plots, themes and characters, but also of the mechanics and aesthetics of poetic composition, and from shared mental structures derived from their common social experience. Audiences are well educated in the highly stylized genre of traditional narrative, and are skilled judges of how well, or not, the performing poet has met the objective requirements of his art.[10]

It follows that the motives of the epic actors for doing and saying what the poet has them do and say are conditioned by the everyday structures and norms of behavior; and, of course, these same awarenesses are the basis for the audiences' own value judgements about actions and motives. Let me interject here that the singer holds the place of honor among the Dark Age craftsmen for his uncanny power to charm his listeners, recognized as supernaturally inspired; his song contains within it the wisdom of the society. His art is then never just entertainment, but serves an important social function by presenting for popular reflection the complexities of life, expressed in terms of conflict and resolution.[11]

The externalized, "objective" narrative form does not allow the poet much scope to editorialize, to make overt his authorial judgements about the behavior of his characters. Thus only rarely, and for the most part with only minor effect, does the oral poet intrude his opinion.[12] Yet he does have opinions, and even in his guise as the self-effacing narrator is able to express them. He conveys his meanings and intentions through his characters' deeds and words, manipulating both the sociological content of the situations and the conventional or expected poetic treatment of these familiar themes, confident that his audience will be looking for, and will appreciate, the variations and nuances that guide them to *this particular* song's representations of character and behavior. So, each performance is a kind of dialogue, issuing from the audience's cultural, ethical, and literary expectations, and the poet's playing with and on those expectations.

2. *Duelling with Gifts*

The struggle, *agôn*, between Agamemnon and Achilles is all about "honor," the highest social value, summed up in the powerful word *timê*; and it is waged entirely within the context of gift-giving. *Timê*, along with its verbs *tiô* and *timaô*, embraces the range of concepts covered by our words honor, dignity, respect, status, and prestige. Since the act of "honoring" is always accompanied by a validating ceremony or gift, the idea of *timê* is indistinguishable from its signs. Thus the abstract noun *timê* is also used concretely to mean rank, for example, the "office" itself of *basileus*. So, too, *geras*, the "prize of honor" awarded to the leader as leader, is frequently a metaphor for his social position.

In a culture where a man's self-image is totally derived from others' opinions of him, any loss of *timê* or *geras* seems unbearable and must be reversed. Accordingly, the *timê*-words are often translated as "compensation," "recompense," "penalty," to convey the Greek idea that one who has been dishonored (*atimos*) will insist on repayment of the portion of honor taken from him. In Homer, to give, take away or pay back *timê* involves a transfer of valuable objects. Thus, in Homeric, as in virtually all archaic societies, gift-giving is a social mechanism of the highest importance. Among the elite particularly, the complicated etiquette of the gift—who gives, who takes, and under what circumstances—is enlisted as a major competitive strategy, to demonstrate, and even to establish, gradations in status and authority.[13]

It is by *giving* gifts especially that one man gains power over another; generous gifts publicly proclaim the giver's potency and, at the same time, put the receiver under obligation. Marcel Mauss, in his 1925 classic, *Essai sur le don*, elegantly stated the essence of the gift-based economy; it is worth quoting in full for its relevance to Homeric society.

> If one hoards, it is only to spend later on, to put people under obligation and to win followers. Exchanges are made as well, but only of luxury objects like clothing and ornaments, or feasts and other things that are consumed at once. Return is made with interest, but that is done in order to humiliate the original donor or exchange partner and not merely to recompense him for the loss that the lapse of time causes him.[14]

It is in this context of calculated generosity that we must view the contest between the two chiefs, each of whom can claim to be the "best of the Achaeans," *aristos Achaiôn*. My argument is this. The narrative structures their *agôn* as a competition in gift-giving. That would have been clear to audiences who daily observed the ritualized display behavior of their *basileis*. As the narrative proceeds, there are constant indications that Achilles is the winner in *timê* all along. This too would have been clear to the listeners at every point in the long story of the Quarrel.

The *Iliad* begins with two gross violations of normal and expected reciprocity on the part of Agamemnon, paramount chief of the combined Greek army at Troy. First, he refuses to accept the generous gifts offered by Chryses, a priest of Apollo, as ransom for his daughter, who had been captured in a raid and awarded as a prize to the chief. Even though the Achaeans shout for him to respect the holy man and give back the woman, he sends Chryses away with harsh threats. It is a terrible and stupid mistake, the first of many, for Apollo immediately avenges the insult by sending a plague on the Achaeans. (1.12–52). Then, to compensate himself for the loss of Chryses' daughter, whom he now must give back, he threatens to take Achilles' spear-prize, Briseis, as compensation (1.116–87). To seize a prize of honor, a *geras*, is an almost unthinkable insult, an act of "negative reciprocity," as Marshall Sahlins would term it, equivalent to raid or plunder against an enemy.[15] The dishonor is greatly compounded by the fact that this *geras* is a woman Achilles regards as his wife (9.335–43). The mere suggestion (1.135–39) enrages Achilles, who counterattacks by verbally assaulting the paramount. The Quarrel is on.

Before we proceed further, we need to digress briefly on the subject of insult, which is intimately bound up in the nexus of honor, status and gift in Homeric society. Insulting words and deeds are the commonest causes of feuds in "shame" cultures, where everything pivots on personal and family honor. Insult situations among high-status warriors, who are particularly touchy about their *timê*, pose a direct danger to social stability, and must be defused as quickly as possible.[16] Normally, a potential *neikos* is headed off either by the rapid intervention of a third party or by a gentle word from the insulter. For example, in *Iliad* 4 Agamemnon accuses Odysseus of shrinking from battle, provoking from him a sharp, angry response. Agamemnon responds with a smile and an apology, promising that "we will make amends afterward if any bad thing has been spoken now," using the verb *areskô*, a word used almost exclusively in Homer for amends in insult situations.[17]

The poems give us two detailed examples of amicable resolution of a potential quarrel. In the Phaeacian games in *Odyssey* 8, Odysseus is verbally insulted by Euryalus (*Od.* 8.158–253); and in the Funeral Games in *Iliad* 23 Antilochus commits insult by cheating Menelaus in the chariot race (*Il.* 23.566–611). In both instances, the insult to honor arouses angry indignation, leading to a public apology and offer of a compensatory gift (*dôron*). The victim good-naturedly accepts the gift and adds a conciliating speech of his own. All seems calculated for an immediate end of the quarrel, with maximum face-saving on both sides. In these situations, the rituals of apology and gift function not only to restore peace but also publicly to affirm or decide status. The young Euryalus offers to "make amends" (*aressomai*) to Odysseus "with words and a gift." His gift (*dôron*) of a fancy sword and scabbard symbolically calls back his insult that Odysseus looked like a merchant, not an athlete, and confers upon the still anonymous stranger his proper status as a warrior (*Od.* 8.396–415).

The situation in the *Iliad* is more complicated. Accused by Menelaus of "shaming my *aretê*," for cheating him out of second place in the chariot race, Antilochus readily apologizes to the older and higher-ranking man, and offers to give him the prize and "some other better thing from my house." Appeased by the apology and show of respect, Menelaus ends by letting Antilochus keep the prize mare, "in order that these men here may know that my spirit is never arrogant and unbending" (23.566–613). By his gracious gesture Menelaus is shown to be big-hearted and generous, as befits a high chief. Antilochus, as the gift-*receiver*, is now even more firmly indebted to Menelaus and his cause.

We note that Menelaus' first angry impulse is to let the "leaders and councillors" decide who was right, but that he hesitates lest a judgement in his favor might later be construed as biased, because he was superior in rank and power. His second thought, to make Antilochus swear before the assembled army that he had not cheated, thereby putting the burden on Antilochus' personal honor, removes the possibility of bad blood between their two close and powerful houses; and Antilochus' immediate apology and Menelaus' benvolence close the incident in perfect balance. Like everything that happens in this book of reconciliation, the race episode symbolizes harmonious restoration of the correct social order: the headstrong young man chastized, the *basileus*' honor kept safe and magnified.

The deference to age and rank displayed by Antilochus becomes all the more interesting when we consider that, just before Menelaus' challenge, the youth vowed he would fight any man that tried to take the mare from him—having in mind Eumelus, an age-mate, to whom Achilles was going to give the second place prize, even though he had come in last, as a consolation for a mishap that cost him the race (23.536–54). In other words, Antilochus was willing to provoke a violent *neikos* with a status-equal, but readily yielded to a superior; quarrels can take place only between social equals—or those who claim to be equals.[18]

Antilochus' anger is directed also at Achilles, whom he accuses of "taking away" his prize, a clear echo of the Quarrel in Book 1, but now with Achilles in the position of Agamemnon and the hotheaded Antilochus as Achilles! Here, though, Achilles smiles, lets Antilochus keep the mare, and gives Eumelus another valuable prize (23.543–65). In these scenes the poet shows, and the audience sees, ideal resolution of insults, challenges and quarrels, achieved through a distribution of gifts and words that enlarges the *timê* of all four men.[19]

We return now to the insult and quarrel of Book 1. From the beginning, the insult situation between Agamemnon and Achilles, heavily freighted with status ambiguity, unfolds in a manner that is the exact negative image of these properly managed incidents. Nestor, the revered elder among the chiefs, tries to mediate, pleading with Agamemnon not to take away Achilles' woman and with Achilles not to wrangle with a superior in rank, and with both to let go their anger (1.275–84). This was the prescribed procedure. Had Agamemnon, as initiator of the quarrel, taken back his threat with a gentle speech, Achilles would have had no choice but to retract his angry insults. But of course, by this point in the *neikos*, they had already dealt each other's pride too much damage for any such quick and friendly solution. Their bloodless duel has become established in the audience's mind as the machine that will drive the dramatic action of the poem. Their—our—interpretation of character, motive and behavior will be conditioned by the poet's representation of the *agôn*, which will continue until the end of Book 23.

Agamemnon, in the space of 300 lines, has committed three highly irregular acts, censured by everyone: mistreatment of a suppliant, compounded by impiety towards the god; gross insult against the leading Achaean warrior; refusal to compromise as established custom demands. These blunders reveal the Agamemnon of *this* poem as seriously deficient in leadership (his actions greatly harm the community of warriors), and as willfully inept at playing the important game of give and take. Most of all, he has shown himself to be greedy and ungenerous, a most serious defect in a gift-based society, where generosity is the "essence of goodness," as Bronislau Malinowski phrased it, and a primary requirement, along with fighting and speaking ability, for leadership.[20] The poet presses this theme throughout Book 1. In his verbal attack on Agamemnon, Achilles calls him "most gain-loving of all men," "clothed in shamelessness, profit-minded," and swears that he will not stay in Troy "dishonored (*atimos*) to pile up your riches and wealth" (1.122, 149, 171; cf. 9.330–36).

The poet reintroduces and strengthens this theme in Book 2, when he has Thersites, the only non-elite warrior given a role in the *Iliad*, use the same charges of greed and ungenerosity against Agamemnon as the grounds for his call for a general revolt (2.225–42). The political subtext of both Achilles' and Thersites' speeches (the one the best, the other the worst of the Achaeans) is that Agamemnon is unfit to lead. Thersites ends his tirade with the flat condemnation: "It is not right for one who is leader (*archos*) to bring the sons of the Achaeans into evils . . . . . let us sail home with our ships and leave him here in Troy to digest his *geras*" (2.233–37). On his side, Achilles had capped his abuse of Agamemnon with the most damning insult of all, *dêmoboros basileus*, a chief so gluttonous that he "eats the people" (1.231).

It is Athena, however, who explicitly defines the nature of their contest. When, in his fury, Achilles reaches for his sword to wipe out the insult, the goddess intervenes to transform the sword duel into a duel of gifts. Standing beside him, invisible to the rest, she says to Achilles,

For thus will I speak out, and this will be its conclusion. One day three times as many spendid gifts (*aglaa dôra*) will come to you because of this outrage (*hubris*). (1.212–14)

By this early point in the story (Book 1, line 214), enough clues have been given to establish for an audience both how the struggle for *timê* will be played out and who the winner will be. They are familiar with the spectacle of "fighting with property," as it has been called—a bloodless, hence socially safe, form of warfare—and will be on the alert for further developments.[21]

Because of the withdrawal of Achilles and the other Myrmidon leaders and warriors, the siege goes badly for the Achaeans. In Book 9, that is about fifteen days after the quarrel, the council of allied chiefs politely but firmly insists that Agamemnon make peace with Achilles. After lecturing Agamemnon for committing insult in the first place, Nestor repeats the customary formula for resolution of insult.

But still, even now, let us consider how we may make amends (*aressamenoi*) and persuade him with soothing gifts and gentle words. (9.111–13)

Agamemnon had previously admitted to the full assembly that he was a victim of *atê*, "destructive folly," inflicted on him by Zeus (2.111, 9.18), and that Zeus had cast him into "futile strifes and quarrels," conceding that he was the one who had started the *neikos* over the girl (2.376–78). Here, in the presence of the chiefs, he frankly admits his grievous mistake (*aasamên*), telling them "I wish to make amends and give back boundless recompense." (9.115–20). What is required by custom, let us be clear, is for him to return Briseis with a public apology and a fitting compensatory gift. Instead, what follows is a gift-attack against Achilles.

Agamemnon reels off the gifts he is offering. Along with Briseis, untouched by him, he swears, will go seven bronze tripods, ten talents of gold, twenty cauldrons, twelve prize-winning horses and seven women—the largest single gift offer in either epic. All this immediately; later, when Troy is taken and the booty divided, Achilles will have his ship full of gold and bronze; and, finally, his pick of Agamemnon's daughters to wife, without having to give the customary bride-gifts (*hedna*), but with gifts to him, "such as no man ever gave along with his daughter," and rule over seven rich settlements on the fringes of his chiefdom, whose inhabitants "will honor him like a god with gifts" (9.121–56).

This is a spectacular gesture, and the audience is supposed to see it as such. In one swoop, Agamemnon shakes off the accusations of greediness that have accumulated around him and makes himself appear a paragon of chiefly generosity. The council of elders (*gerontes*) is impressed. Nestor says, "the gifts you offer lord Achilles are no longer to be despised" (163–64); and the audience members, putting themselves in the elders' place, might well have agreed that this satisfactorily balanced the ledger, especially since Achilles owed the obligations of comradeship to his fellow warriors who were being hard pressed in battle.

But at the same time, the listeners could not have failed to notice two things about the offer that made it less benign than it seemed: first and foremost, the glaringly obvious omission of the indispensable element, a public apology. The embassy is a strictly private affair—from Agamemnon's camp hut to Achilles'—and yet even in this private setting no "gentle words" of apology are reported from the absent offender.[22] Second, according to the rules of reciprocity acceptance of such fabulous treasure-gifts, far exceeding the usual compensation called for in such situations, would have put Achilles under a heavy debt of obligation, in effect turning recompense into a statement of power.

The final part of Agamemnon's offer, to make Achilles his *gambros*, son-in-law, and put him in charge of seven prosperous villages, has seemed to most critics a crowning act of generous compensation. Yet here again, audiences will have recognized a standard epic and mythic motif, adoption by marriage into the household of a powerful chief, a form of marrying-up, typically reserved for wandering adventurers and impecunious suitors. We may think of Odysseus in his guise as a man from Crete, who, though poor and landless, had managed through his *aretê* to marry the daughter of a rich man (*Od.* 14.199–213); or of Othryoneus of Cabesus who, too poor to pay the marriage *hedna*, offered Priam war-service in return for his daughter's hand. He was killed before he could collect his reward, prompting Idomeneus to make a cruel joke about such marriage arrangements as he drags the young man's corpse into the Achaean lines (*Il.* 13.363–82).[23]

James Redfield is surely right in saying, "by his very act of recompense Agamemnon asserts his authority over Achilles," and by the "offered terms of settlement Agamemnon would convert Achilles into his dependent . . . Achilles knows he is being asked to submit."[24] From Achilles' point of view, the offer to make him a service-groom, under the control of his father-in-law, would have appeared as a continuation of the insult; far from honoring him, it formally defines him as inferior in status. This explains his remark to Ajax that Agamemnon has treated him "as if I were some rightless migrant (*atimêtos metanastês*)" (9.648; cf.16.59).

Achilles' immediate reaction to Odysseus' relaying of the offer indicates his awareness: "Hateful to me as the gates of Hades the man who hides one thing in his heart and says another" (9.312–13). This may obliquely include Odysseus himself, although there is nothing deceptive in his perfectly straightforward speech; he is merely the conveyer of the duplicitous offer, which appears friendly, but is really hostile. Agamemnon's "audience," the envoys, understood the situation, of course; that is why they now base their appeal solely on Achilles' obligations to his comrades.[25]

The audience shares the narrator's omniscience here. In this episode, perhaps better than anywhere else in the epic, we can see his method at work; for it is not at all subtle. To make perfectly clear what Agamemnon's motive is, the poet has him say at the end of his catalogue of gifts, "and let him submit to me, inasmuch as I am a greater chief (*basileuteros*) and inasmuch as I say myself to be the elder in birth" (9.160–61). Homer has Odysseus repeat the long gift list (thirty-six lines) word for word to Achilles, but substitute for Agamemnon's insulting conclusion the instrumental Achaean argument:

> But if the son of Atreus has become more hated in your heart, himself and his gifts, at least take pity on the rest of the Pan-Achaeans, worn out amidst the host, who will honor you like a god. For truly you would win very great glory (*kudos*) from them." (9.300–03)

Here the audience knows what the narrator knows and Achilles does not. But the poet presents Achilles as being aware that Odysseus has left out the revealing coda. Presented with such broad clues as these, painted with such plain, bold strokes, contemporary audiences could hardly have missed the poet's intended meaning. Achilles, the embodiment of heroic honor, has no other choice but to refuse, even though this brands him, unwillingly, as a betrayer of *philotês*.

Much has been made of the fact that Achilles questions the heroic ideal of *timê* won by reckless risk of life in battle. It is a brilliant stroke of characterization to have the ideal warrior hero weigh life against booty and posthumous glory and judge in favor of life. The question, which we may be sure many in the audience had pondered to themselves and with others, is perfectly placed in Achilles, for whom alone among epic figures a choice was possible. But his reflections on this topos and his complaints about the *present* political system's failure to distribute *timê* according to merit in no way constitute a denial of his society's values. Throughout the great rejection speech Achilles adheres unswervingly to the core value, revenge for shame, now immensely deepened by the dishonoring offer and by the other chiefs' complicity in it. That his devotion to the honor-shame principle forces him to negate the other imperative of the warrior's ethic, to aid his fellow warriors, is a lamentable, but inevitable consequence of the universally accepted standards of "heroic" behavior.

The interpretation that in having Achilles spurn Agamemnon's gifts the poet holds him guilty of a sin or moral error, caused by a fundamental defect of character, which leads to his punishment later, is sociologically untenable. These are notions based on the ideals of Christian chivalry, not on the demands of an archaic rank society.[26] A quick temper and touchy pride, implacable hatred of one's enemy, fierce resentment at lack of support from *philoi* and *hetairoi*, all of which are at work here, are normal and proper behaviors of a warrior.[27] In fact, it is more correct to say that Achilles' willingness to compromise his honor caused his personal tragedy. His first impulse was to go home to his uncouth Thessalian chiefdom to marry, a point he stresses, a local girl picked out by his father Peleus, and live out a long, though fameless life (9.393–416). It is the pull of his obligations to the community of warriors, expressed variously by the chorus of Odysseus, Phoenix, and Ajax, that decides him to stay in Troy, and on the very next day to send Patroclus into the battle as his surrogate (16.60–65).

Let us briefly recapitulate. Whether they agree with the ambassadors or with Achilles in the excruciating personal dilemma fashioned for him by the poet, the audience understands that Achilles has been presented by an offer he *must* refuse—not, as Cedric Whitman maintains, because Achilles holds to some special "half-realized, inward conception of honor," but simply because Agamemnon has now grossly compounded the original insult.[28] They recognize Agamemnon's tactic—typically wily and typically clumsy (we think of the fiasco of the Dream and Test in Book 2, the very essence of *atê*)—as yet another act of *hubris*. They know that this is just another bout in an ongoing contest over honor and status, expressed in the symbolic language of the gift. They understand that, under the rules of social competition, Achilles' *cholos*, his anger, can now be assuaged only by diminution of Agamemnon's *timê*:

> Not if he gave me gifts as many as there is sand and dust, not even
> so will Agamemnon yet persuade my spirit until he has given back
> to me the whole [price of the] spirit-stinging insult. (9.385–87)

And they are aware as well that by scorning the offer, that is, by foiling Agamemnon's attempt to reduce him to a formal dependent, Achilles has scored a win over his opponent. In being refused, Agamemnon has lost much face.

The Quarrel ends in Book 19, a day and a night after the Embassy. Events have made the choice; Achilles must now reenter the battle to get revenge on Hector and the Trojans for the death of Patroclus. Still, there has to be a formal ceremony of reconciliation before he can rejoin the army. It is not, however, a true reconciliation. The formal proceedings, drawn out for 220 lines (19.56–275), bristle with the same competitive tension of their direct confrontation in Book 1 and their indirect battle in 9. Custom requires, we remember, a public apology from the offender, renunciation of anger by the injured party, public presentation of the compensatory gift, and its acceptance by the victim; all signifying, according to convention, that the former status relationship between the parties has been restored. Each ritual is in fact observed, but the poet's manipulation of the standard elements shows that this is really a continuation of their duel with gifts. Once again, Agamemnon suffers loss of *timê*.

As in Book 1, Achilles takes the initiative, summoning an assembly of all the Greeks. Even the noncombatants, who generally do not attend the *agorê*, come to see and hear. In a short, crisp speech ("a few frigid words" is how Redfield characterizes it ([1975]107), Achilles formally renounces his *cholos*, expressing regret that so many have died, "while I was raging in anger" (verb *apomêniô*). Let us put this strife in the past, he says, "even though it hurts us, beating down the spirit of anger in our breasts, because we must" (19.61–68). The last third of his brief eighteen-line speech is an order to Agamemnon to summon the army quickly to battle (68–73). He is firm, polite, businesslike, and impersonal.

Agamemnon's rambling apology, three and a half times the length of Achilles' speech, true to his character in this poem, is self-serving and oblique (19.78–144):

> Often the Achaeans spoke this word to me and found fault with me;
> but I am not to blame, but Zeus and Moira and Erinys who walks in mist.... (85–87).[29]

Agamemnon's shift of blame onto Atê, that external force which clouds a man's sense of right and makes him err against his will, is in pitiable contrast to Achilles' matter-of-fact acknowledgement that it was his wrath, *mênis*, that sent so many Achaeans to their deaths. However grudgingly, Agamemnon *does* get out the formula: "But since I was blinded (*aasamên*) and Zeus took away my wits from me, I wish to make amends and give back boundless recompense."[30] He ends his speech with a request that Achilles hold off from battle until the gifts are brought out, "so that you may see that I will give you them in satisfying abundance" (144). Thus far, the ceremony, although strained, has been proper.

At this point, however, the situation turns into an almost farcical parody of normal procedures. Achilles replies that Agamemnon may give or keep the *dôra*, as he wishes, but that they should stop wasting time and get on with the battle immediately.[31] Odysseus (who else?) now intervenes, urging that the army have breakfast before fighting; but first off, he says, "let the lord of men Agamemnon bring the gifts into the midst of the assembly, so that all the Achaeans may see them with their eyes and that you may be warmed in your heart," adding that he, Achilles, should now be mollified, and politely rebukes Agamemnon for initiating the quarrel (172–83). Agamemnon immediately agrees, saying:

> Let Achilles remain here the while, eager though he is for Ares, and you, all the rest, stay assembled here until the gifts come from my hut and we swear our oaths with a sacrifice. (188–91)

Achilles again protests the delay; Odysseus insists once more, and finally Briseis and the promised gifts are ceremoniously paraded out and displayed "in the midst of the *agorê*," while a boar is sacrificed as Agamemnon solemnly swears he has not laid a hand on Briseis (199–268).

The significance of this bizarre tug-of-war is not lost on the listeners, who realize that the public display of the fabulous gifts is an essential part of Agamemnon's competitive strategy. This small triumph is his only victory, and he has had to maneuver hard to achieve it. But Achilles does not let him have even this. In place of the customary friendly acknowledgement of the apology and gifts, he delivers, in the form of a prayer to Zeus, a mocking five-line paraphrase of Agamemnon's long dissertation on Atê, and dismisses the assembly, while the Myrmidons collect the gifts and carry them to his ship (270–81).[32]

Let us back up a bit in time. During the embassy to persuade Achilles to accept the gifts in Book 9, Phoenix, his old tutor, told the story of Meleager who, nursing his *cholos* like Achilles, did not come out to save his village until the last minute, and so did not get the gifts he had been offered (9.529–605). Phoenix had warned Achilles then that "if without gifts you go into man-destroying battle, no longer will your *timê* be the same, even though you drive back the battle" (9.604–05). The event has contradicted the prediction of Phoenix, and Athena's prophecy of Book 1, that three times as many gifts would come to Achilles because of the insult, has been fullfilled and exceeded. Achilles has taken great treasure from his rival on his own terms, and without obligation. He has not even acknowledged his acceptance of them. It is a stunning victory.

More victories follow. In Book 23, Achilles' spectacular display of wealth and of generosity in the funeral and games for Patroclus completely eclipses

Agamemnon's public show of the gifts two days before. The funeral itself is an unparalleled holocaust of numerous sheep and cattle, two hunting dogs, four horses and twelve Trojan prisoners, all burned together with Patroclus' corpse on the pyre (23.110–257). In the funeral games immediately following, Achilles distributes his wealth recklessly, increasing prizes and awarding them even to some who do not compete (257–897). It has been pointed out often that his actions bear an unmistakable resemblance to the "potlatch," a lavish competitive feast common among big- man -chief societies, in which huge amounts of food and valuables are eaten, given away, and even destroyed, to show one's superiority over one's rivals.

As Leslie Collins has recently pointed out, the games also offer Achilles an opportunity to act as the Pan-Achaean chief, thus symbolically usurping Agamemnon's rank.[33] Like the paramount chief, Achilles settles disputes, determines status and allocates *timê* in the form of prizes. One of those to whom he gives a prize is Agamemnon, who steps up for the final contest, the spear-throw. Achilles awards him the prize cauldron without a competition, because "we know how much you surpass all others, and how much you are the best (*aristos*) in might and in spear-throwing" (23.890–91).

This marks the true reconciliation, for Achilles honors Agamemnon for precisely that skill he himself excels in, the most important one. It is a gracious compliment and a fitting way to mark the end of their painful progress towards the desired amity. Yet no member of an audience attuned to the use of gifts to calibrate status could have missed the point that a prize (*aethlon*) to be won was converted to a free gift. The Quarrel had begun with Agamemnon churlishly taking away a gift; it ends with Achilles generously bestowing one. Agamemnon leaves the poem under obligation to Achilles.

The interpretation I have advanced, namely that the poet deliberately framed the Quarrel as a duel with gifts, is justified by the fact that the literary situation is precisely about gifts and display, and because we know—from elsewhere in the texts, from later Greek history, and from comparative sociology—that these things had enormous social significance in the Dark Age and Archaic period. We can state this another way. In terms of plot, a physical duel between Achilles and Agamenon was prohibited, obviously, leaving competitive gift-giving as the only other way of representing the titanic struggle between the rivals.

Significant real-life social situations, like insult and competitive gift-giving, are natural themes of traditional poetry, which uses these behavior-revealing occasions to delineate and develop character and motivation. Audiences bring to these fictional situations their collective normative judgements of how people ought to behave in such circumstances and their collective understanding of the conventional poetic handling of these themes and motifs. So, for example, according to the storyteller's symbolic short-hand, the suitors in the *Odyssey*, because they corrupt the important social institutions of feasting and hospitality, are automatically to be recognized as evil and therefore deserving of slaughter.

In the *Iliad*, every twist of the theme of "fighting with property" provides a running commentary on the character and behavior of the rivals. To the collaborating spectators of the *agôn*, who are expertly alert to the signals, the meaning of the interactions between the antagonists is clear. Agamemnon has consistently violated the norms of reciprocity and botched every attempt to outmaneuver Achilles in display and giving. Achilles has played the game flawlessly at every turn, diminishing his rival's *timê* and increasing his own. Achilles, who is indisputably superior to Agamemnon (and to every one else) in warcraft, is revealed as superior to him also in respect to a leader's other ideal quality of princely generosity. Remember, too, that it is through the device of Achilles' magnificent *refusal* of gifts that the poet proves to us his pure adherence to the warrior's fundamental principle, to defend and increase his honor. In that sense, Achilles, often regarded by modern critics as the outsider, the man on the margin of the social order, is revealed as the true insider, the strictest upholder of the traditional heroic code.[34]

There is one final point to make. The duel with gifts serves a deeper artistic purpose. Achilles' most triumphant moments come after he has set aside his obsession with honor and status. His astonishing *aristeia* (20.156–22.394), which in ferocity and brutal efficiency far outshines the battle exploits of all the other heroes combined and brings him his heart's desire of *kleos* and *kudos* (fame and glory), is joyless and meaningless to him, except as revenge. At the moment of his ultimate achievement as a warrior, he is wearily disillusioned with the whole business.[35] Like his *aristeia* his public victories over Agamemnon, the full vindication of his honor, and his symbolic assumption of the ruler's authority are merely the accidents of his grief, unsought and unimportant.

The point of Achilles' unintentional competition for *timê* in Books 19 and 23, like his unintended return to battle, is ironical. Achilles' strange destiny is to be trapped in his ideal-hero image, unable to quit a role he has long questioned and finally repudiated altogether. The duel with gifts functions as the poet's own critical evaluation of the heroic ethos, as he marks out distinctly for the listeners the successive stages of the main hero's perplexity and disillusionment, and his growing awareness and insight. It prepares us for the sublime finale of the *Iliad*, the ransom of Hector's corpse, which tells of a final giving of gifts, a final and symbolically all-embracing resolution of quarrels and renouncing of anger (24.469–688).[36]

Let me summarize briefly the two closely connected propositions I have set forth. First, I have tried to show that an "anthropology of Homer" is possible.

Enough information is now available to reconstruct, not completely, yet adequately, the material and mental realities that made up the common sociological background of poets and audiences. Second, I have argued that since an oral poem exists only as an interaction between singer and listeners, their collective field of expectations is crucial to the process of poetic production. Yet, perhaps because the social basis of that co-creative process has seemed so inaccessible, audience reception has been the least privileged element of Homeric criticism.

That is easy to understand. Already by the early seventh century B.C., the social institutions and values of the ninth- and eighth-century chiefdoms had been radically transformed. By the fifth century, the economy had become "disembedded" almost completely, and exchange and distribution bore only faint traces of the gift-reciprocity that had structured social relations among the pre-polis ancestors. Because of the near total distance from that experience, the working assumption of literary criticism from Hellenistic times on has been that "we"—the reading audience of the moment—are the intended audience, leaving us free to construct our own anachronistic sociologies of Homer, thereby validating interpretations of the poem's aims according to our own cultural preconceptions.

Without a social context we paradoxically ignore a fundamental fact of oral poetry, its embeddedness in the contemporary experience. If I am right about the Great Quarrel, Homer (and his tradition) gave heroic dimension to what was commonplace and recurring in the lives of the Dark Age villagers, yet of extreme interest and importance to them, the insults, quarrels and competitions among the chiefs of the *dêmos*. It cannot be otherwise that the more we understand about how these and other primary sociocultural concerns actually worked in the real world, the keener our literary-critical vision will become.[37]

NOTES

[1] See McDonald and Thomas (1990) 353–59; Snodgrass (1990) 113–36; (1987) 99–102, 108–31.

[2] A good example is the carefully excavated little Dark Age village of Nichoria (c. 1050–750), formerly a larger sub-center of the Bronze Age "kingdom of Pylos." McDonald, Coulson and Rosser (1983) 316–29. A convenient summary of chiefs' houses is Mazarakis Ainian (1988) 105–19. A more general survey is Fagerström (1988).

[3] E.g., Whitely (1991) 184–86.

[4] The originator of the "oral poetry" theory, which revolutionized Homeric studies and has deeply influenced the whole field of oral poetry studies, was Milman Parry (1971); Lord (1960). While the Parry-Lord theory of oral composition has won general acceptance, it is in constant process of refinement and revision. On the current state of the question see Kirk (1985) 1–37; Heubeck (1988) 3–23; Foley (1988). Janko (1982) 228–31 dates the *Iliad* to between 750 and 725 and the *Odyssey* to 743–714; see also Janko (1992) 8–19.

[5] E.g., Coldstream (1977) 18; Snodgrass (1974); Geddes (1984). A more balanced, though still negative view is Whitely (1991) 34–39.

[6]Finley (1974).

[7]The more pressing question today is when to "date" Homeric society. The old view, that it preserves essentially Mycenaean institutions and practices, is now thoroughly discredited; see Dickinson (1986). Finley himself (1978) placed the society of the poems in the tenth and ninth centuries; others believe that it reflects the conditions of the "poet's own day," i.e., the later eighth century (Morris [1986]); others, myself included, see the period from about 850 to about 750 as the most probable time frame of the poems' social "background." For a full discussion of the various views on these matters, see Raaflaub (1991) 205–52.

[8]Redfield (1975) 23, 35–39, 78–79. For oral poetry in general compare Finnegan (1992), who emphasizes the importance both of the audience and the performance. On oral literature as a "reflection of society" and the desirability of contextual analysis, see especially chs. 7 and 8.

[9]We see the lines drawn in Griffin's reaction to Redfield's (1975) "essentially sociological and anthropological approach": (1980)145–46. Firmly committed to an interior, psychological interpretation of motivations, Griffin warns of "the risks in applying too anthropological an analysis to the poem": (1980) 74, note 46. And compare Redfield's "Foreword" in Nagy (1979) vii–xiii. "Sociological and anthropological" readings are appearing in greater numbers, yet, as Martin (1989) 1 notes, while a "fresh emphasis on a sociocultural reading of [Greek] tragedy and comedy" has invigorated these fields and cut them "loose from the bonds of New Criticism…Homer has become for some a haven safe from critical storms."

[10]Compare the perceptive remarks of Martin (1989) 5–7, 47, 89–94, 96, 129, 161, 170, 176, 225, 231–33. Martin focuses on the level of language and "performance" (both by the poet and by the characters he has created); I emphasize here the audiences' sociological expectations. Wyatt (1989) shows that the collaboration extended to the content itself. The oral poet "sang what he wanted, but was constantly checked and corrected by the audience," who could request an episode, object to it or insist on its lengthening (e.g., at *Od.* 1.337–43; 8.98–99, 492, 537–38; Books 9–12); presumably they could also insist on his shortening or omitting an episode (253). Cf. Nagy (1990) 27, 39, 42, 131.

[11]"For among all men who dwell on earth singers have a portion of *timê* and *aidôs*, because the Muse has taught them songs and she loves the tribe of singers" (*Od.* 8.479–81). Cf. *Od.* 8.62–64, 74; 17.518–20; 22.344–48; Hesiod *Theog.* 22–34. On the social functions of Greek epic poetry, see Havelock (1963) 61–95; Russo (1978). I use the terms *Homer, poet, singer* and *narrator* interchangeably, understanding with Richardson (1990) 4 that the "narrator" and the "implied author" are the same. Cf. Edwards (1987) 29–41.

[12]Edwards (1991) 1–6, gives a complete listing by type. See Richardson (1990) 158–66 on the paucity of "genuine narratorial judgments."

[13]To M. I. Finley, again, goes the early credit for recognizing Homeric society as a gift-society: (1978) 61–62, 64–66, 95–98, 117–18, 120–23; see also (1955). While at Columbia University, Finley was greatly influenced by the theory of K. Polanyi (based on the work of earlier economic anthropologists like B. Malinowski, M. Mauss, R. Thurnwald) that in pre-market societies all economic transactions and relations are "embedded" in the total society. Thus, what appears to modern eyes to be "economic" behavior (like exchange and distribution) is motivated by concerns of a noneconomic nature. For an account of Polanyi and his effect on the sociology of exchange and reciprocity in general, and on Finley's ideas in particular, see Humphreys (1969). On how gifts calibrate relative social ranking, see Donlan (1989) 3–4, 6.

[14]Mauss (1967) 73. Cf. Gregory (1982) 55: "Power, authority and status are achieved by giving rather than receiving." An Eskimo proverb states the principle more bluntly, "Gifts make slaves, just as whips make dogs."

[15]Sahlins elaborated and refined Polanyi's posited forms or patterns of economic integration—reciprocity, redistribution and exchange—into a scheme of reciprocity and redistribution closely linked to an underlying set of social relations: (1968) 82–86; (1972) 193–96. Sahlins'

reciprocal transactions occupy a continuum from "generalized reciprocity," i.e., altruistic or "pure" giving, through "balanced reciprocity," where the giver expects an equal or equivalent return, to "negative reciprocity," in which each participant tries to maximize his profit at the other's expense. This last type normatively occurs *outside* the group or community, among strangers or enemies. See Humphreys (1969) 177, 205–06. For an analysis of the types and forms of giving and exchanging in Homer, using this scheme, see Donlan (1982). It turns out, not unexpectedly, that the *quid pro quo* of balanced reciprocity dominates within Homeric society.

[16] There exist, therefore, standard mechanisms for accepting compensatory gifts as requital for serious things like murder and adultery: e.g., *Il.* 9.632–36; 18.497–508; *Od.* 8.332. Personal quarrels not defused can easily escalate into bloodshed. If this is not satisfied by compensation, the inevitable result is either feuds or the exile of the murderer. *Il.* 9.447–84; 15.430–32; 16.570–76; 23.83–90; 24.480–82; *Od.* 14.379–81; 15.222–25, 272–76; 24.430–37. Cf. *Il.* 13.659; 14.482–85; 21.26–28. Odysseus the "Cretan," in somewhat analogous circumstances to the quarrel between Achilles and Agamemnon, responded to the Cretan chief's demand that he give back his war-booty by killing the chief's son in an ambush and fleeing into exile (*Od.*13.258–75).

[17] *Il.* 4.338–63. At *Il.* 23. 473–98, Aias son of Oïleus and Idomeneus start a *neikos* which is quickly nipped in the bud by the mediation of Achilles. Cf. *Od.* 11.543–67, where Odysseus tries to apologize "with soothing words" to the ghost of Aias son of Telamon for unfairly winning the contest for the arms of Achilles.

[18] Unlike Odysseus, when the youthful Diomedes is insulted by Agamemnon as a shirker in battle, he meekly accepts the undeserved reprimand in deference to the chief's rank (*Il.* 4.368–418). Thersites starts a *neikos* with Agamemnon, which of course could not be allowed to continue.

[19] On the "juridical" aspects of these scenes, see Finley (1978) 108–10. Note the political astuteness of Achilles in giving the unclaimed fifth prize to Nestor, father of Antilochus.

[20] In the Trobriand Islands, "The main symptom of being powerful is to be wealthy, and of wealth to be generous. Meanness, indeed, is the most despised vice, and the only thing about which the natives have strong moral views, while generosity is the essence of goodness" Malinowski (1922) 97. On this principle in Homeric society, see Donlan (1982); also (1981–82) 156–57, 163–71.

[21] Qviller (1981) 125 calls competitive gift-giving the "economic corollary to martial contests and fighting."

[22] Achilles never mentions the omission directly, although he does say that Agamemnon, "though shameless as a dog, would not dare to look me in the face" (9.372–73); and at 16.72–73 he tells Patroclus he would now be fighting "if powerful Agamemnon were gentle-minded towards me." See Whitman (1958) 193. Martin (1989) 97 classifies the gift-offer as an abuse of speech. "Agamemnon's gifts alone *should not* persuade Achilles, because he does not accompany them (despite Nestor's warning) with the proper *style*, of 'gentle words'..." Martin notes a further insult; the poet allows Nestor to send Odysseus, Achilles' traditional enemy, as a mouthpiece for Agamemnon.

[23] "And we too would promise and fulfill these things and would give you the best in looks of the daughters of the son of Atreus...if you will sack with us the well-peopled citadel of Ilios...since we are honest marriage-brokers" (377–72). Cf. *Il.* 6.191–95 (Bellerophon); 14.119–24 (Tydeus); *Od.* 7.311–15 (Odysseus).

[24] Redfield (1975) 15–16, 105. The gifts are viewed by most commentators as either contributing positively to Achilles' *timê*, thus exculpating Agamemnon, or else negatively as bribes, thus partially excusing Achilles by placing some burden of blame on the chief. Willcock (1978), at 9.121–56, is typical: "The magnificence of the reparations is a measure of Achilles' honour. He has been insulted; but if he accepts...his status will be higher than before the insult." Cf. Griffin (1980) 99: "The presents are marks of honour (not merely a bribe)." Whitman (1958) 192–93 comes closer to seeing the offer itself as an insult. "[Agamemnon] still must have submission

from Achilles, even if he has to buy it." Where these observations fail is in a lack of understanding of the sociological "language" of gifts. Excessive gifts do not "bribe" (an essentially modern notion), they create a heavy obligation, which translates into a superior-inferior status relationship.

[25] At 9.344-45, 369-76, Achilles specifically accuses Agamemnon of trickery and deceit (verbs *apataô, exapataô*). Richardson (1990) 64 notes that in the narration of the history of Agamemnon's *skêptron* (2.100-08), the symbol of his authority as a *basileus*, the four figures who take possession of it from Zeus to Agamemnon (Hermes, Pelops, Atreus and Thyestes) are associated with trickery and deception.

[26] The Christian moralistic viewpoint was expressed in extreme form by earlier critics; e.g., Bowra (1930): Achilles' "temper" leads him "to disaster and moral degradation"; he has "fallen from heroic standards of virtue" (17); his "wrath is wicked" (18); he has "set himself up against the divine law, and he must expect the consequences" (20); his "character...is the cause of all that happens" (193). Most revealing: "Roland would never have acted, as Achilles acted, from injured pride: that was more the part of Ganelon" (194). Recent critics tone down the rhetoric of sinning, but keep the substance; for Griffin (1980) 74, note 46, Achilles' "passionate emotion" causes him to "override" the heroic code which dictated return to battle as the "appropriate action." Mueller (1984) 46-47 speaks of Achilles' "vindictive intransigence," and his "blind intransigence," which "compounds the initial error."

[27] See the perceptive remarks of Edwards (1987) 232-37. What is problematic is the "success" standard itself. The tension between the self- and family-centered individual and the well-being of the whole community was a persistent structural problem in the pre-polis society (and well beyond), and for that reason is played out over and over again in epic poetry, most searchingly in the Quarrel, but also in the case of Hector and Troy and in the relationship between Odysseus and his *hetairoi* in the *Odyssey*. See in general Adkins (1960).

[28] Whitman (1958) 190. It is excessively "modern," in my opinion, to characterize the Quarrel as merely the "impetus which drove Achilles from the simple assumptions of the other princely heroes onto the path where heroism means the search for the dignity and meaning of the self" (193; cf. 197). Compare A. Parry (1956) 5-6: in his rejection speech, Achilles is searching for some way to express his intuitive sense of the "awful distance between appearance and reality." I emphasize again that the listeners would have had a less complicated psychological reaction. A good corrective is Claus (1975).

[29] See Edwards (1991) 244 on the "ungracious and jealous, not humble or apologetic" tone of the speech, and Agamemnon's obvious "uneasiness and resentment towards Akhilleus."

[30] *Il*. 19.137-38. These lines nearly equal 9.119-20 (see above, 106). Here Agamemnon substitutes "Zeus took away my *phrenes*," for the earlier "yielding to my wretched *phrenes*." That original confession in Book 9, had it been delivered then, either in person or even by the Embassy, would have constituted the necesssary apology to end the *neikos*. Characteristic of Agamemnon's personal style, the force of the original is considerably diluted in its emended public form.

[31] *Il*. 19.146-52. The meaning of the verb *klotopeuein* here, usually rendered, by inference from the context, as "waste time chattering," is unknown; Hesychius glosses the noun *klotopeutês* as *alazôn*, "boaster," which may be significant in this context. Edwards (1991) 254.

[32] Edwards (1991) 266, to the contrary, sees Achilles speaking graciously here, identifying "himself (in effect) with Agamemnon's remarks about the responsibility of Ate, thus implicitly accepting the king's explanation of his conduct." But Achilles has scrupulously avoided the excuse of *atê*, Agamemnon's crutch throughout the poem, for himself. More significantly, he snubs Agamemnon by not addressing him. Achilles also ignores the offer of the "rich feast" promised by Odysseus as part of the compensation/display (19.179-80). When it does take place (23.35-56), it is an insignificant event, completely overshadowed by the huge funeral feast given by Achilles to the Myrmidons just before (23.26-34).

[33]Collins (1988) 102; cf. 99–100. And, of course, Achilles becomes the *de facto* leader of the army in Book 20, since Agamemnon is wounded and cannot fight. We may add that Patroclus' magnificent funeral, which is symbolically Achilles' own, is attended not only by the Myrmidons, but also by the entire Achaean army, making it like the funeral of a paramount *basileus*.

[34]Cf. Redfield (1975) 105. We may note, too, that in refusing the gifts Achilles earned greater *kleos* than if he had accepted, as he himself says at 19.63–64: "But the Achaeans, I think, will long remember the strife (*eris*) between you and me."

[35]See especially 21.99–113. King (1987) 36 has noticed that Achilles never refers to *timê* after Patroclus is killed.

[36]The ransoming of Hector's body provides one final twist in the game of gift-giving and -taking. Despite his stubborn refusal to give back Hector, Achilles gets great treasure gifts in the end (24.229–35). Agamemnon's refusal to let go Chryseis in Book 1 had cost him the "countless ransom" and a payment to Apollo of a hecatomb of bulls and goats.

[37]This paper is based on my 1991 lecture as the John and Helen Condon Symposiast at Loyola University of Chicago. I wish to express again my thanks to the Classical community at Loyola for their *philia*. I am also indebted to Professor Ann Batchelder, whose as yet unpublished paper, "Achilles and Agamemnon: Two Models of Kingship in the *Iliad*," has provided fresh insights into the events of Books 1, 9, 19, and 23.

Works Cited

Adkins, A. W. H. 1960. *Merit and Responsibility*. Oxford.

Bowra, C. M. 1930. *Tradition and Design in the Iliad*. Oxford.

Claus, D. B. 1975. "*Aidôs* in the Language of Achilles." *TAPA* 105: 13–28.

Coldstream, J. N. 1977. *Geometric Greece*. London.

Collins, L. 1988. *Studies in Characterization in the Iliad*. Frankfurt.

Dickinson, O. T. P. K. 1986. "Homer, the Poet of the Dark Age," *Greece and Rome* 33: 20–37.

Donlan, W. 1981–82. "Reciprocities in Homer." *CW* 75: 137–75.
———. 1982. "The Politics of Generosity in Homer." *Helios* 9: 1–15.
———. 1989. "The Unequal Exchange Between Glaucus and Diomedes in Light of the Homeric Gift-Economy." *Phoenix* 43: 1–15.

Edwards, M. W. 1987. *Homer, Poet of the Iliad*. Baltimore and London.
———. 1991. *The Iliad: A Commentary*. Vol. V. Cambridge, Engl.

Fagerström, K. 1988. *Greek Iron Age Architecture*. Göteborg.

Finley, M. I. 1955. "Marriage, Sale and Gift in the Homeric World." *Revue internationale des droits de l'antiquité* 2: 167–94.
———. 1974. "The World of Odysseus Revisited," *PCA* 71: 13–31; reprinted with changes in Finley 1978: 142–58.
———. 1978. *The World of Odysseus*. New York; orig. 1954.

Finnegan, R. 1992. *Oral Poetry: Its Nature, Significance and Social Context.* Bloomington and Indianapolis.

Foley, J. M. 1988. *The Theory of Oral Composition.* Bloomington and Indianapolis.

Fried, M. H. 1967. *The Evolution of Political Society.* New York.

Geddes, A. G. 1984. "Who's Who in 'Homeric' Society," *CQ* 34: 17–36.

Gregory, C. A. 1982. *Gifts and Commodities.* New York and London.

Griffin, J. 1980. *Homer on Life and Death.* Oxford.

Havelock, E. A. 1963. *Preface to Plato.* Cambridge, Mass.

Heubeck, A., S. West, and J. B. Hainsworth. 1988. *A Commentary on Homer's Odyssey.* Vol I. Oxford.

Humphreys, S. C. 1969. "History, Economics, and Anthropology: The Work of Karl Polanyi." *History and Theory* 8: 165–212.

Janko, R. 1982. *Homer, Hesiod and the Hymns.* Cambridge, Engl.
———. 1992. *The Iliad, A Commentary.* Vol. IV. Cambridge, Engl.

King, K. C. 1987. *Achilles. Paradigms of the War Hero from Homer to the Middle Ages.* Berkeley and Los Angeles.

Kirk, G. S. 1985. *The Iliad: A Commentary.* Vol. I Cambridge, Engl.

Lord, A. B. 1960. *The Singer of Tales.* Cambridge, Mass.

Malinowski, B. 1922. *Argonauts of the Western Pacific.* London.

Martin, R. P. 1989. *The Language of Heroes: Speech and Performance in the Iliad.* Ithaca and London.

Mauss, M. 1967. *The Gift*, transl. I. Cunnison. New York.

Mazarakis Ainian, A. J. 1988. "Early Greek Temples: Their Origin and Function." In *Early Greek Cult Practice*, ed. R. Hägg, N. Marinatos, and G. C. Nordquist, 105–19. Stockholm.

McDonald, W. A. and C. G. Thomas. 1990. *Progress into the Past*, 2nd ed. Bloomington and Indianapolis.

McDonald, W. A., W. D. E. Coulson, and J. Rosser, eds. 1983. *Excavations at Nichoria in Southwest Greece* III. Minneapolis.

Morris, I. 1986. "The Use and Abuse of Homer." *CA* 5: 81–138.

Mueller, M. 1984. *The Iliad.* London.

Nagy, G. 1979. *The Best of the Achaeans*. Baltimore and London.
———. 1990. *Greek Mythology and Poetics*. Ithaca and London.

Parry, A. 1956. "The Language of Achilles." *TAPA* 87: 1–7:

Parry, M. 1971. *The Making of Homeric Verse. The Collected Papers of Milman Parry*, ed. A. Parry. Oxford.

Qviller, B. 1981. "The Dynamics of the Homeric Society." *SO* 56: 109–55.

Raaflaub, K. A. 1991. "Homer und die Geschichte des 8. Jh.s v. Chr." In *Zweihundert Jahre Homer-Forschung*, ed. J. Latacz, 205–52. Stuttgart and Leipzig.

Richardson, S. 1990. *The Homeric Narrator*. Nashville.

Redfield, J. M. 1975. *Nature and Culture in the Iliad*. Chicago.

Russo, J. 1978. "How and What, Does Homer Communicate?" In *Communication Arts in the Ancient World*, ed. E. A. Havelock and J. P. Hershbell, 39–52. New York.

Sahlins, M. D. 1968. *Tribesmen*. Englewoods Cliffs, N.J.
———. 1972. *Stone Age Economics*. Chicago.

Service, E. R. 1975. *Origins of the State and Civilization: The Process of Cultural Evolution*. New York.

Snodgrass, A. 1974. "An Historical Homeric Society?" *JHS* 94: 114–25.
———. 1987. *An Archaeology of Greece*. Berkeley, Los Angeles and London.
———. 1990. "Survey Archaeology and the Rural Landscape of the Greek City." In *The Greek City From Homer to Alexander*, ed. O. Murray and S. Price, 113–36. Oxford.

Whitely, J. 1991. *Style and Society in Dark Age Greece*. Cambridge, Engl.

Whitman, C. H. 1958. *Homer and the Heroic Tradition*. Cambridge, Mass.

Willcock, M. M., ed. 1978. *The Iliad of Homer*. Books I–XII. London.

Wyatt, W. F. 1989. "The Intermezzo of *Odyssey* 11 and the Poets Homer and Odysseus." *SMEA* 27: 235–53.

CHIEF AND FOLLOWERS IN PRE-STATE GREECE[*]

As Karl Polanyi knew, Greece just before the city-state is the best documented early-historical example of the embedded economy. In books 9–12 of the *Odyssey*, we are given a rare, animated glimpse into the positive and negative effects of such a system. In these key books we observe Odysseus and his "companions" (*hetairoi*) on their way home from the Trojan War, as told by Homer and narrated by Odysseus himself. Although their adventures take place in a fantasy world, the sociological content of the stories closely reproduces the kinds of relationships between a leader and his followers observed by ethnographers of ranked societies led by big men or low-level chiefs. The rules, norms and behaviours among the community of raiding warriors reflect explicitly or implicitly the value system and the economic, social and political institutions of the village communities in which these men lived.

Before I analyze the Homeric text in detail, let me set the historical and ethnographical stage.[1] The pre-state or state-formative period in Greece dates from approximately 850 to about 750 B.C., roughly the last century of the long Dark Age, so called, which began with the final collapse of the Late Bronze Age kingdoms around 1150 or 1100. Most of the people of that sparsely populated era lived in hamlets and villages of a few dozen to several hundred inhabitants; there were also a select few village clusters on the mainland that formed small towns with populations perhaps in the low thousands. In the Homeric epics, which reflect the society of the pre-state period, these little villages are called *polis* or *astu*, the same names given to the much larger towns and cities of later Greece.

The individual settlements were pretty much self-sufficient economically and were more or less politically autonomous, but were also parts of a larger entity, the *demos*, a word which signified then, as later, both the "people" as an ethnic group and the tribal territory they occupied. A *demos* might consist of a single village and its farmlands and pastures; more typically, however, the *demos* contained a central *polis* and one or more lesser settlements. Politically, the village communities were headed by a chief, *basileus*, distinguished archaeologically by his much bigger house, with its very large living/

feasting hall. To later Greeks the title *basileus* signified a "king" or "monarch," and scholars, almost without exception, so translate it in the Homeric texts. Yet in the Homeric society the *basileus* had very little coercive power over his community and was, as well, subject to displacement by other ambitious men whose family wealth and personal abilities were on par with the chief's. These lesser local chiefs also bore the title of *basileus*.

The political power structure has been aptly described as a series of loosely ranked, competing pyramids, each made up of a *basileus*, his family, close kin, dependents and followers. In practice, a pyramid was often coterminous with a village, although, especially in the larger villages, there might well be several such pyramids. The situation was complicated by the fact that a chief would also recruit followers outside his local base, that is, among the other *poleis* of the *demos*. Note that I have omitted mention of corporate kin groups as functional entities for social and political organization and integration, although they are prominent in ethnographic accounts of living tribal societies. Recent research has cast serious doubt on the existence of a gentilic system of interlocking clans, phratries and internal tribes, once universally believed to form the structure of early Greek communities.[2] In the absence of corporate clans and superclans the emphasis is put squarely on the individual household (the *oikos*) and its concentric circles of retainers and non-kin followers—exactly as we see in Homer.

Despite the looseness of the pyramid system, the Dark Age polity was not an uninhibited political free-for-all among competing groups as has been sometimes suggested. There was never a time in their entire history (including the radical democracies of the fifth and fourth centuries) that the Greeks did not recognize an apical figure who stood above and apart from all other leaders in the *demos* and who gave direction and set policy. In the pre-state period, this chief of chiefs, invariably the ranking chief of the main village, held only a tenuous dominance over the separate segments of the *demos*. He could claim no other title than the generic "*basileus*," and another claimant might easily take his place. Nevertheless, in the epics, the unifying office of paramount *basileus* is supremely important and necessary, and the legitimated holder is a figure of enormous respect and considerable authority.

Thus, Homer's Odysseus was the paramount chief of an ethnic group or tribe called the *Kephallenes* (conventionally anglicized to "Cephallenians"), who inhabited four islands and parts of the mainland opposite them. He was the chief of the main island of Ithaca, his home island, and lived in its main *polis*, also called Ithaca. When he went to Troy, he took with him a contingent of Cephallenian warriors, recruited not only from Ithaca village and island, but also from other parts of his chiefdom. And back home, ninety-six of the 108 suitors and their followers, who hoped to usurp the office of paramount, came from the other islands, which were in effect autonomous political units.

Ethically, this was a warrior culture through and through, and the psychology and behaviours minutely detailed in both the *Iliad* and the *Odyssey* parallel exactly those of the hundreds of small-scale warrior societies known to history and ethnography. A *basileus* was first and foremost a war-leader; there was no other route to elite status and no other way to stay at the top. The economy, like the politics, was bound up in the values of warriorship. This requires some elaboration. The Dark Age Greeks practised a mixed regime of subsistence farming and herding. The elite households shared this mode of life with the non-elite *oikoi*, but on a larger scale: bigger farm plots and work forces including slaves, and larger surpluses. The great distinction, however, between the rich and the average lay in numbers of animals. While most families owned some sheep and goats, a pair of oxen, and perhaps even some cattle (all pastured on common grazing grounds), the truly wealthy had numerous flocks and herds, especially of cattle, the most valued of the herd animals, and horses, the very emblem of a warrior nobility. Animals were considered to be the real wealth and can be said to represent a separate and more or less distinctively elite economic sphere. The other material measurement of prestige was "treasure" (*keimelia*, literally, "things laid up"), costly and scarce display items, principally fine cloth goods and metal objects (bronze, gold, silver, and iron), to which, again, the warrior elite had nearly exclusive access.[3]

Raiding, which ranged from sudden swoops to all-out sieges, and included armed extortion, was the fulcrum of the prestige economy, and was the basis for competition among chiefs. Ambitious warriors collected followers with inducements of profit and glory, sealing the bargain with lavish meat feasts. The object of raids was animals, booty and women, but especially animals. The chief's share, which included an extra leader's portion, replenished and—he would fervently hope—increased his flocks and herds, so that he could continue to give feasts, thereby outdoing his rivals and retaining the loyalty of his followers. The profit of this circular system of slaughtering animals to get animals, which somewhat precariously balanced income and outgo, was, of course, prestige and influence. Large flocks and store rooms full of display goods were proof of warrior excellence, and the mere sight of them ordained respect and subordination. The slaughter of those animals for feasts (including religious sacrificial feasts) was also the main redistributive function of a chief, and so a principal instrument of his social control.

Apart from the raid, the exchange (or "movement") of natural and man-made products occurred through gift-giving and trade. An intricate system, with codified rules about who gives to whom, when, and in what amount, served to validate relationships and regulate and calibrate status.[4] "Treasure" objects, particularly unused bronze tripods and cauldrons, were exchanged exclusively among the elite. These kinds of goods, never used as a purchasing medium, and circulating and re-circulating much like the Kula exchange of the Trobriand islanders, was the currency of prestige. As in most ranked societies, giving was a form of competition, and reputations were made and influence acquired by generous giving. On the other hand, stinginess was antithetical to leadership.

The pace of trade-exchange within the Greek world and with foreigners quickened after 900 B.C. By about 800, long-distance exchange had become regulated to the extent that Greek traders founded and maintained trade settlements in non-Greek lands. Imports were mainly confined to metal and luxury items from the Levant and Egypt—trophies of wealth and success. Only after 700, however, can we legitimately speak of a "trading sector" of the economy, and even then in a very modest sense compared to the later volume of trade.

From this brief description of the later Dark Age society, it is clear that Polanyi's three categories of economic integration—reciprocity, redistribution, and exchange—were totally submerged in institutions and values of a non-economic kind. Almost without exception, every economic (in the more purely materialist sense) gesture was reflexively a social gesture. The exception was a fledgling trading system, which, however, was essentially peripheral to the subsistence economy and quantitatively negligible until the seventh century. Here we should add—as Karl Polanyi pointed out long ago—that while Dark Age chiefs might engage in trade as a side activity of their piracy and mainly in pursuit of raw metals, they despised the occupation of trader on the grounds that it was not a warrior activity.[5]

We give substance and life to these remarks by following Odysseus and his followers (*hetairoi* = "companions," "comrades") on their return from the Trojan War. This portion of the *Odyssey* is neglected as a reflection of the workings of the actual society. I think that is because these episodes contain the most fantastical elements in the epic, which makes them appear remote from real-life experience, and because the milieu is not a settled community, like Ithaca, Troy or Phaeacia, but a roving pirate-band. Yet, as was said above, the *hetairoi*-band is the basic political grouping, and the principal instrument of prestige and profit for its members, especially the chief. Moreover, we can assume a continuity in social relationship from raid to village life. Although things change somewhat when the warriors return home and are reintegrated into their own families, kindreds and villages, with the contrasting pulls of loyalty and energy these present, most *hetairoi* will nonetheless remain loyal to Odysseus and his house, and he to them. Nor is there any reason to think that the operation and motivation of reciprocity and redistribution will differ from peace to raid. What we see, then, in the adventures of Odysseus and his band of *hetairoi*, is the society in its purest, most distilled, form.

Odysseus himself, posing (in one of his many lying tales) as a once powerful Cretan warrior-chief, now a wandering exile, tells how one gathers a following, and why. Unable to settle down into dull domestic life after the Trojan War, and itching for adventure, he says,

> I outfitted nine ships, and the host gathered quickly. Then, for six days my trusty *hetairoi* feasted; and I supplied them with many victims, both for sacrifices to the gods and for them to make feasts for themselves; and on the seventh day we embarked and sailed away from broad Crete...
>
> (*Od.* 14.248–51).

That is the way the "real" Odysseus and the other Greek chiefs would have recruited their companions for raid and war. The word for "feast," *dais*, is from the verb *daio*, "to distribute, divide." This etymology is one of the key semantic indicators of the highly reciprocal nature of the pre-state society.

The first leg of the return voyage is quite realistic—Homer eases his characters (and us, his audience) gradually into the realm of the fantastic—a raid against a Thracian tribe called the Cicones (9.39ff.). The raid began auspiciously; they swooped in from the sea, sacked the main village, killed the men, took away the women and "many possessions" (*ktemata polla*). According to the rule of raiding bands, "We divided it up (verb *daio*), so that no man would go deprived of his equal share" (42).

Immediately, however, troubles start; Odysseus gives the order to run (raids are essentially hit and run), but the men, like "foolish children" (*nepioi*), he says, stay on the beach and feast on the captured sheep, cattle and wine they had hoisted. The next morning reinforcements come from the inland villages of the Cicones. In a day-long battle by the ships they lose six men from each of the twelve ships before they get away.

Here I should say a word about numbers and realism. Twelve ships with (conventionally) fifty men each would be a force of 600 warrior-rowers. This is actually one of the smallest contingents in the Catalogue of Ships in the *Iliad* (Agamemnon, for example, leads 120 ships). Such numbers would have been impossible in the thinly populated Dark Age and highly improbable even for the Archaic period. This poses no problem. We may conjecture that in real life Odysseus' entire Cephallenian chiefdom might have contained five or six thousand people (this would probably be a high estimate), with, say, a total of 800–1,000 men of fighting age. A major chief like Odysseus might easily have been able to gather a troop (the Greek word is *laos*) of 100 or 150 men for a serious raid, i.e., not cattle-lifting and kidnapping, but a full-fledged attack against a prosperous village of 300–400 people, with, say, fifty to seventy-five fighting-age men. So, exaggeration of scale, an epic characteristic, poses no historical problem and does not affect the qualitative picture.

The Cicones episode introduces one of the recurring motifs of the adventures, the tension between the *basileus* and his often unruly *hetairoi*, who resist strict military discipline and regard themselves as equal among one another and nearly equal to their leader. This is the underlying contradiction of power relations in chiefdoms; followers will not always follow obediently. We observe this shifting of the quality and the extent of command authority not only here but throughout both epics. The *Odyssey* provides an especially revealing instance of the chief-people tension in Book 16 (418–48), which also gives us a glimpse into the relations between a paramount chief and a sub-chief. Penelope lectures Antinous, one of the main suitors, on his outrageous behaviour. She reminds him that his father, one of the Cephallenian chiefs, once had to flee the wrath of the *demos* because he had joined up with the Taphian pirates in raiding against the Thesprotians, who at that time were allied to the Cephallenians. The people were angry enough to want to kill him and "eat up his great and pleasant livelihood." Though a chief, Antinous' father was quite vulnerable to the irritation of his people when they felt he had overstepped his authority. He managed to escape their punishment only by fleeing to Odysseus, who protected him until their anger cooled.

So, in this world of uncertain leadership, the extent and quality of control are highly circumstantial; sometimes the leader's authority is complete and unquestioned; at other times the people simply refuse to obey. There are no "constitutional" rules, only the leader's strength of body and character. Thus, in the next adventure, "The Lotus Eaters" (9.82–104), Odysseus is shown as exerting perfect control over his band. When a party of three men, sent to scout the situation, eat the lotus fruit and refuse to return, Odysseus himself goes and drags them out by force and ties them up in the ship and orders his fleet to sail on. Because it is a small mutiny and because the rest of the *hetairoi* agree with his actions, the desired harmony between chief and followers is preserved.

The episode of the Cyclops, which takes up the rest of Book 9 (105–566), begins with an appropriately "primitive" example of reciprocity. The deserted island opposite the land of the Cyclopes, where Odysseus had prudently landed them, was inhabited only by huge herds of wild goats. In this completely "feral" environment, totally removed from the familiar "tamed"

Chief and Followers in Pre-State Greece 351

world of villages, farms and pastures, Odysseus and his men reenact a social ritual as old as human society itself. Dividing into three hunting parties, they soon bring down much game. "Twelve ships followed me, and to each nine goats were allotted; but for me alone they chose out ten" (159–60). Afterwards, they feasted all day on goat-meat and drank the wine they had taken from the Cicones. The only thing that distinguishes this scene from an event in the life of a primitive, egalitarian hunting band—where the catch is divided evenly among everyone—is the "ten for me alone." This extra prize, the *geras*, or leader's special share, tells us we are looking at an established rank society, but in the primordial setting of the world of the pre-civilized Cyclopes—here Homer is a fine anthropologist—the reciprocity is pure. Odysseus does not keep the ten goats but shares them with his companions.[6] He receives his material due as leader, as a *symbolic* gift ratifying his position, which he immediately returns. His "profit" lies in having them to redistribute, building up his fund of good will; what he pockets is the honour, *time*.

On the next day Odysseus convenes an assembly to explain his plan to sail over to the land of the Cyclopes in his own ship, leaving the other eleven in the safety of the deserted island. At this point we should note that in this and all subsequent adventures, the action takes place within the more naturalistic confines of a single ship, and, indeed, with an even smaller number. For when they beached the ship, Odysseus chose "the twelve best of my *hetairoi*," to explore the cave of the Cyclops.

The *hetairoi* "beg" (verb *lissomai*) Odysseus to steal the Cyclops' cheese and his sheep and goats, and quickly leave, but *ou pithomen*, "I did not listen to them," he says (228), hoping in his greed for treasure to see if he can extract some "guest-gifts" (*xeineia*) from the absent owner when he returns. As I have said, this kind of pull and tug forms the usual pattern of the leader-follower relationship. On the one hand, the leader displays those qualities that make him the leader—foresight, prudence, protectiveness—but also bad judgment and recklessness, that go against the common will and good. There should be no doubt in our minds that in portraying this tension and exploring this ambivalence from both perspectives—the rash disobedience of the *hetairoi*, the selfish stubbornness of the *basileus*—the poet is commenting on a *generic* problem.

In some respects Odysseus *is* the ideal chieftain, as in the planning and execution of the blinding of the Cyclops and escape from his cave. The Homeric *archos* ("leader") is ultimately the solitary figure on whom everything hinges. In his own words:

> But I was planning how things might turn out the very best, if I could find some way of escape for my *hetairoi* and for myself. And

> I wove in my mind all sorts of tricks and wiles (as one does in a matter of life and death), for a great evil was near us; and this seemed to my mind the best plan (420–24).

It should be emphasized that in every situation the leader is obligated to put his life on the line. In perfect symmetry with the apportionment of booty, danger is also apportioned in an egalitarian manner. For the perilous task of putting out the Cyclops' eye, four men are picked by casting lots, "and I was numbered fifth among them" (331–35). The leader is both inside and outside the allotment, of course; just as he always gets the extra *geras* he always gets the extra portion of the danger.[7]

Failure of leadership with its socially negative consequences is brought up again in the Polyphemus story. Once more, Odysseus courts disaster by going against the common will (and common sense) for his own personal glory. As they are escaping in their ship, against the entreaties of his companions he taunts the Cyclops, who almost swamps them with huge rocks. Worst of all, by boasting of his name and homeland he allows the giant to name him to his father, Poseidon, who fulfills his prayer to thwart the homecoming and "destroy utterly all his *hetairoi*" (473–542).

The episode of the Cyclops ends, as it had begun, with an example of equal sharing among the group. Odysseus and his surviving shipmates return to the other ships with the Cyclops' sheep. As they had done earlier in the goat hunt, "We divided [the sheep] so that no one would go cheated of his equal share; but my well-greaved *hetairoi* gave the ram to me alone, separate from the division of the sheep, and I sacrificed him on the shore to Zeus" (549–52). In an exact counterpart to the generalized reciprocity observed in egalitarian bands and tribes, all the *hetairoi* share in the spoils, including those who did not take part in the raid. The prize ram, Polyphemus' favourite animal, is fitting symbolic recognition of the leader's cunning and courage. His immediate return of the gift to the giving group completes the circle of reciprocity.

The social function of the rituals of sharing and feasting is to foster the spirit of unity and co-operation within the group. The *geras*, as we see in these examples of purely symbolic presentations, does not violate this spirit. At the same time, the leader's "due" (even if it is, as here, merely honorific and without resemblance to permanent gain), like his "right" to act as the distributor, sustains and strengthens the principle of centricity, of subordination to central authority, without which co-operative social order would be impossible.[8] Thus equal allotment and *geras*, which might appear to express contradictory principles, are a highly complementary means of balancing the conflicting claims of egalitarianism and authoritarianism which are inherent in the chiefdom.

Yet, despite the best efforts to avert it, that contradiction permanently lurks not far below the surface. In both the *Iliad* and the *Odyssey* this tension flares up so frequently that we cannot escape the conclusion that the epic tradition is exploring a recurrent, indeed nagging, social problem. Usually, as we saw in the Cyclops story, and will see again presently, the breakdown in reciprocity is triggered by the fact (or at least perception) that the leader is placing his own wealth and glory-needs before the common good. Just so, in the following episode (10.27–55), Aeolus, the divine keeper of the winds, has given Odysseus a bag containing the contrary winds, with the strict admonition not to open it. Thus protected, the ships sail within sight of Ithaca. Odysseus, weary from his long dutiful stint at the helm, falls asleep and his *hetairoi*, suspecting that Odysseus is holding out on them, grumble among themselves.

> Look, how dear and honoured this man is by the men to whose towns and lands he comes. He is bringing much fine treasure from the booty out of Troy, and we, who have completed the same journey, are returning home with empty hands. And now Aeolus, out of his friendship for him, has given him these gifts. But come, let us quickly see what these are, how much gold and silver are in the bag (10.38–45).

Once more, the built-in adversarial posture, which co-exists with the idealized leader-follower relationship, erupts to threaten the integrity of the group.

Their next adventure, in the land of the Laestrygonian cannibal giants, is a kind of doublet of the Cyclops episode and, for literary purposes, functions essentially as a plot device to lose the other eleven ships (10.76–132). Odysseus' ship, reduced now to a crew of forty-five, sails on, arriving finally at the island of Aeaea, home of the enchantress Circe, where Odysseus and his companions are, as always, the sole representatives of the human social order. This Eden-like environment becomes the setting for yet another mythic reenactment of primitive sharing and solidarity (133–574). Going off alone, to see if there was any sign of civilization, Odysseus comes across a giant stag, kills it, and with heroic effort carries it on his shoulders to his comrades lying on the beach, immobilized by despair, and revives their spirits with the "glorious feast." In this elemental act the twin senses of "divide" and "distribute" that lie behind *dais* are seamlessly combined. According to Elman Service, that is how ranked leadership began in the first place. Such generous service to one's fellows is a "starting mechanism" for the leadership role. By repeated acts of public benefit, an occasional leader comes to occupy a permanent position.[9] In this ultra-simplified setting the poet has Odysseus recreate the very origins of the political order.

Yet order is always poised for disorder in the Homeric world. For the first time, we are introduced to an actual opposing voice in the person of a man named Eurylochus, whom Odysseus describes as a "[close?] relative by marriage" (*peos*) (10.441), possibly his sister's husband, though we can only guess. Eurylochus, who comes off as rather a shirker and whiner, is also, we learn here, Odysseus' second in command. The geographical setting may be a fairy-tale primeval paradise, but the sociological milieu is the familiar one of a small village community.

We first see Eurylochus when, on the next morning (10.205), Odysseus divides his command in two, appointing himself leader of one group of twenty-two men and Eurylochus of the other. As usual, allotment is used to determine which of the two groups will have the dangerous job of exploring. After Eurylochus has lost his men to Circe's enchantments, Odysseus, ever the responsible leader, goes alone to Circe's house, forces her to turn his companions back into men, returns to the rest and announces the good news, that their comrades are alive and feasting in abundance. Eurylochus tries to dissuade them from going to Circe's, predictably blaming Odysseus' bad leadership for the loss of life in the Cyclops' cave: "For those men perished through this man's recklessness (*atasthalie*)" (431–37). This sort of situation, in which a lesser leader challenges the authority of the legitimate paramount, will have been a common occurrence in real life; every villager in the audience will have witnessed a similar scene many times.

Odysseus's immediate impulse—which reminds us again that personal might is literally an essential element of rule in this society—is to kill his challenger, but he is persuaded not to by the rest. We note that the confrontation doesn't end badly; Eurylochus goes along after all, in fear and shame. He doesn't even lose his rank, for twice more we see him in delegated positions of responsibility (11.23–24, 12.195–96).

In his final and fateful appearances as the self-appointed spokesman for the group, Eurylochus again shows how easily a chief's authority is subverted by a forceful opposing voice from below, especially when it purports to speak for the common good. Having escaped, though with losses, from the hideous trials of Charybdis and Scylla (12.234–59), there awaits the last test of the forbidden Cattle of the Sun. Even though their survival thus far was due to Odysseus' good leadership ("my courage, planning and intelligence," is how he puts it, 12.211), the men are exhausted and totally demoralized. So, when Odysseus wisely orders them not to land on the island of the Sun, but row past, "the spririt was broken within them, and immediately Eurylochus answered me with hateful words," giving an impassioned and persuasive speech to the effect that in a night sail they would all perish. "And the rest of the companions gave assent" (*eneon alloi hetairoi*), a standard formula for agreement to an opinion voiced in assembly.

Odysseus reluctantly gives in: "you [plural] force [*biazete*] me, one man alone" (297), but still has sufficient authority to make them swear an oath not to eat the Cattle of the Sun. When they are becalmed on the island for a month, and starving, Eurylochus delivers another persuasive speech for slaughtering the cattle, which ends: "'I would rather lose my life once and for all gulping at a wave than to pine slowly away on a deserted island.' So spoke Eurylochus, and the rest of the companions gave assent" (12.340–52).

I doubt there exists a clearer description in all of ethnography of a low-level chiefdom, and of its internal stresses, than in these books of the *Odyssey*. The chief possesses considerable authority, but he must bend to the collective will of the fighting men, who are naturally disposed to be critical of his leadership. It is important that we understand that the epic tradition constantly underscores the fact that the leader-people tension is the cause of social dysfunction. Odysseus is consistently represented as being as good a leader as a people could realistically hope for; yet the message is unmistakable, that personal leadership is fragile and unstable and that the intrinsic opposition between the two social vectors of autocracy on the one hand and egalitarianism on the other, is a frequent prescription for social breakdown.

We may add an Odyssean postscript that highlights this problem. None of the *hetairoi* made it back to Ithaca. Had Odysseus returned with his followerband intact, the constitutional crisis that had been brewing at home would have dissolved immediately. As it was, Telemachus, a boy just becoming a man, was in a very precarious position, with no brothers, cousins or kinsmen by marriage to help him stave off the suitors, but only a handful of *hetairoi* loyal to the house, too few and too old to be of much use, and a populace that naturally blamed Odysseus for the loss of their sons, husbands and brothers.[10] And so, when Odysseus returned alone he had to lay low and scheme. By his fabled cunning and by recruiting a rag-tag band of followers from his loyal slaves he saved his chieftainship and the preeminence of the house of Laertes. Still, it took the intervention of the gods to prevent a civil war and restore the established order.[11]

In the event, the low-level chiefdom form of polity, which, despite its inherent instability, was quite serviceable in the simple conditions of the Dark Age, was doomed to vanish in the face of a whole new set of conditions, often referred to as a "social revolution." As the population rose sharply in the eighth century and land became a scarce good, the prestige economy, based on large herds and raids for animals and booty, rapidly gave way to an agricultural economy based on exclusive landownership, surplus cereal and oil production, and wage labour. Those changes not only ended the social organization by follower-bands, they also saw the replacement of the traditional morality of reciprocity and sharing, of the sort we have observed in the story of Odysseus, by a value of exploitation.[12]

How the historically unique polity of the mature city-state evolved out of the thick stew of change, growth and conflict, is a matter of lively discussion and controversy. Historians of this process, which unfolds during the Archaic period (roughly 750–490) and well into the Classical period (roughly 490–350), would do well to order the kaleidoscope of events and transitions on the three Polanyian categories of reciprocity (whose imperative was a major social–psychological force in this period), redistribution (which took on some very interesting forms in the developing city–state) and market exchange (whose evolutionary effect became strong, if not decisive, late in the fifth century). When we look at Archaic and Classical history in this way, the break between the pre-historical Dark Age and the historical era seems much less severe than how it is represented in the history books. The citizen-soldier of the democratic city-state is imprinted with the egalitarian ethic of Odysseus' *hetairoi*-band.

NOTES

* The original version of this paper was delivered at the fourth International Karl Polanyi Conference, held in Montréal in November 1992.

[1] The following sketch of the Dark Age society is my own interpretation of the evidence, for which see Donlan 1981–82; 1985; 1989. On the controversial question of the relation of epic poetry to the actual society, see Raaflaub 1991; Morris 1986 (both with ample bibliography).

[2] Roussel 1976; Bourriot 1976.

[3] On the various "spheres" of the "multi-centric" Homeric economy, marked by different institutionalization and different moral values (which have numerous anthropological parallels), see Donlan 1981. This concept goes back to Polanyi's distinction between "general-purpose" and "special-purpose" money.

[4] On gift-giving in Homeric society see M. I. Finley's *World of Odysseus* (Finley 1978). This short book, first published in 1954, introduced the ideas of Polanyi and the "substantivist" school of economic history into the study of Homeric society and began a new chapter in the historiography of early Greece.

[5] Polanyi 1951, 25–26.

[6] On equal share and the leader's extra due, see *Od.* 14.229–34; *Il.* 11.677–705.

[7] See Finley 1978, 96–97.

[8] Sahlins 1972, 189–90.

[9] Service 1965, 149; Sahlins 1972, 208.

[10] As Eurylochus had done, Eupeithes, the father of the suitor Alcinous, takes control of the people by whipping up sentiment against Odysseus in the assembly for losing "many good men and the hollow ships" in the return (24.426–88; cf. 462–66).

[11] 24.472–86: Zeus decrees that the Ithacans should swear an oath for Odysseus "to be *basileus* forever" and that they should all "love one another as before, and let wealth and peace abound." Cf. 546–48.

[12] Already by the turn of the eighth to the seventh century, Hesiod in *Works and Days* is complaining about the greed of the *basileis* and their disregard for "justice" (*dike*), the abstract quality of balanced reciprocity.

REFERENCES

Bourriot, Felix. 1976. *Recherches sur la nature du génos: étude d'histoire sociale athénienne. Périodes archaïque et classique.* Paris: H. Champion.

Donlan, Walter. 1981. "Scale, Value, and Function in the Homeric Economy." *American Journal of Ancient History* 6:101–17.

———, 1981–82. "Reciprocities in Homer." *Classical World* 75:137–75.

———, 1985. "The Social Groups of Dark Age Greece." *Classical Philology* 80:293–308.

———, 1989. "The Pre-State Community in Greece." *Symbolae Osloenses* 64:5–29.

Finley, Moses I. 1978. *The World of Odysseus.* 2d rev. ed. New York: Viking.

Morris, Ian. 1986. "The Use and Abuse of Homer." *Classical Antiquity* 5:81–138.

Polanyi, Karl. 1951. "Reciprocity and Redistribution in Homeric Greece." Chapter One of an unpublished work in progress by Polanyi, which resides in the archive of the Karl Polanyi Institute of Political Economy in Montreal under the title *Greek Manuscript*.

Raaflaub, Kurt. 1991. "Homer und die Geschichte des 8. Jh. v. Chr." In *Zweihundert Jahre Homer-Forschung: Ruckblick und Ausblick*, edited by Joachim Latcz, 205–55. Stuttgart and Leipzig: B.G. Teubner.

Roussel, Denis. 1976. *Tribu et cité: études sur les groupes sociaux dans les cités grecques aux époques archaïque et classique.* Paris: Les Belles Lettres.

Sahlins, Marshall D. 1972. *Stone Age Economics.* Chicago: Aldine.

Service, Elman. 1965. *Primitive Social Organization: An Evolutionary Perspective.* New York: Random House.

BIBLIOGRAPHY OF WORKS BY THE AUTHOR

ARTICLES AND BOOK CHAPTERS

"A Note on *Aristos* as a Class Term," *Philologus* 113 (1969) 268–70.

"Simonides, fr. 4D and P.Oxy. 2432," *Transactions and Proceedings of the American Philological Association* 100 (1969) 73–95.

"Character Structure in Homer's *Iliad*," *Journal of General Education* 21 (1970) 259–69.

"The Foundation Legends of Rome: An Example of Dynamic Process," *The Classical World* 64 (1970) 109–14.

"Changes and Shifts in the Meaning of *Demos* in the Literature of the Archaic Period," *La Parola del Passato* 135 (1970) 381–95.

"Archilochus, Strabo and the Lelantine War," *Transactions and Proceedings of the American Philological Association* 101 (1970) 131–42.

"Classical Mythology in the High School: A Modest Proposal," *The Classical Journal* 66 (1970) 347–49.

"Homer's Agamemnon," *The Classical World* 65 (1971) 109–15.

"The Role of *Eugeneia* in the Aristocratic Self-Image During the Fifth Century B.C.," in *Classics and the Classical Tradition,* edited by E. Borza and R. Carrubba (University Park, PA: The Pennsylvania State University, 1973) 63–78.

ARTICLES on "Hesiod," "Sappho," "Menander," in *The Encyclopedia of World Biography* (New York: McGraw-Hill, 1973) 250–52; 340–42; 404–06.

"The Tradition of Anti-Aristocratic Thought in Early Greek Poetry," *Historia* 22 (1973) 145–54.

"The Origin of Καλὸς κἀγαθός," *The American Journal of Philology* 94 (1973) 365–74.

"The Charge at Marathon: Herodotus 6.112," *The Classical Journal* 71 (1976) 339–43 (co-authored with James Thompson).

"Hard Facts, Straight Talk, and How to Keep Your Virtue in a Cruel World," *Classical Outlook*, Supplement 67 (1976) 1–5.

"Towards a Better Understanding of Ancient Societies," *Helios* 4 (1976) 3–15.

TRANSLATION. Ch. 16 of *A Composite Translation of a Life of George Washington in Latin Prose, by Francis A. Glass, A.M. of Ohio*. Edited by J. F. Latimer (Washington DC: The George Washington University, 1976) 62–65.

"Social Vocabulary and Its Relationship to Political Propaganda in Fifth-Century Athens, *Quaderni Urbinati di Cultura Classica* 27 (1977) 95–111.

PREFACES. To five-volume series of *Reprints of the* Classical World *Bibliographies,* edited by W. Donlan. "Garland Reference Library of the Humanities" (New York and London: Garland, 1978).

"The Structure of Authority in the *Iliad*, " *Arethusa* 12 (1979) 51–70.

"The Charge at Marathon Again," *The Classical World* 72 (1979) 419–20 (co-authored with James Thompson).

"A Brief History of The Classical Association of the Atlantic States and *The Classical World*: 1907–1980," *The Classical World* 75 (1981) 3–25.

"Reciprocities in Homer," *The Classical World* 75 (1981–82) 137–75.

"The Politics of Generosity in Homer," *Helios* 9 (1982) 1–15.

"Scale, Value, and Function in the Homeric Economy," *American Journal of Ancient History* 6 (1981) 101–17 (publ. in 1984).

"The Social Groups of Dark Age Greece," *Classical Philology* 80 (1985) 293–308.

"Pistos Philos Hetairos," in *Theognis of Megara. Poetry and the Polis*, edited by T. J. Figuera and G. Nagy (The Johns Hopkins University Press, 1985) 223–44.

"Teach the Romans with the Latin: Roman Culture through Intermediate Latin Texts," *Texas Classics in Action* (Summer, 1985) 21–27.

"Two modes of distribution in Dark Age Greece"; "Renfrew's model of the origin of civilization," in *The Boundaries of Civilization in Space and Time*, edited by M. Melko and L. R. Scott (University Press of America, 1987) 157–59; 208–10.

"The Unequal Exchange Between Glaucus and Diomedes in Light of the Homeric Gift Economy," *Phoenix* 43 (1989) 1–15.

"The Pre-State Community in Greece," *Symbolae Osloenses* 64 (1989) 5–29.

"Homeric *Temenos* and Land Tenure in Dark Age Greece," *Museum Helveticum* 46 (1989) 129–45.

"Duelling with Gifts in the *Iliad*: As the Audience saw It," *Colby Quarterly* 29 (1993) 155–72.

"The Village Community of Ancient Greece: Neolithic, Bronze and Dark Ages," *Studi Micenei ed Egeo-Anatolici* 31 (1993) 61–71 (co-authored with Carol G. Thomas).

"Chief and Followers in Pre-State Greece," in *From Political Economy to Anthropology: Situating Economic Life in Past Societies*, edited by David Tandy and Colin A. M. Duncan (Black Rose Books. 1994) 34–51.

"The Homeric Economy," in *A New Companion to Homeric Studies*, edited by Ian Morris and Barry Powell (E. J. Brill, 1997) 649–667.

REVIEW ARTICLE of *Homer and the Sacred City*, by Stephen Scully (Cornell University Press, 1990) in *Arion* 5 (1997) 218–228.

"The Relations of Power in the Pre-State and Early State Polities," in *The Development of the Polis in Archaic Greece*, edited by Lynette G. Mitchell and P. J. Rhodes (Routledge, 1997) 39–48.

"Political Reciprocity in Dark Age Greece: Odysseus and his *hetairoi*," in *Reciprocity in Ancient Greece*, edited by Christopher Gill, Norman Postlethwaite, and Richard Seaforth (Oxford University Press, 1998) 51–71.

Ancient Greece: A Political, Social, and Cultural History, co-authored with Stanley Burstein, Sarah Pomeroy, and Jennifer Roberts (Oxford University Press, 1999).

Reviews

Schools of Hellas, by Kenneth J. Freeman (Teachers College Press, 1969) in *Journal of General Education* 23 (1971) 77–79.

Archilochus of Paros, by H.D. Rankin (Noyes Press, 1977) in *Helios* 7 (1979) 75–82.

Douleia. Esclavage et Pratiques Discursives dans l' Athènes Classique, by M.-M. Mactoux (Annales littéraires de l' Université de Besancon 250, 1980) in *The American Historical Review* 87 (1982) 753–54.

Basileus. The Evidence for Kingship in Geometric Greece, by Robert Drews (Yale University Press, 1983) in *The Classical World* 77 (1983) 201–02.

The Poems of Hesiod. Translated, with Introduction and Comments, by R. M. Frazer (University of Oklahoma Press, 1983) in *The Classical World* 77 (1984) 387–88.

Poesia e Pubblico nella Grecia Antica. Da Omero al V Secolo, by Bruno Gentili (Editio Laterza, 1984) in *The Classical World* 79 (1985) 63–64.

Conventions of Form and Thought in Early Greek Epic Poetry, by William G. Thalmann (The Johns Hopkins University Press, 1984) in *The Classical World* 79 (1986) 340–41.

Bibliography

Individual and Community: The Rise of the Polis 800–500 B.C., by Chester G. Starr (Oxford University Press, 1986) in *The Classical World* 80 (1987) 451.

Myth and Mind, by Harvey Birenbaum (University Press of America, 1988) in *The Classical World* 83 (1989) 58–59.

Die Entdeckung der Freiheit. Zur historischen Semantik und Gesellschaftsgeschichte eines politischen Grundbegriffs der Griechen, by Kurt Raaflaub (Verlag C. H. Beck, 1985) in *Classical Philology* 85 (1990) 55–60.

Civilization of the Ancient Mediterranean. Greece and Rome. Three volumes: edited by Michael Grant and Rachel Kitzinger (Charles Scribner's Sons, 1988) in *The American Historical Review* 95 (1990) 466–68.

Homer's The Odyssey. Edited, with an introduction, by Harold Bloom (Chelsea House Publishers, 1988) in *The Classical World* 84 (1990) 73.

Greek Mythology and Poetics, by Gregory Nagy (Cornell University Press, 1990) in *The Classical World* 84 (1991) 69–70.

Oral Tradition and Written Record in Classical Athens, by Rosalind Thomas (Cambridge University Press, 1989) in *Philosophy and Rhetoric* 25 (1992) 298–303.

Adelskultur und Polis-gessellschaft. Studien zum griechischen Adel in archaischen und klassischen Zeit, by Elke Stein-Hölkeskamp (Franz Steiner Verlag, 1989) in *American Journal of Philology* 113 (1992) 137–40.

Women in Greek Tragedy: An Anthropological Approach, by Synnove des Bouvrie (Norwegian University Press, 1991) in *The Classical World* 86 (1992) 143.

Apollo the Wolf-god, by Daniel E. Gershenson (Journal of Indo-European Studies, Monograph No 8, 1991) in *The Classical* World 87 (1994) 321–22.

Archaic Greek Poetry: An Anthology, translated by Barbara Hughes Fowler (The University of Wisconsin Press, 1992) in *The Classical World* 89 (1996) 227.

Heat and Lust: Hesiod's Midsummer Festival Scene Revisited, by J. C. B. Petropoulos (Rowman and Littlefield, 1994) in *The Classical* World 90 (1996) 61–62.

The Tyrant's Writ. Myths and Images of Writing in Ancient Greece, by Deborah Tarn Steiner (Princeton University Press, 1994) in *The Classical Bulletin* 72 (1996) 78–80.

Sardonic Smile: Nonverbal Behavior in Homeric Epic, by Donald Lateiner (University of Michigan Press, 1995) in *The Classical Journal* 92 (1996) 77–79.

"Moral Codes and Social Structure in Ancient Greece," by Joseph M. Bryant (SUNY Press, 1996) in *The American Historical Review* 102 (1997) 1456–1457.